Allahabad High Court

Group D Exam

Latest Edition
Practice Kit

16 Tests
08 Mock Test
08 Sectional Test

Based On Real Exam Pattern

✓ Thoroughly Revised and Updated

✓ Detailed Analysis of all MCQs

Title	: Allahabad High Court Group D Exam
Author Name	: Mr. Rohit Manglik
Published By	: EduGorilla Community Pvt. Ltd.
Publishers Address	: 12/651, First Floor Opp. Arvindo Park, Near Jama Masjid, Indira Nagar, Lucknow, Uttar Pradesh-226016, India

Copyright EduGorilla

Disclaimer EduGorilla

ROHIT MANGLIK
CEO, EduGorilla

Dear Applicants,

People say *"Success comes to those who work hard."* But I've seen people working hard for their exams day in and day out for marginal success. While others succeed in their examinations by putting in just half the work. So are they God Gifted? No! I believe that it's because they work *smart* and not just *hard*. Similarly, for your exams, you should strategize your preparation so as to increase the likelihood of success. Well with EduGorilla get ready to increase your *chances of selection* in your exam by *16x*.

EduGorilla helps you in not only working *hard* but also working in a *smart and strategic* manner. With EduGorilla's preparation package, you get a chance to make your exam preparation easy, and a fun learning path towards selection. Finding the right path to your preparations can be difficult if you don't know in which direction to head. Don't worry, we have you covered! EduGorilla will be your guide to success in your journey. With our Preparation Package, you can prepare strategically and beat the exam in just one attempt.

EduGorilla's Preparation Package includes-

- **Test Series**
- **Books**

Our preparation package is handcrafted as per the latest changes, expert opinions, and students' discretion. Thus, enabling you to get through each stage of the selection process for your exam.

Our Books are designed by the teachers and experts of the respective exam with a combined 150+ years of experience; to provide you with easy, efficient, and effective learning. Our books are smart, in the sense that not only do they give you the answers to the questions but also provide similar questions for practice.

EduGorilla's competent Test Series gives you real-time experience and confidence through which you can clear your offline or online exam in just one attempt. We currently host 83,000+ mock tests for 1,440+ competitive and academic exams.

Thus, EduGorilla misses no chance to assist you in your preparation and covers all stages of the exam, so that you don't have to look anywhere else.

We provide complete preparation packages for defense, banking, teaching, and other National & State-Level exams. Hence, it doesn't matter which exam you aspire to because you will reach your success.

ALL THE BEST !
Let EduGorilla be your Guide to Success.

Rohit Manglik,
Founder and CEO, EduGorilla

INTRODUCTION

EduGorilla focuses on guiding students to succeed in their examinations. With that in mind, our book, titled "Allahabad High Court : Group D Exam", has been drafted through the collective efforts of our distinguished experts with 150+ years of combined experience. This book consists of questions that are created following the latest changes in the syllabus and exam pattern. We compiled the book on the basis of questions that are most likely to appear in the Allahabad High Court Group D Exam Book. Through EduGorilla's "Allahabad High Court : Group D Exam" your chances of success will increase 16x.

EduGorilla does this through our Complete Preparation Package. This package consists of well-conceptualized and structured content in the form of questions that are tailor-made according to your needs and will help you practice for exams in a smart way by pinpointing all the necessary information. It also provides hints and solutions, along with a smart answer sheet for your self-evaluation. You can assess your shortcomings and work accordingly on areas that may require more of your attention.

EduGorilla promises to help you succeed in your examination and accomplish your dream goals. We believe in our aspirants and see them at the top of the merit list. And the first step towards the top is to start preparing with us. EduGorilla's "Allahabad High Court : Group D Exam" includes the following attributes.

➤ Well-Researched Content

➤ Top-Notch Quality

➤ Detailed Answers and Analysis

➤ Smart Answer Sheet

➤ Exam Relevant Questions

Therefore, EduGorilla fortifies your preparation and makes it durable enough to help you stand tall and beat the examination.

Allahabad High Court Group D Exam Book
Scan QR code for Eligibility, Exam Pattern, Syllabus and more.

Book ID: 1203

TABLE OF CONTENTS

Hindi

Q.1 "तृषा ने खाना लगाया"। में कौन सा काल है?
A. सामान्य भूतकाल
B. संदिग्ध भूतकाल
C. संभाव्य भविष्य काल
D. संदिग्ध वर्तमान काल

Q.2 किस वाक्य में विराम चिन्हों का प्रयोग सही किया गया है?
A. राजा-दशरथ, के चार पुत्र थे।
B. दोनों साथ-साथ खेलते, खाते, पढ़ते और टहलते है।
C. राधिका बहुत खुश हुई "वह माँ बननेवाली थी न"
D. दोनों साथ साथ खेलते, खाते, पढ़ते, और टहलते है।

Q.3 इनमें से भाववाचक संज्ञा कौन सी है?
A. अच्छा
B. मधुर
C. सुंदर
D. अच्छाई

Q.4 'थाली का बैंगन' मुहावरे का अर्थ है:
A. कभी यहाँ और कभी वहाँ बैठे रहना।
B. कभी एक पक्ष और कभी दूसरे कोने में रहना।
C. कभी एक पक्ष और कभी दूसरे पक्ष में रहना।
D. कभी एक पक्ष और कभी दूसरे पिंजरे में रहना।

Q.5 'तोता डाली पर बैठा है' इस वाक्य में कौन-सा कारक है?
A. करण
B. सम्बन्ध
C. अधिकरण
D. अपादान

Q.6 इनमें से कौन सा शब्द 'गार' प्रत्यय से बना शब्द है?
[MP Sub Inspector (MPSI), 2017]
A. मदगार
B. मददगार
C. कमगार
D. कामगार

Q.7 'दुबई कितना सुंदर देश है।' रेखांकित पद ____ है।
[Allahabad High Court Review Officer (RO), 2017]
A. प्रविशेषण
B. संख्यावाची विशेषण
C. परिमाण वाचक विशेषण
D. विधेय विशेषण

Q.8 निम्नलिखित में से कौनसा शब्द अनिश्चियवाचक सर्वनाम नहीं है?
A. कुछ
B. किसी
C. कोई
D. किसका

Q.9 निम्नलिखित में से जीभ के मध्य भाग से निकलने वाला स्वर कौन सा है?
A. ई
B. ऊ
C. आ
D. अ

Q.10 जो एक या एक से ज्यादा वस्तुओं अथवा व्यक्तियों का बोध कराता हो उसे क्या कहते हैं?
[UP Police ASI, 2018]
A. मिथ्यावचन
B. सत्यवचन
C. बहुवचन
D. एकवचन

Q.11 'ब्रह्मास्त्र' का संधि-विच्छेद है:
A. ब्रह्म + अस्त्र
B. ब्रह्मा + अस्त्र
C. बह्म + अस्त्र
D. ब्रह्मः + अस्त्र

Q.12 'तरल' का विलोम शब्द है:
[UP Police Sub Inspector, 2021]
A. सरल
B. ठोस
C. तीक्ष्ण
D. जटिल

Q.13 निम्नलिखित में से कौन-सा मिश्र वाक्य है?

[UPTET Science and Maths, 2019], [UPTET Social Studies, 2019]
A. यज्ञदत्त देवदत्त को व्याकरण पढ़ता है।
B. वह उड़ती हुई चिड़िया पहचानता है।
C. उसमें न पत्ते थे, न फुल थे।
D. मैंने सुना है कि आपके देश में अच्छा राजप्रबंध है।

Q.14 निम्नलिखित प्रश्न में, चार विकल्प दिए गए हैं, जिनमें से एक शब्द दिए गए शब्द का सही तन्द्भव रूप है।
'अम्लिका'
A. आंवला
B. आमला
C. इमली
D. ईमली

Q.15 "जिसे भय नहीं है" इस वाक्यांश के लिए एक सार्थक शब्द दीजिए।
A. बहादुर
B. श्रेष्ठ
C. निर्दय
D. निर्भय

Q.16 कम बोलने वाले व्यक्ति इस वाक्यांश के लिए एक सार्थक शब्द दीजिए।
A. मितभाषी
B. व्याख्याता
C. मितव्ययी
D. वाचाल

Ques (17-18):निर्देश: दिए गए विकल्पों में से सही विकल्पों का चयन करके वाक्य पूर्ण करें।

Q.17 बड़ा ____ लड़का है, काले साँप को भी पकड़ लेता है।
A. मूर्ख
B. निःशंक
C. निर्भिक
D. बेवकूफ

Q.18 हमें एक अत्यंत मानवीय, न्यायशील, सत्यप्रेम तथा सौहार्द्र के प्रति ____ समाजसूत्र का निर्माण करना है।
A. प्रेम
B. विशुद्ध
C. प्रबुद्ध
D. समृद्ध

Q.19 निम्नलिखित में से अशुद्ध वर्तनी का चयन कीजिए:-
A. नुकसानदेह
B. नौकरी
C. निलंवित
D. निःशुल्क

Q.20 "इंद्र" का पर्यायवाची शब्द क्या है?
A. बाजीगर
B. राजराज
C. मधवा
D. विनायक

Q.21 दिए गए विकल्पों में से निम्नलिखित वाक्य का भेद बताइए।
वाह ! भारत ने विश्वकप जीत लिया।
A. विस्मयादिबोधक वाक्य
B. इच्छाबोधक वाक्य
C. विधानवाचक वाक्य
D. निषेधवाचक वाक्य

Q.22 निम्नलिखित में से अर्द्धविराम का चिह्न कौन-सा है?
A. :-
B. _
C. -
D. ;

Q.23 'संकल्प' शब्द में उपसर्ग बताइए।
A. सम्
B. सक्
C. सन्
D. सन्क

Q.24 'दिखावा कुछ और गुण कुछ भी नहीं' का अर्थ प्रकट करने के लिए सर्वोचित लोकोक्ति है:
A. नौ सौ चूहे खाके बिल्ली हज को चली
B. ढोल के अंदर पोल
C. नाच न जाने आँगन टेढ़ा
D. अधजल गगरी छलकत जाए

Q.25 'भय' किस रस का स्थायी भाव है?
A. अद्भुत रस
B. वीभत्स रस
C. रौद्र रस
D. भयानक रस

English

Ques (26-33):Direction: Select the most appropriate option to fill in the blank.

Q.26 Neither of the brothers has brought _______ notebook.
A. Their   **B.** Hers   **C.** His   **D.** You

Q.27 My house is _____________as yours.
[Sainik School Entrance Class VI, 2018]

A. big   **B.** as big   **C.** bigger   **D.** biggest

Q.28 You ___ book the tickets for the play in advance; they sell out quickly.
A. must   **B.** should   **C.** have to   **D.** would

Q.29 I expected to fail the exam, but I ______ after all.
A. passes   **B.** passed
C. pass   **D.** will be passing

Q.30 He refused to work _____ the new boss.
A. from   **B.** into   **C.** under   **D.** between

Q.31 Her parents are anxious ____ her safety.
A. to   **B.** about   **C.** at   **D.** for

Q.32 It's also the ______ and most nerve-wracking purchase you'll make as well.
A. scarier   **B.** scary
C. most scariest   **D.** scariest

Q.33 I ______ my work before the boss called me.
A. am finishing   **B.** finish
C. was finishing   **D.** had finished

Q.34 Choose the correctly punctuated sentence.
A. Stop, Are you out of your mind.
B. Stop; Are you out of your mind?
C. Stop! Are you out of your mind?
D. Stop! Are you out of your mind!

Q.35 Which of the following words is a material noun?
[UPTET Paper - I, 2018]

A. Cow   **B.** Gold   **C.** Air   **D.** Class

Q.36 Out of the given words, one word is misspelt find the misspelt word.
A. Malignancy   **B.** Frequency
C. Emergancy   **D.** Consistency

Q.37 Choose the correct option which has the same relation as that given in the words.
Dexterity :: Ability :: Timid : _______
A. Bold   **B.** Energetic
C. Afraid   **D.** Agility

Ques (38-39):Direction: Choose the correct word that is opposite in meaning to the word.

Q.38 Discourage
A. Crushed   **B.** Demoralize
C. Dishearten   **D.** Encourage

Q.39 Consecutive
A. Discontinuous   **B.** Successive
C. Following   **D.** Succeeding

Q.40 Choose the word that can substitute the given sentence.
The art or practice of garden cultivation and management is known as
A. Demography   **B.** Aviculture
C. Horticulture   **D.** Apiculture

Q.41 Direction: Change the gender of the underlined noun and rewrite the sentence:
When her <u>aunt</u> died, Katie moved in with Carmen.
A. brother   **B.** father   **C.** uncle   **D.** mother

Q.42 Direction: Which of the words is not an adjective?
A. learn   **B.** beautiful
C. fast   **D.** enormous

Q.43 Direction: Write the full form of:
Couldn't
A. cannot   **B.** would not
C. could not   **D.** could

Q.44 Direction: Choose the meaningful word from the given jumbled words:
URTHT
A. truht   **B.** thurt   **C.** turth   **D.** truth

Q.45 Direction: Identify the interjection in the following sentence:
Oh, what a beautiful house!
A. Oh   **B.** what   **C.** beautiful   **D.** house

Q.46 Read the given statement carefully and choose the correct tense.
I feel great!
A. Past Perfect   **B.** Simple Past
C. Simple Present   **D.** Future Progressive

Q.47 Direction: Choose the correct option:
The basic _____ (principal/principle) was that those who worked _____ (quite/quiet) hard would be rewarded.
A. principal, quiet   **B.** principal, quite
C. principle, quite   **D.** principle, quiet

Ques (48-49):Direction: Select the most appropriate synonym of the given word.

Q.48 Maintain
A. Care   **B.** Ignore   **C.** Release   **D.** Neglect

Q.49 Bias
A. Prejudice   **B.** Justice
C. Advantage   **D.** Tolerance

Q.50 Direction: Fill in the blank with the correct form of the verb.
We _____ for a drive next week.

A. went
B. will go
C. will have been going
D. had gone

General Studies

Q.51 Kerala Tourism won the coveted Responsible Tourism Global Award at London World Travel Mart in Nov 2022, for which of the following project?
A. CLEAN CITY, GREEN CITY project
B. STREET project
C. WELCOME TO THE KERALA project
D. All of these

Q.52 Who among the following has won the gold medal in Badminton women's singles in CWG 2022?
A. Michelle Li
B. Carolina Marin
C. Tai Tzu-Ying
D. P. V. Sindhu

Q.53 Which Indian Institute of Management (IIM) has launched country's first Agri Land Price Index in June 2022?
A. IIM Bangalore
B. IIM Calcutta
C. IIM Lucknow
D. IIM Ahmedabad

Q.54 The fifth Bangladesh-India Cultural meet concluded in which city?
A. New Delhi
B. Rajshahi
C. Shillong
D. Dhaka

Q.55 "Handmade Paper" is selected as a product from the _____ district of Uttar Pradesh under the "One district One Product" scheme.
A. Amethi
B. Jalaun
C. Deoria
D. Kushinagar

Q.56 Patari tribe is found in which district of Uttar Pradesh?
A. Sonbhadra
B. Prayagraj
C. Lalitpur
D. Mahoba

Q.57 Where is the "Electronics City" being established in the state of Uttar Pradesh?

[UPSSSC Forest Guard, 2015]

A. Agra
B. Noida
C. Bareli
D. Kanpur

Q.58 Shilling is the currency of _______.
A. Jordan
B. Kenya
C. Israel
D. Kiribati

Q.59 Introversion-Extraversion trait of personality is propounded by:
[Rajasthan Teachers Eligibility Test - Level 1 Primary Level (RTET), 2017]

A. Hans Eysenck
B. R.B. Cattle
C. Gordon Allport
D. Carl Jung

Q.60 In Jal Jeevan Survekshan-2023 which of the following districts of Uttar Pradesh topped in giving tap water connections?
A. Bulandshahr
B. Bareilly
C. Mirzapur
D. Shahjahanpur

Q.61 Major General _________, who amputated his leg on battlefield, launched his new book 'Cartoos Saab: A Soldier's Story of Resilience in Adversity' in November 2022.
A. Anil Chauhan
B. Yogendra Dimri
C. Ajai Singh
D. Ian Cardozo

Q.62 Dandiya Raas is a famous dance form of:
A. Andhra Pradesh
B. Gujarat
C. Mizoram
D. Haryana

Q.63 What is the full form of "EVM"?
A. Electronic Voting Machines
B. Electrical Voters Machines
C. Electrical Vote Machines
D. Electronic Vote Machines

Q.64 Boundary Line between India & Afghanistan:
A. Durand Line
B. Seigfried Line
C. Radcliffe Line
D. Mason-Dixon Line

Q.65 The first death anniversary day of Sri Rajiv Gandhi was observed as the:
A. National Integration Day
B. Peace and Love Day
C. Secularism Day
D. Anti-Terrorism Day

Q.66 In which country is the Great Pyramid of Giza located?
A. Syria
B. Egypt
C. Saudi Arab
D. Iran

Q.67 Who was known as 'Devanampriya Priyadarshi'?
A. Ashoka Maurya
B. Bindusara Maurya
C. Chandragupta Maurya
D. Mahapadma Nanda

Q.68 Which dynasty was the first dynasty of the Delhi Sultanate?
A. Khilji Dynasty
B. Slave Dynasty
C. Tughlaq Dynasty
D. Sayyid Dynasty

Q.69 The Black soil is also known as _______ soil.
A. Bhangar
B. Humus
C. Crystalline
D. Regur

Q.70 The name India is derived from the ______ river.
A. Indus
B. Irrawaddy
C. Brahmaputra
D. Ganges

Q.71 Which of the following is a physical change?
[MP Jail Prahari, 2018]

A. Melting of ice
B. Milk is set into curd
C. Ripening of fruits
D. Grapes get fermented

Q.72 The metal used to make lightning conductors is:
A. Iron
B. Aluminum
C. Copper
D. Zinc

Q.73 Deficiency of vitamin A causes:
A. Vision issues during night time
B. Scurvy
C. Beri Beri
D. Rickets

Q.74 Uttar Pradesh Textile Technology Institute is located in which of the following city?
A. Kanpur
B. Moradabad
C. Lucknow
D. Faizabad

Q.75 "Uttar Priyadarshi" play was written by________.
A. Sachchidananda Vatsyayan
B. Vidya Niwas Mishra
C. Kaifi Azmi
D. Majrooh Sultanpuri

Mathematics

Q.76 Given HCF of ($16,100$) $= 4$, what is the LCM of ($16,100$)?

[RRB/RRC Group D, 2018]

A. 400
B. 398
C. 440
D. 300

Q.77 Find HCF of 726 and 462.
A. 66
B. 67
C. 68
D. 69

Q.78 Rohan borrows Rs. $6,000$ from Mohit at 3% per annum on simple interest. He pays Rs. 240 as interest, when will he pay the debt?
A. 14 months
B. 15 months
C. 16 months
D. 18 months

Q.79 The tens and units digits of a number are the same. When the number is added to its reverse, the sum is 110. What is the number?
A. 44
B. 33
C. 55
D. 66

Q.80 If $\sqrt{2^n} = 32$, then n is equal to:
A. 2
B. 4
C. 6
D. 10

Q.81 If the mean of distribution 10, 8, 15, 12, K, 25 is 12, find the value of K.
A. 2
B. 1
C. 4
D. 3

Q.82 If $n \times \left(\frac{4}{9}\right)$ of $1620 = (n+1)$ of 72, then 125% of n is:
A. $\frac{1}{36}$
B. $\frac{5}{36}$
C. $\frac{25}{9}$
D. $\frac{9}{25}$

Q.83 The value of $\frac{2}{5} \times 350 + 30\%$ of 250 is:
A. 115
B. 125
C. 215
D. 225

Q.84 If $x - \frac{2}{x} = 15$, then what is the value of $\left(x^2 + \frac{4}{x^2}\right)$?
A. 223
B. 227
C. 229
D. 221

Q.85 Find the value of x.
$x\%$ of $60 = 48$
A. 70
B. 65
C. 80
D. 40

Q.86 The cost price of an item is 25% less than the marked price. At how much percentage above the cost price has the item been marked?
A. 36
B. 30
C. 35
D. $33\frac{1}{3}$

Q.87 Correct expression of $1.\overline{23} = ?$
A. $\frac{56}{33}$
B. $\frac{122}{99}$
C. $\frac{123}{99}$
D. $\frac{66}{33}$

Q.88 Evaluate: $0.6\overline{23}$
A. $6\frac{23}{999}$
B. $\frac{623}{999}$
C. $\frac{617}{990}$
D. $6\frac{23}{990}$

Q.89 $78 - [5 + 3$ of $(25 - 2 \times 10)] =?$
A. 58
B. 38
C. 48
D. 56

Q.90 Which of the following numbers is completely divisible by 99?
A. 51579
B. 51557
C. 55036
D. 49984

Q.91 Which of the following is not a prime number?
A. 853
B. 953
C. 553
D. 653

Q.92 Find the number whose 8 times is 8 less than 40.
A. 2
B. 3
C. 4
D. 5

Q.93 What is the conversion of 460 cm $+0.6$ km $+20$ m $=$
A. 72560 cm
B. 62460 cm
C. 62760 cm
D. 68700 cm

Q.94 The sum of the square of the sides of a rhombus is 1600 cm^2. What is the side of the rhombus?
A. 25 cm
B. 10 cm
C. 15 cm
D. 20 cm

Q.95 If the diameter of a sphere is 56 cm, then what is its surface area? (Take $\pi = \frac{22}{7}$)
A. 9856 cm^2
B. 9556 cm^2
C. 9756 cm^2
D. 9806 cm^2

Q.96 The value of $0.9 \div (0.3 \times 0.3)$ is:

[Jawahar Navodaya Entrance Class VI, 2020]

A. 0.01
B. 0.1
C. 1
D. 10

Q.97 What will come in place of the question mark?
$\frac{15}{7}$ of 70% of $0.15 =?$
A. 0.225
B. 0.256
C. 0.656
D. 0.144

Q.98 What will come at the place of question mark?
4, 7, 12, 19, 28, ?
A. 49
B. 36
C. 30
D. 39

Q.99 Find the least number which will leaves remainder 5 when divided by $8, 12, 16$ and 20.

A. 240 **B.** 245 **C.** 265 **D.** 235

Q.100 What will come in place of question mark '?' in the following question?

$$2112 + 692 \times 2 - 1111 \times 5 + 7324 \times 8 = ?$$

A. 56533 **B.** 57533 **C.** 49533 **D.** 45653

// Smart Answer Sheet //

Correct   Indicates percentage of students who answered questions correctly.

Skipped   Indicates percentage of students who skipped questions.

Q.	Ans.	Correct / Skipped	Q.	Ans.	Correct / Skipped	Q.	Ans.	Correct / Skipped	Q.	Ans.	Correct / Skipped	Q.	Ans.	Correct / Skipped
1	A	42.07 % / 4.14 %	17	C	78.62 % / 6.21 %	33	D	44.14 % / 15.86 %	49	A	29.66 % / 15.86 %	65	D	28.97 % / 15.17 %
2	B	59.31 % / 4.83 %	18	C	25.52 % / 6.2 %	34	C	46.21 % / 15.17 %	50	B	52.41 % / 14.49 %	66	B	62.07 % / 15.86 %
3	D	52.41 % / 5.52 %	19	C	68.97 % / 3.44 %	35	B	63.45 % / 16.55 %	51	B	15.17 % / 15.17 %	67	A	33.79 % / 15.18 %
4	C	67.59 % / 6.2 %	20	C	31.03 % / 6.9 %	36	C	40.0 % / 15.17 %	52	D	51.72 % / 15.87 %	68	B	49.66 % / 13.79 %
5	C	55.86 % / 5.52 %	21	A	77.93 % / 2.76 %	37	C	24.83 % / 11.03 %	53	D	18.62 % / 15.86 %	69	D	42.07 % / 15.17 %
6	B	88.28 % / 4.82 %	22	D	78.62 % / 6.21 %	38	D	62.76 % / 16.55 %	54	B	12.41 % / 15.18 %	70	A	55.86 % / 13.11 %
7	D	25.52 % / 5.51 %	23	A	51.03 % / 6.21 %	39	A	48.97 % / 16.55 %	55	B	24.83 % / 15.17 %	71	A	54.48 % / 14.49 %
8	D	29.66 % / 5.51 %	24	B	50.34 % / 7.59 %	40	C	42.76 % / 13.79 %	56	A	37.93 % / 14.48 %	72	C	34.48 % / 15.86 %
9	D	24.14 % / 5.52 %	25	D	61.38 % / 6.21 %	41	C	46.9 % / 16.55 %	57	B	66.9 % / 14.48 %	73	A	62.07 % / 14.48 %
10	C	81.38 % / 6.9 %	26	C	33.1 % / 15.87 %	42	A	33.79 % / 16.55 %	58	B	27.59 % / 15.17 %	74	A	52.41 % / 14.49 %
11	A	34.48 % / 7.59 %	27	B	42.76 % / 15.86 %	43	C	69.66 % / 16.55 %	59	A	19.31 % / 14.48 %	75	A	40.69 % / 15.17 %
12	B	70.34 % / 6.21 %	28	B	28.97 % / 15.17 %	44	D	63.45 % / 16.55 %	60	D	18.62 % / 13.79 %	76	D	22.76 % / 15.86 %
13	D	52.41 % / 4.83 %	29	B	53.79 % / 15.87 %	45	A	51.03 % / 17.25 %	61	D	19.31 % / 15.17 %	77	A	42.76 % / 15.86 %
14	C	28.28 % / 7.58 %	30	C	57.24 % / 15.86 %	46	C	56.55 % / 12.42 %	62	B	76.55 % / 13.79 %	78	C	38.62 % / 16.55 %
15	D	82.76 % / 6.21 %	31	D	24.14 % / 15.00 %	47	C	29.66 % / 16.55 %	63	A	75.17 % / 15.17 %	79	C	62.76 % / 12.41 %
16	A	57.93 % / 5.52 %	32	D	24.14 % / 15.86 %	48	A	62.07 % / 15.86 %	64	A	53.1 % / 13.8 %	80	D	30.34 % / 13.8 %

Q.	Ans.	Correct		Q.	Ans.	Correct		Q.	Ans.	Correct		Q.	Ans.	Correct		Q.	Ans.	Correct
		Skipped				Skipped				Skipped				Skipped				Skipped
81	A	40.69 %		85	C	49.66 %		89	A	37.93 %		93	B	41.38 %		97	A	43.45 %
		13.79 %				17.93 %				16.55 %				16.55 %				16.55 %
82	B	45.52 %		86	D	44.83 %		90	A	42.76 %		94	D	33.1 %		98	D	60.0 %
		13.79 %				16.55 %				16.55 %				17.24 %				15.17 %
83	C	44.83 %		87	B	28.97 %		91	C	28.97 %		95	A	32.41 %		99	B	55.17 %
		16.55 %				12.41 %				15.86 %				15.87 %				15.17 %
84	C	27.59 %		88	C	25.52 %		92	C	53.1 %		96	D	30.34 %		100	A	30.34 %
		15.86 %				17.93 %				15.18 %				16.56 %				15.87 %

Performance Analysis

Avg. Score (%)	41.0%
Toppers Score (%)	99.0%
Your Score	

//Hints and Solutions//

1. "तृषा ने खाना लगाया"। में सामान्य भूतकाल है।

सामान्य भूतकाल: क्रिया के जिस रूप से काम के सामान्य रूप से बीते हुए समय में होने का बोध हो, उसे सामान्य भूतकाल कहते है।

अत: विकल्प (A) सही है।

2. "दोनों साथ-साथ खेलते, खाते, पढ़ते और टहलते हैं।" वाक्य में विराम चिन्हों का प्रयोग सही किया गया है। साथ साथ के मध्य में हाइफ़न(-) का चिह्न लगेगा। खेलते, खाते, शब्द पे ज़ोर देने के लिए अल्प विराम प्रयोग किया है।

अल्प विराम का प्रयोग: एक अल्पविराम आमतौर पर समन्वय वाक्यांशों (यानी क्रियाविशेषण) को अलग करने के लिए प्रयोग किया जाता है। यदि क्रिया और विषय अलग हो रहे थे, उदाहरण के लिए, "महिला ने कहा कि उसे कल बैठक में पहनने के लिए एक पोशाक होगी," अल्पविराम क्रमशः "कहा" और "से" शब्दों पर जोर देने में मदद करता है।

अत: विकल्प (B) सही है।

3. अच्छाई भाववाचक संज्ञा है। जो शब्द किसी चीज़ या पदार्थ की अवस्था, दशा या भाव का बोध कराते हैं, उन शब्दों को भाववाचक संज्ञा कहते हैं। जैसे- बचपन, बुढ़ापा, मोटापा, मिठास, उमंग, चढ़ाई, थकावट, मानवता, चतुराई, जवानी, लम्बाई, मित्रता, मुस्कुराहट, अपनापन, परायापन, भूख, प्यास, चोरी, क्रोध, सुन्दरता आदि।

अत: विकल्प (D) सही है।

4. 'थाली का बैंगन' मुहावरे का अर्थ है: कभी एक पक्ष और कभी दूसरे पक्ष में रहना।

- वाक्य प्रयोग: आजकल के नए-नए नेता तो थाली के बैंगन हैं।

मुहावरा: हिन्दी में ऐसे वाक्यांशों को मुहावरा कहा जाता है, जो अपने साधारण अर्थ को छोड़कर विशेष अर्थ को व्यक्त करते हैं।

उदाहरण: अंक भरना: स्नेह से लिपटा लेना।

अत: विकल्प (C) सही है।

5. 'तोता डाली पर बैठा है' इस वाक्य में अधिकरण कारक है। अन्य विकल्प असंगत है।

कारक		
* संज्ञा या सर्वनाम के जिस रूप से उनका (संज्ञा या सर्वनाम का) क्रिया से सम्बन्ध सूचित हो, उस रूप को 'कारक' कहते हैं। * संज्ञा अथवा सर्वनाम को क्रिया से जोड़ने वाले चिह्न अथवा परसर्ग ही कारक कहलाते हैं।		
कारक	**परिभाषा**	**उदाहरण**
सम्बन्ध कारक	शब्द के जिस रूप से संज्ञा या सर्वनाम के संबंध का ज्ञान हो, उसे सम्बन्ध कारक कहते है।	जैसे- सीता का भाई आया है। वह किसका भाई है ? गीता का।
अधिकरण कारक	शब्द के जिस रूप से क्रिया के आधार का ज्ञान होता है, उसे अधिकरण कारक कहते है।	जैसे- मोहन मैदान में खेल रहा है। मनमोहन छत पर खेल रहा है।
करण कारक	वाक्य में जिस शब्द से क्रिया के सम्बन्ध का बोध हो, उसे करण कारक कहते हैं।	जैसे- वह कुल्हाड़ी से वृक्ष काटता है। मुझे अपनी कमाई से खाना मिलता है। साधुओं की संगति से बुद्धि सुधरती है।
अपादान कारक	संज्ञा के जिस रूप से किसी वस्तु के अलग होने का भाव प्रकट होता है, उसे	जैसे- हिमालय से गंगा निकलती है। मोहन ने घड़े से
	अपादान कारक कहते है।	पानी ढाला। बिल्ली छत से कूद पड़ी चूहा बिल से बाहर निकला।

अत: विकल्प (C) सही है।

6. मददगार शब्द 'गार' प्रत्यय से बना शब्द है।

मददगार = मदद + गार। इसमें कृत् प्रत्यय है।

प्रत्यय वे शब्द हैं जो दूसरे शब्दों के अन्त में जुड़कर, अपनी प्रकृति के अनुसार, शब्द के अर्थ में परिवर्तन कर देते हैं। प्रत्यय शब्द दो शब्दों से मिलकर बना है – प्रति + अय। प्रति का अर्थ होता है 'साथ में, पर बाद में' और अय का अर्थ होता है "चलने वाला", अत: प्रत्यय का अर्थ होता है साथ में पर बाद में चलने वाला।

उदाहरण: ता, औना, अन, अत

श्रो + ता = श्रोता

अत: विकल्प (B) सही है।

7. जो विशेषण विशेष्य और क्रिया के बीच आये, वहाँ विधेय विशेषण होता हैं। जैसे- मेरा कुत्ता लाल हैं।, मेरा लड़का आलसी है।

उपर्युक्त वाक्य का रेखांकित पद 'सुंदर' विधेय विशेषण है। यह वाक्य के विधेय पद 'देश' की विशेषता बताता है।

अत: विकल्प (D) सही है।

8. किसका शब्द प्रश्न का बोध कराता है अतः यह प्रश्नवाचक सर्वनाम है।

अन्य सभी विकल्प अनिश्चितता का बोध कराते हैं। अतः अनिश्चियवाचक सर्वनाम के उदाहरण हैं।

अत: विकल्प (D) सही है।

9. 'अ' स्वर का उच्चारण जीभ के मध्य भाग से किया जाता है। जीभ के उपयोग के आधार पर स्वर तीन प्रकार से उच्चारित होते हैं:

- अग्र स्वर – इसके उच्चारण में जीभ का अगला भाग कार्य करता है। जैसे- इ, ई, ए, ऐ।
- मध्य स्वर – जिनके उच्चारण में जीभ का मध्य वाला भाग कार्य करता है। जैसे- अ।
- पश्च स्वर – जिनके उच्चारण में जीभ का पिछला भाग कार्य करता है। जैसे- आ, उ, ऊ, ओ, औ।

अत: विकल्प (D) सही है।

10. जो एक या एक से ज्यादा वस्तुओं अथवा वयक्तियों का बोध कराता हो उसे बहुवचन कहते हैं।

जो शब्द एक ही वस्तु/व्यक्ति का बोध कराता है, उसे 'एकवचन' कहते हैं। मिथ्यावचन और सत्यवचन परस्पर विलोमार्थी शब्द हैं।

अत: विकल्प (C) सही है।

11. 'ब्रह्मास्त' का संधि-विच्छेद है - ब्रह्म + अस्त।

'ब्रह्मास्त' में दीर्घ संधि है।

जब दो शब्दों की संधि करते समय (अ, आ) कै साथ (अ, आ) ही तो 'आ' बनता है, जब (इ, ई) के साथ (इ, ई) हो तो 'ई' बनता है, जब (उ, ऊ) के साथ (उ, ऊ) हो तो 'ऊ' बनता है। उसे दीर्घ संधि कहते है। जैसे- विद्या + अभ्यास = विद्याभ्यास (आ + अ = आ) आदि।

अत: विकल्प (A) सही है।

12. 'तरल' का विलोम शब्द ठोस है।

किसी शब्द का विलोम शब्द उस शब्द के अर्थ से उल्टा या विपरीत अर्थ वाला होता है।

शब्द	विलोम
तरल	ठोस
सरल	जटिल/कठिन
तीक्ष्ण	कुन्द

अतः विकल्प (B) सही है।

13. 'मैंने सुना है कि आपके देश में अच्छा राजप्रबंध है।' एक मिश्र वाक्य है। यह प्रधान वाक्य और आश्रित वाक्य से मिलकर बना है।

अतः विकल्प (D) सही है।

14. दिए गए विकल्पों में से 'अम्लिका' शब्द का शुद्ध तद्भव रूप 'इमली' है। अन्य विकल्प अनुचित हैं।

- इमली स्त्रीलिंग शब्द है।
- यह एक खट्टा फल जिसकी चटनी बनाई जाती है।
- इमली को 'चिंचा या तेतर' भी कहा जाता है।

अतः विकल्प (C) सही है।

15. 'जिसे भय नहीं है' वाक्यांश के लिए एक शब्द है- निर्भय

अन्य विकल्प-

- बहादुर- जो वीर हो
- श्रेष्ठ- जो पद में सबसे बड़ा हो
- निर्दय- जिसके अंदर दया नहीं हो

अतः विकल्प (D) सही है।

16. कम बोलने वाले व्यक्ति वाक्यांश के लिए एक सार्थक शब्द - मितभाषी होगा।

अन्य विकल्पों का विश्लेषण:-

- व्याख्याता वह जो किसी विषय की व्याख्या करता हो
- मितव्ययी वह जो कम खर्च करता हो
- वाचाल बहुत अधिक बोलने वाला

अतः विकल्प (A) सही है।

17. पूर्ण वाक्य है- बड़ा निर्भीक लड़का है, काले साँप को भी पकड़ लेता है।

- दिए गए विकल्पों में से रिक्त स्थान के लिए उचित शब्द 'निर्भीक' होगा।
- 'निर्भीक' विशेषण शब्द है जिसका अर्थ 'निडर' होता है।
- निः + भीक = निर्भीक। यह विसर्ग संधि का उदाहरण है।

अन्य शब्द -

- मूर्ख - नासमझ
- बेवकूफ - नासमझ
- निःशंक - बिना शंका का

अतः विकल्प (C) सही है।

18. हमें एक अत्यंत मानवीय, न्यायशील, सत्यप्रेम तथा सौहार्द्र के प्रति प्रबुद्ध समाजसूत्र का निर्माण करना है।

- प्रबुद्ध का अर्थ है : ज्ञानी , जाग्रत
- अन्य विकल्प असंगत है।

अतः विकल्प (C) सही है।

19. उपरोक्त विकल्पों में 'निलंवित' शब्द वर्तनीगत अशुद्ध है।

इसका शुद्ध रूप है 'निलंबित'।

जिसका अर्थ होता है- पदच्युत किया गया।

अतः विकल्प (C) सही है।

20. "इंद्र" का पर्यायवाची शब्द 'मधवा' है।

'इंद्र' का अन्य पर्यायवाची शब्द है - सुरपति, पुरंदर, वासव, महेंद्र, देवराज, सुराधिप, शचीपति, शक्र, शतमन्यु।

- 'जादूगर' का पर्यायवाची शब्द है - बाजीगर, ऐंद्रजालिक।
- 'कुबेर' का पर्यायवाची शब्द है - किन्नरेश, यक्षराज, धनद, धनाधिप, राजराज।
- 'गणेश' का पर्यायवाची शब्द है - लंबोदर, एकदंत, मूषकवाहन, गजवदन, गजानन, विनायक, गणपति, विघ्ननाशक।

अतः विकल्प (C) सही है।

21. वाह ! भारत ने विश्वकप जीत लिया। इसमें विस्मयादिबोधक वाक्य है।

ऐसे वाक्य जिनमे हमें आश्चर्य, शोक, घृणा, अत्यधिक खुशी, स्तब्धता आदि भावों का बोध हो, ऐसे वाक्य विस्मयादिबोधक वाक्य कहलाते हैं। इन वाक्यों में जो शब्द विस्मय के होते हैं उनके पीछे (!) विस्मयसूचक चिन्ह लगता है। इस चिन्ह से हम इस वाक्य की पहचान कर सकते हैं।

अतः विकल्प (A) सही है।

22. अर्द्धविराम का चिह्न - (;) है।

जब बीच में हल्का सा विराम लेना हो पर वाक्य को खत्म न किया जाये तो वहाँ पर अर्द्ध विराम (;) चिन्ह का प्रयोग किया जाता है।

उदाहरण - जिसे मैंने अपना दोस्त समझा; वही आस्तीन का सांप निकला।

अतः विकल्प (D) सही है।

23. 'संकल्प' शब्द में 'सम्' उपसर्ग का प्रयोग हुआ है। 'सम्' उपसर्ग से बनने वाले अन्य शब्द हैं - संस्कृत, संस्कार, संगीत, संहार आदि हैं।

उपसर्ग उस अक्षर या अक्षर समूह को कहते हैं जो किसी शब्द के पहले जुड़कर उसके अर्थ में परिवर्तन लाता है।

अतः विकल्प (A) सही है।

24. "ढोल के अंदर पोल", लोकोक्ति का अर्थ 'दिखावा कुछ और गुण कुछ भी नहीं' हैं।

वाक्य प्रयोग- कविता अंग्रेजी में कुछ भी बोलती रहती है, अभी उससे पूछो कि 'सेंटेन्स' कितने प्रकार के होते हैं 'तब ढोल के भीतर पोल' दिखना शुरू हो जाएगा।

अतः विकल्प (B) सही है।

25. भयानक रस'भय' नामक स्थायी भाव 'भयानक रस' का है।

जब किसी भयानक व्यक्ति या वस्तु को देखने, उससे संबन्धित वर्णन सुनने या किसी दुखद घटना का स्मरण करने से मन में जो व्याकुलता उत्पन्न होती है उसे भयानक रस कहते हैं।

अतः विकल्प (D) सही है।

26. Correct sentence: Neither of the brothers has brought his notebook.

- Pronouns that stand for the three persons are known as personal pronouns.
- For eg.- I, me, we, her, it, they, them, etc.

- When each, every, neither, either. anyone is used as the subject, 3rd person singular is used as a possessive case.
- For eg.- Each one is doing his duty properly.
- We will thus use the possessive pronoun 'his' to fill in the blank.

Hence, the correct option is (C).

27. My house is **as big** as yours.

The given sentence needs to be filled with the most suitable adjective. Looking at 'as yours' we can understand that the sentence is about a comparison between the size of houses and is to a positive degree. 'As' states equality here, which means both the houses are of the same size. Thus we can say 'as big as'.

Hence, the correct option is (B).

28. Correct sentence: You 'should' book the tickets for the play in advance; they sell out quickly.

Modal Verbs show us the attitude of the speaker to what is being said or done. The term "modal" means expressing mood and mood is a way to express the attitude of the speaker.

- Option (B) is the correct answer because it expresses the mood of duty or correctness.
- Option (A) suggests obligation.
- Option (C) is similar to option (A).
- Option (D) expresses unsure certainty with which certain act is to be done in future.

Hence, the correct option is (B).

29. Correct sentence: I expected to fail the exam, but I passed after all.

The given sentence is in simple past form. Simple past tense tells us about an action completed in the past time. For writing sentences in simple past form, the general rule followed:

- Subject + 2nd form of the verb + object.

Hence, the correct option is (B).

30. Correct sentence: He refused to work under the new boss.

The meaning of the phrase "work under someone" is to have someone else supervise or manage your work or perform some work while physically underneath someone or something. The given sentence says that the person objected to working under the supervision of the new manager.

Hence, the correct option is (C).

31. The correct sentence: Her parents are anxious for her safety.

- The above sentence is an example of a preposition.
- A preposition is a word used to link nouns, pronouns, or phrases to other words within a sentence.
- 'Anxious for' indicates a positive concern or a desire for something.
- 'Anxious about' refers to the subject of worry, and 'anxious at' refers to the cause of worry.

- 'Anxious to' also indicates eagerness and is followed by a verb.
- The given sentence implies that her parents have a concern for her safety.
- Thus, the appropriate preposition to be filled in the blank will be 'for'.

Hence, the correct option is (D).

32. Correct sentence: It's also the scariest and most nerve-wracking purchase you'll make as well.

- Now 'scary' is an adjective that has two syllables.
- Adjectives with two syllables can form the superlative by adding -est.
- Also, for adjectives ending in y, change the 'y' to an 'i' before adding the ending.
- So, 'scariest' is the superlative degree of the adjective and is appropriate for the given blank.
- Also, the same degree of adjectives are used on either side of a conjunction (here, and).

Hence, the correct option is (D).

33. Correct Sentence: I had finished my work before the boss called me.

The correct word to be used in the filler is had finished. The sentence is in the past perfect tense which follows the following structure:

- Subject + had + past participle + the rest of the sentence

Hence, the correct option is (D).

34. The given sentence is in the tone of exclamation and interrogative.

Here 'stop' conveys a strong emotion to halt a certain act.

'Stop' is followed by an exclamation mark,

- Stop!

Further, 'Are you out of your mind' is a question sentence and it should be followed by a question mark (?).

- Are you out of your mind?

Correct sentence: 'Stop! Are you out of your mind?'

Hence, the correct option is (C).

35. Gold is a material noun because gold is a material.

Material nouns are materials or substances out of which things are made.

Cows and air are not materials and class is not something you can make something of.

Thus, the correct answer is gold.

Hence, the correct option is (B).

36. Emergancy is the misspelt word.

Correct spelling is the emergency.

Emergency: a serious, unexpected, and often dangerous situation requiring immediate action.

Hence, the correct option is (C).

37. The above-given pair of words i.e. Dexterity: Ability are synonyms of each other.

Timid(adjective) - showing a lack of courage or confidence; easily frightened.

The correct synonym of Timid is Afraid.

Afraid(adjective) - feeling fear or anxiety; frightened.

Therefore, the correct pair will be Dexterity: Ability :: Timid : Afraid.

Hence, the correct option is (C).

38. The correct word that is opposite in meaning to the word discourage is encourage.

Discourage - cause (someone) to lose confidence or enthusiasm.

Encourage - give support, confidence, or hope to (someone).

Hence, the correct option is (D).

39. The correct word that is opposite in meaning to the word consecutive is discontinuous.

The meaning of the word 'Consecutive' is 'following one after the other in regular order; continuous'.

The meaning of the word 'discontinuous' is 'not continuous or having gaps'.

From the given meanings, we can understand that 'discontinuous' is the antonym of the given word.

Hence, the correct option is (A).

40. The art or practice of garden cultivation and management is known as horticulture.

Horticulture - the science and art of growing fruits, vegetables, flowers, or ornamental plants.

For Example - The treatment in horticulture of the peach and nectarine is the same in every respect.

Hence, the correct option is (C).

41. An opposite word can be defined as a word that expresses a meaning as opposed to the meaning of a particular word.

In this case, the two words are called antonyms of each other.

Let us explore the antonyms of the given options:

- Brother: Sister
- Father: Mother
- Uncle: Aunt
- Mother: Father

Therefore, the gender of the underlined noun is "uncle."

Hence, the correct option is (C).

42. Learn is not an adjective.

Adjectives describe or modify that is, they limit or restrict the meaning of—nouns and pronouns.

They may name qualities of all kinds: huge, red, angry, tremendous, unique, rare, etc. An adjective usually comes right before a noun: "a red dress," or "fifteen people."

- Learn: (Verb) (to get knowledge, a skill, etc. (from somebody/something).
- Beautiful: (Adjective) (very pretty or attractive; giving pleasure to the senses.
- Fast: Adjective, (Adverb) (able to move or act at great speed.
- Enormous: (Adjective) (very big or very great.

Therefore, the word which is not an adjective is "learn."

Hence, the correct option is (A).

43. The full form of couldn't is could not.

"Couldn't" is the usual spoken form of 'could not.'

It is also the short form of "could not."

Example: I couldn't find my keys this morning.

Hence, the correct option is (C).

44. The meaningful word from the words "URTHT" is "truth."

"Truth" means what is true; the facts.

Example: Please tell me the truth.

Hence, the correct option is (D).

45. An interjection is a part of speech used to convey or express sudden feelings and emotions.

Oh (Exclamation): used for reacting to something that somebody has said, for emphasizing what you are saying, or when you are thinking of what to say next.

Hence, the correct option is (A).

46. The correct tense I feel great! is Simple Present.

Let us see the structure of the given options:

Past Perfect: Subject + had + V3 + Object.

Example: She had left the city.

Simple Past: Subject + V2 + Object.

Example: She left the city.

Simple Present: Subject + V2(s/es) + Object

Example: She leaves the city.

Future Progressive: Subject + will + be + the present participle (the root verb + -ing)

Example: She will be leaving the city.

"I" is a singular pronoun and takes a plural verb "feel".

Hence, the correct option is (C).

47. The basic principle was that those who worked quite hard would be rewarded.

Principle (noun): a basic truth that explains or controls how something happens or works.

Quite (Adverb): not very; to a certain degree; rather.

The given sentence wants to convey that the main premise was that individuals who worked really hard would be rewarded.

Hence, the correct option is (C).

48. The most appropriate synonym of the given word is care.

Maintain: cause or enable (a condition or situation) to continue.

Care: the provision of what is necessary for the health, welfare, maintenance, and protection of someone or something.

Hence, the correct option is (A).

49. The meaning of 'Bias' is inclination or prejudice toward or against one person or group, especially in a way considered to be unfair.

Prejudice: an unfair and unreasonable opinion or feeling, especially when formed without enough thought or knowledge.

Therefore, the exact synonym of the given word 'Bias' is 'Prejudice.'

Hence, the correct option is (A).

50. We will go for a drive next week.

In simple future tense, the first form of the verb(V_1) is used with 'will/shall.' In the above sentence, the verb 'will go' is used as the action will take place in the future.

Hence, the correct option is (B).

51. Kerala Tourism won the coveted Responsible Tourism Global Award at London World Travel Mart in Nov 2022, for its STREET Project.

The 'STREET' initiative is a water protection and conservation project in the Tourism sector implemented with public participation. STREET is an acronym for Sustainable, Tangible, Responsible, Experiential, Ethnic & Tourism hubs & it was implemented in March 2022.

Hence, the correct option is (B).

52. P. V. Sindhu won the gold medal in Badminton women's singles in CWG 2022.

- P. V. Sindhu is the first and only Indian to become the badminton world champion and only the second individual athlete from India to win two consecutive medals at the Olympic Games.
- PV Sindhu defeated Michelle Li of Canada in the final badminton match of women's singles at the Commonwealth Games 2022 in Birmingham, to win gold on 8 August 2022.
- She beat Michelle Li by 21-15 and 21-13.
- She rose to a career-high world ranking of no. 2 in April 2017.

- Sindhu broke into the top 20 of the BWF World Rankings in September 2012, at the age of 17.

Hence, the correct option is (D).

53. The Indian Institute of Management Ahmedabad in collaboration with Indian agri-land marketplace SFarmsIndia has announced the launch of IIMA-SFarmsIndia Agri Land Price Index (ISALPI). It is a first-of-its-kind land price index that will record and present 'quality controlled' data of prices of agricultural land across the country.

Hence, the correct option is (D).

54. The fifth Bangladesh -India cultural meet concluded on 28 February 2022 in Rajshahi. The function was presided over by the Mayor of Rajshahi city AHM Khairuzzaman Liton. The four-day event between $25 - 28$ February was held to celebrate the birth centenary of Bangabandhu Sheikh Mujibur Rahman, the golden jubilee of the liberation of Bangladesh, and the 50th year of Bangladesh India Friendship.

Hence, the correct option is (B).

55. One District, One Product Programme aims to encourage indigenous and specialized products and crafts in India. It was first started by the Uttar Pradesh government. This scheme will provide job opportunities to 25 lakh unemployed candidates across the state.

Improvement in product quality and skill development is one of the main objective of the One District, One Product Programme. Uttar Pradesh government had launched this scheme on 24 January 2018.

"Handmade Paper" is selected as a product from the Jalaun district of Uttar Pradesh under the "One District One Product" scheme.

Hence, the correct option is (B).

56. The Patari is a community found mainly in the Sonbhadra district of Uttar Pradesh, India.

According to the tribe itself, the Patari are by origin Gond tribals, who were ritual specialists and advisers to the Gond kings. They belong to the Devgond sub-division.

The Patari once spoke Chhattisgarhi, but now speaks Hindi.

The Patari are further divided into four sub-divisions, each of which has separate totemistic septs called kuris.

The Patari are priests, locally known as Baigas, of a number of tribal grouping in south-east Uttar Pradesh such as the Majhwar, Chero, and Bhuiyar.

Hence, the correct option is (A).

57. Noida is the "Electronics City" being established in the state of Uttar Pradesh

The Yogi Adityanath government plans to establish separate clusters for companies from Taiwan, Japan, and South Korea as these three countries have a strong base in electronics. A team from Yamuna Expressway Authority in which the "Electronic City" is located will be traveling to these countries to interact with potential investors. The government is looking at a possible investment of Rs. 40,000 crore in the "Electronics City".

Hence, the correct option is (B).

58. Shilling is the currency of Kenya.

The shilling is a historical coin, and the name of a unit of modern currencies formerly used in the United Kingdom, Ireland, Australia, New Zealand and other British Commonwealth countries.

Currently the shilling is used as a currency in five east African countries: Kenya, Tanzania, Uganda, Somalia, as well as the de facto country of Somaliland.

Hence, the correct option is (B).

59. Introversion-Extraversion trait of personality is propounded by Hans Eysenck.

Hans Eysenck (1916-1997): British psychologist Hans Eysenck developed a model of personality basic upon just three universal traits; Introversion/Extroversion, Neuroticism/Emotional stability, and Psychoticism. Eysenck sees only two major types or traits as underlying personality structure: introversion-extraversion and stability-neuroticism. Introversion involves directing attention to inner experiences. while extraversion relates to focusing attention outward on other people and the environment. So, a person high in introversion might be quiet and reserved, while an individual high in extraversion might be sociable and outgoing.
Hence, the correct option is (A).

60. Shahjahanpur has topped in giving tap water connections.

In Jal Jeevan Survekshan-2023 several Uttar Pradesh districts have done well including Shahjahanpur, Bulandshahr, Bareilly, and Mirzapur. Shahjahanpur with 689,990 marks stood first in two categories. It was ranked on top in the aspirant category for ensuring 28,419 tap connections. Bulandshahr is in second place in the best performance category and placed third in the fast-moving districts.

Hence, the correct option is (D).

61. Major General Ian Cardozo, who amputated his leg on battlefield, launched his new book in November 2022.

The book is titled 'Cartoos Saab: A Soldier's Story of Resilience in Adversity.' He was the first war-disabled officer of the Indian Army to command a battalion and a brigade. It recounts Major General Ian Cardozo's painstaking efforts as a war-disabled officer to command a battalion.

Hence, the correct option is (D).

62. Dandiya Raas is a traditional folk dance of Gujarat and Rajasthan. It is associated with scenes from Holi and the Leela of Krishna and Radha in Vrindavan. It is a featured dance of the evening of Navratri in western India.

Hence, the correct option is (B).

63. The full form of "EVM" is Electronic Voting Machine.

An electronic Voting Machine (EVM) is an electronic device for recording votes. Electronic Voting Machines (EVMs) have been in use in Indian general and state elections since the 1999 elections in part for the implementation of electronic voting.

Hence, the correct option is (A).

64. The Durand Line was established in 1893 AD in the Hindukush, which passed through the tribal areas of Afghanistan and British India, outlining their areas of influence. In modern times this line is the boundary line between Afghanistan and Pakistan. The line was named after Sir Mortimer Durand, who had persuaded the Amir of Afghanistan Abdur Rahman Khan to consider it a boundary line. Perhaps this can be called a solution to the Indo-Afghan border problem for the rest of the British period.

Hence, the correct option is (A).

65. The first death anniversary of Shri Rajiv Gandhi was observed as Anti-Terrorism Day. After the assassination of the young Prime Minister of India Rajiv Gandhi on 21 May 1997, former Prime Minister VP Singh had announced to celebrate this day as Anti-Terrorism Day. Since that day it is celebrated as National Anti-Terrorism Day.

Hence, the correct option is (D).

66. The Great Pyramid of Giza, also known as the Pyramid of Cheops or Khufu, is located in Egypt and was built between 2560-2540 BC. The Giza Pyramid Complex or the Giza Pyramid Complex is an archaeological site on the Giza Plateau on the outskirts of the Egyptian capital, Cairo. This complex of ancient monuments includes three pyramidal complexes known as the Great Pyramids, a large-scale sculpture in the form of the Great Sphinx, several cemeteries, a workers' village, and an industrial complex.

Hence, the correct option is (B).

67. Ashoka Maurya was known as 'Devanampriya Priyadarshi'.

"Devanampriya" refers to the 'beloved to the gods' and "Priyadarshi" refers to the one who regards everyone amiably.

Hence, the correct option is (A).

68. Slave Dynasty was the first dynasty of the Delhi Sultanate.

The Delhi Sultanate was ruled over by five dynasties. These five dynasties were: the Slave dynasty (1206-90), Khilji dynasty (1290-1320), Tughlaq dynasty (1320-1412), Sayyid dynasty (1414-50), and Lodhi dynasty (1451-1526).

Hence, the correct option is (B).

69. The Black soil is also known as Regur soil.

- It covers a major part of the Deccan plateau including the states of Andhra Pradesh, Gujarat, Madhya Pradesh, Maharashtra, and Tamil Nadu.
- It is also known as black cotton soil.
- These are impermeable, deep, and, clayey and are rich in alumina, magnesia, iron, and lime.
- Some of the crops grown on it include cotton, jowar, wheat, linseed, etc.

Hence, the correct option is (D).

70. The name India is derived from the Indus river.

- It originates in the Tibetan region from a glacier near Bokhar Chu near Mansarovar Lake.
- In Tibet, it is known as Singi Khamban or Lion's mouth.
- In Jammu and Kashmir, its Himalayan tributaries are Zanskar, Dras, Gilgit, etc.
- The tributaries which join Indus at various places are Jhelum, Chenab, Ravi, Beas, and Sutlej.

Hence, the correct option is (A).

71. The melting of ice is a physical change.

- The change that does not lead to changes in the chemical composition of a substance is termed physical change.
- Physical changes lead to changes in physical properties and are generally reversible in nature.
- Examples of physical changes are the melting of ice, transition into gas, textural changes, changes in size, shape, color, etc.

Hence, the correct option is (A).

72. The metal used to make lightning conductors is copper.

Lightning rod:

- It is a metal rod mounted on top of a building that is electrically bonded using a wire or electrical conductor to interface with ground or "earth" through an electrode, engineered to protect the building in the event of a lightning strike.
- If lightning targets the building it will strike the rod and be conducted to the ground through the wire, instead of passing through the building, where it could start a fire or cause electrocution.
- Copper is a very good electrical conductor.

Hence, the correct option is (C).

73. A deficiency of vitamin A causes vision issues during night time.

- Vitamin A also called Retinol.
- Its deficiency causes hyperkeratosis and keratomalacia.
- Food rich in vitamin A are eggs, fish, milk, yogurt, etc.

Hence, the correct option is (A).

74. Uttar Pradesh Textile Technology Institute (Earlier known as Government Central Textile Institute) is located in Kanpur.

It is a premier textile institute in North India. However in 1937, Govt. Central Textile Institute came into existence in its present form by the merger of two premier textile institutes i.e., one at Kanpur and the other at Roorkee i.e., Department of Textile Technology.

Hence, the correct option is (A).

75. "Uttar Priyadarshi" play was written by Sachchidananda Vatsyayan.

Sachchidananda Vatsyayan was popularly known by his pen name Agyeya. Sachchidananda Vatsyayan was born in Kushinagar District, Uttar Pradesh.

Hence, the correct option is (A).

76.

2	6,100
2	3,50
3	3,25
5	1,25
5	1,5
	1,1

$6 = 2 \times 3$
$100 = 2 \times 2 \times 5 \times 5$
LCM of 6 and $100 = 2 \times 2 \times 3 \times 5 \times 5 = 300$
Hence, the correct option is (D).

77. Factor of $726 = 2 \times 3 \times 11 \times 11$

Factor of $426 = 2 \times 3 \times 7 \times 11$

So, HCF $(726,426) = 2 \times 3 \times 11 = 66$

Hence, the correct option is (A).

78. Given:

Principal $(P) =$ Rs. $6,000$

Rate $(R) = 3\%$

Simple interest $(SI) =$ Rs. 240

Time $(T) =?$

We know that:

Simple interest $SI = \frac{P \times R \times T}{100}$

$\Rightarrow 240 = \frac{6000 \times 3 \times T}{100}$

$\Rightarrow 240 = 180T$

$\Rightarrow T = \frac{4}{3}$ years

$\Rightarrow T = \left(\frac{4}{3}\right) \times 12$ months

$\Rightarrow T = 16$ months

$\therefore$ Rohan will pay the debt after 16 months.

Hence, the correct option is (C).

79. Let the units digit be x.

Then the tens digit is also x.

Therefore the number is $10x + x = 11x$.

On reversing the order of the digit the number is $10x + x = 11x$.

Hence by the given condition, we have,

$$11x + 11x = 110$$

$$22x = 110$$

$$x = 5$$

Therefore the required number is $11x = 11 \times 5 = 55$.

Hence, the correct option is (C).

80. Given,

$$\sqrt{2^n} = 32$$

$$\Rightarrow (2^n)^{\frac{1}{2}} = 32$$

$$\Rightarrow 2^{\frac{n}{2}} = 32$$

$$\Rightarrow 2^{\frac{n}{2}} = 2^5$$

By comparing powers, we get

$$\Rightarrow \frac{n}{2} = 5$$

$$\Rightarrow n = 10$$

Hence, the correct option is (D).

81. Given,

The mean of distribution $10, 8, 15, 12, K, 25 = 12$

As we know,

$$\text{Mean} = \frac{\text{Sum of all numbers}}{\text{Total numbers}}$$

$$\therefore \frac{(10+8+15+12+K+25)}{6} = 12$$

$$\Rightarrow 70 + K = 72$$

$$\Rightarrow K = 2$$

$\therefore$ The value of $K = 2$

Hence, the correct option is (A).

82. Given:

$$n \times \left(\frac{4}{9}\right) \text{ of } 1620 = (n+1) \text{ of } 72$$

$$\Rightarrow n \times 4 \times 180 = (n+1) \times 72$$

$$\Rightarrow n \times 180 = (n+1) \times 18$$

$$\Rightarrow n \times 10 = n + 1$$

$$\Rightarrow 10n - n = 1$$

$$\Rightarrow n = \frac{1}{9}$$

Now,

$$125\% \text{ of } \frac{1}{9}$$

$$125\% = 100\% + 25\%$$

$$= \frac{100}{100} + \frac{25}{100}$$

$$= 1 + \frac{1}{4}$$

$$= \left(1 + \frac{1}{4}\right) \times \frac{1}{9}$$

$$= \frac{5}{36}$$

So, 125% of $n = \frac{5}{36}$

Hence, the correct option is (B).

83. Given:

$$= \frac{2}{5} \times 350 + 30\% \text{ of } 250$$

$$= \frac{2}{5} \times 350 + \frac{30}{100} \times 250$$

$$= 140 + 75$$

$$= 215$$

Hence, the correct option is (C).

84. Given:

$$x - \frac{2}{x} = 15$$

We know that,

$$\left(A - \frac{1}{A}\right)^2 = A^2 - 2 + \frac{1}{A^2}$$

Now,

$$x - \frac{2}{x} = 15$$

$$\Rightarrow x^2 - 4 + \frac{4}{x^2} = 225 \text{ (Squaring both side)}$$

$$\Rightarrow x^2 + \frac{4}{x^2} = 229$$

Hence, the correct option is (C).

85. Given:

$$x\% \text{ of } 60 = 48$$

$$\Rightarrow \left(\frac{x}{100}\right) \times 60 = 48$$

$$\Rightarrow \frac{3x}{5} = 48$$

$$\Rightarrow x = 80$$

Hence, the correct option is (C).

86. Given:

The cost price of an item is 25% less than the marked price.

Let the marked price be $100a$.

So, cost price $= 100a - 100a \times 25\%$

$\Rightarrow 75a$

Now,

Marked price is $(100a - 75a) = 25a$ extra than the cost price

So, required $\% = \left(\dfrac{25a}{75a}\right) \times 100$

$\Rightarrow 33\dfrac{1}{3}$

$\therefore$ Required answer is $33\dfrac{1}{3}\%$.

Hence, the correct option is (D).

87. Given:

$x = 1.\overline{23}$

$\Rightarrow x = 1.232323 \quad \ldots(1)$

$\Rightarrow 100x = 123.232323\ldots \quad \ldots(2) \quad$ [Equation 1×100]

Substracting equation (1) from (2), we get,

$99x = 122$

$\Rightarrow x = \dfrac{122}{99}$

$\therefore ? = \dfrac{122}{99}$

Hence, the correct option is (B).

88. Let $x = 0.6\overline{23} \quad \ldots(1)$

Multiply by 10 in equation (1),

$10x = 6 + 0.232323\ldots \quad \ldots(2)$

Multiply by 1000 in equation (1),

$1000x = 623 + 0.2323\ldots \quad \ldots(3)$

Subtract equation (2) from equation (3),

$990x = 617$

$\Rightarrow x = \dfrac{617}{990}$

Hence, the correct option is (C).

89. Given:

$78 - [5 + 3 \text{ of } (25 - 2 \times 10)]$

$= 78 - [5 + 3 \text{ of } (25 - 20)]$

$= 78 - [5 + 3 \text{ of } (5)]$

$= 78 - [5 + 15]$

$= 78 - [20]$

$= 58$

Hence, the correct option is (A).

90. We know that,

Divisibility rule of 9:

The addition of digits of a given number must be divisible by 9.

Divisibility rule of 11:

The difference of sums of the digits in odd and even places is zero or multiple of 11.

Now,

99 can be written as,

$\Rightarrow 99 = 9 \times 11$

Now by taking options,

Option (A),

For 9,

$\Rightarrow 51579 = 5 + 1 + 5 + 7 + 9 = 27$

27 which is divisible by 9,

So the number is divisible by 9.

For 11,

$\Rightarrow 51579 = (5 + 5 + 9) - (1 + 7)$

$\Rightarrow 19 - 8 = 11$

So the number is divisible by 11.

$\therefore 51579$ is divisible by 99.

Hence, the correct option is (A).

91. We know that,

Prime numbers: A number that has only two factors one and itself is called a Prime number.

$\Rightarrow 853 = 1 \times 853$

853 is a prime number.

$\Rightarrow 953 = 1 \times 953$

953 is a prime number.

$\Rightarrow 553 = 1 \times 7 \times 79$

553 is not a prime number, because it has more than two factors.

$\Rightarrow 653 = 1 \times 653$

653 is a prime number.

$\therefore 553$ is not a prime number.

Hence, the correct option is (C).

92. Let the number be x.

According to the question,

$8x = 40 - 8$

$\Rightarrow 8x = 32$

$\Rightarrow x = 4$

Hence, the correct option is (C).

93. We know that,

1 km $= 1000$ m

1 m $= 100$ cm

Now,

460 cm $+0.6$ km $+20$ m

$\Rightarrow 500$ cm $+(0.6 \times 100000)$ cm $+(20 \times 100)$ cm

$\Rightarrow 460$ cm $+60000$ cm $+2000$ cm

$\Rightarrow 62460$ cm

Hence, the correct option is (B).

94. Given:

The sum of the square of the sides of a rhombus $= 1600$ cm^2

Let the side of the rhombus be a.

Sum of the side of rhombus $= 4a$

Now,

According to the question,

$4a^2 = 1600$ cm^2

$\Rightarrow a^2 = \left(\dfrac{1600}{4}\right)$

$\Rightarrow a^2 = 400$

$\Rightarrow a = 20$ cm

$\therefore$ The side of the rhombus is 20 cm.

Hence, the correct option is (D).

95. Given:

Diameter of a sphere $= 56$ cm

We know that,

The surface of a sphere $= 4\pi R^2$ (R is the radius of the sphere)

Radius $=$ Diameter $\div 2$

Radius of the sphere $= \dfrac{56}{2} = 28$ cm

Now, the surface area of the sphere $= 4\pi \times 28^2$

$\Rightarrow 9856$ cm^2

$\therefore$ Its surface area is 9856 cm^2.

Hence, the correct option is (A).

96. Given:

$0.9 \div (0.3 \times 0.3)$

$= 0.9 \div (0.09)$

$= \dfrac{0.9}{0.09} = \dfrac{0.90}{0.09} = \dfrac{90}{9} = 10$

The value of $0.9 \div (0.3 \times 0.3)$ is 10.

Hence, the correct option is (D).

97. Given:

$\dfrac{15}{7}$ of 70% of $0.15 = ?$

$\Rightarrow \dfrac{15}{7} \times \dfrac{70}{100} \times \dfrac{15}{100} = ?$

$\Rightarrow \dfrac{15}{7} \times \dfrac{7}{10} \times \dfrac{3}{20} = ?$

$\Rightarrow ? = \dfrac{3}{2} \times \dfrac{3}{20} = \dfrac{9}{40}$

$\Rightarrow ? = 0.225$

$\therefore$ The required value is 0.225.

Hence, the correct option is (A).

98. Given,

$4, 7, 12, 19, 28, ?$

First term : 4

Second term: $4 + 3 = 7$

Third term : $7 + 5 = 12$

Fourth term : $12 + 7 = 19.$

Fifth term : $19 + 9 = 28.$

Therefore,

Next Terms : $28 + 11 = 39$

Hence, the correct option is (D).

99. We have to find the Least number, therefore we find out the LCM of $8, 12, 16$ and 20.

$8 = 2 \times 2 \times 2$

$12 = 2 \times 2 \times 3$

$16 = 2 \times 2 \times 2 \times 2$

$20 = 2 \times 2 \times 5$

LCM $= 2 \times 2 \times 2 \times 2 \times 3 \times 5 = 240$

This is the least number which is exactly divisible by $8, 12, 16$ and 20

Thus, Required number which leaves remainder 5 is,

$240 + 5 = 245$

Hence, the correct option is (B).

100. Given,

$\Rightarrow 2112 + 692 \times 2 - 1111 \times 5 + 7324 \times 8 =?$

$\Rightarrow 2112 + 1384 - 5555 + 58592 =?$

$\Rightarrow ? = 62088 - 5555 = 56533$

$\therefore ? = 56533$

Hence, the correct option is (A).

Hindi

Ques (1-2):निर्देश: निम्नलिखित प्रश्न में दिए गए वाक्य के लिए एक शब्द चुनिए।

Q.1 'जो विनीत या नरम न हो'

A. प्रियभाषी   B. अभूतपूर्व   C. अविनीत   D. सर्वव्यापक

Q.2 जिसे किसी वस्तु की इच्छा न हो

A. निःस्पृह   B. निस्पृहीन   C. नीस्पृह   D. निःस्पृहा

Q.3 निम्नलिखित में कौन सा विकल्प सही है?

A. आश्रिता ने पत्र लिखा – पूर्ण भूतकाल
B. लड़की गाँव जाती है – सामान्य वर्तमानकाल
C. लड़का जा रहा है – अपूर्ण भूतकाल
D. पिताजी जाएंगे – संभाव्य भविष्यतकाल

Q.4 दिए गए विराम चिह्नों में से अर्द्ध विराम चिह्न है:

A. ,   B. :   C. :-   D. ;

Q.5 जब किसी कथन को अलग दिखाना हो तो किसका प्रयोग करते हैं?

A. योजक चिह्न   B. उपविराम चिह्न
C. आदेश चिह्न   D. रेखांकन चिह्न

Q.6 समुदायवाचक संज्ञा किसे कहते हैं?

A. जो शब्द किसी एक जाति के व्यक्तियों, वस्तुओं के समूह का बोध कराते है।
B. वह शब्द जो किसी द्रव्य, धातु या पदार्थ का बोध कराते हैं।
C. वे शब्द जिनसे भाव का बोध होता है।
D. इनमें से कोई नहीं

Q.7 'आँसू पीकर रह जाना' मुहावरे का सही अर्थ है-

[UPSSSC Junior Assistant, 2020]

A. आँसू बहने न देना।
B. अन्न के अभाव में आँसू से भूख मिटाना।
C. गुस्सा होना।
D. चुपचाप दुःख सह लेना।

Q.8 'आँधी आवे बैठ गंवावे' लोकोक्ति का उपयुक्त अर्थ है:

[UPSSSC Junior Assistant, 2020]

A. संकट से मुँह फेरना
B. विपरीत परिस्थिति में उपयुक्त समय आने का इंतजार करना
C. विपत्ति से टकराने का हौसला रखना
D. आँधी के बाद पानी बरसने का इंतजार करना

Q.9 इनमें से कर्म कारक का चिह्न कौन-सा है?

[UP Police Sub Inspector, 2021]

A. को   B. ने   C. से   D. में

Q.10 'अलंकार' में किस उपसर्ग का प्रयोग है?

[UPTET Paper - I, 2018]

A. अलु   B. अल   C. अलन्   D. अलम्

Q.11 'संकल्प' शब्द में उपसर्ग बताइए:

[UPTET Paper - I, 2018]

A. सम्   B. सक्   C. सन्   D. सन्क

Q.12 'पर्वतीय' कौन-सा विशेषण है?

[UPSSSC Village Development Officer, 2018]

A. गुणवाचक विशेषण   B. संख्यावाचक विशेषण
C. परिमाण वाचक विशेषण   D. सार्वनामिक विशेषण

Q.13 निम्नलिखित प्रश्न में, चार विकल्पों में से, उस सही विकल्प का चयन करें जो बताता है कि – वह सर्वनाम का भेद नहीं है।

A. पुरूषवाचक सर्वनाम   B. निश्चयवाचक सर्वनाम
C. प्रश्नवाचक सर्वनाम   D. जातिवाचक सर्वनाम

Ques (14-15):निर्देश: रिक्त स्थान की पूर्ति कीजिए।

Q.14 भाव दशा के कारण वचन में आये परिवर्तन को _____ कहते हैं।

A. वाचिक उद्दीपन   B. वाचिक अनुभाव
C. वाचिक विभव   D. वाचिक आलंबन

Q.15 पल्लवन में सूत्र वाक्य, विचार या भाव को _____।

A. मात्रा विस्तार दिया जाता है
B. मात्र विस्तार दिया जाता है
C. मात्र विस्तार नहीं दिया जाता है
D. मात्र विस्तारा दिया जाता है

Q.16 स्वर तंत्रियों के आधार पर व्यंजनों को कितने वर्गों में बाँटा गया है?

A. एक   B. दो   C. तीन   D. चार

Q.17 अकारांत स्त्रीलिंग शब्द का बहुवचन बनाने के लिए क्या किया जाता है?

[UPSSSC Junior Assistant, 2020]

A. अन्त्य स्वर के बदले 'ओं' कर देते हैं।
B. अन्त्य स्वर के साथ 'अयें' लगा देते हैं।
C. अन्त्य स्वर के बदले 'ऐं' कर देते हैं।
D. अन्त्य स्वर के बदले आएँ कर देते हैं।

Q.18 निम्न में से शुद्ध वर्तनी वाले शब्द का चयन कीजिए।

A. वाल्मीकी   B. वाल्मिकि   C. वालमीकी   D. वाल्मिकि

Q.19 'यथोचित' का सही संधि-विच्छेद है-

[UPSSSC Junior Assistant, 2020]

A. यथो + उचित   B. यथा + उ + चित
C. यथा + उचित   D. यथा + ओचित

Q.20 'रति' किस रस का स्थायी भाव है?

A. शांत रस   B. वीर रस
C. श्रृंगार रस   D. वीभत्स रस

Q.21 'मूर्त' शब्द का विलोम है-

[UPSSSC Junior Assistant, 2020]

A. अमूर्त   B. प्रतिमूर्त   C. सम्मूर्त   D. अदृष्ट

Q.22 कौन सा शब्द 'व्योम' का पर्यायवाची नहीं है?

A. अन्तरिक्ष   B. अम्बर   C. पीयूष   D. नभ

Q.23 "ईश्वर तुम्हें सफलता प्रदान करे।" यह किस प्रकार का वाक्य है?

[Rajasthan Teachers Eligibility Test - Level 1 Primary Level (RTET), 2015]

A. संकेतवाचक
B. विधानवाचक
C. इच्छावाचक
D. इच्छावाचक

Q.24 निम्नलिखित में से कौन सा शब्द तत्सम नहीं है?

[UPSSSC Junior Assistant, 2020]

A. परतीत
B. प्रतीत
C. प्रतिमान
D. प्रतिबिम्ब

Q.25 निम्नलिखित में से कौन सा शब्द तद्भव है?

[UPSSSC Junior Assistant, 2020]

A. उल्लास
B. उच्छ्वास
C. निःश्वास
D. उजास

English

Ques (26-33):Direction: Fill in the blank in the given sentence by choosing the correct option.

Q.26 A person suffering from chronic neurodegenerative disease _______ short-term memory loss.
A. experienced
B. has experienced
C. is experiencing
D. experiences

Q.27 In all probability, it _______ rain tonight.
A. will
B. can
C. may
D. ought

Q.28 Owing to his consistent practice he is _______ well in this particular sport.
A. getting at
B. getting off
C. getting on
D. getting in

Q.29 Annu, though ill-equipped for the project, had _______ tried her best.
A. for
B. nevertheless
C. last
D. if

Q.30 You have to submit a copy of _______ school leaving certificate.
A. hers
B. yours
C. theirs
D. your

Q.31 I wish I _______ a car. It would make life so much easier.
A. have
B. had
C. would have
D. will have

Q.32 "He lived a hand _______ mouth existence, surviving on just a few rupees a week".
A. in
B. to
C. for
D. inside

Q.33 Only a small fraction are convicts; the rest are _______.
A. Undertrials
B. Underpopulated
C. Understated
D. Underwhelmed

Q.34 Choose the correctly punctuated sentence.
A. What a beautiful house!
B. What a beautiful house?
C. What a beautiful house.
D. What a beautiful house,

Q.35 Choose the correctly punctuated sentence.
A. You should listen to her? otherwise you will regret.
B. You should listen to her, otherwise you will regret.
C. You should listen to her. otherwise you will regret.
D. You should listen to her! otherwise you will regret.

Q.36 Direction: Please choose one of the 4 alternatives that can be substituted for the given sentence.

A person who believes in God.

[Intelligence Bureau Security Assistant, 2019]

A. Theist
B. Cynic
C. Atheist
D. none of these

Q.37 Choose the correctly spelled word.
A. Simanticist
B. Semanticist
C. Simenticist
D. Symanticist

Q.38 Direction: Identify the tense used in the sentence given below.

Shakespeare has written dramas appealing to all people of all ages.
A. Simple Present
B. Present Continuous
C. Past Perfect
D. Present Perfect

Q.39 Direction: Find out the adjective of the given word.

Custom
A. Customer
B. Customise
C. Customary
D. Costume

Q.40 Direction: Match the following verbs to their past participle:

Simple Present	Past participle
1. Write	a. Wrote
2. Wear	b. Wore
3. Wake	c. Woke

A. 1-a, 2-c, 3- b
B. 1-b, 2- a, 3-b
C. 1-b, 2-a, 3-c
D. None of these

Q.41 Direction: Identify the interjection in the given sentence.

Uh-oh! Dude, I think we're in serious trouble.
A. Dude
B. Trouble
C. Uh-oh
D. Think

Q.42 Direction: A word with letters jumbled has been given. Choose the correct order of letters from the options.

SPTRECE
A. RESTPCE
B. RESTPEC
C. SPTCERE
D. RESPECT

Q.43 Direction: Change the gender of the underlined noun and rewrite the sentence:

My brother is going out of town.
A. My niece is going out of town.
B. My aunt is going out of town.
C. My uncle is going out of town.
D. My sister is going out of town.

Q.44 Direction: Choose the correct alternative which is related to the third term in the same way as the second term is related to the first term.

Sheep : Lamb :: Butterfly : ?
A. Caterpillar
B. Nymph
C. Tadpole
D. Larva

Q.45 Direction: Fill in the blank with the correct pronoun.

I have nobody _____ I can confide in.

A. whom **B.** who **C.** which **D.** whose

Q.46 Direction: Fill in the blanks with the correct prepositions.

The tourists were ___ the car; the car was passing _____ the tunnel.

A. in, through **B.** on, through
C. at, through **D.** under, through

Ques (47-48):Direction: In the following question, out of the given alternatives, choose the one which best expresses the meaning of the given word.

Q.47 Assertion

A. Discussion **B.** Rejection
C. Declaration **D.** Continuation

Q.48 Sentiment

A. Antipathy **B.** Concrete
C. Hatred **D.** Feeling

Ques (49-50):Direction: In the following question, choose the word opposite in meaning to the given word.

Q.49 Conducive

A. Favourable **B.** Unfavourable
C. Propitious **D.** Opportune

Q.50 Audacious

A. Vulgar **B.** Extinct **C.** Timid **D.** Fickle

General Studies

Q.51 In which of the following divisions of Uttar Pradesh the first Samajwadi Abhinav School was established?

A. Allahabad **B.** Aligarh
C. Agra **D.** Varanasi

Q.52 Which large metropolitan region of Uttar Prdesh has highest population?

A. Lucknow **B.** Kanpur
C. Ghaziabad **D.** Gorakhpur

Q.53 Slow left-arm spinner Kuldeep Yadav belongs to which district of Uttar Pradesh?

A. Kanpur **B.** Agra
C. Gaziabad **D.** Meerut

Q.54 Prime Minister Modi will lay the foundation stone of the development work of Chittaura Lake. It is in which district of Uttar Pradesh?

A. Moradabad **B.** Gorakhpur
C. Mau **D.** Bahraich

Q.55 The Kampil Fair is celebrated in which of the following districts?

A. Agra **B.** Farrukhabad
C. Kanpur **D.** Hamirpur

Q.56 Which of the following hills lie between India and Myanmar ?

A. Mount Everest **B.** Garo
C. Naga **D.** Khasi

Q.57 State Highways are maintained by:

A. State Government
B. Central Government
C. Central and State Governments jointly
D. Private parties selected by the State Governments

Q.58 _______has become the fastest human calculator in the world after bagging the gold for India in the Mental Calculation World Championship at Mind Sports Olympiad.

A. Anand Mahindra
B. Kiran Karnik
C. Uday K Sondhi
D. NeelaKantha Bhanu Prakash

Q.59 _______ is the currency of North Korea.

A. Yen **B.** Dinar **C.** Dollar **D.** Won

Q.60 Who is known as the father of the Blue Revolution in India?

A. Verghese Kurien **B.** Sam Pitroda
C. Hiralal Chaudhuri **D.** M.S. Swaminatha

Q.61 In which stadium the final match of IPL 2022 was played?

A. Eden Garden
B. Wankhede stadium
C. Arun Jetaly stadium
D. Narendra Modi Stadium

Q.62 Who was the Mughal ruler participated in the revolt of 1857 and was later exiled to Rangoon?

A. Bahadur Shah Zafar **B.** Akbar II
C. Ahmad Shah **D.** Shah Alam II

Q.63 The city of lakes is:

A. Jodhpur **B.** Raipur **C.** Udaipur **D.** Mewar

Q.64 Dhanvantri and Kalidasa were in the court of which Gupta Emperor?

A. Kumar Gupta I **B.** Samudra Gupta
C. Chandra Gupta II **D.** Skanda Gupta

Q.65 Which of the following regions of India is known as a cold desert?

A. Marusthali
B. Tirunelveli region of Tamil Nadu
C. Kachchha region
D. Ladakh

Q.66 Which is the most suitable cash crop for black soil?

A. Cotton **B.** Tea **C.** Jute **D.** Oilseeds

Q.67 The Tropic of Cancer does NOT pass through which of the following Indian states?

A. Chhattisgarh **B.** Assam
C. Tripura **D.** Jharkhand

Q.68 Identify A in the given diagram:

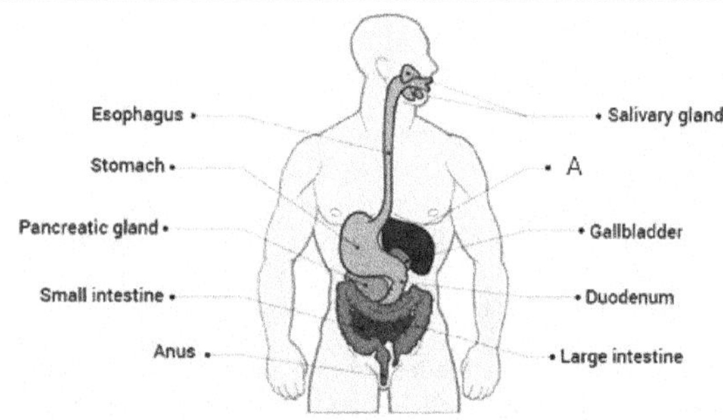

A. Liver   **B.** Kidney   **C.** Lungs   **D.** Trachea

Q.69 Identify A, B, and C in the given diagram:

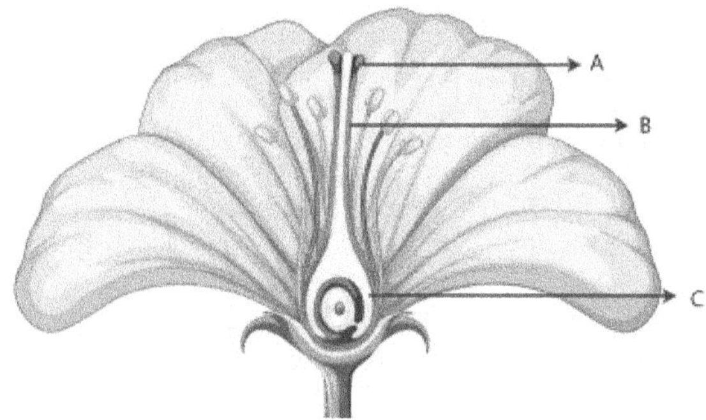

A. A. Ovary B. Style C. Stigma
B. A. Stigma B. Style C. Ovary
C. A. Style B. Style C. Stigma
D. A. Style B. Gynoecium C. Stigma

Q.70 What is the rank of India in the 2022 Global Innovation Index, released in September 2022?
A. 30th   **B.** 10th   **C.** 20th   **D.** 40th

Q.71 Wayanad Wildlife Sanctuary is located in _________.
A. Andhra Pradesh   **B.** Tamil Naidu
C. Karnataka   **D.** Kerala

Q.72 The first "Amrit Sarovar" in India was inaugurated in which state of India?
A. Karnataka   **B.** Assam
C. Madhya Pradesh   **D.** Uttar Pradesh

Q.73 Former India cricketer Yuvraj Singh has been appointed as the brand ambassador for the 3rd T20 World Cup for the Blind. The 3rd T20 World Cup for the Blind will be held in _________.
A. India   **B.** Bangladesh
C. Australia   **D.** New Zealand

Q.74 Which state has been awarded 'Ayushmann Utkrishta award 2022'?
A. Andhra Pradesh   **B.** Uttar Pradesh
C. Karnataka   **D.** Himachal Pradesh

Q.75 Who won the title of Emerging player of the season in IPL 2022?
A. Dinesh Karthik   **B.** Umran Malik
C. Jos Buttler   **D.** Evin Lewis

Mathematics

Q.76 Two numbers are in ratio $1:2$ and their HCF is 16. Their LCM is:

[RRB (NTPC), 2017]

A. 16   **B.** 23   **C.** 32   **D.** 60

Q.77 The difference between the area of the circumcircle and the incircle of an equilateral triangle is $66m^2$, then find out the area of triangle $\left(\pi = \frac{22}{7}\right)$
A. $21\sqrt{3}$ m^2 **B.** $14\sqrt{3}$ m^2
C. 21 m^2 **D.** 24 m^2

Q.78 The sum of 5 consecutive numbers is 140. Find the highest number.
A. 26   **B.** 30   **C.** 40   **D.** 28

Q.79 What is the square root of 3920?
A. $28\sqrt{5}$ **B.** $26\sqrt{5}$
C. $24\sqrt{5}$ **D.** None of these

Q.80 Ram buys 70 articles for Rs. 890 and sold 60 articles for Rs. 890. What is his gain percent?
A. $17\frac{1}{3}\%$ **B.** 25%   **C.** 20%   **D.** $16\frac{2}{3}\%$

Q.81 Find the mean of the given data {a, b, a, a, b, a, b, c, a, b, a, c, a, b, a}, where a is less than b and b is less than c.
A. $\frac{(3a+2b+4c)}{9}$ **B.** $\frac{(8a+4b+2c)}{15}$
C. $\frac{(8a+5b+2c)}{15}$ **D.** $\frac{(8a+5b+c)}{15}$

Q.82 The difference between a number and $\frac{2}{7}$th of the number is 100. The number is:
A. 130   **B.** 140   **C.** 150   **D.** 160

Q.83 Simplify: $(2^2)^3 \times (2^3)^2$
A. 4096   **B.** 4046   **C.** 3096   **D.** 3046

Q.84 Find the value of 121 ÷ 5 + (8740 ÷ 5 - 4) ÷ 5.
A. 373   **B.** 473
C. 543   **D.** None of these

Q.85 Direction: Simplify the following expression:
2.06 - 3.16 + 4.59 - 1.79
A. 1.75   **B.** 1.65   **C.** 1.80   **D.** 1.70

Q.86 Find the value of k if $(-5)^{k+2} \times (-5)^4 = (-5)^9$.
A. 3   **B.** 4   **C.** 1   **D.** 2

Q.87 Simplify: 21 × (23 - 12) - {(-1 × 10) + 21}
A. 210   **B.** 190   **C.** 220   **D.** 0

Q.88 Find the H.C.F of 2.1, 10.5, 1.89
A. 0.21   **B.** 1.05   **C.** 0.3   **D.** 0.6

Q.89 If the length of a diagonal of a square is 12 cm, then its area will be?
A. $24\sqrt{2}\ cm^2$ **B.** $24\ cm^2$
C. $72\ cm^2$ **D.** $36\ cm^2$

Q.90 If P% of P is 36, then P is equal to:

[UPTET Paper - I, 2018]

A. 3600   **B.** 60   **C.** 15   **D.** 600

Q.91 The smallest number, which, when divided by 16 or 12 or 8, leaves remainder 6 in each case, is:

A. 102   **B.** 78   **C.** 54   **D.** 70

Q.92 Find the smallest 4 digit number which is divisible by 12, 15 and 18.

A. 1040   **B.** 1000   **C.** 1080   **D.** 1020

Q.93 What is the difference between the sum of the place value and real value of 9 and the sum of the place value and real value of 7 in 9876?

A. 8932   **B.** 8392   **C.** 8931   **D.** 8391

Q.94 What will be the simple interest at Rs. 720 at the rate of 9% per annum for 5 years?

A. Rs. 250   **B.** Rs. 520   **C.** Rs. 540   **D.** Rs. 324

Q.95 What will come in place of a question mark (?) in the following number series?

9, 13, 21, 33, ?, 69

A. 47   **B.** 48   **C.** 49   **D.** 50

Q.96 If $a + b = 7$ and $ab = 12$, then what will be the value of $a^2 + b^2$?

A. 40   **B.** 25   **C.** 39   **D.** 45

Q.97 The greatest two digit even number when added to smallest three digit prime number gives:

A. 198   **B.** 199   **C.** 200   **D.** 201

Q.98 The product of two numbers is 0.432. If one of them is 1.6, what is the other number?

A. 0.027   **B.** 0.27   **C.** 2.7   **D.** 27

Q.99 What should be subtracted from sum of 16.7 and 12.38 to obtain 10.09?

A. 17.89   **B.** 18.99   **C.** 16.98   **D.** 20.09

Q.100 The difference of the place value and the face value of the number 3 in 12345 is:

A. 0   **B.** 295   **C.** 297   **D.** 405

// Smart Answer Sheet //

Correct — Indicates percentage of students who answered questions correctly.

Skipped — Indicates percentage of students who skipped questions.

Q.	Ans.	Correct / Skipped	Q.	Ans.	Correct / Skipped	Q.	Ans.	Correct / Skipped	Q.	Ans.	Correct / Skipped	Q.	Ans.	Correct / Skipped
1	C	54.5 % / 1.72 %	17	C	61.48 % / 1.65 %	33	A	47.52 % / 1.77 %	49	B	58.19 % / 1.41 %	65	D	52.37 % / 1.32 %
2	A	65.75 % / 1.68 %	18	B	67.8 % / 1.86 %	34	A	83.55 % / 0.0 %	50	C	61.97 % / 1.92 %	66	A	52.42 % / 1.67 %
3	B	22.65 % / 4.51 %	19	C	56.74 % / 1.64 %	35	B	80.58 % / 0.0 %	51	A	40.54 % / 1.16 %	67	B	53.46 % / 1.02 %
4	D	82.67 % / 0.0 %	20	C	79.35 % / 0.0 %	36	A	44.5 % / 1.99 %	52	B	58.91 % / 1.58 %	68	A	63.74 % / 1.51 %
5	B	76.23 % / 0.0 %	21	A	82.41 % / 0.0 %	37	B	56.51 % / 1.55 %	53	A	41.55 % / 1.39 %	69	B	50.59 % / 1.54 %
6	A	55.21 % / 1.77 %	22	C	46.61 % / 1.89 %	38	D	59.07 % / 1.97 %	54	D	61.98 % / 1.44 %	70	D	57.58 % / 1.22 %
7	D	68.74 % / 1.81 %	23	C	15.0 % / 3.03 %	39	C	46.98 % / 1.72 %	55	B	82.54 % / 0.0 %	71	D	66.69 % / 1.13 %
8	B	79.68 % / 0.0 %	24	A	76.99 % / 0.0 %	40	D	54.5 % / 1.9 %	56	C	42.64 % / 1.72 %	72	D	66.84 % / 1.78 %
9	A	60.3 % / 1.49 %	25	D	78.0 % / 0.0 %	41	C	66.36 % / 1.91 %	57	A	76.47 % / 0.0 %	73	A	52.65 % / 1.63 %
10	D	84.68 % / 0.0 %	26	D	60.01 % / 1.17 %	42	D	51.94 % / 1.26 %	58	D	62.49 % / 1.53 %	74	B	67.74 % / 1.02 %
11	A	46.28 % / 1.92 %	27	A	40.43 % / 1.51 %	43	D	68.46 % / 1.46 %	59	D	18.68 % / 3.43 %	75	B	68.84 % / 1.96 %
12	A	42.46 % / 1.52 %	28	C	56.45 % / 1.56 %	44	A	62.57 % / 1.72 %	60	C	76.32 % / 0.0 %	76	C	58.21 % / 1.36 %
13	D	80.43 % / 0.0 %	29	B	46.37 % / 1.83 %	45	A	55.03 % / 1.55 %	61	D	56.84 % / 1.64 %	77	A	46.97 % / 1.3 %
14	B	52.59 % / 1.43 %	30	D	54.11 % / 1.18 %	46	A	57.16 % / 1.36 %	62	A	49.01 % / 1.81 %	78	B	80.74 % / 0.0 %
15	B	78.35 % / 0.0 %	31	B	67.37 % / 1.35 %	47	C	45.82 % / 1.34 %	63	C	78.09 % / 0.0 %	79	A	56.84 % / 1.73 %
16	B	43.39 % / 1.88 %	32	B	58.61 % / 1.24 %	48	D	48.56 % / 1.26 %	64	C	62.28 % / 1.36 %	80	D	41.42 % / 1.17 %

Q.	Ans.	Correct	Skipped	Q.	Ans.	Correct	Skipped	Q.	Ans.	Correct	Skipped	Q.	Ans.	Correct	Skipped	Q.	Ans.	Correct	Skipped
81	C	44.76 %	1.14 %	85	D	41.19 %	1.98 %	89	C	51.86 %	1.11 %	93	A	59.73 %	1.67 %	97	B	53.8 %	1.48 %
82	B	77.34 %	0.0 %	86	A	47.31 %	1.61 %	90	B	56.18 %	1.2 %	94	D	67.15 %	1.32 %	98	B	45.24 %	1.84 %
83	A	62.03 %	1.54 %	87	C	41.29 %	1.19 %	91	C	67.75 %	1.28 %	95	C	57.42 %	1.57 %	99	B	45.63 %	1.03 %
84	A	67.85 %	1.46 %	88	A	82.24 %	0.0 %	92	C	45.62 %	1.35 %	96	B	40.28 %	1.46 %	100	C	64.6 %	1.75 %

Performance Analysis

Avg. Score (%)	**53.0%**
Toppers Score (%)	**75.0%**
Your Score	

//Hints and Solutions//

1. दिये गए विकल्पों में से 'जो विनीत या नरम न हो' के लिए एक शब्द 'अविनीत' है।

'अविनीत' का पर्यायवाची: अभद्र, अशिष्ट, असभ्य, अकुलीन होगा।

'अविनीत' का विलोम 'विनीत' होगा।

अतः विकल्प (C) सही है।

2. 'जिसे किसी वस्तु की इच्छा न हो' वाक्यांश के लिए सार्थक शब्द 'निःस्पृह' है।

निःस्पृह – अर्थ: जिसे किसी प्रकार का लोभ या लालसा न हो।

उदाहरण: सच्चे साधु-संत निस्पृह होते हैं।

अतः विकल्प (A) सही है।

3. दिए गये विकल्पों में 'लड़की गाँव जाती है – सामान्य वर्तमानकाल' सही विकल्प है क्योंकि सामान्य वर्तमानकाल अर्थात क्रिया के जिस रूप से क्रिया का वर्तमान समय में सामान्य रूप से होने का पता चले। इसमें क्रिया के साथ ता है, ते है, ती है आदि आते है।

अतः विकल्प (B) सही है।

4. ' ; ' अर्द्ध विराम चिह्न है।

विराम चिह्न: विराम चिह्न का अर्थ ठहराव, रुकना है, अर्थात वाक्य लिखते समय विराम को प्रकट करने के लिए लगाए जाने वाले चिह्न को विराम चिह्न कहते हैं।

अतः विकल्प (D) सही है।

5. जब किसी कथन को अलग दिखाना हो तो 'उपविराम चिह्न' का प्रयोग करते हैं। उपविराम चिह्न (:) होता है।

अन्य विकल्प:

- योजक चिह्न (-)
- आदेश चिह्न (:-)
- रेखांकन चिह्न (_)

अतः विकल्प (B) सही है।

6. जिन संज्ञा शब्दों से किसी भी व्यक्ति या वस्तु के समूह का बोध होता है, उन शब्दों को समूहवाचक या समुदायवाचक संज्ञा कहते हैं।

अतः विकल्प (A) सही है।

7. 'आँसू पीकर रह जाना' मुहावरे का सही अर्थ चुपचाप दुःख सह लेना है।

वाक्य- सबके सामने बिना वजह जली-कटी सुनकर भी राजू आंसू पीकर रह गया।

अतः विकल्प (D) सही है।

8. 'आँधी आवे बैठ गंवावे' लोकोक्ति का उपयुक्त अर्थ 'विपरीत परिस्थिति में उपयुक्त समय आने का इंतजार करना' है।

वाक्य: परीक्षा की तिथि ज्ञात होने पर भी तैयारी न करना, आंधी आवे बैठ गंवावे के समान है।

अतः विकल्प (B) सही है।

9. दिये गये विकल्पों में 'को' परसर्ग कर्म कारक का चिन्ह है।

संज्ञा या सर्वनाम के जिस रूप से वाक्य के अन्य शब्दों के साथ उनका संबंध सूचित हो उसे कारक कहते हैं। हिंदी व्याकरण में कुल 8 प्रकार के कारकों का विधान किया गया है, जो परसर्ग सहित इस प्रकार हैं-

कारक	परसर्ग
कर्ता	ने
कर्म	को
करण	से/के द्वारा
सम्प्रदान	के लिए
अपादान	से (अलगाव)
संबंध	का, के, की, ना, ने, नी, रा, रे, री
अधिकरण	में, पर
सम्बोधन	हे!, ओ!, अरे!, अजी!

अतः विकल्प (A) सही है।

10. 'अलंकार' में 'अलम्' उपसर्ग का प्रयोग किया गया है।

'अलम्' का अर्थ 'पर्याप्त' होता है।

उपसर्ग: उपसर्ग ऐसे शब्दांश जो किसी शब्द के पूर्व जुड़ कर उसके अर्थ में परिवर्तन कर देते हैं या उसके अर्थ में विशेषता ला देते हैं।

उदाहरण: प्र + हार = प्रहार, 'हार' शब्द का अर्थ है पराजय। परंतु इसी शब्द के आगे 'प्र' शब्दांश को जोड़ने से नया शब्द बनेगा - 'प्रहार' (प्र + हार) जिसका अर्थ है चोट करना।

अतः विकल्प (D) सही है।

11. 'संकल्प' शब्द में 'सम्' उपसर्ग का प्रयोग हुआ है।

'सम्' उपसर्ग से बनने वाले अन्य शब्द हैं- संस्कृत, संस्कार, संगीत, संहार आदि हैं।

उपसर्ग: उपसर्ग उस अक्षर या अक्षर समूह को कहते हैं जो किसी शब्द के पहले जुड़कर उसके अर्थ में परिवर्तन लाता है।

जैसे- प्र, सु, अति, अधि, अनु नि, आदि।

अतः विकल्प (A) सही है।

12. 'पर्वतीय' में 'गुणवाचक विशेषण' है।

वे शब्द जो संज्ञा या सर्वनाम के गुण, धर्म, स्वभाव आदि का बोध कराते हैं, गुणवाचक विशेषण कहलाते हैं।

जैसे- बलशाली, पुराण, नया, तीक्ष्ण, कमजोर, मोटा, दुर्बल, पठारी आदि।

अतः विकल्प (A) सही है।

13. सर्वनाम उस विकारी शब्द को कहते है, जो पूर्वापरसंबंध से किसी भी संज्ञा के बदले आता है।

सर्वनाम के छः भेद होते है-

- पुरुषवाचक सर्वनाम
- निश्चयवाचक सर्वनाम
- अनिश्चयवाचक सर्वनाम
- संबंधवाचक सर्वनाम
- प्रश्नवाचक सर्वनाम
- निजवाचक सर्वनाम

अतः विकल्प (D) सही है।

14. 'भाव दशा के कारण वचन में आये परिवर्तन को वाचिक अनुभव कहते हैं।'

काव्य में नायक अथवा नायिका द्वारा भाव-दशा के कारण वचन में आए परिवर्तन को वाचिक अनुभव कहते हैं।

अतः विकल्प (B) सही है।

15. पल्लवन में सूत्र वाक्य, विचार या भाव को मात्र विस्तार दिया जाता है।

किसी निर्धारित विषय जैसे सूत्र-वाक्य, उक्ति या विवेच्य-बिन्दु को उदाहरण, तर्क आदि से पुष्ट करते हुए प्रवाहमयी, सहज अभिव्यक्ति-शैली में मौलिक, सारगर्भित विस्तार देना पल्लवन कहलाता है। इसे विस्तारण, भाव-विस्तारण, भाव-पल्लवन आदि भी कहा जाता है।

सूत्र रूप में लिखी या कही गई बात के गर्भ में भाव और विचारों का एक पुंज छिपा होता है। विद्वान् जन एक पंक्ति पर घंटों बोल लेते हैं और कई बार तो एक पूरी पुस्तक ही रच डालते हैं। यही कला 'पल्लवन' कहलाती है।

अतः विकल्प (B) सही है।

16. स्वर तंत्रियों के आधार पर व्यंजनों को दो वर्गों में बाँटा गया है - घोष व्यंजन और अघोष व्यंजन।

- घोष व्यंजन: जिन वर्णों के उच्चारण में केवल नाद(मधुर ध्वनि) का उपयोग होता है, उन्हें घोष वर्ण कहते हैं। इनकी संख्या 31 होती है। इसमें सभी स्वर अ से ओ तक और ग, घ, ङ , झ, ञ, ड, ढ, ण, द, ध, न, ब, भ, म, य, र, ल, व, ह है।
- अघोष व्यंजन - जिन वर्णों के उच्चारण में नाद(मधुर ध्वनि) की जगह केवल श्वाँस का उपयोग होता है, उन्हे अघोष वर्ण कहते हैं। इनकी संख्या 13 होती है। जो इस प्रकार है: क, ख, च, छ, ट, ठ, त, थ, प, फ, श, ष, स।

अतः विकल्प (B) सही है।

17. अकारांत स्त्रीलिंग शब्द का बहुवचन बनाने के लिए अन्त्य स्वर के बदले 'एँ' कर देते हैं।

जैसे - गाय - गायें, बात - बातें, बहन - बहनें, रात - रातें, आदि।

अतः विकल्प (C) सही है।

18. दिए गए विकल्पों में 'वाल्मीकि' शब्द की वर्तनी शुद्ध है। अन्य सभी शब्दों की वर्तनी त्रुटि पूर्ण हैं।

'वाल्मीकि' का अर्थ 'ऋषि का नाम' है। 'वाल्मीकि' संस्कृत रामायण के प्रसिद्ध रचयिता हैं जो आदिकवि के रूप में प्रसिद्ध हैं। उन्होंने संस्कृत मे रामायण की रचना की।

वाक्य - महर्षि वाल्मीकि को प्राचीन वैदिक काल के महान ऋषियों की श्रेणी में प्रमुख स्थान प्राप्त है।

अतः विकल्प (B) सही है।

19. 'यथोचित' का सही संधि विच्छेद "यथा + उचित" (अ/आ + उ = ओ) है।

इसमें गुण संधि है इसमें अ, आ के बाद इ, ई हो तो ए, उ, ऊ हो तो ओ, तथा ऋ हो तो अर् हो जाता है। उदाहरण : महा + इंद्र = महेंद्र।

गुण संधि का सूत्र आद्गुण: होता है। यह संधि स्वर संधि के भागो में से एक है।

अतः विकल्प (C) सही है।

20. 'रति' श्रृंगार रस का स्थायी भाव है।

श्रृंगार रस की विशेषताएँ निम्नलिखित है:

- नायक और नायिका के मन में संस्कार रूप में स्थित रति या प्रेम जब रस की अवस्था को पहुँचकर आस्वादन के योग्य हो जाता है, तब वह 'श्रृंगार रस' कहलाता है।
- श्रृंगार रस को रसराज कहा जाता है।
- श्रृंगार रस का विषय नायक या नायिका है।
- उद्दीपन विभाव – नायिका के कुच, नितम्बादि अंग, एकान्त, वन-उपवन, चन्द्र-ज्यौत्स्ना, वसन्त, पुष्प, नायिका अथवा अनुभाव की चेष्टाएँ – हावभाव, तिरछी चितवन, मुस्कान।

- संचारी भाव – तैंतीस संचारियों में उग्रता, मरण, आलस्य, जुगुप्सा को छोड़कर शेष सभी संचारी भाव, मुख्यतः लज्जा, शर्म, चपलता।

अतः विकल्प (C) सही है।

21. दिए गए विकल्पों में से 'मूर्त' शब्द का विलोम शब्द 'अमूर्त' होगा।

मूर्त तत्सम शब्द है जिसका अर्थ 'आकार वाला' होता है।

'मूर्त' शब्द में 'अ' उपसर्ग के योग से 'अमूर्त' शब्द बना जिसका अर्थ 'अप्रत्यक्ष या निराकार' होगा।

अतः विकल्प (A) सही है।

22. 'व्योम' का पर्यायवाची शब्द 'पीयूष' नहीं है। 'पीयूष' शब्द 'अमृत' का पर्यायवाची है। अन्य विकल्प 'अंतरिक्ष, अम्बर और 'नभ' व्योम के ही पर्यायवाची हैं।

अतः विकल्प (C) सही है।

23. "ईश्वर तुम्हें सफलता प्रदान करे।" वाक्य में कोई व्यक्ति किसी अन्य व्यक्ति के लिए इच्छा व्यक्त कर रहा है। इस प्रकार यह 'इच्छावाचक' वाक्य है।

इच्छावाचक वाक्य अर्थात ऐसे वाक्य जिनसे हमें वक्ता की कोई इच्छा, कामना, आकांशा, आशीर्वाद आदि का बोध हो।

अतः विकल्प (C) सही है।

24. 'परतीत' शब्द तत्सम शब्द नहीं है।

- परतीत तद्भव शब्द है जिसका तत्सम रूप 'प्रतीत' होगा।
- अन्य सभी शब्द तत्सम हैं।

अतः विकल्प (A) सही है।

25. 'उजास' शब्द तद्भव है जिसका अर्थ प्रकाश या उजाला होता है।

- उजास का तत्सम उज्ज्वल है।
- अन्य सभी शब्द तत्सम हैं।

अतः विकल्प (D) सही है।

26. Complete sentence: A person suffering from chronic neurodegenerative disease **experiences** short-term memory loss.

The given sentence is giving a general information about what happens to a person diagnosed with neurodegenerative disease.

Present Indefinite Tense represents an action which is regular or normal or true and uses the base form of the verb. In case of the third person singular number, 's or es' is added with the verb.

- Example: We watch movies in this Cineplex.

Among the given options, **'experiences'** is the verb form of present indefinite tense.

Hence, the correct option is (D).

27. In all probability, it **will** rain tonight.

Let us explore the given options:

Will is used for expressing a strong intention or assertion about the future.

Can means to have the opportunity or possibility to.

May is used when admitting that something is so before making another, more important point.

Ought is used to indicate something that is probable.

Hence, the correct option is (A).

28. Owing to his consistent practice he is **getting on** well in this particular sport.

'Getting on' is a phrasal verb that means perform or make progress in a specified way. Example: She is getting on well in her new job.

In the given sentence, the phrasal verb is used to show his progress in a particular sport.

Hence, the correct option is (C).

29. The most appropriate word to fill in the given blank is 'nevertheless'.

- The word **'nevertheless'** means 'in spite of that. Example: It was a cold, rainy day. **Nevertheless,** more people came than we had expected.
- We use **'nevertheless'** when saying something that contrasts with what has just been said.

Hence, the correct option is (B).

30. In the given sentence, we have to use a possessive adjective.

Possessive adjectives are used when we have to show who or what owns something.

Examples of the possessive adjective: are my, our, your, his, her, its, and their.

Possessive adjectives are used before nouns in a sentence to modify the noun.

Here the word school is a noun so we need to use 'your' to show possession.

The complete sentence is: You have to submit a copy of your school leaving certificate.

Hence, the correct option is (D).

31. We use the past perfect to talk about wishes for the past:

- For example: I wish I had worked harder when I was at school.

In the given sentence, the wish is mentioned for the past.

So, the answer will be "I wish I had a car. It would make life so much easier".

Hence, the correct option is (B).

32. "He lived a hand **to** mouth existence, surviving on just a few rupees a week."

A hand-to-mouth existence is a way of life in which you have hardly enough food or money to live on. To live (from) hand to mouth is a phrase which means to have just enough money to live on and nothing extra.

Hence, the correct option is (B).

33. The given sentence is talking about a fraction of people who are guilty and the others.

Therefore, the most appropriate word to be filled in the blank is 'Undertrials'.

The word 'Undertrials' means People who are being held in custody awaiting trial for a crime.

- Example: The Supreme Court ordered the release of undertrials who have already served half their sentence.

Complete Sentence: Only a small fraction are convicts; the rest are undertrials.

Hence, the correct option is (A).

34. What a beautiful house!

Option (A) is a correctly punctuated sentence.

Option (B) is incorrect. The question mark is used after asking a question. Example: What is her name?

Option (C) is incorrect. A full stop is used at the end of a sentence. Example: She is my sister.

Option (D) is incorrect. A comma is used when someone is directly addressed/to separate two clauses/to separate ideas, objects, names in a sentence. Example: I will go to Goa, Mumbai and Pune.

Hence, the correct option is (A).

35. You should listen to her, otherwise you will regret.

Option (A) is incorrect. The question mark is used after asking a question. Example: What is her name?

Option (B) is a correctly punctuated sentence.

Option (C) is incorrect. A full stop is used at the end of a sentence. Example: She is my sister.

Option (D) is incorrect. The exclamation mark is used to express wonder, surprise or to emphasize. Example: I have found the lost photo album!

Hence, the correct option is (B).

36. A 'Theist' is a person who believes in the existence of a god or gods, specifically of a creator who intervenes in the universe.

Example: 'I am a hardcore theist and the person most close to me is my God'.

Hence, the correct option is (A).

37. 'Semanticist' is the correct spelling of the word.

It means 'the branch of semiotics dealing with the relations between signs and what they denote'.

Hence, the correct option is (B).

38. The Present Perfect tense is a verb tense which is primarily used to express an action that took place at some indefinite time in the past. The present perfect tense can also be used to express an action that began in the past and continues now.

The verb structure Present Perfect tense aspect usually follows is: has/have (depending on the subject) + Past Participle form of the verb.

1. For example, 'He and his wife have travelled all over the world.'
2. For example, 'My dog has stolen the cat's food.'

The given sentence follows the structure of the Present Perfect verb structure.

Hence, the correct option is (D).

39. Let's see the meaning of the options given.

- Customary(Adjective): According to custom
- Customer(Noun): A person who buys goods or services in a shop, restaurant, etc.
- Customise(Verb): Modify (something) to suit a particular individual or task.
- Costume(Noun): A set or style of clothes worn by people in a particular country or in a particular historical period.

Thus, the adjective form of Custom is 'Customary'.

Hence, the correct option is (C).

40. The past forms of the words are given. The past participle forms are as follows,

Write = Written

Wear = Worn

Wake = Woken

Hence, the correct option is (D).

41. Interjection is a part of speech which is more commonly used in informal language than in formal writing or speech. Basically, the function of interjections is to express emotions or sudden bursts of feelings. They can express a wide variety of emotions such as excitement, joy, surprise, or disgust.

Different kinds of interjections:

Adjectives that are used as interjections.

Nice! You got a perfect score in your GRE!

Nouns or noun phrases that are used as interjections.

Holy cow! I forgot to bring my wallet!

Short clauses that are used as interjections.

Rishi is our mechanical engineering professor. Oh, the horror!

Some sounds can work as interjections as well.

Yay! I got the job!

In this sentence, the interjection is that of sound: uh-oh!

Hence, the correct option is (C).

42. SPTRECE is the jumbled form of RESPECT.

Respect means that you accept somebody for who they are, even when they're different from you or you don't agree with them.

Hence, the correct option is (D).

43. The feminine gender of the noun brother is sister.

Let's look at the gender change of the other option:

Noun	Gender	Changed gender

Niece	Feminine	Nephew
Aunt	Feminine	Uncle
Sister	Feminine	Brother

Therefore, after understanding the above table it is clear that the correct answer is option (D).

Hence, the correct option is (D).

44. 1st word is "name of the animal" and 2nd word is "young ones of that animal".

- Sheep : Lamb

Here, 'Lamb' is the young one of the 'Sheep'.

Similarly,

- Butterfly : Caterpillar

Here, 'Caterpillar' is the young one of the 'Butterfly'.

Hence, the correct option is (A).

45. Here, in the given fill-in-the-blank the most appropriate answer is 'whom'.

'Whom' is used instead of 'who' as the object of a verb or preposition.

- Example: I met a man with whom I used to work.

Correct Sentence: I have nobody whom I can confide in.

Hence, the correct option is (A).

46. In the given blanks, the correct prepositions are 'in, though' i.e. option (A) is the correct answer.

The preposition 'in' is used with something that surrounds.

- The group will meet at 7:30 in the park.

The preposition 'through' is used for a movement inside something.

- They walked slowly through the woods. (the wood means 'forest')

So, the correct sentence is" The tourists were in the car; the car was passing through the tunnel.

Hence, the correct option is (A).

47. The word 'Assertion' means a solemn and often public declaration of the truth or existence of something.

- The synonyms of the word 'Assertion' are "declaration, affirmation, claim".
- From the synonym of the given word, we can say that the word 'Declaration' is the same in meaning.
- The word 'Declaration' means a formal or explicit statement or announcement.

Let's see the meaning of other given options:

WORDS	MEANING
Discussion	a conversation or debate about a specific topic
Rejection	the dismissing or refusing of a proposal, idea, etc
Continuation	the action of carrying something on overtime or the state of being carried on

Hence, the correct option is (C).

48. The most appropriate synonym of the given word 'Sentiment' is 'Feeling'.

- Sentiment: feelings such as pity, romantic love, sadness, etc. that influence somebody's action or behaviour (sometimes in situations where this is not appropriate).
    - Example: There's no room for sentiment in business.
- Feeling: something that you feel in your mind or body.
    - Example: I've got a funny feeling in my leg.

Let's look at the meaning of other words:

- Antipathy: a strong feeling of not liking somebody/something; dislike.
- Concrete: real or definite; not only existing in the imagination.
- Hatred: a very strong feeling of not liking somebody/something; hate.

Hence, the correct option is (D).

49. The word 'Conducive' is an adjective; it means making a certain situation or outcome likely, possible or favourable.

- For example, A quiet room is a more conducive atmosphere for studying.

The marked option 'Unfavourable' means not giving you an advantage or a good chance of success.

- For example, Current conditions in the state are very unfavourable for new businesses.

So, we can say that 'Unfavourable' can function as the opposite word of 'Conducive.'

- Favourable: giving one the advantage or a good chance of success.
- Propitious: giving or indicating a good chance of success.
- Opportune: (of a time) especially convenient or appropriate for a particular action or event.

Hence, the correct option is (B).

50. The word 'Audacious'(adjective) means- "willing to take risks or do something shocking".

- E.g. He described the plan as ambitious and audacious.

Let's have a look at the meaning of the words that are given in the options:

- Vulgar(adjective)- "rude and likely to upset or anger people, especially by referring to sex and the body in an unpleasant way".
- Extinct(adjective)- "not now existing".
- Timid(adjective)- "shy and nervous; without much confidence; easily frightened".
- Fickle(adjective)- "always changing your mind or your feelings so you cannot be trusted".

Therefore, as per the points mentioned above, we find that 'Timid' is the correct antonym of the given word.

Hence, the correct option is (C).

51. On 23rd April 2016, the then chief Minister of Uttar Pradesh, Akhilesh Yadav inagurated the states's first Samajwadi Abhinav Vidyalaya in Dandupur, Allahabad.

These schools will be from Class VI to Class XII where 35 students at maximum will be enrolled in Class VI to Class VIII each while around 40 students will be admitted in Class IX to Class XII.

Hence, the correct option is (A).

52. Kanpur has the highest population in the large metropolitan region category.

- Kanpur, a city in Uttar Pradesh, is believed to get its name from Kanh-pur which means the town of Krishna or Kanha.
- Some of the theories also suggest that it got its name from Karnapur, the town of Karna.
- Kanpur is the second largest populous city of UP.

Hence, the correct option is (B).

53. Kuldeep Yadav (born 14 December 1994) is an Indian international cricketer from the Kanpur district.

- He plays for India and for Uttar Pradesh in domestic cricket and for Kolkata Knight Riders in the IPL.
- He became the second Indian other than Bhuvneshwar Kumar and the third spinner other than Imran Tahir and Ajantha Mendis to take 5-wicket hauls in all three formats.
- On September 21, 2017, he became the third bowler for India to take a hat-trick in an ODI after Chetan Sharma and Kapil Dev.

Hence, the correct option is (A).

54. Chittaura Lake, also known as Ashtwarka jheel is a lake in Uttar Pradesh. It is situated about 8 km from Bahraich city, on Gonda road, near Jittora or Chittaura village.

A small river, Teri Nadi, flows from this lake.

Chittaura Jheel is a Hindu pilgrimage site. According to local legends, Ashtwarka Muni, the Guru of Maharaja Janak used to live here in his ashram.

The area beside the lake is also the site of an 11th-century battle between the Hindu king Suhaldev and the Muslim invader Ghazi Saiyyad Salar Masud.

Hence, the correct option is (D).

55. The Kampil Fair is a Jain fair that is held each year in the Farrukhabad district of Uttar Pradesh.

- This fair derives its name from the place Kampil where it is celebrated.
- Kampil is an ancient historical town that finds mention in our epics.

- The place was earlier known as Kampilya and was the capital of King Draupad.

Hence, the correct option is (B).

56. Naga Hills lie between India and Myanmar. Garo and Khasi hills are lower hills that lie between Assam & Bangladesh. Mount Everest lies on the Nepal-China border.

Hence, the correct option is (C).

57. State Highways are the responsibility of State Governments and are maintained through various agencies. The state highways are usually roads that link important cities, towns and district headquarters within the state and connect them with National Highways or state highways of neighbouring states.

Hence, the correct option is (A).

58. Hyderabad's Neelkantha Bhanu Prakash (20 years) has become the first Indian to win a gold medal at the Mental Calculation World Championship 2020 at Mind Sports Olympiad (MSO), held in London. He holds the 4 world and Limca records of 'fastest human calculator' in the world.

Hence, the correct option is (D).

59. North Korean Won is the currency of North Korea. It is subdivided into 100 chon. Vaughan is issued by the Central Bank of the Democratic People's Republic of Korea. Won is associated with the Chinese Yuan and the Japanese Yen.

Hence, the correct option is (D).

60. Hiralal Chaudhuri is known as the father of the Blue Revolution in India.

Revolution	Related to	Father of the Revolution
White	Milk Production	Verghese Kurien
Blue	Fish Production	Hiralal Chaudhuri and Arun Krishnan
Green	Food Grain	M.S. Swaminathan
Silver	Egg Production	Indira Gandhi

Hence, the correct option is (C).

61. The Indian Premier League (IPL) 2022 ended with Gujarat Titans (GT) lifting the trophy by defeating inaugural champions Rajasthan Royals (RR) at the Narendra Modi Stadium, Ahmedabad.

The Indian Premier League (IPL) 2022, was the 15th edition of the professional Twenty20 cricket league established by the Board of Control for Cricket in India (BCCI). IPL 2022 Sponsorer was TATA.

Hence, the correct option is (D).

62. Bahadur Shah Zafar (1837-1857): Also known as Bahadur Shah-II. He was the last Mughal emperor of India who reigned from 1837-58. For most of his reign, he was a client of the British and was without real authority. He was chosen as a nominal leader of the revolt of 1857. After the rebellion was put down by the British, he was exiled to Rangoon in Burma(Myanmar) and later he died there.

Hence, the correct option is (A).

63. The city of Udaipur, which previously served as the Mewar Kingdom's capital, is located in Rajasthan, a state in western India. In addition to being a popular tourist destination, Udaipur is also well-known for its Rajput-era architecture, history, culture, and gorgeous locales. It is known as the "city of lakes" because of its sophisticated lake system. Maharana Udai Singh II built a number of artificial lakes to surround it in 1559.

Thus, the city of the lake is Udaypur.

Hence, the correct option is (C).

64. The court of Chandra Gupta II was made even more illustrious by the fact that it was graced by the navaratna.

- A group of nine who excelled in the literary arts.
- Dhanvantri and Kalidasa were in the court of Chandra Gupta II.
- Kalidasa is the immortal poet and playwright of India and a peerless genius whose works became famous worldwide in the modern world.
- Dhanvantri was a Great Physician.

Hence, the correct option is (C).

65. Ladakh is the cold desert of India which lies in the Greater Himalayas. Ladakh is towards the east of Jammu & Kashmir. Ladakh shares borders with China. The cold desert in Ladakh is enclosed by the Zanskar mountains in the south and the Karakoram mountain range in the north.

Hence, the correct option is (D).

66. Cotton is the most suitable cash crop for black soil. The largest producer of cotton in India is Maharashtra followed by Gujarat and Telangana. The largest producer of cotton in the world is India followed by China and the United States of America (USA).

- The cash crop is also known as profit crop is an agricultural crop that is grown to sell for profit.
- Some examples of cash crops are tea, coffee, rubber, coconut, and spices.
- Black soil which is found in India is rich in metals such as Aluminium, Magnesium, Lime, Calcium, and Iron.
- It is deficient in Phosphorous, Potassium, Nitrogen, and organic matter.
- The black soil is also called regur and black cotton soils because cotton is the most important crop grown on these soils.
- This soil is mainly found in Tamil Nadu, Maharashtra, Gujarat, Madya Pradesh, Andhra Pradesh, and parts of Karnataka.
- It has the highest water-retaining capacity.
- The texture of the black soil is Clayey.

Hence, the correct option is (A).

67. Tropic of cancer does not pass through the state of Assam.

Tropic of Cancer (23½° North) passes through the middle of the country.

- The location of the country is in the northern and eastern hemispheres.
- It divides India into two almost equal climatic zones, namely the northern region and the southern region.
- It passes through the states of Gujarat, Rajasthan, Madhya Pradesh, Chhattisgarh, Jharkhand, West Bengal, Tripura, and Mizoram.

Hence, the correct option is (B).

68. In the given figure (A) will be replaced by liver.

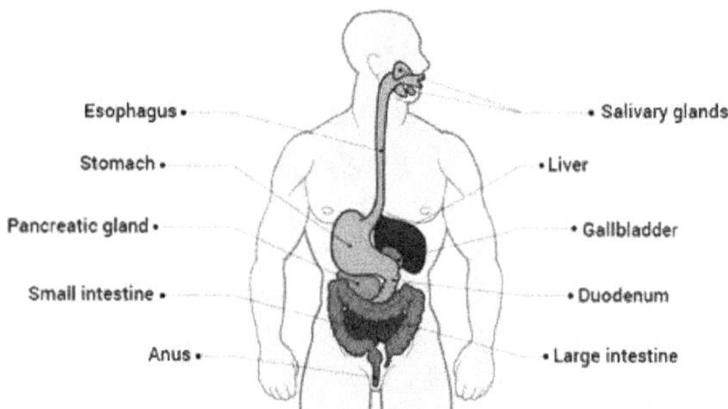

The digestive system plays a significant role in the digestion process, which is composed of the alimentary canal and other associated glands. The alimentary canal is divided into five main parts- Salivary glands, Esophagus, Stomach, Gallbladder, Duodenum, Pancreatic gland, Liver, Small intestine, large intestine and Anus.

Hence, the correct option is (A).

69. The gynoecium is the female reproductive part of the flower and is essential for plant sexual reproduction.

Ovary, style, and stigma are the three parts of the gynoecium. The ovary is the swollen basal portion containing ovules. Stigma is the portion that receives pollen grains during pollination. Style is the portion that connects stigma and ovary.

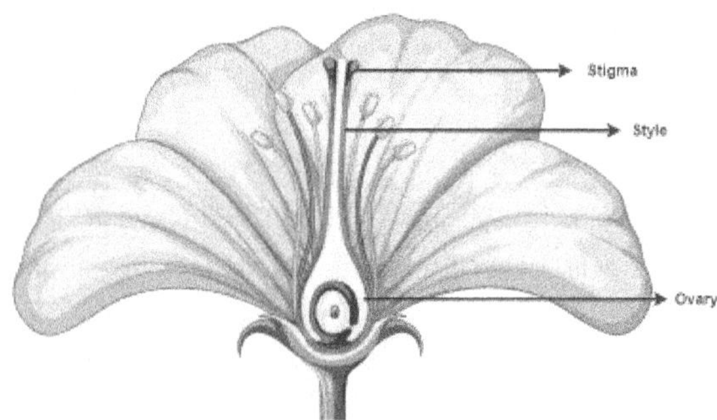

Hence, the correct option is (B).

70. India climbed six notches to 40th position in the Global Innovation Index 2022, according to a report by the Geneva-based World Intellectual Property Organization. Turkiye and India entered the top 40 for the first time, placing at 37th and 40th, respectively. Switzerland has topped the ranking for the 12th consecutive year. The Index was started in 2007 was created by Soumitra Dutta.

Hence, the correct option is (D).

71. Wayanad Wildlife Sanctuary is located in Kerala.

- Wayanad Wildlife Sanctuary (WWS) is an integral part of the Nilgiri Biosphere Reserve.
- It was established in 1973.
- Nilgiri Biosphere Reserve was the first from India to be included in the UNESCO designated World Network of Biosphere Reserves (designated in 2012).

Hence, the correct option is (D).

72. Union Minister of Minority Affairs Mukhtar Abbas Naqvi inaugurated India's first "Amrit Sarovar" in Patwai, Rampur, Uttar Pradesh.

- On 24th April 2022, mission Amrit Sarovar was launched by PM Modi. The mission aims to develop and rejuvenate 75 water bodies in each district of India.
- The technical support for this mission is provided by the Bhaskaracharya National Institute for Space Application and Geo-informatics.
- The Mission Amrit Sarovar is expected to be completed by 15th August 2023. The mission is a part of the Azadi ka Amrit Mahotsav celebration.

Hence, the correct option is (D).

73. The Cricket Association for the Blind in India (CABI) has announced former India cricketer Yuvraj Singh as the brand ambassador for the 3rd T20 World Cup for the Blind. The 3rd T20 World Cup for the Blind will be held in India from 5 to 17 Dec 2022. Participating countries are: India, Nepal, Bangladesh, Australia, South Africa, Pakistan, and Sri Lanka.

Hence, the correct option is (A).

74. Uttar Pradesh has been awarded Ayushmann Utkrishta award 2022 for adding various health facilities to health facility register.

It is the best performing state in the country with 28728 Health facilities added to National health facility register. It is also the second best State in creating Ayushmann Bharat health account (ABHA) with almost 2 crores ABH Accounts.

Hence, the correct option is (B).

75. Umran Malik won the title of Emerging player of the season in IPL 2022.

- He hails from Gujjar Nagar in Jammu.
- He is also known as Jammu Express.
- He played for the Sunrisers Hyderabad in IPL.

Hence, the correct option is (B).

76. Given,

Ratio of two numbers $= 1:2$

HCF $= 16$

As we know,

If we multiply HCF of any two numbers with their respective ratio, then we will get the numbers.

$\therefore$ First number $= 1 \times 16 = 16$

Second number $= 2 \times 16 = 32$

HCF $\times$ LCM $=$ First number $\times$ Second number

$\Rightarrow 16 \times$ LCM $= 16 \times 32$

$\Rightarrow$ LCM $= \dfrac{16 \times 32}{16}$

$\Rightarrow$ LCM $= 32$

So, their LCM is 32.

Hence, the correct option is (C).

77. Let the radius of circumcircle be R and radius of incircle be r,

Given that,

$$\pi R^2 - \pi r^2 = 66$$

$$R^2 - r^2 = 66 \times \frac{7}{22} = 21$$

We know that,

$$R = \frac{a}{\sqrt{3}} \text{ and } r = \frac{a}{2\sqrt{3}}$$

(a is side of equilateral triangle)

$$\Rightarrow \frac{a^2}{3} - \frac{a^2}{12} = 21$$

$$\Rightarrow \frac{3a^2}{12} = 21$$

$$\Rightarrow a^2 = 21 \times 4$$

Area of an equilateral triangle:

$$= \frac{\sqrt{3}}{4}a^2 = \frac{\sqrt{3}}{4} \times 21 \times 4 = 21\sqrt{3} \text{ m}^2$$

Hence, the correct option is (A).

78. Let the 5 consecutive numbers be $x, x + 1, x + 2, x + 3, x + 4$.

$$x + x + 1 + x + 2 + x + 3 + x + 4 = 140$$

$$5x + 10 = 140$$

$$5x = 130$$

$$x = 26$$

Therefore the numbers are $26, 27, 28, 29, 30$.

So, highest number is 30

Hence, the correct option is (B).

79. Given:

We have a number 3920.

Prime factorization of $3920 = 2 \times 2 \times 2 \times 2 \times 7 \times 7 \times 5$

Only 5 is left unpaired.

$\therefore$ The square root of 3920 is $28\sqrt{5}$.

Hence, the correct option is (A).

80. Given:

CP (Cost price) of 70 article $=$ Rs. 890

SP (Selling price) of 60 article $=$ Rs. 890

Profit $\% = \dfrac{\text{(Selling price-Cost price)}}{\text{Cost price}} \times 100$

CP of 70 article is 890

$\Rightarrow$ CP of 420 article = Rs. 5340

$\Rightarrow$ SP of 60 article $= 890$

$\Rightarrow$ SP of 420 article = Rs. 6230

Profit $= 6230 - 5340 =$ Rs. 890

$\therefore$ Profit $\% = \dfrac{890}{5340} \times 100$

$$= 16\frac{2}{3}\%$$

Hence, the correct option is (D).

81. Concept:

$$\text{Mean} = \dfrac{\text{Total sum of all values}}{\text{Number of values}}$$

Calculations:

Sum of the given data
$= a + b + a + a + b + a + b + c + a + b + a + c + a + b + a$

$$\Rightarrow 8a + 5b + 2c$$

Number of values $= 15$

$$\text{Mean} = \dfrac{(8a + 5b + 2c)}{15}$$

Hence, the correct option is (C).

82. Let the number be X.

$$\Rightarrow X - \frac{2X}{7} = 100$$

$$\Rightarrow \frac{7X - 2X}{7} = 100$$

$$\Rightarrow X = 140$$

Hence, the correct option is (B).

83. Given:

$(2^2)^3 \times (2^3)^2$

Concept:

$(a^b)^c = (a)^{bc}$

Calculation:

Here,

$= (2^2)^3 \times (2^3)^2$

$= (2)^6 \times (2)^6$

$= 64 \times 64$

$= 4096$

Hence, the correct option is (A).

84. Given:

? = 121 ÷ 5 + (8740 ÷ 5 - 4) ÷ 5

$\Rightarrow$? = 121 ÷ 5 + 1744 ÷ 5

$$\Rightarrow ? = \frac{121}{5} + \frac{1744}{5}$$

$$\Rightarrow ? = \frac{1865}{5} = 373$$

Hence, the correct option is (A).

85. Given:

2.06 - 3.16 + 4.59 - 1.79

= 2.06 + 4.59 - 3.16 - 1.79

= 6.65 - 4.95

= 1.70

∴ Required answer is 1.70.

Hence, the correct option is (D).

86. Given:

$(-5)^{k+2} \times (-5)^4 = (-5)^9$

$$(-5)^{k+2} = \frac{(-5)^9}{(-5)^4}$$

$(-5)^{k+2} = (-5)^{(9-4)}$

$(-5)^{k+2} = (-5)^5$

k + 2 = 5

k = 5 - 2 = 3

∴ The answer is 3.

Hence, the correct option is (A).

87. Given:

21 × (23 - 12) - {(-1 × 10) + 21}

= 21 × (11) - [-10 + 21]

= 231 - 11

= 220

∴ The required answer = 220

Hence, the correct option is (C).

88. First remove the decimal by multiplying each term by 100

Then terms will be 210, 1050, 189

Factors of 210 are 2, 5, 3, 7

Factors of 1050 are 2, 3, 5, 5, 7

Factors of 189 are 3, 3, 3, 7

$\Rightarrow$ H.C.F will be 3 × 7 = 21

Now divide 21 by 100

∴ We get 0.21.

Hence, the correct option is (A).

89. Given: Length of a diagonal of a square $= 12 \ cm$

Concept: Diagonal of a square $= \sqrt{2} \times$ side

Area of a square $=$ side $\times$ side

Calculation:

Diagonal $= \sqrt{2} \times$ side

∴ $\sqrt{2} \times$ side $= 12$

$\Rightarrow$ side $= 6\sqrt{2} \ cm$

Area $= 6\sqrt{2} \times 6\sqrt{2}$

$\Rightarrow$ Area $= 72 \ cm^2$

So, the area of square will be $72 \ cm^2$.

Hence, the correct option is (C).

90. If P% of P is 36

$$\Rightarrow \frac{P}{100} \times P = 36$$

$\Rightarrow P^2 = 36 \times 100$

$\Rightarrow P = \sqrt{3600}$

$\Rightarrow P = 60$

∴ The value of P is 60.

Hence, the correct option is (B).

91. The number when divided by 16 or 12 or 8 leaves a remainder of 6.

∴ The number when divided by LCM of 16 or 12 or 8 that is 48 should also leave a remainder of 6

$\Rightarrow$ When number is divided by 48, then remainder = 6

∴ Number = 48n + 6, where n ∈ N

∴ Smallest number which satisfies the given conditions = 48 × 1 + 6 = 48 + 6 = 54

Hence, the correct option is (C).

92. We all know that smallest 4 digit number = 1000

LCM of 12, 15 and 18 = 180

1000 ÷ 180 ⇒ Remainder = 100

Difference of LCM – Remainder = 180 – 100 = 80

∴ Required Number = 1000 + 80 = 1080

Hence, the correct option is (C).

93. Concept:

Place value is defined as the digit multiplied by wherever it is placed, either by hundreds or thousands. Face value or real value is simply defined as the digit itself within a number.

For example: in 256, the place value of 2 is 200 and the face value of 2 is 2.

Calculation:

Place value and face value of 9 in 9876 = 9000 and 9 respectively

Sum of place value and face value = 9000 + 9 = 9009

Place value and face value of 7 in 9876 = 70 and 7 respectively

Sum of place value and face value = 70 + 7 = 77

Difference between the sums = 9009 - 77

= 8932

Hence, the correct option is (A).

94. Given:

Principal = Rs. 720

Rate = 9%

Time = 5 years

Formula:

Simple Interest (SI) $= \dfrac{P \times t \times R}{100}$

Where P = Principal

R = Rate of interest

t = Time

Calculation:

$SI = \dfrac{720 \times 9 \times 5}{100}$

$\Rightarrow SI = \dfrac{32400}{100}$

$\Rightarrow SI = Rs.\ 324$

∴ The Simple interest is Rs. 324.

Hence, the correct option is (D).

95. Given:

9, 13, 21, 33, ?, 69

The given series follows the following pattern.

⇒ 9 + 4 = 13

⇒ 13 + 8 = 21

⇒ 21 + 12 = 33

⇒ 33 + 16 = 49

⇒ 49 + 20 = 69

∴ 49 will come on the place of ?.

Hence, the correct option is (C).

96. Given:

a + b = 7 and ab = 12

Formula:

$(a + b)^2 = a^2 + b^2 + 2ab$

According to the question,

$(a + b)^2 = a^2 + b^2 + 2ab$

$\Rightarrow (7)^2 = a^2 + b^2 + 2 \times 12$

$\Rightarrow 49 = a^2 + b^2 + 24$

$\Rightarrow a^2 + b^2 = 49 - 24 = 25$

Hence, the correct option is (B).

97. An even number is one which is divisible by 2.

A prime number is one which has exactly two factors.

Calculation:

The greatest two digit even number is 98.

The smallest three digit prime number is 101.

On adding, we get,

= 98 + 101

= 199

Hence, the correct option is (B).

98. Given:

The product of the two numbers is 0.432.

One of them is 1.6

Calculation:

Let the other number be P.

According to the question,

1.6 × P = 0.432

⇒ P = 0.27

∴ The other number is 0.27.

Hence, the correct option is (B).

99. Let x be the required number.

⇒ Sum of 16.7 and 12.38 = 29.08

Since x is subtracted from the above sum to obtain 10.09 thus,

⇒ 29.08 – x = 10.09

⇒ x = 18.99

Hence, the correct option is (B).

100. Given:

The number = 12345

The face value of 3 = 3

The place value of 3 in 12345 = 3 × 100 = 300

⇒ The required difference = 300 - 3 = 297

∴ The required result will be 297.

Hence, the correct option is (C).

Hindi

Q.1 निर्देश: दिए गए वाक्य के लिए एक शब्द का चयन कीजिए।
'जो परिणय सूत्र में न बँधा हो'

A. अज्ञ
B. अभियोगी
C. सद्यःपरिणीत
D. अपरिणीत

Q.2 'रेखा घर में है' वाक्य में कारक पहचानिए।

A. कर्ता
B. करण
C. अधिकरण
D. कर्म

Q.3 रिक्त स्थान को भरने के लिए उपयुक्त शब्द का चयन करें।
नेता ने बहुत ही बढ़िया _______ दिया।

A. वाद-विवाद
B. प्रवचन
C. आख्यान
D. भाषण

Q.4 निर्देश: रिक्त स्थान को भरने के लिए उपयुक्त शब्द का चयन करें।
साहिल को पाँच _______ दूध चाहिए।

A. लीटर
B. मीटर
C. किलो
D. दर्जन

Q.5 'आगरा' का बहुवचन होगा-

A. आगरे
B. आगरों
C. आगरें
D. बहुवचन नहीं होगा

Q.6 निम्नलिखित में से शुद्ध वर्तनी वाला शब्द कौन सा है?

[SSC Constable (GD), 2021]

A. संसारीक
B. सांसारीक
C. सांसारिक
D. संसारिक

Q.7 'विद्यार्थी' का सही संधि-विच्छेद है-

[UPSSSC Junior Assistant, 2020]

A. विद्या + रथी
B. विद्या + अर्थी
C. विद् + अर्थी
D. विद्या + आर्थी

Q.8 'सम्मुख' शब्द का विलोम है-

[UPSSSC Junior Assistant, 2020]

A. विमुख
B. प्रमुख
C. पार्श्व
D. समक्ष

Q.9 'वाह! कितना सुन्दर दृश्य है।' वाक्य का प्रकार है?

[Rajasthan Teachers Eligibility Test - Level 1 Primary Level (RTET), 2017]

A. संदेहवाचक
B. विस्मयादिबोधक
C. संकेतार्थक
D. प्रश्नवाचक

Q.10 निम्नलिखित में से कौन सा शब्द तत्सम नहीं है?

[UPSSSC Junior Assistant, 2020]

A. किशन
B. कटि
C. कर्क
D. कृशकाय

Q.11 निम्नलिखित में से कौन सा शब्द तद्भव नहीं है?

[UPSSSC Junior Assistant, 2020]

A. दाँत
B. अधर
C. आँख
D. कान

Q.12 रस के कितने अंग हैं:

A. पांच
B. नौ
C. चार
D. तीन

Q.13 'पसीना पसीना होना' मुहावरे का सही अर्थ है:

A. क्रोधित होना
B. बहुत थक जाना
C. प्यासा होना
D. भयभीत होना

Q.14 'जैसी करनी वैसी भरनी' लोकोक्ति का उपयुक्त अर्थ है:

A. अपने किए का फल पाना
B. कम श्रम में अधिक लाभ प्राप्त करना
C. काम करने से बचाना
D. दूसरो को कष्ट देना

Q.15 निर्देश: वाक्यांश के लिए एक शब्द बताइए:
"किसी की सहायता करने वाला"

A. सहायक
B. सहृदय
C. सहचर
D. सहकार

Q.16 विराम-चिह्न की दृष्टि से शुद्ध वाक्य का चयन कीजिए।

A. मेरी मित्र जो एक, लेखिका है, आजकल एक पुस्तक लिख रही है।
B. मेरी मित्र जो, एक लेखिका है, आजकल एक पुस्तक लिख रही है।
C. मेरी मित्र, जो एक लेखिका है, आजकल एक पुस्तक लिख रही है।
D. मेरी मित्र जो एक लेखिका है, आजकल एक पुस्तक लिख रही है।

Q.17 निम्नलिखित प्रश्न में, चार विकल्पों में से, उस विकल्प का चयन करें जो विराम चिह्न युक्त वाक्य का सही विकल्प हो।

A. देवियों, आप हमारे देश की आशाएँ है!
B. देवियो-आप हमारे देश की आशाएँ है!
C. देवियो आप हमारे देश की आशाएँ है
D. देवियो, आप हमारे देश की आशाएँ है।

Q.18 'अत्युक्ति' में उपसर्ग है:

A. अत्य
B. अत
C. अति
D. अत्यु

Q.19 'गुजारा' में प्रत्यय बताये।

A. आऊ
B. आडी
C. अक
D. आ

Q.20 "मैं उस लड़की से मिला था जिसकी किताब खो गई थी।"– यह किस प्रकार का वाक्य है?

A. सरल वाक्य है।
B. मिश्र वाक्य है।
C. संयुक्त वाक्य है।
D. कर्तृवाच्य वाक्य है।

Q.21 वाक्य के कितने प्रकार है?

[UP Police Constable, 2018]

A. तीन
B. चार
C. एक
D. कोई प्रकार नहीं

Q.22 हिंदी वर्णमाला में स्वरों की संख्या है?

A. आठ
B. नौ
C. ग्यारह
D. चौदह

Q.23 दिए गए विकल्पों में से कौन सा विकल्प काल का भेद नहीं है?

A. वर्तमान काल
B. रीतिकाल
C. भूतकाल
D. भविष्यत काल

Q.24 'परदेसिया' शब्द में कौनसा प्रत्यय है?

A. इया
B. इय
C. आइय
D. सिया

Q.25 निम्नलिखित में से 'अधोलोक' का पर्यायवाची क्या है?

A. वायु
B. गगन
C. पाताल
D. परलोक

English

Q.26 Direction: Choose which part of speech the underlined part belongs to.

<u>Bravo</u>! Well done players.

A. Interjection **B.** Adjective
C. Verb **D.** Adverb

Q.27 Choose the correctly punctuated sentence.
A. However, David did not achieve his goal.
B. However; David did not achieve his goal.
C. However: David did not achieve his goal.
D. However! David did not achieve his goal.

Q.28 Direction: Choose the correctly punctuated sentence.
A. How do you prepare a burger,
B. How do you prepare a burger!
C. How do you prepare a burger?
D. How do you prepare a burger.

Q.29 Direction: Choose the appropriate word that can substitute the sentence or phrase given below.

To stay with to the end
A. See-through
B. See about
C. See a person through
D. Set about

Q.30 Direction: Fill in the blank with the appropriate option given below.

She was beaten _______ a bat.
A. on **B.** with **C.** to **D.** of

Q.31 Select the option that spells the word correctly.
A. Profesor **B.** Professar
C. Professor **D.** Proffesor

Q.32 Direction: In each of the following questions find out the alternative which will replace the question mark.

Carbon : Diamond :: Corundum : ?
A. Garnet **B.** Ruby **C.** Pukhraj **D.** Pearl

Q.33 Direction: Identify the part of speech the underlined word belongs to.

She <u>yelled</u> when she hit her toe.
A. Verb **B.** Noun
C. Conjunction **D.** Adverb

Ques (34-35):Directions: Select the most appropriate antonym of the given word.

Q.34 Modest
A. Unhappy **B.** Conceited
C. Sullen **D.** Glum

Q.35 INSTANT
A. Similar **B.** Gradual **C.** Prompt **D.** Diverse

Ques (36-37):Direction: Select the most appropriate synonym of the given word.

Q.36 PLEASANT
A. Tiresome **B.** Tedious

C. Refreshing **D.** Exasperating

Q.37 PRIORITY
A. Inference **B.** Deference
C. Subservience **D.** Preference

Q.38 Direction: Select the correct form of the tense for the given sentence.

Anand goes to TCS every day.
A. Simple Present **B.** Present perfect
C. Past perfect **D.** Future perfect

Q.39 Direction: In the following question, out of the four alternatives, choose the one which can be substituted for the given sentence.

The life history of a person written by himself.
A. Essay **B.** Biography
C. Travelogue **D.** Autobiography

Q.40 Direction: Change the gender of the underlined noun and rewrite the sentence:

Her <u>brother</u> was a vamp.
A. Her <u>aunt</u> was a vamp.
B. Her <u>niece</u> was a vamp.
C. Her <u>sister</u> was a vamp.
D. Her <u>uncle</u> was a vamp.

Q.41 Which of the words is not an adjective?
A. Snake **B.** Happy **C.** Faster **D.** Long

Q.42 Direction: Fill in the blank with the plural form of the word given in the bracket:

They had to travel everywhere by ______. (bus)
A. busis **B.** buses **C.** busses **D.** busess

Q.43 Directions: Fill in the blanks with the correct prepositions.

I was born ________ Thursday, the 25th of March.
A. in **B.** at **C.** on **D.** since

Q.44 Direction: Insert proper preposition in the sentence.

He hinted ____ some loss of treasure.
A. of **B.** for **C.** with **D.** at

Q.45 Direction: Select the most appropriate option to fill in the blank.

I watched him _____.
A. fell **B.** fall **C.** to falling **D.** to fell

Q.46 Direction: Choose the appropriate word to fill in the blank.

What time is the news _____ T.V.?
A. in **B.** with **C.** on **D.** at

Q.47 Direction: Choose which part of speech the underlined word belongs to:

<u>Time</u> is money.
A. Noun **B.** Pronoun
C. Verb **D.** Adjective

Q.48 Direction: Choose the correct option:

I met my friend while I _____ the road.

A. am crossing   **B.** crossed

C. were crossing   **D.** was crossing

Q.49 Direction: Fill in the blank with the correct conjunction.

I obeyed her _______ she should be angry.

A. because   **B.** so   **C.** if   **D.** lest

Q.50 Direction: Choose the appropriate word to fill in the blank.

Is everyone______ (here/hear)? Do we have a full ___(compliment/complement)?

A. here, complement   **B.** here, compliment

C. hear, compliment   **D.** hear, complement

General Studies

Q.51 Which of the following country's lunar probe mission has found evidence of water on the moon in January 2022?

A. India   **B.** China   **C.** Russia   **D.** Japan

Q.52 Amongst all the States of India, what is the rank of U.P. area-wise?

A. First   **B.** Second   **C.** Third   **D.** Fourth

Q.53 The Regional Centre of the Lalit Kala Akademi (National Academy of Art) in Uttar Pradesh is located at _____.

[UPSSSC Village Development Officer, 2018]

A. Allahabad   **B.** Lucknow

C. Aligarh   **D.** Kanpur

Q.54 UNESCO added Ajanta Caves to the list of World Heritage Sites in 1983. It is located in _______.

A. Maharashtra   **B.** Tamilnadu

C. Gujarat   **D.** Madhya Pradesh

Q.55 Penicillin, the first antibiotic, was discovered by:

A. Jonas Salk   **B.** Edward Jenner

C. Louis Pasteur   **D.** Alexander Fleming

Q.56 Who is the author of the book named "Wings of fire"?

A. Dr. A.P.J. Abdul Kalam

B. Dr. Indu Anand

C. Arunima Sinha

D. Rajdeep Sardesai

Q.57 Who among the following is the poet who composed 'Buddhacharita', a biography of Buddha?

A. Ashvaghosh   **B.** Bhavabhuti

C. Vasumitra   **D.** Nagarjuna

Q.58 Capital of the kingdom of the Pallavas was _____.

A. Mysore   **B.** Madras

C. Kannauj   **D.** Kanchipuram

Q.59 Which state is not a part of the 'Seven Sisters' of North East?

A. Meghalaya   **B.** Sikkim

C. Arunachal Pradesh   **D.** Tripura

Q.60 Which country will host the Southeast Asian Games (SEA) in 2027?

A. Malaysia   **B.** Singapore

C. Thailand   **D.** Myanmar

Q.61 Who has become the first-ever Indian brand ambassador of luxury brand Louis Vuitton?

A. Aamir Khan   **B.** Disha Patani

C. Shahrukh Khan   **D.** Deepika Padukone

Q.62 India's first 'Amrit Sarovar' has come up in which state?

A. Gujarat   **B.** Punjab

C. Odisha   **D.** Uttar Pradesh

Q.63 In October 2022, the financial Action Task Force (FATF) has removed which country from its grey list after four years?

A. Oman   **B.** Pakistan

C. Saudi Arabia   **D.** Indonesia

Q.64 Which country will be invited by India as the guest country during its G-20 presidency in 2023?

A. Bangladesh   **B.** Thailand

C. Myanmar   **D.** Nepal

Q.65 Which of the following song forms are sung in the rainy season in Uttar Pradesh?

A. Birha   **B.** Rasia   **C.** Chaiti   **D.** Kajri

Q.66 The deficiency of which vitamin causes night blindness?

A. Vitamin A   **B.** Vitamin B_1

C. Vitamin C   **D.** Vitamin E

Q.67 A thin wire that gives off light from the bulb is called _____.

A. Terminal   **B.** Tip   **C.** Source   **D.** Filament

Q.68 Saina Nehwal is associated with which field?

A. Engineering   **B.** Sports

C. Army   **D.** Education

Q.69 Gateway of India is in ________.

A. Mumbai   **B.** Chennai

C. Bangalore   **D.** New Delhi

Q.70 Bhoksa people speak _____ language.

A. Sanskrit language   **B.** Garo language

C. Khasia language   **D.** Buksa language

Q.71 Maad soil is found in which part of Uttar pradesh?

A. Northern Uttar Pradesh

B. Southern Uttar Pradesh

C. Eastern Uttar Pradesh

D. None of the above

Q.72 What is the currency of Malaysia?

A. Malaysian Dinar   **B.** Malaysian Dollars

C. Malaysian Euro   **D.** Malaysian Ringgit

Q.73 Identify the given leaf.

A. Neem
B. Rose
C. Banana leaf
D. None of these

Q.74 In which river Mata Tila Dam is situated?
A. Narmada **B.** Son **C.** Cane **D.** Betwa

Q.75 Which city does not traditionally hold Kumbha Mela?
A. Ujjain
B. Varanasi
C. Haridwar
D. Prayagraj

Mathematics

Q.76 The product of the two prime numbers is 493. What will the $L.C.M$ of these two numbers?
A. 493
B. 17
C. 29
D. None of these

Q.77 A sum of Rs. 15000 amounts to Rs. 18600 in 4 years at simple interest. What is the rate of interest?
A. 6.5% **B.** 5% **C.** 6% **D.** 8%

Q.78 The unequal side of an isosceles triangle is $3\ cm$ more than one of its equal sides. If the perimeter of the triangle is $18\ cm$, find the length of the equal sides.
A. $3\ cm$ **B.** $8\ cm$ **C.** $5\ cm$ **D.** $6\ cm$

Q.79 The sum of twice a number and thrice its reciprocal is $\dfrac{25}{2}$. What is the number?

[Territorial Army Officer, 2021]

A. 7 **B.** 6 **C.** 5 **D.** 4

Q.80 The divisor is 25 times the quotient and 5 times the remainder. If the quotient is 16, the dividend is:
A. 6400 **B.** 6480 **C.** 480 **D.** 960

Q.81 Which of the following number is divisible by 11?
A. 1516 **B.** 1452 **C.** 1011 **D.** 1121

Q.82 In an election, out of $70,000$ eligible voters $42,000$ cast their vote. Calculate the percentage of voters casting their votes.
A. 60 percent
B. 55 percent
C. 61 percent
D. 59 percent

Q.83 The length of a rectangular field is twice its breadth. If the area of the field is 288 sq.m., the length of the field is:
A. 14 m **B.** 12 m **C.** 24 m **D.** 16 m

Q.84 Express $11.\overline{330}$ as a vulgar fraction.
A. $11\frac{109}{330}$ **B.** $11\frac{327}{330}$ **C.** $11\frac{109}{990}$ **D.** $11\frac{330}{900}$

Q.85 What will be the square root of $\sqrt{12996}$?
A. 106 **B.** 126 **C.** 124 **D.** 114

Q.86 The value of $\dfrac{(10(1+13-4-8)}{5}$
A. 2.5 **B.** 1.5 **C.** 2.2 **D.** 4

Q.87 648 ÷ 54 × 14 = ?
A. 134 **B.** 146 **C.** 152 **D.** 168

Q.88 $60 + 5 \times \dfrac{12}{\left(\frac{180}{3}\right)} =?$
A. 60 **B.** 120 **C.** 13 **D.** 61

Q.89 100 + 50 × 2 = ?
A. 75 **B.** 150 **C.** 200 **D.** 300

Q.90 If three-fifths of 60% of a number is 36, the number is:
A. 100 **B.** 90 **C.** 80 **D.** 75

Q.91 Find the LCM of $16, 18, 24$ and 36.
A. 144 **B.** 145 **C.** 154 **D.** 14

Q.92 Direction: Find the missing term in the following series?
$100, 200, 310, 430, ?$
A. 506 **B.** 512 **C.** 560 **D.** 566

Q.93 Ramu bought an article at Rs. 900. He sold it at Rs. 600. Find his profit or loss percent.
A. $33\frac{1}{3}\%$ **B.** 30% **C.** 45% **D.** 51%

Q.94 Find the median of the given set of numbers $2,6,6,8,4,2,7,9$
A. 6 **B.** 8 **C.** 4 **D.** 5

Q.95 What is the sum of the natural numbers up to 17?
A. 153 **B.** 72 **C.** 90 **D.** 81

Q.96 Find the number of all prime numbers less than 55.
[RRB (NTPC), 2020]
A. 15 **B.** 17 **C.** 18 **D.** 16

Q.97 The sum of two numbers is 23 and their product is 216. Find the sum of their squares.
A. 961 **B.** 313 **C.** 97 **D.** 529

Q.98 The circumference of a circle is given as $308\ m$. What is the area of the circle?

$$\left[\text{Use } \pi = \frac{22}{7}\right]$$

A. $7646\ m^2$ **B.** $7546\ m^2$ **C.** $7556 m^2$ **D.** $7446\ m^2$

Q.99 Directions: Choose the Roman representation for: 18.

A. VII   **B.** IX   **C.** XX   **D.** XVIII

Q.100 Write 0.18 in fraction :

A. $\frac{18}{100}$ **B.** $\frac{18}{10}$ **C.** $\frac{18}{1000}$ **D.** $\frac{2}{1000}$

// Smart Answer Sheet //

Correct Indicates percentage of students who answered questions correctly.

Skipped Indicates percentage of students who skipped questions.

Q.	Ans.	Correct / Skipped	Q.	Ans.	Correct / Skipped	Q.	Ans.	Correct / Skipped	Q.	Ans.	Correct / Skipped	Q.	Ans.	Correct / Skipped
1	D	86.44 % / 0.0 %	17	D	65.75 % / 1.52 %	33	A	51.92 % / 1.66 %	49	D	68.98 % / 1.92 %	65	D	50.55 % / 1.44 %
2	C	43.73 % / 1.55 %	18	C	52.85 % / 1.96 %	34	B	45.77 % / 1.53 %	50	A	41.43 % / 1.28 %	66	A	68.19 % / 1.58 %
3	D	80.94 % / 0.0 %	19	D	68.39 % / 1.52 %	35	B	49.54 % / 1.76 %	51	B	43.46 % / 1.31 %	67	D	41.48 % / 1.85 %
4	A	86.76 % / 0.0 %	20	B	54.24 % / 1.78 %	36	C	65.24 % / 1.32 %	52	D	78.73 % / 0.0 %	68	B	59.06 % / 1.58 %
5	D	79.34 % / 0.0 %	21	A	45.53 % / 1.66 %	37	D	45.25 % / 1.17 %	53	B	81.15 % / 0.0 %	69	A	67.61 % / 1.58 %
6	C	40.97 % / 1.25 %	22	C	53.82 % / 1.13 %	38	A	49.96 % / 1.84 %	54	A	83.59 % / 0.0 %	70	D	60.53 % / 1.25 %
7	B	47.02 % / 1.72 %	23	B	43.13 % / 1.03 %	39	D	43.36 % / 1.48 %	55	D	80.88 % / 0.0 %	71	B	54.3 % / 1.5 %
8	A	42.61 % / 1.19 %	24	A	45.65 % / 1.85 %	40	C	45.13 % / 1.62 %	56	A	87.75 % / 0.0 %	72	D	59.59 % / 1.53 %
9	B	20.53 % / 3.06 %	25	C	69.75 % / 1.46 %	41	A	65.26 % / 1.12 %	57	A	59.41 % / 1.12 %	73	A	43.71 % / 1.69 %
10	A	81.0 % / 0.0 %	26	A	84.23 % / 0.0 %	42	B	56.3 % / 1.18 %	58	D	47.35 % / 1.32 %	74	D	63.88 % / 1.24 %
11	B	89.59 % / 0.0 %	27	A	85.57 % / 0.0 %	43	C	45.14 % / 1.05 %	59	B	55.19 % / 1.26 %	75	B	60.92 % / 1.36 %
12	C	58.06 % / 1.46 %	28	C	84.96 % / 0.0 %	44	D	64.12 % / 1.7 %	60	A	66.46 % / 1.52 %	76	A	83.92 % / 0.0 %
13	B	64.4 % / 1.96 %	29	A	47.3 % / 1.31 %	45	B	50.84 % / 1.13 %	61	D	58.97 % / 1.88 %	77	C	82.05 % / 0.0 %
14	A	61.34 % / 1.7 %	30	B	42.06 % / 1.38 %	46	C	55.9 % / 1.13 %	62	D	60.28 % / 1.97 %	78	C	54.2 % / 1.79 %
15	A	54.01 % / 1.7 %	31	C	57.76 % / 1.8 %	47	A	66.15 % / 1.6 %	63	B	42.62 % / 1.77 %	79	B	57.34 % / 1.03 %
16	C	59.99 % / 1.03 %	32	B	56.66 % / 1.84 %	48	D	60.71 % / 1.86 %	64	A	46.35 % / 1.89 %	80	B	43.23 % / 1.3 %

Q.	Ans.	Correct / Skipped
81	B	41.06 %
		1.14 %
82	A	58.65 %
		1.95 %
83	C	65.95 %
		1.01 %
84	A	58.42 %
		1.11 %

Q.	Ans.	Correct / Skipped
85	D	61.2 %
		1.99 %
86	D	57.33 %
		1.73 %
87	D	49.26 %
		1.34 %
88	D	55.28 %
		1.88 %

Q.	Ans.	Correct / Skipped
89	C	53.33 %
		1.51 %
90	A	62.61 %
		1.48 %
91	A	51.59 %
		1.22 %
92	C	51.41 %
		1.24 %

Q.	Ans.	Correct / Skipped
93	A	57.71 %
		1.01 %
94	A	55.79 %
		1.94 %
95	A	68.8 %
		1.67 %
96	D	78.4 %
		0.0 %

Q.	Ans.	Correct / Skipped
97	C	69.49 %
		1.22 %
98	B	47.2 %
		1.75 %
99	D	60.79 %
		1.59 %
100	A	42.03 %
		1.65 %

Performance Analysis

Avg. Score (%)	46.0%
Toppers Score (%)	58.0%
Your Score	

//Hints and Solutions//

1. 'अपरिणीत' अर्थात 'जो परिणय सूत्र में न बँधा हो'।

'अज्ञ' का अर्थ क्या है - जो कुछ भी नहीं जानता हो।

अभियोगी : जिस पर अभियोग लगाया गया हो।

अल्पज्ञ : जो बहुत थोड़ा जानता हो।

अतः विकल्प (D) सही है।

2. दिये गए विकल्पों में से 'रेखा घर में है' में अधिकरण कारक है।

अधिकरण का मतलब आश्रय होता है, संज्ञा का वह स्वरूप जिसमें किया कि आधार का बोध होता हो, उसे अधिकरण कारक कहते हैं। अधिकरण कारक में विभक्ति चिन्ह में, भीतर, अंदर, ऊपर, बीच, इत्यादि शब्दों का प्रयोग होता है।

कर्ता - जो क्रिया का सम्पादन करे।

करण - जिस माद्यम से क्रिया का सम्पादन होता है।

कर्म - जिस पर क्रिया का फल पड़े।

अतः विकल्प (C) सही है।

3. भाषण, यहाँ सही विकल्प हैं, अन्य विकल्प असंगत है। वाक्य के अनुसार भाषण यहाँ सही उत्तर है, क्योंकि नेताओं द्वारा किए गये संवाद को भाषण कहा जाता है। इसलिए, भाषण यहाँ सही विकल्प होगा।

अतः विकल्प (D) सही है।

4. लीटर, यहाँ सही विकल्प हैं, अन्य विकल्प असंगत है। चूँकि सभी द्रव्य पदार्थों को लीटर में मापा जाता है, इसलिए, उचित विकल्प 'लीटर' होगा।

अतः विकल्प (A) सही है।

5. 'आगरा' का बहुवचन नहीं होगा।

किसी स्थान या जगह का कोई बहुवचन नहीं होता है।

अतः सही विकल्प (D) है।

6. शुद्ध वर्तनी वाला शब्द 'सांसारिक' है।

सांसारिक का अर्थ है: संसार संबंधी, लौकिक।

शुद्ध वर्तनी का अर्थ है: शब्दों में मात्राओं का सही प्रयोग करके सही शब्द लिखना। जैसे अकाश – आकाश, इद – ईद, उष्मा- ऊष्मा आदि।

अतः विकल्प (C) सही है।

7. 'विद्यार्थी' का सही संधि विच्छेद विद्या + अर्थी (आ + अ = आ) है।

इसमें दीर्घ स्वर संधि है। इस संधि को हम हस्व संधि भी कह सकते हैं।

दीर्घ स्वर संधि: जब दो शब्दों की संधि करते समय (अ, आ) के साथ (अ, आ) हो तो 'आ' बनता है, जब (इ, ई) के साथ (इ, ई) हो तो 'ई' बनता है, जब (उ, ऊ) के साथ (उ, ऊ) हो तो 'ऊ' बनता है।

जैसे: पुस्तक + आलय = पुस्तकालय बनता है। यहाँ अ + आ मिलकर आ बनाते हैं।

अतः विकल्प (B) सही है।

8. 'सम्मुख' का विलोम शब्द 'विमुख' होता है।

सम्मुख का अर्थ: सामने, समक्ष, आगे, आदि।

विमुख का अर्थ: विरत, प्रतिकूल, आदि।

'मुख' शब्द में 'वि' उपसर्ग लगाकर 'विमुख' शब्द का निर्माण हुआ है।

अतः विकल्प (A) सही है।

9. 'वाह! कितना सुन्दर दृश्य है।' यह विस्मयादिबोधक वाक्य का उदाहरण है। विस्मयादिबोधक वाक्य अर्थात ऐसे शब्द जो वाक्य में आश्चर्य, हर्ष, शोक, घृणा आदि भाव व्यक्त करने के लिए प्रयुक्त हों। ऐसे शब्दों के साथ विस्मयादिबोधक चिन्ह (!) का प्रयोग किया जाता है। जैसे: अरे!, ओह!, शाबाश!, काश! आदि।

अतः विकल्प (B) सही है।

10. 'किशन' शब्द तत्सम नहीं है। 'किशन या किसन' का तत्सम 'कृष्ण' होता है। अन्य सभी शब्द तत्सम रूप में हैं।

अन्य विकल्प:

- 'कटि' का तद्भव शब्द 'कमर' है।
- 'कर्क' का तद्भव शब्द 'केकड़ा' है।
- 'कृशकाय' का तद्भव शब्द 'कमजोर' है।

अतः विकल्प (A) सही है।

11. दिए गए शब्दों में से 'अधर' शब्द तद्भव नहीं है यह तत्सम शब्द है।

- 'अधर' का तद्भव 'ओठ' होता है।
- अन्य सभी शब्द तद्भव रूप में हैं।

अतः विकल्प (B) सही है।

12. रस के चार अंग हैं।

स्थाई भाव	स्थाई भाव रस का पहला एवं सर्वप्रमुख अंग है। भाव शब्द की उत्पत्ति ' भ् ' धातु से हुई है। जिसका अर्थ है संपन्न होना या विद्यमान होना। आचार्य भरतमुनि ने स्थाई भाव आठ ही माने हैं – रति, हास्य, शोक, क्रोध, उत्साह, भय, जुगुप्सा और विस्मय। वर्तमान समय में इसकी संख्या 9 कर दी गई है तथा निर्वेद नामक स्थाई भाव की परिकल्पना की गई है।
विभाव	रस का दूसरा अनिवार्य एवं महत्वपूर्ण अंग है। भावों का विभाव करने वाले अथवा उन्हें आस्वाद योग्य बनाने वाले कारण विभाव कहलाते हैं। विभाव कारण हेतु निर्मित आदि से सभी पर्यायवाची शब्द हैं। विभाव का मूल कार्य सामाजिक हृदय में विद्यमान भावों की महत्वपूर्ण भूमिका मानी गई है। विभाव के अंग – १ आलंबन विभाव और २ उद्दीपन विभाव
अनुभाव	रस योजना का तीसरा महत्वपूर्ण अंग है। आलंबन और उद्दीपन के कारण जो कार्य होता है उसे अनुभव कहते हैं। शास्त्र के अनुसार आश्रय के मनोगत भावों को व्यक्त करने वाली शारीरिक चेष्टाएं अनुभव कहलाती है। भावों के पश्चात उत्पन्न होने के कारण इन्हें अनुभव कहा जाता है। अनुभवों की संख्या 4 कही गई है – सात्विक, कायिक, मानसिक और आहार्य। इनकी संख्या 8 मानी गई है – स्तंभ, स्वेद, रोमांच, स्वरभंग, कंपन, विवरण, अश्रु, प्रलय
संचारी भाव	मानव रक्त संचरण करने वाले भाव ही संचारी भाव कहलाते हैं यह तत्काल बनते हैं एवं मिटते हैं संचारी भावों की संख्या 33 मानी गई है – निर्वेद, स्तब्ध, गिलानी, शंका या भ्रम, आलस्य, दैन्य, चिंता, स्वप्र, उन्माद, बीड़ा, सफलता, हर्ष, आवेद, जड़ता, गर्व, विषाद, निद्रा, स्वप्र, उन्माद, त्रास, धृति, समर्थ, उग्रता, व्याधि, मरण, वितर्क आदि।

अतः विकल्प (C) सही है।

13. 'पसीना पसीना होना' मुहावरे का सही अर्थ 'बहुत थक जाना' है।

पसीना पसीना होना मुहावरे से बना वाक्य:-

- सुबह से लगातार काम करते-करते तो मैं पसीना- पसीना हो गया हूं।

अन्य विकल्पों का विश्लेषण:-

- क्रोधित होना के लिए मुहावरा है - 'आग बबूला होना'।
- भयभीत होना के लिए मुहावरा है - 'पसीना छूटना'।

- प्यासा होना के लिए मुहावरा है - 'गला सूखना'।

अतः विकल्प (B) सही है।

14. 'जैसी करनी वैसी भरनी' लोकोक्ति का उपयुक्त अर्थ 'अपने किए का फल पाना' है।

लोकोक्ति का वाक्य प्रयोग:-

- शेर ने जानवरों को पकड़ने के लिए गड्ढा खोदा और उसे पत्तों से ढक दिया, लेकिन अज्ञानतावश वह स्वयं ही उस गड्ढे में गिर गया, इसे कहते हैं जैसी करनी वैसी भरनी।
- बहुत अधिक प्रचलित और लोगों के मुँहचढ़े वाक्य लोकोक्ति के तौर पर जाने जाते हैं। इन वाक्यों में जनता के अनुभव का निचोड़ या सार होता है। इनकी उत्पत्ति एवं रचनाकार ज्ञात नहीं होते।

अन्य विकल्पों का विश्लेषण:-

- कम श्रम में अधिक लाभ प्राप्त करना - के लिए लोकोक्ति हो सकती है - आम के आम, गुठलियों के दाम।
- काम करने से बचाना - फेर से भागना।
- दूसरो को कष्ट देना - के लिए लोकोक्ति या मुहावरा है - कान सेकना।

अतः विकल्प (A) सही है।

15. किसी की सहायता करने वाले को 'सहायक' कहते हैं।

जो हृदयवान हो 'सहृदय' कहलाता है। साथ चलने वाला 'सहचर' तथा साथ कार्य करने वाला 'सहकार' कहलाता है।

अतः विकल्प (A) सही है।

16. अन्य विकल्पों में "अल्प विराम" सम्बंधित अशुद्धि है।

शुद्ध वाक्य : मेरी मित्र, जो एक लेखिका है, आजकल एक पुस्तक लिख रही है।

उपर्युक्त वाक्य में तीन अलग - अलग वाक्यों को अल्प विराम के द्वारा जोड़ा गया है।

वाक्य : मेरी मित्र

वाक्य : जो एक लेखिका है

वाक्य : आजकल एक पुस्तक लिख रही है।

अन्य विकल्पों में विराम चिन्ह उचित स्थान पर नहीं है।

अतः विकल्प (C) सही है।

17. उपर्युक्त विकल्पों में से विकल्प "देवियो, आप हमारे देश की आशाएँ हैं।" सही है तथा अन्य विकल्प असंगत हैं।

- "देवियो, आप हमारे देश की आशाएँ हैं।" वाक्य सही है।
- देवियो के आगे अल्पविराम सम्बोधन करने के कारण लगा है।
- तथा अंत में पूर्ण विराम लगेगा।

अतः विकल्प (D) सही है।

18. 'अत्युक्ति' शब्द में 'अति' उपसर्ग है।

इसका उचित संधि विच्छेद 'अति + उक्ति = अत्युक्ति' होगा।

यह यण संधि का उदाहरण है।

जो शब्दांश शब्दों के प्रारम्भ में जुड़ कर उनके अर्थ में कुछ विशेषता लाते हैं, वे उपसर्ग कहलाते हैं।

अतः विकल्प (C) सही है।

19. 'गुजारा' में 'आ' प्रत्यय है।

प्रत्यय उस शब्दांश को कहते हैं, जो किसी शब्द के अंत में आकर उस शब्द के विभिन्न अर्थ में प्रकट करते हैं। प्रत्यय शब्द के अंत में आता है, जैसे 'भला' शब्द के अंत में आई प्रत्यय लगाकर 'भलाई' शब्द बनता है।

अतः विकल्प (D) सही है।

20. जिस वाक्य में एक से अधिक वाक्य मिले हों, किन्तु एक प्रधान उपवाक्य तथा शेष आश्रित उपवाक्य हों, मिश्रित वाक्य कहलाता है।

- प्रधान उपवाक्य - 'मैं उस लड़की से मिला था'
- आश्रित उपवाक्य - 'जिसकी किताब खो गयी थी'

अतः विकल्प (B) सही है।

21. वाक्य तीन प्रकार के होते हैं सरल वाक्य, सयुंक्त वाक्य तथा मिश्र वाक्य इसलिए विकल्प (A) सही है।

वाक्य के प्रकार
सरल वाक्य: सरल वाक्य में एक उद्देश्य के साथ-2 केवल एक ही समायिका और एक विधेय होते हैं सरल वाक्य कहलाते हैं। उदाहरण:- बच्चे क्रिकेट खेलते हैं।
संयुक्त वाक्य: दो या दो से अधिक सरल वाक्य योजक शब्दों के द्वारा जुड़कर बनते हैं संयुक्त वाक्य को विभाजित करने पर पुनः सरल वाक्य प्राप्त होते हैं। उदाहरण:- राम आया और सो गया।
मिश्र वाक्य: जिन वाक्यों में एक प्रधान उपवाक्य और इस उपवाक्य पर एक या एक से अधिक आश्रित उपवाक्य होते हैं यह सभी आपस में कि, जो, की, इतना, उतना, इधर, उधर, कब, कितना, जब ,तब जैसा, वैसा, वह, आदि, शब्दों, से जुड़े होते हैं।

अतः विकल्प (A) सही है।

22. स्वरों की कुल संख्या - 11 (अ, इ, उ, ऋ, आ, ई, ऊ, ए, ऐ, ओ, औ)

- हस्व स्वरों की कुल संख्या - 6 (अ, इ, उ, ऋ)
- दीर्घ स्वरों की कुल संख्या - 7 (आ, ई, ऊ, ए, ऐ, ओ, औ)

अतः विकल्प (C) सही है।

23. 'रीतिकाल' काल का भेद नहीं बल्कि हिन्दी साहित्य के काल विभाजन का भेद है।

अन्य सभी काल के भेद हैं।

सामान्यत: हिन्दी साहित्य के इतिहास को चार भागों में विभाजित किया गया है-

- आदिकाल
- भक्ति काल
- रीतिकाल और
- आधुनिक काल

अतः विकल्प (B) सही है।

24. 'परदेसिया' शब्द में 'इया' प्रत्यय है।

- परदेसिया = परदेस + इया (प्रत्यय)।
- 'इया' प्रत्यय से अन्य शब्द - दिवालिया, सवालिया, नगरिया आदि।

अतः विकल्प (A) सही है।

25. 'अधोलोक' का पर्यायवाची 'पाताल' है। इसका अन्य पर्यायवाची शब्द 'रसताल' है। अन्य विकल्प असंगत हैं। इसलिए, सही विकल्प 'पाताल' है।

परलोक - देवलोक

भू-लोक - पृथ्वी लोक

गगन - व्योम

वायु - पवन

अत: विकल्प (C) सही है।

26. The underlined part belongs to Interjection.

The underlined word **'bravo'** is used to express 'well done'. So, it is an **interjection**.

Interjection: It is used to show a sudden feeling of happiness, anger, sorrow, etc. Example - Alas! I am ruined.

Hence, the correct option is (A).

27. However, David did not achieve his goal.

- The comma (,) is used to separate ideas or elements. Also, it is used after the salutation, or when a brief pause is required after a word or phrase. In the question, we require a brief pause after however as it is the introductory adverb.

- A semicolon (;) is used when we need to separate independent clauses and to show a close relationship between them.

- A colon (:) is used to provide a pause before introducing related information, or when we want to define or introduce something and join unequal parts of sentences.

- An exclamation mark (!) is used to denote a sudden outcry or emphasis.

Hence, the correct option is (A).

28. How do you prepare a burger?

- Question mark (?) is used after asking a question. So, it is a correctly punctuated sentence.

- A comma is used when someone is directly addressed/to separate two clauses/to separate ideas, objects, names in a sentence. For example, I will go to Goa, Mumbai, and Pune.

- The exclamation mark is used to express wonder, surprise or to emphasize. For example, I have found the lost photo album!

- A full stop is used at the end of a sentence. For example, She is my sister.

Hence, the correct option is (C).

29. See-through means to stay with to the end or until completion; persevere: to see a difficult situation through.

Other words:

See about means attend to or deal with something.

See a person through means to cause or help someone to manage or survive

Set about means to start doing something with vigor or determination.

Hence, the correct option is (A).

30. She was beaten **with** a bat.

With used to show the way in which somebody does something.

Example: He behaved **with** great dignity.

Hence, the correct option is (B).

31. Professor is the correctly spelled word.

Professor means a university teacher of the highest level.

Example: The professor is an academic rank at universities and other post-secondary education and research institutions in most countries.

Hence, the correct option is (C).

32. As Diamond is made of Carbon similarly Ruby is made of Corundum.

Hence, the correct option is (B).

33. The underlined word 'yelled' is a verb that means 'shouted in a loud, sharp way'. For example, You heard me losing my temper and yelling at her.

As we have to identify which part of speech the word belongs to, we need to know the significance of the parts of speech.

Parts of Speech:

- A category to which a word is assigned in accordance with its syntactic functions.

- In English, the main parts of speech are noun, pronoun, adjective, determiner, verb, adverb, preposition, conjunction, and interjection.

Here, the word 'yelled' is an action. So, 'yelled' will be categorized as a verb.

Hence, the correct option is (A).

34. The most appropriate antonym of the given word 'Modest' is 'Conceited'.

Modest: not talking too much about your own abilities, good qualities, etc.

- Example: She got the best results in the exam but she was too modest to tell anyone.

Conceited: excessively proud of oneself; vain.

- Example: He's so conceited—he thinks he's the best at everything!

Hence, the correct option is (B).

35. Let's see the meanings of the given words:

- Instant→ Happening immediately.

- Similar→ Of the same kind in appearance.

- Gradual→ Taking place over an extended period.

- Prompt→ cause or bring about.

- Diverse→ widely varied

- So according to the meaning of the given words the correct sentence is 'Gradual'

Hence, the correct option is (B).

36. The most appropriate synonym of the given word 'Pleasant' is 'Refreshing'.

Let's look at the meaning and examples of the given words:

Words	Meaning	Example
Pleasant	enjoyable, attractive, friendly, or easy to like	Harold did his best to be pleasant to the old man.
Refreshing	making you feel less hot or tired	There's nothing more refreshing on a hot day than a cold beer.
Tiresome	annoying and making you lose patience	He has the tiresome habit of finishing your sentences for you.
Tedious	boring and tiring, esp. because long or often repeated	Learning a new computer program can be a tedious process.
Exasperating	annoying, because we can do nothing to solve a problem	It's so exasperating when he won't listen to a word that I say.

Hence, the correct option is (C).

37. The word 'Priority' means 'the state of being more important than somebody/something or of coming before somebody/something else'.

The synonyms of the word 'Priority' are "preference, antecedency, anteriority, precedence, precedency, antecedence, precession.".

From the synonym of the given word, we can say that the word 'Preference' is the most similar in meaning.

The word 'Preference' means 'an interest in or desire for one thing more than another'.

Hence, the correct option is (D).

38. The given sentence 'Anand goes to TCS every day' is in the Simple Present Tense.

We know that the structure of the Simple Present Tense. is

Structure: Sub + V_1 + s/es + Obj

Example: He goes to the temple daily.

By comparing the given sentence with this structure we can say that the sentence is in the Simple Present Tense.

Hence, the correct option is (A).

39. Autobiography- an account of a person's life written by that person

- Essay- a short piece of writing on a particular subject
- Biography- an account of someone's life written by someone else
- Travelogue- a movie, book, or illustrated lecture about the places visited and experiences encountered by a traveler

Hence, the correct option is (D).

40. Correct Sentence: Her <u>sister</u> was a vamp.

The feminine gender of '<u>brother</u>' is '<u>sister</u>'.

Hence, the correct option is (C).

41. Let's look at the meaning of the given words and to which part of speech do they belong:

- Snake (noun) - a long limbless reptile which has no eyelids, a short tail, and jaws that are capable of considerable extension. Some snakes have a venomous bite.
- Happy (adjective) - feeling or showing pleasure or contentment.
- Faster (adjective) - comparative degree of 'fast'.
- Long (adjective) - measuring a great distance from end to end.

Hence, the correct option is (A).

42. Correct sentence: They had to travel everywhere by buses.

- The plural of "bus" is "buses."
- "Busses" is an archaic plural now considered a spelling mistake.

Hence, the correct option is (B).

43. Correct sentence is- I was born on Thursday, the 25th of March.

The meaning of the preposition 'on' is- used for saying the day or date when something happens

- Example- He's coming home on Wednesday.

The meaning of the preposition 'in' is- within an area, city, or country

- Example- The books are printed in Hong Kong.

The meaning of the preposition 'at' is- in a particular place

- Example- There's a telephone box at the crossroads.

Hence, the correct option is (C).

44. Correct Sentence: He hinted at some loss of treasure.

- Here, in the given sentence the most appropriate preposition is 'at'.
- In the given sentence 'hinted at' is a phrasal verb.
- It means 'to talk about (something) in an indirect way

Example: He's been hinting at the possibility of running for mayor.

Therefore, as per the points mentioned above, we find that the correct answer is Option (D).

Hence, the correct option is (D).

45. The main verb of the sentence is 'watched' with this verb we always use the bare infinitive that is don't use 'to + v_1'

There are some other verbs that take the bare infinitive- Watch, Let, help, etc.

So the correct sentence is- I watched him fall.

Hence, the correct option is (B).

46. The sentence is What time is the news <u>on</u> T.V.?

- In general, we use on for a surface.

- The preposition "on" is used to show something that is "located in the general surface area."

- The characters on TV can be seen on the surface area of the TV.

- Thus, the preposition 'on' should be used.

Hence, the correct option is (C).

47. As we have to identify the part of the speech of the word, we need to know the significance of the parts of the speech.

Parts of speech:

- A category to which a word is assigned in accordance with its syntactic functions.

- In English, the main parts of speech are noun, pronoun, verb, adjective, adverb, preposition, conjunction, and interjection.

Let's understand the definitions of parts of speech given in the options:

Parts of speech	Function	Example
Noun	It is the name of a person, place, animal, feeling, etc.	Ram is a good boy. Meena is studying
Pronoun	To replace a noun to avoid repetition.	Shalini is Intelligent. She can stand first.
Verb	It is the word that expresses the action word in the sentence.	Let's work hard. It is very competitive.
Adjective	It is used to qualify the noun or the pronoun in the sentence.	Khushbu is an intelligent girl. She is a nice girl.

Thus the correct answer is: Noun

Hence, the correct option is (A).

48. Complete Sentence: I met my friend while I <u>was crossing</u> the road.

The past continuous tense, also known as the past progressive tense, refers to a <u>continuing action or state that was happening at some point in the past.</u>

- Example: Ritesh was watching television yesterday evening.

"I were" is called the subjunctive mood, and is used when <u>we're are talking about something that isn't true or when we wish something will true or some condition</u>. If not a subjunctive one then we use "I was" <u>instead</u> of "I were".

Formula for past continuous tense:

- Subject + was/were + Ving + Object

Hence, the correct option is (D).

49. Correct Sentence: I obeyed her lest she <u>should</u> be angry.

- In the given sentence, the most appropriate conjunction to fill-in-the-given blank is 'lest'.

- Lest is generally followed by a verb clause in the subjunctive mood.

- The word 'should' is just a way to put a clause into the future subjunctive.

- Here, the word 'subjunctive mood' means 'a form that refers to actions that are possibilities rather than facts'.

- The conjunction 'lest' means 'in order to prevent any possibility that something will happen'.

- 'Lest...should' is a pair of conjunction. We can use 'lest' without 'should' also but in that case, we have to use the base form of the verb.

Hence, the correct option is (D).

50. Let us see the meanings of the words in the brackets:

- Here(adverb) : in, at, or to this place or position.

- Hear(verb) : perceive with the ear the sound made by (someone or something).

- Complement(noun) : a thing that contributes extra features to something else in such a way as to improve or emphasize its quality.

- Compliment(noun) : a polite expression of praise or admiration.

Correct sentence : Is everyone here? Do we have a full complement.

Hence, the correct option is (A).

51. China's Chang'e 5 lunar lander has found the first-ever on-site evidence of water on the surface of the moon.

The study was published in the journal Science Advances. It revealed that the lunar soil at the landing site contains less than 120 parts-per-million (ppm) water or 120 grams of water per ton, and a light, vesicular rock carries 180 ppm, which is much drier than that on Earth.

Hence, the correct option is (B).

52. Uttar Pradesh with an area of 240928 sq. km ranks 4th in India. Rajasthan with an area of 342240 sq. km is first, Madhya Pradesh with an area of 308252 sq. km is 2nd Maharashtra with an area of 307713 sq. km is third.

Hence, the correct option is (D).

53. The Regional Centre of the Lalit Kala Akademi (National Academy of Art) in Uttar Pradesh is located at Lucknow.

- The office of the Lalit Kala Akademi is located at Lal Baradari Bhawan which is a historical monument.

- State Lalit Kala Akademi, U.P. was established on 8th February 1962 under the Department of Culture, Govt. of Uttar Pradesh as a fully funded autonomous body.

- The Lalit Kala Akademi or the National Academy of Art is India's National Academy of fine arts.

- Its main motive is to promote and propagate an understanding of Indian art in the country as well as outside the country.

Hence, the correct option is (B).

54. The Ajanta Caves are 30 rock-cut Buddhist caves which are located in Aurangabad, Maharashtra.

- These caves are built under the Patronage of two dynasties namely the Satvahana Dynasty and the Vakataka Dynasty.

- The caves include paintings and rock-cut sculptures of the Buddhist religion.

- Earlier, these caves are protected by the Archaeological Survey of India and in 1983 Ajanta Caves are included in the UNESCO World Heritage Site.

Hence, the correct option is (A).

55. Alexander Fleming was a Scottish physician, microbiologist, and pharmacologist who is credited with discovering the first antibiotic, Penicillin.

For this discovery, Alexander Fleming was awarded the Nobel Prize in Physiology or Medicine in 1945.

Hence, the correct option is (D).

56. Dr. APJ Abdul Kalam is the author of the book 'Wings of Fire'.

The story tells us about Kalam's rise from a humble lower-middle-class family & his narrative of India's efforts in rocketry & space technology.

Hence, the correct option is (A).

57. Ashvaghosh is the poet who composed 'Buddhacharita', a biography of Buddha.

- Ashvaghosha was a philosopher and poet who is considered India's greatest poet before Kalidasa (5th century) and the father of Sanskrit drama.

- He popularized the style of Sanskrit poetry known as kavya.

- Ashvaghosha adorned the court of Kanishka.

- He was born in Saketa in northern India.

- Though Pali language literature was popular in Buddhism, Ashvaghosha wrote in Classical Sanskrit.

- Ashvaghosha spoke at length on Mahayana (Greater Vehicle) Buddhist doctrine at the fourth Buddhist council, which he helped organize.

- Buddhacharita written by Ashvaghosha is an epic on the life of the Buddha.

- He also wrote Saundarananda, with the theme of conversion of Nanda, Buddha's half-brother, so that he might reach salvation.

- He is also thought to be the author of the Sutralankara.

Hence, the correct option is (A).

58. Capital of the kingdom of the Pallavas was kanchipuram.

- The Pallavas emerged as a formidable power in the South around the 4th century AD and were at the height of their power in the seventh century AD.

- They were able to sustain their rule for about 500 years.

- They built great cities, centres of learning, temples, and sculptures and influenced a large part of Southeast Asia in culture.

Hence, the correct option is (D).

59. Sikkim state is not a part of the 'Seven Sisters' of North East.

Important Facts about Seven Sisters:

- Largest Area - Arunachal Pradesh

- Smallest Area - Tripura

- Highest population - Assam

- Lowest Population - Mizoram

- Highest population density - Assam

- Lowest Population density - Arunachal Pradesh

- Highest literacy - Mizoram

- Lowest Literacy - Arunachal Pradesh

- World's biggest river island - Majuli located in Assam

- India's longest bridge - Bhupen Hazarika Bridge built on the Lohit river in Assam.

Hence, the correct option is (B).

60. Malaysia will host the 2027 SEA Games and Singapore the 2029 edition.

- The 2021 Games in the Vietnamese capital Hanoi were delayed six months because of Covid and are set to officially open 19 May 2022.

- The 2023 SEA Games are scheduled to be held in Cambodia and 2025 will be in the Thailand's capital Bangkok.

Hence, the correct option is (A).

61. Actress Deepika Padukone has become the first-ever Indian brand ambassador of luxury brand Louis Vuitton.

- It saw Padukone joining actors Emma Stone and Zhou Dongyu for promotional shots.

- She was named part of an eight-member jury presided by French actor Vincent Lindon at 75th Cannes Film Festival.

Hence, the correct option is (D).

62. India's first 'Amrit Sarovar' has come up in Uttar Pradesh's Rampur.

- India's first "Amrit Sarovar" was inaugurated by the Union Minister for Minority Affairs Mukhtar Abbas Naqvi on 13 May 2022.

- PM Narendra Modi had called for having at least 75 ponds in every district in the 75th year of India's Independence, calling them 'Amrit Sarovar'.

- The pond will not only help in protecting the environment and conserving water but will also be an attraction for people.

Hence, the correct option is (D).

63. In October 2022, the financial Action Task Force (FATF) has removed Pakistan country from its grey list after four years.

- Pakistan has been on the Paris-based watchdog's grey list for deficiencies in its counter-terror financing and anti-money laundering regimes since June 2018.
- The decision was taken by the FATF in its plenary held in Paris on 21 October 2022.

Hence, the correct option is (B).

64. As part of the G-20 tradition of inviting some Guest Countries, India has decided to invite Bangladesh as a Guest Country to take part in the G-20 meeting during its Presidency.

- Apart from Bangladesh, India will also invite Egypt, Mauritius, Netherlands, Nigeria, Oman, Singapore, Spain & UAE as Guest Countries.
- India will assume the Presidency of G-20 for one year from Dec 2022 to Nov 2023.

Hence, the correct option is (A).

65. Kajri song forms are sung in the rainy season in Uttar Pradesh.

- Kajri is one of the renowned folk songs of Uttar Pradesh.
- Kajri is generally sung by the women in Uttar Pradesh in the Bhojpuri language.
- Kajri is sung as the ode to the dark clouds which nurtures and devastates, brings life, and sometimes death.
- Kajri is often used to describe the longing of a maiden for her lover.

Hence, the correct option is (D).

66. The deficiency of Vitamin A causes night blindness. Vitamin A is found in a range of different foods including carrots, spinach, broccoli, milk, egg, liver and fish.

Hence, the correct option is (A).

67. A thin wire that gives off light from the bulb is called filament.

- The filament of the light bulb is made of tungsten metal.
- Tungsten is used in the manufacturing of filament due to its highest value of melting point.
- Incandescent lamps are filament lamps.
- The filament is enclosed in a bulb to protect the filament from the issues of oxidation.
- Argon, Nitrogen is the gases used to fill a filament lamp.
- The lifespan of a filament lamp is 1000 hours.

Hence, the correct option is (D).

68. Saina Nehwal is associated with sports field.

- Saina Nehwal is a female Indian singles badminton player.
- A former world no. 1, she has won over 24 international titles, including eleven titles in the Superseries.
- While she reached the 2nd world ranking in 2009, it was only in 2015 that she was able to cross the No. 1 world ranking.
- Nehwal is the first Indian to win two Commonwealth Games singles gold medals (2010 and 2018).
- In 2016, Padma Bhushan, India's third-highest civilian award, was awarded to her by the Government of India (GoI).

Hence, the correct option is (B).

69. Gateway of India is in mumbai.

- The Gateway of India is located in Mumbai.
- It was constructed in 1924.
- The main objective behind the construction of the Gateway of India was to commemorate the visit of King George V and Queen Mary to Bombay (Mumbai).
- In March 1911, Sir George Sydenham Clarke, who was then the Governor of Bombay, laid down the monument's foundation.
- The architectural design of the Gateway of India was done by the architect George Wittet.

Hence, the correct option is (A).

70. Bhoksa people speak Buksa language.

The Bhoksa people are indigenous people who have been granted the status of the Scheduled Tribes. They speak Buksa language which can be compared to Rana Tharu. After abandoning their animist traditions, they are now basically Hindus. They use Brahmin priests for all their religious activities and worship the tribal deity of Shakumbari Devi.

Hence, the correct option is (D).

71. Maad soil is usually found in the Southern part of Uttar Pradesh.

- Maad soil contains silica(60%), Iron(15%), aluminum(25%).
- In this type of soil, agriculture is difficult.
- The Southern Plateau was made up in the Pre-Cambrian period also known as Bundelkhand and Baghelkhand regions.

Hence, the correct option is (B).

72. The currency of Malaysia is the Malaysian ringgit. It is further divided into 100 sen. The Malaysian ringgit is issued by the central bank of Malaysia (Bank Negara Malaysia). Dinar is a monetary unit used in several Middle Eastern countries, including Algeria, Bahrain, Iraq, Jordan, Kuwait, Libya, and Tunisia.

Hence, the correct option is (D).

73. Given leaf is Neem.

Neem contains chemicals that might help reduce blood sugar levels, heal ulcers in the digestive tract, prevent pregnancy, kill bacteria, and prevent plaque from forming in the mouth.

Hence, the correct option is (A).

74. Mata Tila Dam is situated on Betwa river.

- Mata Tila Dam is located in the Lalitpur district in Uttar Pradesh.
- Mata Tila Dam was built in 1958.
- It was built on the Betwa River.
- The dam has the capacity to generate about 45 MW of power.
- The maximum storage capacity of the dam is 1132 mcm.

Hence, the correct option is (D).

75. Varanasi city does not traditionally hold Kumbha Mela.

- Kumbh Mela or Kumbha Mela is a mass Hindu pilgrimage of faith in which Hindus gather to bathe in a sacred or holy river.
- Traditionally, four fairs are widely recognized as the Kumbh Melas:
- The Haridwar Kumbh Mela, the Allahabad Kumbh Mela, the Nashik-Trimbakeshwar Simhastha, and Ujjain Simhastha.
- These four fairs are held periodically at one of the following places by rotation: Haridwar, Allahabad (Prayaga), Nashik district (Nashik and Trimbak), and Ujjain. (Hence option 2 correct)
- At any given place, the Kumbh Mela is held once in 12 years.
- There is a difference of around 3 years between the Kumbh Melas at Haridwar and Nashik; the fairs at Nashik and Ujjain are celebrated in the same year or one year apart.

Hence, the correct option is (B).

76. If there are two numbers a and b,

Then, $a \times b = LCM$ of $(a, b) \times HCF$ of (a, b)

According to the question $a \times b = 493$

And we know that HCF for two prime numbers is $= 1$

So,

$$493 = LCM \text{ of } (a, b) \times 1$$

$$\Rightarrow LCM \text{ of of these two numbers } (a, b) = 493$$

Hence, the correct option is (A).

77. Given:

$$P = \text{Rs. } 15000$$

$$A = \text{Rs. } 18600$$

$$T = 4 \text{ years}$$

Where,

A is amount,

P is principle,

SI is simple interest,

N is total number of years,

R is rate,

We know that:

$$SI = A - P$$

$$SI = 18600 - 15000 = \text{Rs. } 3600$$

$$SI = \frac{(P \times N \times R)}{100}$$

$$\Rightarrow 3600 = \frac{(15000 \times 4 \times R)}{100}$$

$$\Rightarrow R = \frac{360000}{60000} = 6$$

$\therefore$ Rate of interest is 6%.

Hence, the correct option is (C).

78. Let the length of the equal sides be $x \, cm$.

Then the length of the unequal sides will be $(x + 3) cm$.

Perimeter of an isosceles triangle is $18 \ldots x + x + 3 + x = 18$

$$3x + 3 = 18$$

$$3x = 15$$

$$\therefore x = 5$$

Therefore the equal sides of the triangle are $5 \, cm$ and the unequal side is $8 \, cm$.

Hence, the correct option is (C).

79. Let number be x then its reciprocal be $\frac{1}{x}$.

According to the question,

$$2x + \frac{3}{x} = \frac{25}{2}$$

$$\Rightarrow 2x^2 + 3 = \frac{25x}{2}$$

$$\Rightarrow 4x^2 + 6 = 25x$$

$$\Rightarrow 4x^2 - 25x + 6 = 0$$

$$\Rightarrow (4x - 1)(x - 6) = 0$$

$$\Rightarrow x = 6, \frac{1}{4}$$

Value of number cannot be a fraction.

So, the number is 6.

Hence, the correct option is (B).

80. Given,

Quotient is 16 and the divisor is 25 times the quotient.

$\Rightarrow$ Divisor $= 25 \times 16 = 400$

Also, divisor is 5 times the remainder.

$\Rightarrow$ Remainder $= \dfrac{\text{divisor}}{5}$

$\Rightarrow$ Remainder $= \dfrac{400}{5} = 80$

We know that, dividend $=$ quotient $\times$ divisor $+$ remainder

$\Rightarrow$ Dividend $= 16 \times 400 + 80$

$\Rightarrow$ Dividend $= 6480$

Hence, the correct option is (B).

81. Concept:

Divisibility Rule of 11:

If the difference between the sum of the digits at odd places and the sum of the digits at even places of the number, is 0 or divisible by 11, then the given number is also divisible by 11.

Option (A): 1516

(5 + 6) - (1 + 1)

$\Rightarrow$ 11 - 2 = 9

Option (B): 1452

(4 + 2) - (1 + 5)

$\Rightarrow$ 6 - 6 = 0

So, it is divisible by 11.

Option (C): 1011

(1 + 0) - (1 + 1)

$\Rightarrow$ 1 - 2 = -1

Option (D): 1121

(1 + 1) - (1 + 2)

$\Rightarrow$ 2 - 3 = -1

$\therefore$ 1452 is divisible by 11.

Hence, the correct option is (B).

82. Given:

Eligible voters $= 70000$, cast their votes $= 42000$

Formula used:

$\%$ of voters $= \dfrac{\text{number of votes casted}}{\text{eliqible votes}} \times 100$

$\%$ of voters $= \dfrac{42000}{70000} \times 100$

$= \dfrac{42}{70} \times 100$

$= 6 \times 10$

$= 60\%$

$\therefore$ The answer is 60%.

Hence, the correct option is (A).

83. Given:

The length of a rectangular field is twice its breadth.

The area of the field is 288 sq.m.

Concept used:

Area of a rectangle = Length × Breadth

Let the length and breadth of the rectangular field be 2d and d meter respectively.

According to the concept,

2d × d = 288

$\Rightarrow$ 2d² = 288

$\Rightarrow$ d² = 144

$\Rightarrow$ d = ± 12

$\Rightarrow$ d = +12 (length can't be negative)

$\Rightarrow$ 2d = 24

$\therefore$ The length of the field is 24 meter.

Hence, the correct option is (C).

84. Given:

$11.3\overline{30}$

Concept used:

Firstly, write down the repeated digits only once in numerator and then place as many lines in the denominator as the number of digits repeating and the number which is not marked consider zero for that number in the denominator and subtract the total number by the number which is not marked after the decimal part.

$11 + \dfrac{(330-3)}{990}$

$11 + \dfrac{327}{990}$

$11 + \dfrac{109}{330}$

$\therefore$ The answer is $11\dfrac{109}{330}$.

Hence, the correct option is (A)

85. Given:

$\sqrt{12996}$

Division method

```
    .   114|
       ─────────
1  |  1 29 96
   |  1
   ──────────────
21 |    029
   |     21
   ──────────────
224|    896
   |    896
   ──────────────
           0
```

∴ The value of $\sqrt{12996}$ is 114.

Hence, the correct option is (D).

86. Given:

$$\frac{(10(1+13-4-8)}{5}$$

Using the BODMAS rule:

$$\Rightarrow \frac{10\left(1+13-4-8\right)}{5}$$

$$\Rightarrow \frac{10\left(14-4-8\right)}{5}$$

$$\Rightarrow \frac{10\left(14-12\right)}{5}$$

$$\Rightarrow 10 \times \frac{2}{5}$$

$$\Rightarrow \frac{20}{5} = 4$$

Hence, the correct option is (D).

87. Given:

$648 \div 54 \times 14 = ?$

$\Rightarrow 648 \div 54 \times 14$

$\Rightarrow 12 \times 14$

$\Rightarrow 168$

So, the correct answer is "168".

Hence, the correct option is (D).

88. Given:

$$60 + 5 \times \frac{12}{\left(\frac{180}{3}\right)}$$

$$\Rightarrow 60 + 5 \times 12 \times \frac{3}{180}$$

$$\Rightarrow 60 + \left(\frac{180}{180}\right)$$

$$\Rightarrow 60 + 1$$

Hence, the correct option is (D).

89. Given:

$\Rightarrow 100 + 50 \times 2$

$\Rightarrow 100 + 100$

$\Rightarrow 200$

∴ The correct answer is 200.

Hence, the correct option is (C).

90. Formula Used:

$$X\% = \frac{X}{100}$$

Let the number be x

$$\Rightarrow \frac{3}{5} \times \frac{60}{100} \times x = 36$$

$$\Rightarrow \frac{9x}{25} = 36$$

$$\Rightarrow x = 100$$

∴ The correct answer is 100.

Hence, the correct option is (A).

91. Factor of $16 = 2 \times 2 \times 2 \times 2$

Factor of $18 = 2 \times 3 \times 3$

Factor of $24 = 2 \times 2 \times 2 \times 3$

Factor of $36 = 2 \times 2 \times 3 \times 3$

So, LCM $= 2 \times 2 \times 2 \times 2 \times 3 \times 3 = 144$

Hence, the correct option is (A).

92. Given,

$$100 + 100 = 200$$

$$200 + 110 = 310$$

$$310 + 120 = 430$$

$$430 + 130 = 560$$

Hence, the correct option is (C).

93. Given:

$$CP = \text{Rs. } 900$$

$$SP = \text{Rs. } 600$$

$$\text{Loss } \% = \frac{\text{Loss}}{CP} \times 100$$

$$\text{Loss } = CP - SP$$

$$\Rightarrow \text{Loss } = 900 - 600$$

$$\Rightarrow \text{Loss } = 300$$

$$\text{Loss } \% = \frac{300}{900} \times 100$$

$$= \frac{1}{3} \times 100$$

$$= 33\frac{1}{3}\%$$

$\therefore$ Loss $\%$ is $33\frac{1}{3}\%$.

Hence, the correct option is (A).

94. Given values $2,6,6,8,4,2,7,9$

Arrange the observations in ascending order:

$2,2,4,6,6,7,8,9$

Here, $n = 8 =$ even

As we know, If n is even then,

Median $=$

$$\frac{\text{value of } \left(\frac{n}{2}\right)^{th} \text{ observation + value of } \left(\frac{n}{2}+1\right)^{th} \text{ observation}}{2}$$

$$= \frac{4^{th} \text{ observation } + 5^{th} \text{ observation}}{2}$$

$$= \frac{6+6}{2} = 6$$

So, Median $= 6$

Hence, the correct option is (A).

95. Given:

The sum of the natural numbers up to 17

Formula used:

Sum of n natural numbers $= \dfrac{n(n+1)}{2}$

Now,

Sum of n natural numbers $= \dfrac{n(n+1)}{2}$

$$\Rightarrow \left[\frac{17(17+1)}{2}\right]$$

$$\Rightarrow \frac{(17 \times 18)}{2}$$

$$\Rightarrow (17 \times 9)$$

$$\Rightarrow 153$$

$\therefore$ The required number is 153.

Hence, the correct option is (A).

96. Prime numbers less than 55 = 2, 3, 5, 7, 11, 13, 17, 19, 23, 29, 31, 37, 41, 43, 47, 53

$\therefore$ The required no of prime numbers is 16.

Hence, the correct option is (D).

97. Given:

Sum of two numbers is 23

The product of two numbers is 216

Formula used:

$a^2 + b^2 = (a + b)^2 - 2ab$

Let p and q be the numbers,

p + q = 23

pq = 216

By using the above formula,

$p^2 + q^2 = (23)^2 - 2 \times 216$

$p^2 + q^2 = 529 - 432 = 97$

The sum of the squares of the number is 97.

Hence, the correct option is (C).

98. Given:

The circumference of a circle is given as $308\ m$.

Concept used:

The circumference of a circle $= 2\pi R$

The area of a circle $= \pi R^2$

Where R is the radius.

Let the radius of the circle be R meter.

According to the question,

$$2\pi R = 308$$

$$\Rightarrow 2 \times \frac{22}{7} \times R = 308$$

$$\Rightarrow R = 49$$

$$\Rightarrow \pi R^2 = \frac{22}{7} \times 49^2$$

$$\Rightarrow \pi R^2 = 7546$$

$\therefore$ The area of the circle is $7546\ m^2$.

Hence, the correct option is (B).

99. Roman equivalent of 18 is XVIII.

Hence, the correct option is (D).

100. 0.18 in fraction,

$$0.18 \times \frac{100}{100} = \frac{18}{100}$$

Hence, the correct option is (A).

Hindi

Q.1 निर्देश: वाक्यांश के लिए एक शब्द का चयन कीजिये।

जिस पर अनुग्रह किया गया हो:

A. अनुग्रिहित   B. अनुगढ़ित
C. अनुगृहीत   D. अनुगरिहीत

Q.2 निर्देश: वाक्यांश के लिए एक शब्द का चयन कीजिये।
जो उत्तर ना दे सके

A. निउत्तर   B. निरुत्तर   C. निरउत्तर   D. निरत्तर

Q.3 निम्नलिखित वाक्य में कौन सा वाक्य पूर्ण भूतकाल है?

A. यदि पढ़ा होता तो पास हो जाते
B. सचिन लिख रहा है
C. पंडित जी ने गीता समाप्त कर दी होगी
D. मैं कल मंजू के घर गयी थी

Q.4 किसी के कहे कथन या वाक्य को या रचना के अंश को ज्यों का त्यों प्रस्तुत करने के लिए जिस विराम चिह्न का प्रयोग किया जाता है उसे कहते हैं:
[Rajasthan Teachers Eligibility Test - Level 1 Primary Level (RTET), 2021]

A. निर्देशक चिह्न   B. उद्धरण चिह्न
C. विवरण चिह्न   D. हंस पद

Q.5 निर्देश: दिए गए वाक्य में उपयुक्त विराम चिह्न का चयन कीजिए।
क्या आप दिल्ली के रहनेवाले हैं

A. विस्मयादिबोधक   B. योजक
C. लोप   D. प्रश्नवाचक

Q.6 पंडित की भाववाचक संज्ञा है:

A. पंडिताई   B. पंडिताइन
C. पांडित्य   D. इनमें से कोई नहीं

Q.7 'किताब का कीड़ा होना' का उपयुक्त अर्थ है-
[UPSSSC Junior Assistant, 2020]

A. बहुमूल्य वस्तु को नष्ट करने वाला
B. अनुपयुक्त जगह रहने वाला
C. बहुत अधिक पढ़ने वाला
D. ज्ञान का दुश्मन

Q.8 'कच्चा चिट्ठा खोलना' का उपयुक्त अर्थ है-
[UPSSSC Junior Assistant, 2020]

A. सारा भेद खोल देना
B. कच्चे काम को पक्का करना
C. भेद छिपाना
D. कान का कच्चा होना

Q.9 'खबरदार ! उससे बात नहीं करनी।' यह किस कारक का विकल्प होगा?

A. अपादान कारक   B. संबंध कारक
C. सम्बोधन कारक   D. संप्रदान कारक

Q.10 'विनियंत्रण' शब्द में उपसर्ग है:

A. विन   B. वि   C. विनिय   D. विनियां

Q.11 'पर' उपसर्ग किसमें है:

A. परिचय   B. परसाल   C. पराजय   D. प्रकंप

Q.12 इस कबूतर को पिंजरे से निकालो इसमें कौन सा विशेषण हैं?

A. गुणवाचक विशेषण
B. निश्चित संख्यावाचक विशेषण
C. अनिश्चित संख्यावाचक विशेषण
D. सार्वनामिक विशेषण

Q.13 हिन्दी में कुल कितने सर्वनाम हैं?
[UPSSSC Village Development Officer, 2018]

A. 9   B. 10   C. 11   D. 12

Q.14 निर्देश: रिक्त स्थान को भरने के लिए सबसे उपयुक्त शब्द का चयन करें।
बन्दूक एक बहुत ही उपयोगी __________ है।
[SSC Constable (GD), 2021]

A. वस्त्र   B. शास्त्र   C. शस्त्र   D. सर्वत्र

Q.15 निर्देश: रिक्त स्थान भरने के लिए सबसे उपयुक्त शब्द का चयन करें।
________खाना तैयार करती हैं।
[SSC Constable (GD), 2021]

A. भैया   B. लड़की   C. बहू   D. बहुएँ

Q.16 निम्नलिखित में से अनुनासिक स्वर का उदाहरण कौन सा है?

A. अँ   B. ख   C. है   D. इ

Q.17 'घोड़ा' शब्द का बहुवचन शब्द होगा-

A. घोड़ों   B. घोड़ें   C. घोड़े   D. घोड़ै

Q.18 सही वर्तनी वाले शब्द का चयन करें।

A. स्थायीत्व   B. स्थायित्व   C. इस्थायित्व   D. स्थाईत्व

Q.19 'नाविक' का सही संधि-विच्छेद है-
[UPSSSC Junior Assistant, 2020]

A. नौ + विक   B. ना + विक
C. नौ + इक   D. न + आविक

Q.20 भयंकर प्राकृतिक दृश्यों को देखकर अथवा प्राणों के विनाशक बलवान् शत्रु को देखकर भय उत्पन्न होना कौन-सा रस है?

A. हास्य रस   B. वीभत्स रस
C. भयानक रस   D. वीर रस

Q.21 'वक्ता' शब्द का विलोम है-
[UPSSSC Junior Assistant, 2020]

A. आयोजक   B. प्रयोजक   C. श्रोता   D. व्याख्याता

Q.22 निम्नलिखित में से कौन सा शब्द तत्सम नहीं है?
[UPSSSC Junior Assistant, 2020]

A. धृष्ट   B. पृष्ठ   C. पानिप   D. पंक

Q.23 निम्नलिखित में से कौन सा शब्द तत्सम नहीं है?
[UPSSSC Junior Assistant, 2020]

A. गायक **B.** नायक **C.** शावक **D.** उपखान

Q.24 "जो कलम तुम्हारे पास है वह मेरी है।" वाक्य का प्रकार बताइये।
A. मिश्रित **B.** सरल
C. संयुक्त **D.** विस्मयादिबोधक

Q.25 "मैंने उसे उठाया और खाना खिलाया।" वाक्य का प्रकार बताइये।
A. सरल **B.** संयुक्त
C. मिश्रित **D.** आज्ञावाचक

English

Ques (26-33):Direction: Fill in the blanks with an appropriate word.

Q.26 The bamboo clumps flower all at the same time only once _______ the plant's lifetime.
A. in **B.** into **C.** on **D.** over

Q.27 I am looking forward _____ you.
A. to seeing **B.** to see
C. to have seen **D.** for seeing

Q.28 Neither the boys nor the teacher _______ present.
A. is **B.** are
C. were **D.** have been

Q.29 _____ team member is expected to obey the rules of the competition.
A. All **B.** None **C.** Every **D.** Either

Q.30 Robert is ______ European.
A. one **B.** a **C.** an **D.** the

Q.31 This is in conformity _______ the rules laid down by the Corporation.
A. for **B.** against **C.** about **D.** with

Q.32 Children _______ online for more than a year now.
A. study **B.** are studying
C. have been studying **D.** studied

Q.33 He has been behaving in an eccentric manner ______.
A. later **B.** late **C.** early **D.** lately

Q.34 Direction: Identify the interjection in the given sentence.
Wow! John hit the ball far.
A. Wow **B.** John **C.** Hit **D.** Far

Q.35 Choose the correctly punctuated sentence.
A. All the passengers, with the driver, is killed in the accident.
B. All the passengers, with the driver, be killed in the accident.
C. All the passengers, with the driver, were killed in the accident.
D. All the passengers, with the driver, was killed in the accident.

Q.36 Choose the correctly punctuated sentence.
A. Between you and me, Mr Sharma is not to be trusted.
B. Between you and I, Mr Sharma is not to be trusted.
C. Between I and me, Mr Sharma is not to be trusted.
D. Between you and you, Mr Sharma is not to be trusted.

Q.37 Direction: Please choose one of the 4 alternatives that can be substituted for the given sentence.

Story of an individual by himself.
A. Biography **B.** Autobiography
C. History **D.** None of these

Q.38 Select the word spelled incorrectly.
A. mischeif **B.** belief **C.** thief **D.** grief

Q.39 Which word is an abstract noun?
"Honesty is the best policy."
A. Best **B.** Honesty **C.** Policy **D.** The

Q.40 Direction: Identify the tense used in the given sentence.
"Someone picked my pocket."
A. Present indefinite tense
B. Past indefinite tense
C. Past perfect tense
D. Present perfect tense

Ques (41-42):Direction: Select the most appropriate synonym of the given word.

Q.41 Assembly
A. Gathering **B.** Inquire
C. Conduct **D.** Accused

Q.42 Chore
A. Thief **B.** Relief **C.** Colour **D.** Task

Ques (43-44):Direction: Choose the word which best expresses the opposite meaning of the word.

Q.43 Arrogant
A. Humble **B.** Cowardly
C. Egoistic **D.** Gentlemanly

Q.44 EARN
A. Win **B.** Obtain **C.** Lose **D.** Derserve

Q.45 Direction: Choose the correct option to replace the word(s) given in brackets.
"Ten candidates _______ for the interview."
A. turned up **B.** turned down
C. turned over **D.** turned out

Q.46 Direction: In the following question, select the related word from the given alternatives.
Grain : Warehouse : : Water : ?
A. Drink **B.** Dam **C.** Canal **D.** River

Q.47 Direction: Choose the correct alternative to fill in the blank.
It is _______ useful _______ ornamental.
A. Whether, or **B.** Both, or
C. Neither, nor **D.** Either, but also

Q.48 Direction: Select the word which means the same as the group of words given.

An imaginary, perfect state or place
A. Utopia
B. Dystopia
C. Arcadia
D. Nostalgia

Q.49 Direction: Change the gender of the underlined noun and rewrite the sentence.

My <u>father</u> is going.
A. My <u>mother</u> is going.
B. My <u>sister</u> is going.
C. My <u>aunt</u> is going.
D. My <u>sister in law</u> is going.

Q.50 Direction: Choose the meaningful word from the given jumbled words.

EMUOARYHJE
A. Mother
B. Mather
C. Mothar
D. Motar

General Studies

Q.51 How many times a state of emergency has been declared in India since independence?

[UP Police Sub Inspector, 2017]

A. Thrice
B. Once
C. Twice
D. Four Times

Q.52 Byanjana Dwadashi festival is celebrated in which of the following state?
A. Assam
B. Odisha
C. Madhya Pradesh
D. Karnataka

Q.53 Omkareshwar temple is located on the banks on _____ river.
A. Narmada
B. Tapti
C. Gomti
D. Ganga

Q.54 When we move from top to down in Periodic table, size of alkali metals:
A. Increases
B. Decreases
C. No change
D. Either increases or decreases

Q.55 Which of the following country's national currency is Ngultrum?
A. Myanmar
B. Afghanistan
C. Bhutan
D. Hong Kong

Q.56 All the planets move around the sun in _________.
A. Circular path
B. Rectangular path
C. Elliptical path
D. Hyperbolic path

Q.57 Who has won gold medal in Men's Rapid Fire Pistol event at the 36th National Games at Ahmedabad in Gujarat on 30 September 2022?
A. Anish Bhanwala
B. Ankur Goyal
C. Gurmeet
D. Satish Gupta

Q.58 Saint Kabir Das, who was famous poet was belong to which place in Uttar Pradesh?
A. Varanasi
B. Allahabad
C. Kanpur
D. Lucknow

Q.59 Which of the following is the oldest university in Uttar Pradesh?
A. Aligarh Muslim University
B. Banaras Hindu University
C. Mahatma Gandhi vidyapeeth
D. Allahabad University

Q.60 Which of the following cities are the main centers of the leather industry in Uttar Pradesh?
A. Agra
B. Etawah
C. Kanpur
D. Both (A) and (C)

Q.61 The famous Sufi Saint Sheikh Salim Chisti's Dargah is situated at _____ in Uttar Pradesh.
A. Jaunpur
B. Kannauj
C. Fatehpur Sikri
D. Barabanki

Q.62 Who has been appointed as ombudsman under Mahatma Gandhi National Rural Employment Guarantee Scheme (MGNREGA)?
A. S L Thaosen
B. Ajay Kumar Srivastava
C. Swarup Kumar Saha
D. N J Ojha

Q.63 Which of the following rivers the "Chitrakote" water fall is located?
A. Yamuna River
B. Mandakini River
C. Indravati River
D. Narmada River

Q.64 In which city, Union Minister Sarbananda Sonowal has inaugurated the Chabahar Day conference in July 2022?
A. Chennai
B. Chabahar
C. Gandhinagar
D. Mumbai

Q.65 Who has been appointed as the new chairman of the International Aluminium Institute (IAI) on 6 June 2022?
A. Swaroop Kumar Saha
B. Miles Prosser
C. Ben Kahrs
D. Satish Pai

Q.66 Which of the following states launched Cheerag Scheme?
A. Uttar Pradesh
B. Haryana
C. Assam
D. Jharkhand

Q.67 Who has achieved the feat of becoming the first one star rider of the country?
A. Suman Lata
B. Seema Mishra
C. Swati Rathod
D. Saima Syed

Q.68 Ashoka Pillar of Allahabad provided information about which ruler?
A. Chandragupta Maurya
B. Samudragupta
C. Chandragupta Maurya II
D. Chandragupta Maurya I

Q.69 The Tropic of Cancer does not pass through which of the following state?

A. Mizoram   **B.** Tripura
C. Odisha   **D.** Madhya Pradesh

Q.70 Who was sworn in for a second term as president of Angola on 15 September 2022?
A. Jeremias Chitunda
B. Arlete Chimbinda
C. Abdelmadjid Tebboune
D. Joao Lourenco

Q.71 Which of the following has started the revolt of 1857?
A. The landlords   **B.** The soldiers
C. The farmers   **D.** Plantation workers

Q.72 A passenger in a moving bus is thrown forward when the bus suddenly stops. This is explained:
A. by Newton's first law
B. by Newton's second law
C. by Newton's third law
D. by the principle of conservation of momentum

Q.73 Graphite is commonly known as _______.
A. Fool's Gold   **B.** Black Gold
C. Black Lead   **D.** Soft Diamond

Q.74 Jayaprabha Menon is famous for which of the following classical dances?
A. Odissi   **B.** Mohiniyattam
C. Kathakali   **D.** Kuchipudi

Q.75 Where is Manjira Crocodile Wildlife Sanctuary situated?
A. Tamil Nadu   **B.** Odisha
C. Telangana   **D.** Kerala

Mathematics

Q.76 Find the HCF of 513, 1107 and 783.
A. 19   **B.** 22   **C.** 27   **D.** 21

Q.77 What should be the simple interest obtained on an amount of Rs. 5760 at the rate of 6 p.a. after 3 years?
A. Rs. 1036.8   **B.** Rs. 1666.8
C. Rs. 1336.8   **D.** Rs. 1063.8

Q.78 A man sold a bicycle for an amount, which was greater than Rs. 988 by half the price he paid for it and made a profit of Rs. 300. How much did he buy the bicycle for?
A. 1376   **B.** 1300   **C.** 1476   **D.** 1576

Q.79 Direction: What should come in place of the question mark '?' in the following number series?

72, 56, 42, 30, 20, ?
A. 22   **B.** 26   **C.** 12   **D.** 62

Q.80 If $2365A$ is divisible by 9, then find the value of A.
A. 2   **B.** 3   **C.** 0   **D.** 1

Q.81 In three consecutive even numbers, the sum of the first two numbers is 14 more than the third number. Find the smallest number.

A. 16   **B.** 18   **C.** 20   **D.** 14

Q.82 If the sum of two consecutive even numbers is 66, then the smaller one is:
A. 34   **B.** 32   **C.** 42   **D.** 24

Q.83 Simplify $36 - [18 - \{14 - (15 - 4 \div 2 \times 2)\}]$.
A. 40   **B.** 30   **C.** 20   **D.** 21

Q.84 A student gets 170 marks which is equivalent to 34%. If he gets 200 marks then what will the equivalent percent of marks?
A. 50%   **B.** 40%   **C.** 45%   **D.** 55%

Q.85 If a man were to sell his chair for Rs. 720, he would lose 25%. To gain 25% he should sell it for:
A. Rs. 1200   **B.** Rs. 1000   **C.** Rs. 960   **D.** Rs. 900

Q.86 Divide $150.75 \div 0.6$.
A. 251.25   **B.** 2512.5   **C.** 25125   **D.** 25.125

Q.87 Write the Roman numerals for 900.
A. CM   **B.** M   **C.** C   **D.** CMVIII

Q.88 Numerals that can be repeated in the Roman system are:
A. I, X and C   **B.** I, V and X
C. V, L and D   **D.** D

Q.89 The sum of the prime numbers between 90 and 100 is:
A. 97   **B.** 100   **C.** 99   **D.** 95

Q.90 The number of composite number between 101 and 120 are:
A. 11   **B.** 12   **C.** 13   **D.** 14

Q.91 Find the average of $80, 90, 100, 110, 120, 130$.
A. 100   **B.** 105   **C.** 110   **D.** 115

Q.92 Solve $\frac{2}{3} + \frac{1}{11}$.
A. $\frac{25}{33}$ **B.** $\frac{15}{21}$ **C.** $\frac{18}{25}$ **D.** $\frac{21}{37}$

Q.93 Simplify $16 - 2 \div 7 + 6 \times 2$.
A. $27\frac{5}{7}$ **B.** $27\frac{2}{9}$ **C.** $27\frac{1}{7}$ **D.** $27\frac{2}{3}$

Q.94 If two numbers are 101 and 151. Find their HCF.
A. 1   **B.** 101   **C.** 151   **D.** 251

Q.95 The cost of 3 envelopes is ₹ 15. Find the cost of 5 envelopes.
A. ₹ 20   **B.** ₹ 25   **C.** ₹ 30   **D.** ₹ 40

Q.96 If $\frac{2x}{3} = 18$, then x is equal to:
A. 36   **B.** 54   **C.** 32   **D.** 27

Q.97 If the perimeter of a square is 36 cm, then its area is:
A. 6 cm ^{2} **B.** 9 cm ^{2} **C.** 18 cm ^{2} **D.** 81 cm ^{2}

Q.98 If the area of a rectangular plot is 180 sq. m and its length is 15 m, then its breadth is:

A. 12 m   **B.** 14 cm   **C.** 60 m   **D.** 9 m

Q.99 What is the square root of $3920?$

A. $28\sqrt{5}$ **B.** $26\sqrt{5}$

C. $24\sqrt{5}$ **D.** None of these

Q.100 Solve $25 + \dfrac{3}{100} + \dfrac{4}{1000} = ?$

A. 25.34   **B.** 25.304   **C.** 25.034   **D.** 25.0034

// Smart Answer Sheet //

Correct Indicates percentage of students who answered questions correctly.

Skipped Indicates percentage of students who skipped questions.

Q.	Ans.	Correct / Skipped
1	C	58.52 % / 1.11 %
2	B	49.16 % / 1.16 %
3	D	83.88 % / 0.0 %
4	B	57.35 % / 1.63 %
5	D	86.54 % / 0.0 %
6	C	62.62 % / 1.29 %
7	C	46.25 % / 1.55 %
8	A	77.46 % / 0.0 %
9	C	68.67 % / 1.19 %
10	B	69.81 % / 1.21 %
11	B	88.05 % / 0.0 %
12	D	64.9 % / 1.69 %
13	C	40.59 % / 1.43 %
14	C	58.2 % / 1.97 %
15	D	47.74 % / 1.96 %
16	A	54.4 % / 1.52 %

Q.	Ans.	Correct / Skipped
17	C	83.17 % / 0.0 %
18	B	79.95 % / 0.0 %
19	C	44.81 % / 1.56 %
20	C	40.07 % / 1.19 %
21	C	46.85 % / 1.44 %
22	C	79.81 % / 0.0 %
23	D	49.64 % / 1.98 %
24	A	48.22 % / 2.0 %
25	B	68.58 % / 1.92 %
26	A	58.05 % / 1.25 %
27	A	44.08 % / 1.6 %
28	A	50.03 % / 1.78 %
29	C	54.87 % / 1.96 %
30	B	85.31 % / 0.0 %
31	D	59.61 % / 1.3 %
32	C	63.82 % / 1.32 %

Q.	Ans.	Correct / Skipped
33	D	67.85 % / 1.07 %
34	A	86.89 % / 0.0 %
35	C	89.98 % / 0.0 %
36	A	49.99 % / 1.64 %
37	B	84.22 % / 0.0 %
38	A	52.94 % / 1.89 %
39	B	83.13 % / 0.0 %
40	B	52.58 % / 1.93 %
41	A	25.84 % / 4.72 %
42	D	54.1 % / 1.61 %
43	A	63.8 % / 1.3 %
44	C	52.28 % / 1.48 %
45	A	56.82 % / 1.78 %
46	B	68.65 % / 1.05 %
47	C	69.91 % / 1.12 %
48	A	42.04 % / 1.81 %

Q.	Ans.	Correct / Skipped
49	A	40.12 % / 1.46 %
50	A	47.02 % / 1.64 %
51	A	80.9 % / 0.0 %
52	B	16.78 % / 3.42 %
53	A	45.17 % / 1.63 %
54	A	61.95 % / 1.67 %
55	C	63.44 % / 1.48 %
56	C	44.13 % / 1.27 %
57	A	54.71 % / 1.93 %
58	A	41.66 % / 1.52 %
59	D	68.1 % / 1.51 %
60	D	56.79 % / 1.71 %
61	C	49.8 % / 1.49 %
62	D	48.43 % / 1.88 %
63	C	68.86 % / 1.17 %
64	D	44.46 % / 1.77 %

Q.	Ans.	Correct / Skipped
65	D	53.05 % / 1.46 %
66	B	61.25 % / 1.31 %
67	D	42.98 % / 1.05 %
68	B	63.07 % / 1.42 %
69	C	44.29 % / 1.73 %
70	D	55.55 % / 1.99 %
71	B	40.52 % / 1.29 %
72	A	59.06 % / 1.15 %
73	C	56.09 % / 1.46 %
74	B	45.65 % / 1.16 %
75	C	61.72 % / 1.96 %
76	C	59.06 % / 1.07 %
77	A	88.22 % / 0.0 %
78	A	51.6 % / 1.75 %
79	C	30.12 % / 3.49 %
80	A	55.21 % / 1.56 %

Q.	Ans.	Correct / Skipped
81	A	50.01 %
		1.03 %
82	B	81.62 %
		0.0 %
83	D	49.16 %
		1.86 %
84	B	40.17 %
		1.27 %

Q.	Ans.	Correct / Skipped
85	A	55.49 %
		1.39 %
86	A	46.52 %
		1.72 %
87	A	47.78 %
		1.61 %
88	A	42.37 %
		1.63 %

Q.	Ans.	Correct / Skipped
89	A	87.85 %
		0.0 %
90	D	64.67 %
		1.95 %
91	B	83.44 %
		0.0 %
92	A	86.33 %
		0.0 %

Q.	Ans.	Correct / Skipped
93	A	81.26 %
		0.0 %
94	A	76.61 %
		0.0 %
95	B	89.59 %
		0.0 %
96	D	82.76 %
		0.0 %

Q.	Ans.	Correct / Skipped
97	D	88.4 %
		0.0 %
98	A	67.72 %
		1.93 %
99	A	48.34 %
		1.35 %
100	C	43.67 %
		1.27 %

Performance Analysis

Avg. Score (%)	54.0%
Toppers Score (%)	71.0%
Your Score	

//Hints and Solutions//

1. दिए गए विकल्पों में से 'जिस पर अनुग्रह किया गया हो' उसके लिए उचित शब्द 'अनुगृहीत' होगा।

अर्थात जिस पर अनुग्रह किया गया हो के लिए एक शब्द अनुगृहीत है।

अनुगृहीत शब्द का अर्थ: उपकृत, एहसानमंद, कृतज्ञ।

अतः विकल्प (C) सही है।

2. 'जो उत्तर न दे सके' वाक्यांश के लिए एक शब्द 'निरुत्तर' होता है। अर्थात जो उत्तर न दे सके के लिए एक शब्द निरुत्तर है।

निरुत्तर का अर्थ: अनुत्तर, अनूतर, ज़बानबंद, बेजवाब, लाजवाब

उदाहरण: निरुत्तर छात्र एक दूसरे का मुँह देख रहे थे।

अतः विकल्प (B) सही है।

3. दिए गए विकल्पों में पूर्ण भूत काल का उदाहरण "मैं कल मंजू के घर गयी थी।" है।

पूर्ण भूतकाल: क्रिया के जिस रूप से काम के कुछ समय पूर्व ही पूरा होने का पता चले अर्थात काम अभी-अभी समाप्त हुआ कहते है।

उदाहरण:

- वह सो चूका था।
- वह रो चूका था।
- वह गा चूका था।

अतः विकल्प (D) सही है।

4. किसी और के लिखे गए वाक्य का प्रयोग करने के लिए उद्धरण चिह्न प्रयुक्त होता है।

जैसे - हरिवंश राय बच्चन ने कहा है - "मन का हो तो अच्छा, मन का न हो तो भी अच्छा"

अवतरण चिन्ह या उद्धरण चिन्ह	गांधी जी ने कहाँ था "अहिंसा परम धर्म है"	'....' "..."

अतः विकल्प (B) सही है।

5. वाक्य "क्या आप दिल्ली के रहनेवाले हैं" में 'प्रश्नवाचक चिन्ह का प्रयोग होता है।

प्रश्नवाचक चिन्ह (?)	बातचीत के दौरान जब किसी से कोई बात पूछी जाती है अथवा कोई प्रश्न पूछा जाता है, तब वाक्य के अंत में प्रश्नसूचक-चिन्ह का प्रयोग किया जाता है।	तुम्हारी माताजी का नाम क्या है ?

अतः विकल्प (D) सही है।

6. 'पंडित' शब्द की भाववाचक संज्ञा 'पांडित्य' होगी जिससे पंडिताई के भाव का बोध हो रहा है।

जिन शब्दों से किसी प्राणी या पदार्थ के गुण भाव स्वभाव के अवस्था का बोध होता है, उन्हें भाववाचक कहते हैं।

जैसे- बचपन, बुढ़ापा, मोटापा, मिठास, उमंग, चढ़ाई, थकावट, मानवता, चतुराई, जवानी, लम्बाई, मित्रता, मुस्कुराहट, अपनापन, परायापन, भूख, प्यास, चोरी, क्रोध, सुन्दरता आदि।

अतः विकल्प (C) सही है।

7. 'किताब का कीड़ा होना' का उपयुक्त अर्थ 'बहुत अधिक पढ़ने वाला' है।

वाक्य प्रयोग- विद्यार्थी को केवल किताब का कीड़ा नहीं होना चाहिए, बल्कि स्वस्थ शरीर और उन्नत मस्तिष्क वाला होनहार युवक होना चाहिए।

अतः विकल्प (C) सही है।

8. 'कच्चा चिट्ठा खोलना' का उपयुक्त अर्थ 'सारा भेद खोल देना है।

वाक्य प्रयोग- न्यूज़ चैनल ने नामी नेता का कच्चा चिट्ठा जनता के सामने खोल दिया।

अतः विकल्प (A) सही है।

9. 'खबरदार! उससे बात नहीं करनी।' यह सम्बोधन कारक का उदाहरण है।

संज्ञा या जिस रूप से किसी को पुकारने तथा सावधान करने का बोध हो, उसे सम्बोधन कारक कहते हैं।

इसका सम्बन्ध न क्रिया से और न किसी दूसरे शब्द से होता है।

यह वाक्य से अलग रहता है।

इसके लिए (!) इस चिह्न का प्रयोग किया जाता है।

अतः विकल्प (C) सही है।

10. 'विनियंत्रण' शब्द में 'वि' उपसर्ग है।

विनियंत्रण शब्द में मूल शब्द 'नियंत्रण' है और 'वि' उपसर्ग के योग से यह शब्द निर्मित हुआ है।

जो शब्दांश शब्दों के प्रारम्भ में जुड़ कर उनके अर्थ में कुछ विशेषता लाते हैं, वे उपसर्ग कहलाते हैं।

अतः विकल्प (B) सही है।

11. दिए गए विकल्पों में 'परसाल' शब्द में 'पर' उपसर्ग है।

'परसाल' शब्द 'पर + साल = परसाल'

परसाल का अर्थ पिछले साल या अगले साल है।

जो शब्दांश शब्दों के प्रारम्भ में जुड़ कर उनके अर्थ में कुछ विशेषता लाते हैं, वे उपसर्ग कहलाते हैं।

अतः विकल्प (B) सही है।

12. इस कबूतर को पिंजरे से निकालो इसमें सार्वनामिक विशेषण हैं।

ऐसे सर्वनाम शब्द जो संज्ञा से पहले लगकर उस संज्ञा शब्द की विशेषण की तरह विशेषता बताते हैं, वे शब्द सार्वनामिक विशेषण कहलाते हैं। यह शब्द सर्वनाम के लिए विशेषण का काम करते हैं। जैसे: मेरी पुस्तक , कोई बालक , किसी का महल , वह लड़का , वह बालक , वह पुस्तक , वह आदमी , वह लडकी आदि।

अतः विकल्प (D) सही है।

13. हिंदी में कुल '11' सर्वनाम हैं।

हिंदी के मूल सर्वनाम 11 हैं, जैसे- मैं, तू, आप, यह, वह, जो, सो, कौन, क्या, कोई, कुछ।

सर्वनाम उन शब्दों को कहा जाता है, जिन शब्दों का प्रयोग संज्ञा अर्थात किसी व्यक्ति, वस्तु स्थान आदि, के नाम के स्थान पर करते हैं। इसके अंतर्गत मै, तुम, तुम्हारा, आप, आपका, इस, उस, यह, वह, हम, हमारा ,आदि शब्द आते हैं।

अतः विकल्प (C) सही है।

14. बन्दूक एक बहुत ही उपयोगी **शस्त्र** है।

संपूर्ण वाक्य: बन्दूक एक बहुत ही उपयोगी 'शस्त्र' हैं।

शस्त्र मतलब हथियार, कोई ऐसा यंत्र और औजार, जिससे युद्ध के समय शत्रु पर प्रहार किया जाता है।

- शास्त्र का अर्थ है: ज्ञान की कोई शाखा या हिंदू धर्म के पवित्र ग्रंथ।
- वस्त्र का अर्थ है: मतलब कपड़ा, पहनावा, परिधान और पोशाक।

- सर्वत्र का अर्थ है: हर स्थान पर और पूर्ण रूप से।

अतः विकल्प (C) सही है।

15. बहुएँ खाना तैयार करती हैं।

दिया गया वाक्य बहुवचन में है इसलिए रिक्त स्थान में बहुवचन शब्द का प्रयोग किया जाएगा।

संपूर्ण वाक्य: बहुएँ खाना तैयार करती हैं।

'करती हैं' के साथ बहू और लड़की नहीं आ सकता, क्योंकि यह दोनों एक वचन शब्द हैं।

भैया गलत उत्तर है क्योंकि 'करती' शब्द के साथ स्त्रीलिंग शब्द आएगा, और भैया पुल्लिंग शब्द है।

अतः विकल्प (D) सही है।

16. जिन स्वरों के उच्चारण में मुख के साथ-साथ नासिका की भी सहायता लेनी पड़ती है अर्थात् जिन स्वरों का उच्चारण मुख और नासिका दोनों से किया जाता है वे अनुनासिक स्वर कहलाते हैं। इनका चिह्न चन्द्रबिन्दु (ॅं) है। 'अँ' अनुनासिक स्वर का उदाहरण है। जैसे-हँसना, आँख।

अतः विकल्प (A) सही है।

17. बहुवचन - शब्द के जिस रूप से उसके एक से अधिक होने का बोध हो, वह बहुवचन कहलाते हैं।

'घोड़ा' शब्द का बहुवचन शब्द 'घोड़े' होगा।

अतः विकल्प (C) सही है।

18. यहां सही वर्तनी वाला शब्द - "स्थायित्व" । है। अन्य विकल्प असंगत हैं।

'स्थायीत्व, इस्थायित्व, स्थाईत्व' यह तीनों स्थायित्व शब्द की गलत वर्तनी है।

इन तीनों की सही वर्तनी 'स्थायित्व' शब्द में दिखाई देती है।

स्थायित्व शब्द का अर्थ है- स्थाई या पक्का होने का भाव।

अत: विकल्प (B) सही है।

19. 'नाविक' का सही संधि-विच्छेद 'नौ + इक' है। यहाँ औ + ई = आव् में परिवर्तित होने के कारण अयादि संधि है।

अयादि संधि: ए, ऐ, ओ, औ के बाद कोई भिन्न स्वर जाता है तो 'ए' का अय, 'ऐ' का आय्, 'ओ' का अव् तथा 'औ' का आव् हो जाता है, इसे अयादि संधि कहते हैं।

अतः विकल्प (C) सही है।

20. भयंकर प्राकृतिक दृश्यों को देखकर अथवा प्राणों के विनाशक बलवान् शत्रु को देखकर भय उत्पन्न होना भयानक रस है।

भयानक रस की विशेषताएँ निम्नलिखित है:

- भयानक रस का स्थायी भाव भय है।
- भयंकर प्राकृतिक दृश्यों को देखकर अथवा प्राणों के विनाशक बलवान् शत्रु को देखकर उसका वर्णन सुनकर भय उत्पन्न होता है।
- जैसे- "एक ओर अजगरहि लखि, एक ओर मृगराय। बिकल बटोही बीच ही, परयौ मूर्छा खाय।।"

अत: विकल्प (C) सही है।

21. 'वक्ता' का विलोम शब्द 'श्रोता' होता है।

वक्ता के पर्यायवाची शब्द हैं - वाचक, व्याख्याता, भाषणकर्त्ता, तकरीर करने वाला।

श्रोता के पर्यायवाची शब्द हैं - सुनने वाला, श्रवणकर्ता।

अतः विकल्प (C) सही है।

22. दिए गए शब्दों में से 'पानिप' शब्द तत्सम नहीं है।

पानिप का अर्थ पानी होता है। अन्य सभी विकल्प तत्सम शब्द हैं।

अतः विकल्प (C) सही है।

23. दिए गए शब्दों में से 'उपखान' शब्द तत्सम नहीं है। अन्य सभी शब्द तत्सम हैं।

तत्सम शब्द संस्कृत भाषा के दो शब्दों, तत् + सम् से मिलकर बना है। तत् का अर्थ है – उसके, तथा सम् का अर्थ है – समान। अर्थात – ज्यों का त्यों। जिन शब्दों को संस्कृत से बिना किसी परिवर्तन के ले लिया जाता है, उन्हें तत्सम शब्द कहते हैं।

तत्सम शब्द में ध्वनि परिवर्तन नहीं होता है। जैसे – आम्र, अग्नि, अमूल्य, क्षेत्र, अज्ञान, अन्धकार, चंद्र, बांग्ला, मराठी, गुजराती, हिंदी, पंजाबी, कन्नड़, तेलगु, मलयालम आदि।

अतः विकल्प (D) सही है।

24. "जो कलम तुम्हारे पास है वह मेरी है।" मिश्रित वाक्य है।

जिस वाक्य में एक से अधिक वाक्य मिले हों, किन्तु एक प्रधान उपवाक्य तथा शेष आश्रित उपवाक्य हों, मिश्रित वाक्य कहलाता है।

"जो कलम तुम्हारे पास है" यह प्रधान उपवाक्य है, "वह मेरी है।" यह आश्रित उपवाक्य है। इसलिए यह एक मिश्रित वाक्य होगा।

उदाहरण: मुझे तुम पर विश्वास है कि तुम परीक्षा में पास हो जाओगे।

अतः विकल्प (A) सही है।

25. "मैंने उसे उठाया और खाना खिलाया।" संयुक्त वाक्य है।

जिस वाक्य में दो या दो से अधिक उपवाक्य मिले हों, परन्तु सभी वाक्य प्रधान हो तो ऐसे वाक्य को संयुक्त वाक्य कहते हैं।

उदाहरण: महेश खेलता है और रमेश पढता है।

अतः विकल्प (B) सही है।

26. Correct sentence: The bamboo clumps flower all at the same time only once **in** the plant's lifetime.

The preposition 'in' is also used to express a period of time during which an event happens.

In the given sentence, we can see that the plant's lifetime is the period of time during which the event of flowering takes place.

- 'Into' is used for expressing movement or action with the result that someone or something becomes enclosed or surrounded by something else.
- 'On' is used when an object is physically in contact with and supported by a surface.
- 'Over' is used when the motion or position of an object is higher than another object but there is no physical contact between the two.

Hence, the correct option is (A).

27. Correct sentence: "I am looking forward **to seeing** you."

- Some words use V_1+ing after them.
- The given sentence is erroneous for the wrong usage of the main verb after the phrase looking forward.
- Gerund: It is denoted by 'V_1+ing'

For example:

Swimming is good exercise.

I learnt cooking.

When there are certain phrases in the sentence like addicted to, accustomed to, look forward to, taken to, with a view to, etc., then gerund is used with them.

Hence, the correct option is (A).

28. Correct sentence: 'Neither the boys nor the teacher **is** present.'

- If the subject is made up of both singular and plural words connected by or, nor, either ...or, neither ... nor, not only ... but also, the verb agrees with the nearer part of the subject. For example,
- 'Neither the salesmen nor the buyer is in favour of the proposed change.'
- 'Neither the buyer nor the salesmen are in favour of the proposed change.'
- In the given sentence, two subjects 'the boys' and 'the teacher' are connected with 'neither... nor.'
- As a result, the verb following will concord with its nearer subject, i.e. 'the teacher' and the verb will be third person singular.

Hence, the correct option is (A).

29. Correct sentence: '**Every**' is used with singular nouns to refer to all the members of a group of things or people.

 Example:

- Every player wants to be in a winning team.
- We know every student in the school.
- According to the explanation and example that are given above, 'Every' is the correct choice for the blank.

Here, in the given sentence 'team member' is a singular noun. So, the usage of 'Every' is correct.

Hence, the correct option is (C).

30. Correct sentence: Robert is **a** European.

We use articles 'a' and 'an' for specific identity who is not known.

- Article 'a' for consonant sound words.
- Article 'an' for vowel sound words.

We use 'the' for specific identities that are known to us. 'One' is the number indicating a single unit.

For the given sentence, 'a' article will be grammatically and contextually correct. This is because it begins with a vowel e but it begins with the pronunciation yu.

Hence, the correct option is (B).

31. Correct sentence: This is in conformity with the rules laid down by the Corporation.

"With" means in the company or presence of somebody/something or in connection with; in the case of.

- Example: Be careful with the glasses.

In the given sentence, the conformity is in connection with the rules laid by the Corporation.

Thus, from the above explanation, it is clear that the correct preposition to use is "with."

Hence, the correct option is (D).

32. Correct sentence: Children **have been studying** online for more than a year now.

The given sentence is talking about an incident that started in the past and is continuing at the present time.

- So, we need to write this sentence in the Present Perfect Continous Tense.
- The present perfect continuous tense (also known as the present perfect progressive tense) shows that something started in the past and is continuing at the present time.
- The present perfect continuous is formed using the construction has/have been + the present participle (root + -ing).
- Example: I have been reading War and Peace for a month now.

Hence, the correct option is (C).

33. Correct Sentence: He has been behaving in an eccentric manner **lately**.

First of all, the given sentence is in the present perfect tense.

We need to choose the appropriate adverb from the given options which will be filled in the given blank.

Let us explore the given options:

- Later: Later is an adverb that means at a time in the near future; soon or afterward.
- Late: Later is an adverb that means after the expected, proper, or usual time.
- Early: in or during the first part of a period of time, before the usual or expected time.

The marked option 'Lately' is used for recent states, and repeated events, it goes mostly with the present perfect.

So, from the given usage of different adverbs, the most appropriate adverb is 'Lately'.

Hence, the correct option is (D).

34. 'Wow!' is an interjection used in the above statement which is used to express surprise or admiration. Interjections are usually accompanied by an exclamation mark (!)

Whereas other options are not the form of interjections

Hence, the correct option is (A).

35. The correct answer is 'All the passengers, with the driver, were killed in the accident.'

A subject remains singular or plural regardless of any intervening expressions; the verb always maintains concord with that subject.

- For example, Gagan, as well as the rest of her family, was late.

The reported events usually take past tense.

- For example, The Indian team left for New Zealand yesterday.

Considering the above points and after reading the given variants of the sentence, we can see that the correct sentence is:

'All the passengers, with the driver, were killed in the accident.'

Hence, the correct option is (C).

36. The Object of a verb or of a preposition, when it is a pronoun, should be in the objective form.

- Example - Between you and me affairs look dark.

The phrase 'Between you and me' contains a preposition: the word between. That means it requires an object pronoun, or the word me, which functions as the object of the preposition.

The objective form of the Pronoun 'I' is 'me'.

Thus, the grammatically correct sentence is 'Between you and me, Mr Sharma is not to be trusted'.

Hence, the correct option is (A).

37. 'Autobiography' is the biography of a person narrated by himself or herself.

Example: Gandhi Ji's autobiography, which he had titled 'My experiments with Truth' can be rated as one of the most popular and the most influential books in recent history.

Hence, the correct option is (B).

38. 'Mischeif' is spelled incorrectly.

Mischief meaning: bad behaviour (usually of children) that is not very serious

The correct spelling is 'Mischief' which means "a specific injury or damage attributed to a particular agent".

Example: She wanted to explain how much mischief might be done by such reports.

Hence, the correct option is (A).

39. The word 'honesty' is an abstract noun. This word refers to the quality or characteristic of being honest and truthful.

Abstract nouns includes nouns which express ideas, concepts or qualities that cannot be seen or experienced. Examples include words like anger, liberty, freedom etc.

Hence, the correct option is (B).

40. Simple past tense is the tense used in the sentence "Someone picked my pocket".

- Simple tenses are the verbs used to describe things that had already occurred in the past.
- In simple past tense, the action present in it will always be done stating it past tense.
- The verbs which are being used should also be in simple past tense only.

- Usually, the simple past tense verbs end with "-ed".
- In the sentence, "Someone picked my pocket", "picked" is the verb used in the past tense.

Hence, the correct option is (B).

41. Assembly is the action of gathering together for a common purpose.

Often used to describing a gathering of people the word assembly can also refer to putting something together, such as a machine or a piece of furniture.

From the meaning of the given words, we can say that gathering is the synonym of assembly.

Hence, the correct option is (A).

42. The meaning of the given words:

Chore: a job or a piece of work that is often boring or is unpleasant but needs to be done regularly.

Task: a piece of work to be done.

So, from the meaning of the given words we can say that task is the synonyms of chore.

Hence, the correct option is (D).

43. Arrogant means 'a sense that one is more important or able than one actually is.

'Humble' means 'having a modest or low estimate of one's importance.

So, from the meaning of the words, we can say that humble is the opposite of arrogant.

Hence, the correct option is (A).

44. The meaning of the given words:

- EARN means to obtain money.
- LOSE means to be deprived of or to cease to have money.
- WIN means to be victorious.
- OBTAIN means to get something.
- DESERVE means to be worthy of.

From the meaning of the given words, we can say that lose is the antonym of earn.

Hence, the correct option is (C).

45. The given blank needs a phrasal verb that means to show up for the interview.

So, turned up which means (of a person) to arrive is the correct phrasal verb for the given blank.

The sentence would become: "Ten candidates turned up for the interview."

The meaning of the other options are as follows -

- turned down - to refuse or decline a request. - My credit card application was turned down by the bank because of my bad credit.

- turned over - to change position so that the other side is facing toward the outside or the top. - The car skidded and turned over.
- turned out - to happen in a particular way. - Despite our worries everything turned out well.

Hence, the correct option is (A).

46. The first word denotes a class of objects stored in the structure defined in the second word.

The grain is stored in a warehouse.

Similarly, Water is stored in a dam.

Hence, the correct option is (B).

47. By reading the sentence, we can see that the fillers need a pair of correlative conjunctions which indicate similar in their sense/polarity (both positive or negative).

- In the given options, the only correct correlative pair of conjunctions is 'neither... nor' which is used when you are talking about two or more things that are not true or that do not happen.
- So, the correct choice for the words to fill the blanks is 'neither, nor' and the correct sentence: 'It is neither useful nor ornamental.'

Hence, the correct option is (C).

48. The most appropriate word for the given group of words is 'utopia'.

It means 'a place or state that exists only in the imagination, where everything is perfect.'

- Example: We weren't out to design a contemporary utopia.

Hence, the correct option is (A).

49. The feminine of a **father** is a mother.

The word **father** describes a man.

Hence, the correct option is (A).

50. The meaningful word from the words "EMUOARYHJE" is "mother".

"Mother" is important member of a family. a woman in relation to her child or children. etc.

Example: I want to see your mother.

Hence, the correct option is (A).

51. Three times a state of emergency has been declared in India since independence.

The first State of emergency was imposed during the India-China war between 26 October 1962 to 10 January 1968, it was the time when "the security of India" was declared as being "threatened by external aggression".

The second State of emergency was also proclaimed during the Indo-Pakistan war between 3 to 17 December 1971, later it was extended with the third proclamation that was imposed by Prime Minister Indira Gandhi on 25th June 1975. This 'emergency' was imposed because of the perceived threat of internal disturbance.

The third Emergency ended as dramatically as it had begun, resulting in a defeat of the Congress in the Lok Sabha elections of 1977.

Hence, the correct option is (A).

52. The festival of Vyasan Dwadashi is celebrated in Odisha in the direction of promoting food security.

Dishes Dwadashi festival:

- The festival is a culinary and indulgent celebration with at least 701 dishes being prepared.
- It is in the month of Margashira (mid-December to mid-January) that different types of food (dishes) are prepared on the 12th day (Dwadashi) of the Shukla Paksha or the growing phase of the moon.
- The festival is reminiscent of an episode in the Mahabharata where Yashoda finds her son Krishna pale and emaciated.

Hence, the correct option is (B).

53. Omkareshwar Mahadev Temple is situated on the northern bank of Narmada.

It is located in Khandwa district of Madhya Pradesh. It is situated in the middle of the river Narmada on an island called Mandhata or Shivpuri. It is one of the twelve Jyotirlingas of Lord Shiva.

Hence, the correct option is (A).

54. When we move from top to down in Periodic table, size of alkali metals increases.

Alkali metals are the elements present in group 1 in the periodic table. They are very reactive metals and their reactivity increases as we move down the group from top to bottom because of an increase in the atomic size. Alkali metals have one electron in their respective valence shells. They have a strong tendency to lose this electron and acquire the stable configuration of the nearest noble gas. Thus, the reactivity of alkali metals depends upon their ability to lose electrons.

Since their tendency to lose electrons increases down the group hence their reactivity increases down the group.

Hence, the correct option is (A).

55. The national currency of Bhutan is the Ngultrum.

Bhutan is a small country located between Tibet and India in the mountainous region of the Himalayas. It is a landlocked country situated between China and India. The currency of Bhutan is the Bhutanese Ngultrum. Dzongkha is the only official national language in Bhutan.

Hence, the correct option is (C).

56. All the planets move around the sun in an Elliptical path.

When an object moves or revolves around the other object in an elongated path and not in a circular motion, it is called an Elongated path or Elliptical orbit.

Hence, the correct option is (C).

57. On September 30, 2022, shooter Anish Bhanwala of Karnal district of Haryana won the gold medal in shooting at the 36th National Games being held in Ahmedabad, Gujarat.

Anish Bhanwala is an Indian shooter. He is from Karnal, Haryana. They compete in the 25m Rapid Fire Pistol, 25m Pistol and 25m Standard Pistol events. Anish has been a part of the Indian shooting team since 2017.

Hence, the correct option is (A).

58. Saint Kabir Das was the famous Hindi poet of the 15th century, who belongs to the Varanasi in Uttar Pradesh.

- He was born in the 1425A.D in Varanasi.
- His early life was in a Muslim family, but he was strongly influenced by his teacher, the Hindu bhakti leader Ramananda.
- Kabir's legacy survives and continues through the Kabir Panth, a religious community that recognizes him as its founder and is one of the Sant Mat sects.
- Kabir's main composition was Sakhi, Sbad, Ramani.
- Kabir's verses were found in Sikhism's scripture Guru Granth Sahib.

Hence, the correct option is (A).

59. The University of Allahabad is a public central university located in Allahabad(now Prayagraj), Uttar Pradesh, India.

- It was established on 23 September 1887, it is one of the oldest modern universities in India.
- Its origins lie in the Muir Central College, named after Lt. Governor of North-Western Provinces, Sir William Muir in 1876.
- At one point, it was known as the "Oxford of the East".
- Its Central University status was re-established through the University of Allahabad Act 2005 by the Parliament of India.
- The foundation stone of the Muir Central College was laid by Governor-General of India, Lord Northbrook on 9 December 1873.

Hence, the correct option is (D).

60. The main center of the Leather industry in Uttar Pradesh is in Kanpur but the leather shoes, suitcases are manufactured in Agra, Bareilly, Lucknow, and Meerut.

Kanpur is very famous for leather industry in the world. The main mineral of the district is sand. Sand is available in abundance on the banks of the river Ganges, which is used in the construction of houses, bridges and roads, etc. Brick soil is also available in Kanpur Nagar.

Agra is famous for its leather work. Many leather products like shoes, belts, bags are manufactured here. The raw material is mainly imported from Kanpur, Kolkata, Chennai, Taiwan and China.

Hence, the correct option is (D).

61. The Dargah of the famous Sufi saint Sheikh Salim Chishti is located in Fatehpur Sikri, Uttar Pradesh.

The site houses the dargah of Sufi saint Salim Chishti (1478 - 1572), successor of Khwaja Moinuddin Chishti of Ajmer, where he lived in a cave on the ridge at Sikri. The mausoleum was built by Akbar to honor the Sufi saint.

Hence, the correct option is (C).

62. N J Ojha has been appointed as the Ombudsman for two years under the Mahatma Gandhi National Rural Employment Guarantee Scheme.

An ombudsman has the power to receive complaints from MGNREGA workers, consider such complaints, pass awards within 30 days from the date of receipt of complaints and issue directions to conduct on-the-spot inquiries and delay in payment of wages or unemployment Also initiate 'suo moto' proceedings in case of any complaints including issues relating to payment of allowances.

Hence, the correct option is (D).

63. The Chitrakote Falls is situated on the Indravati river. It is located in the Indian state of Chattisgarh.

- Chitrakote Falls is fondly known as the "Niagara Falls of India" because of its unbelievable width.
- It falls from a height of 30 meters and is almost as wide as 985 ft, which is one-third of the magnanimous Niagara Falls.

Hence, the correct option is (C).

64. Union Minister Sarbananda Sonowal inaugurated the Chabahar Day Convention on 31 July 2022 in Mumbai.

The opening ceremony was attended by dignitaries from Kazakhstan, Iran, Tajikistan, Kyrgyzstan, Uzbekistan, Turkmenistan and Afghanistan.

"Chabahar Day" is celebrated to mark the launch of INSTC - India's vision to make cargo movement economical between India and Central Asia. The Chabahar port in Iran is a commercial transit hub for the region and Central Asia in particular.

Hence, the correct option is (D).

65. Satish Pai has been appointed as the new chairman of the International Aluminium Institute (IAI) on 6 June 2022.

The International Aluminium Institute (IAI), the only body representing the global primary aluminium industry, has announced the appointment of Satish Pai as its new Chairman. He is the Managing Director of Hindalco Industries, one of the world's largest integrated producers of aluminium.

Hence, the correct option is (D).

66. Haryana Government recently launched the Haryana Cheerag Scheme. Under the scheme, government will provide free education to Economically Weaker section (EWS) students of Government schools in private school. Cheerag Scheme stands for, "Chief Minister Equal Education Relief, Assistance and Grant".

Hence, the correct option is (B).

67. Saima Syed has achieved the feat of becoming the country's first one-star rider.

- Saima Syed is a Horse Rider of Nagaur, Rajasthan.
- She has created a new history in the country by achieving the feat of becoming a One Star Rider by qualifying with a bronze medal in the 80 km Endurance Race.
- Saima Syed is the first woman horseman in the country to have received this category.
- Saima Syed has achieved the feat of becoming a One Star Rider by qualifying with a bronze medal in the 80 km Endurance Race.

Hence, the correct option is (D).

68. The Ashoka Pillar of Allahabad included the political and military achievements of Gupta Emperor Samudragupta (350-375 CE). It is also a source of the Geopolitical landscape of that era.

- It almost completely circles the pillar and is written around the Minor Edicts of Ashoka.
- This inscription is also known as "Prayag Prashasti" and is considered one of the important historical documents of the classical Gupta age.
- Harisena who was the court poet of Samudragupta mentioned his achievements on Prayag Prashasti.

Hence, the correct option is (B).

69. The Tropic of Cancer does not pass through Odisha. The Tropic of Cancer is an imaginary line north from the Equator at an angle of 23.50 degrees. Tropic of Cancer passes through 16 countries, 3 continents and 6 water bodies. The Tropic of Cancer passes through the 8 Indian states of Gujarat, Rajasthan, Madhya Pradesh, Chhattisgarh, Jharkhand, West Bengal, Tripura, Mizoram.

Hence, the correct option is (C).

70. Joao Lourenco was sworn in for a second term as president of Angola on 15 Sept 2022.

Lourenco, 68, was sworn in alongside Esperanca da Costa, Angola's first female vice president in the capital, Luanda. The ruling MPLA party garnered 51% of the votes and 124 seats in the 220-member parliament in the Aug 24 election. Angola is a country located on the west coast of Southern Africa.

Hence, the correct option is (D).

71. The soldiers has started the revolt of 1857.

The revolt of 1857 was the conscious beginning of the Independence struggle against the colonial tyranny of the British. The revolt began on May 10, 1857, at Meerut as a sepoy mutiny. It was initiated by sepoys in the Bengal Presidency against the British officers.

Hence, the correct option is (B).

72. Newton's laws of motion-

Newton's first law states that, if a body is at rest or moving at a constant speed in a straight line, it will remain at rest or keep moving in a straight line at constant speed unless it is acted upon by force.

- This postulate is known as the law of inertia. The law of inertia was first formulated by Galileo Galilei for horizontal motion on Earth and was later generalized by René Descartes.
- Before Galileo, it had been thought that all horizontal motion required a direct cause. Still, Galileo deduced from his experiments that a body in motion would remain in motion unless a force (such as friction) caused it to come to rest.

Hence, the correct option is (A).

73. Graphite is also known as Black Lead and Plumbago. The term black lead usually refers to a powdered or processed graphite, matte black in color. Graphite is a crystalline allotrope of carbon in which carbons are arranged in hexagonal structure. It is good conductor of electricity and this makes it useful in electronic products such as electrodes, batteries, and solar panels.

Hence, the correct option is (C).

74. Jayaprabha Menon is famous for the Mohiniyattam .

Jayaprabha Menon has notched a reputation non-pareil in the firmament of Indian Classical dances. Her performances of Mohiniyattam have been eloquent demonstrations of talents groomed by venerated Gurus like Kalamandalam Saraswathy, C V Chandrasekhar, and Bharathy Shivaji. Jayaprabha Menon is the director of the International Academy of Mohiniyattam, New Delhi.

"Mohiniyattam is a solo dance tradition from Kerala, performed by a young woman named Prakriti, to dedicate herself to the temple deity through dance and music.

Hence, the correct option is (B).

75. The Manjira Crocodile Wildlife Sanctuary is situated in Medak district Telangana state.

- The Manjira sanctuary is situated along the mighty river Manjeera.
- The Manjira sanctuary was established in June 1978.
- In 1974, the mugger crocodile had reached the threshold of extinction in Telangana, with only four pairs of mugger crocodiles remaining in the Manjira wildlife sanctuary.
- Today there are approximately 400 to 600 crocodiles in the sanctuary helped by a crocodile breeding program that is carried out here.

Hence, the correct option is (C).

76. $513 = (3 \times 3 \times 3) \times 19$

$1107 = (3 \times 3 \times 3) \times 41$

$783 = (3 \times 3 \times 3) \times 29$

∴ The HCF of 513, 1107 and 783 is 27.

Hence, the correct option is (C).

77. Given:

Amount (P) = 5760, Rate (R) = 3 and Time (T)=6

As we know,

$$\text{Simple Interest } = \frac{P \times R \times T}{100}$$

Therefore, required Simple Interest $= \dfrac{5760 \times 3 \times 6}{100}$

= Rs. 1036.8

Hence the correct option is (A).

78. Let the Cost Price be Rs. x

Then Sell Price $= 988 + \dfrac{1}{2}x$

Profit = Rs. 300

By the given condition,

Sell Price = Cost Price + Profit

$$988 + \frac{1}{2}x = x + 300$$

Multiplying by 2 on both sides

$$2 \times 988 + x = 2x + 600$$

$$1976 + x = 2x + 600$$

$$1976 - 600 = 2x - x$$

$$\therefore x = 1376$$

Hence, the correct option is (A).

79. The relation between the numbers is as follows:

72 - 56 = 16

56 - 42 = 14

42 - 30 = 12

30 - 20 = 10

20 - 12 = 8

Thus, the number which complete the series is 12.

Hence, the correct option is (C).

80. Given:

$2365A$ is divisible by 9.

If the sum of all the digits is divisible by 9, then the number is also divisible by 9.

Sum of all the digits $= 2 + 3 + 6 + 5 + A$

$$\Rightarrow 16 + A$$

As the number is divisible by 9, so $16 + A$ is also divisible by 9.

Multiple of 9 nearest to 16 is 18.

$$\Rightarrow 16 + A = 18$$

$$\Rightarrow A = 18 - 16$$

$$\Rightarrow A = 2$$

$\therefore$ The value of A is 2.

Hence, the correct option is (A).

81. Given:

There are three consecutive even number and the sum of the first two is 14 more than the third one.

The three consecutive even number are (x + 2), (x + 4) and (x + 6).

According to the question,

The sum of the first two terms is 14 more than the third.

$\therefore$ (x + 2) + (x + 4) = (x + 6) + 14

$\Rightarrow$ x = 14

So, the numbers are 16, 18, and 20 where 16 is the smallest number.

$\therefore$ The smallest number is 16.

Hence, the correct option is (A).

82. Let the smaller numbers be x

The other numbers are (x + 2)

According to the question,

x + (x + 2) = 66

$\Rightarrow$ 2x = 64

$\Rightarrow$ x = 32

$\therefore$ The smaller one is 32.

Hence, the correct option is (B).

83. Given,

$$36 - [18 - \{14 - (15 - 4 \div 2 \times 2)\}]$$

$$= 36 - \left[18 - \left\{14 - \left(15 - \frac{4}{2} \times 2\right)\right\}\right]$$

$$= 36 - [18 - \{14 - 11\}]$$

$$= 36 - [18 - 3]$$

$$= 36 - 15$$

$$= 21$$

Hence, the correct option is (D).

84. Given,

170 marks are equivalent to 34%.

Let the total marks be x.

According to the question,

$$\frac{34x}{100} = 170$$

$$\Rightarrow x = 500$$

$$\Rightarrow \frac{200}{500} \times 100 = 40$$

$\therefore$ 200 marks is equivalent to 40%.

Hence, the correct option is (B).

85. Let the Cost price of the Chair is x.

Selling Price $= x - 25\%$ of x

$$720 = 0.75x$$

$$x = \frac{720}{0.75}$$

$$\Rightarrow x = 960$$

Cost Price $=$ Rs. 960

So, To gain 25%, SP would be $= 960 + 25\%$ of 960

$$= 960 + \frac{25}{100} \times 960$$

$$= 960 + \frac{1}{4} \times 960$$

$$= 960 + 240$$

$$= \text{Rs. } 1200$$

Hence, the correct option is (A).

86. Given,

$$150.75 \div 0.6$$

$$= \frac{150.75}{0.6}$$

$$= \frac{150.75 \times 10}{0.6 \times 10}$$

$$= \frac{1507.5}{6}$$

$$= 251.25$$

Hence, the correct option is (A).

87. The Roman numerals are represented by the following letters:

$$\text{I} = 1$$

$$\text{V} = 5$$

$$\text{X} = 10$$

$$\text{L} = 50$$

$$\text{C} = 100$$

$$\text{D} = 500$$

$$\text{M} = 1000$$

If a numeral is followed by another numeral of lower denomination, the two are added together.

if it is preceded by one of lower denomination, the smaller numeral is subtracted from the greater.

900 can be written as $(1000 - 100)$.

$$900 = 1000 - 100$$

$$900 = M - C$$

Therefore, $900 =$ CM

Hence, the correct option is (A).

88. Numerals that can be repeated in the Roman system are I, X and C.

- V can be used once in the Roman system.
- Similarly, L and D can be used only once in the Roman System.
- But I, X and C can be repeated in the Roman system to represent certain numbers.

I is written as 1, X is written as 10 and C is written as 100.

Thus, the numerals that can be repeated in the Roman system are I, X and C.

Hence, the correct option is (A).

89. Prime numbers are those numbers which are only divisible by itself and one.

97 is the only prime number between 90 and 100.

So, the sum $= 97$

Hence, the correct option is (A).

90. A composite number is a positive integer that has atleast one positive divisor other than one or the number itself. In other words, a composite number is any integer greater than one that is not a prime number

Now between 101 and 120, numbers are $102, 104, 105, 106, 108, 110, 111, 112, 114, 115, 116, 117, 118, 119$

So, the number of composite number between 101 and 120 are 14.

Hence, the correct option is (D).

91. Given,

Numbers $= 80, 90, 100, 110, 120, 130$

$$\text{Average} = \left(\frac{\text{Sum of Values}}{\text{Number of Values}}\right)$$

$$= \frac{80 + 90 + 100 + 110 + 120 + 130}{6}$$

$$= \frac{630}{6}$$

$$= 105$$

Hence, the correct option is (B).

92. Given:

$$\frac{2}{3} + \frac{1}{11}$$

After taking LCM of Denominators,

$$= \frac{22}{33} + \frac{3}{33}$$

$$= \frac{22+3}{33}$$

$$= \frac{25}{33}$$

Hence, the correct option is (A).

93. Given,

$$16 - 2 \div 7 + 6 \times 2$$

$$= 16 - \frac{2}{7} + 6 \times 2$$

$$= 16 - \frac{2}{7} + 12$$

$$= 28 - \frac{2}{7}$$

$$= \frac{196-2}{7}$$

$$= \frac{194}{7}$$

$$= 27\frac{5}{7}$$

Hence, the correct option is (A).

94. Given,

Two numbers are 101 and 151.

$101, 151$ doesn't any common factor.

So, HCF is 1.

Hence, the correct option is (A).

95. Given,

Cost of 3 envelopes $= 15$

Cost of 1 envelope $= \frac{15}{3}$

Cost of 1 envelope $= 5$

Cost of 5 envelope $= 5 \times 5$

$$= ₹\ 25$$

Hence, the correct option is (B).

96. Given,

$$\frac{2x}{3} = 18$$

Multiply 3 on both the sides, we get

$$2x = 18 \times 3$$

$$\Rightarrow 2x = 54$$

Divide both side by 2, we get

$$\Rightarrow x = 27$$

Hence, the correct option is (D).

97. Given,

Perimeter of a square $= 36$ cm

As we know,

Perimeter of a square $= 4 \times$ length of a side

$$\Rightarrow 4 \times \text{length of a side} = 36$$

$$\Rightarrow \text{length of a side} = \frac{36}{4} = 9 \text{ cm}$$

Area of a square $= (\text{Length of a side })^2 = (9 \text{ cm })^2 = 81 \text{ cm}^2$

Hence, the correct option is (D).

98. Given,

Length $= 15m$

Let Breadth $= x$

Area of a rectangle $= 180$ sq . m

As we know,

Area of a rectangle $=$ Length $\times$ Breadth

$$180 = \text{Length} \times \text{Breadth}$$

$$\Rightarrow 180 = \text{Length} \times x$$

$$\Rightarrow 180 = 15 \times x$$

$$\Rightarrow x = \frac{180}{15}$$

$$\Rightarrow x = 12 \text{ m}$$

So, its breadth is 12m.

Hence, the correct option is (A).

99. Given:

We have a number 3920.

Prime factorization of $3920 = 2 \times 2 \times 2 \times 2 \times 7 \times 7 \times 5$

Only 5 is left unpaired.

$\therefore$ The square root of 3920 is $28\sqrt{5}$.

Hence, the correct option is (A).

100. Given,

$$25 + \frac{3}{100} + \frac{4}{1000}$$

$$= 25 + 0.03 + 0.004$$

$$= 25.034$$

So, the value of $25 + \dfrac{3}{100} + \dfrac{4}{1000}$ is 25.034.

Hence, the correct option is (C).

Mock Test 05

Hindi

Ques (1-2):निर्देश: दिए गए शब्दों के लिए एक शब्द बताइए।

Q.1 'कार्य करने वाला व्यक्ति'

A. कार्यकर्ता
B. कल्पनातीत
C. केन्द्राभिमुख
D. कामचोर

Q.2 'जो स्त्री सूर्य भी न देख सकें'

A. विदुषी
B. अलक्ष्या
C. असूर्यपश्या
D. शास्त्रज्ञा

Q.3 दिए गए वाक्य का सही काल निर्धारण कीजिए।
वह कानपुर जा रहा था।

A. भूतकाल
B. वर्तमान काल
C. भविष्य काल
D. सामान्य भविष्य

Q.4 दो समान शब्दों के मध्य लगाया जाने वाला चिन्ह है:

A. -
B. ?
C. ,
D. इनमे से कोई नहीं

Q.5 वाक्य के बीच में आए शब्दों अथवा पदों का अर्थ स्पष्ट करने के लिए किस विराम चिन्ह का प्रयोग किया जाता है?

A. अल्पविराम
B. विस्मयादिबोधक-चिह्न
C. कोष्ठक चिह्न
D. त्रुटि-चिह्न

Q.6 जिस संज्ञा पद से किसी वर्ग के प्राणियों वस्तु या संस्थानों का बोध होता है वह है:

A. व्यक्तिवाचक
B. भाववाचक
C. जातिवाचक
D. अस्थान वाचक

Q.7 'घड़ों पानी पड़ना' मुहावरे का अर्थ होगा?

A. काँपना
B. सर्दी लगना
C. नहाना
D. लज्जित होना

Q.8 "एक पन्थ दो काज" लोकोक्ति का अर्थ बताइये।

A. ज्यादा बढ़ा-चढ़ाकर बोलना
B. मुसीबत आना
C. चोट लगना
D. एक काम से दूसरा काम हो जाना

Q.9 'से' किस कारक का चिह्न है?

A. करण कारक
B. कर्म कारक
C. संबंध कारक
D. कर्ता कारक

Q.10 'संहार' में किस उपसर्ग का प्रयोग है?

A. सम्
B. सन
C. सनह
D. सम्ह

Q.11 'सावधानी' में कौन-सा प्रत्यय है?
[UPSSSC Village Development Officer, 2018]

A. नी
B. धानी
C. ई
D. आनी

Q.12 मेरे तो गिरधर गोपाल दूसरो न कोई। जाके सिर मोर मुकुट मेरो पति सोई ।।
दी गई पँक्तियों में किस रस का प्रयोग किया गया है?

A. रौद्र रस
B. वीर रस
C. श्रृंगार रस
D. करुण रस

Q.13 'उबटन' शब्द का तत्सम रूप क्या है?

A. उपलेपन
B. उद्वर्तन
C. उद्रवतन
D. उपः लेपन

Q.14 दिये गये विकल्पों में से तन्दव शब्द का चयन कीजिए।

A. झीना
B. दंश
C. युवान
D. यज्ञोपवीत

Q.15 'यशोदा' का सन्धि विच्छेद है:

A. यशो + दा
B. यश + दा
C. यशः + दा
D. य + शोदा

Q.16 नीचे दिए गए वाक्य का प्रकार बताये।
"ईश्वर तुम्हें सफलता दें।"

A. प्रश्नवाचक वाक्य
B. विस्मयवाचक वाक्य
C. निषेधवाचक वाक्य
D. इच्छावाचक वाक्य

Q.17 निम्नलिखित वाक्य में प्रयुक्त विशेषण का प्रकार बताइए।
"उस मैदान में पाँच लड़के खेल रहे हैं।"

A. संख्यावाचक विशेषण
B. गुणवाचक विशेषण
C. परिमाणवाचक विशेषण
D. संबंधवाचक विशेषण

Q.18 निम्न में निश्चयवाचक सर्वनाम कौन सा है?

A. वह
B. तुम
C. आप
D. मैं

Ques (19-20):निर्देश: सही शब्द का चयन करते हुए रिक्त स्थान की पूर्ति कीजिए।

Q.19 आपसे सादर _______ है कि आप हमारे समारोह में पधारें।

A. अनुग्रह
B. कामना
C. अनुरोध
D. आरक्षण

Q.20 उसे मेरी सफलता से _______ है।

A. ईर्ष्या
B. द्वेष
C. स्पर्द्धा
D. क्रोध

Q.21 मात्रा के आधार पर स्वर कितने प्रकार के होते हैं?

A. 2
B. 3
C. 4
D. 6

Q.22 दिए गए शब्द का बहुवचन चुनिए।
आँख

A. आँख
B. आँखे
C. अखियाँ
D. इनमे से कोई नहीं

Q.23 निर्देश: सही वर्तनी वाले शब्द का चयन करें।

A. शौकाकुल
B. शोकाकुल
C. शोककुल
D. शौककुल

Q.24 दिए गए शब्द का पर्यायवाची शब्द बताइए।
'अश्व'

A. घोड़ा
B. ड्ग
C. अभिलाषा
D. मघवा

Q.25 निम्नलिखित में से कौन-सा शब्द 'कृतज्ञ' का विलोम शब्द है?

A. कृतघ्न
B. संसारी
C. भय
D. वक्र

English

Ques (26-27):Direction: Read the given statement carefully and choose the correct tense.

Q.26 The peon is ringing the bell.

A. Present indefinite tense

"

B. Present continuous tense
C. Past continuous tense
D. Present perfect tense

Q.27 It rains all year round here.
A. Present continuous tense
B. Present indefinite tense
C. Past continuous tense
D. Present perfect tense

Q.28 Which of the words is not an adjective?
A. Beautiful   **B.** Enormous
C. Dog   **D.** Silly

Ques (29-36):Direction: Complete the sentence by choosing the most appropriate option from those given below:

Q.29 Ram as well as his brothers _______coming today.
A. are   **B.** were
C. is   **D.** have been

Q.30 He picked up a piece ___ wood.
A. in   **B.** on   **C.** of   **D.** by

Q.31 Is there _________ fitness centre near your house?
[Intelligence Bureau Security Assistant, 2019]
A. an   **B.** the
C. a   **D.** None of these

Q.32 He has hardly read ___________ book.
[Intelligence Bureau Security Assistant, 2019]
A. many   **B.** all
C. the   **D.** None of these

Q.33 Give me ___ apple.
A. a   **B.** an
C. the   **D.** None of these

Q.34 He is superior _____ me.
A. from   **B.** to   **C.** by   **D.** in

Q.35 We were prevented _____ seeing the prisoner.
A. from   **B.** to   **C.** on   **D.** at

Q.36 I have been to ________________ doctor, whose name figured in the Times of India.
[Intelligence Bureau Security Assistant, 2019]
A. the   **B.** an
C. any   **D.** None of these

Ques (37-38):Direction: In the question below, a sentence is given with two blanks that indicate that some parts are missing. Identify the correct pair of words that fit in the sentence to make it grammatically and contextually correct.

Q.37 A ________ and a ________ can never be just friends.
A. father, son   **B.** mother, daughter
C. boy, girl   **D.** man, pet

Q.38 We are ___________ to go out for a picnic tomorrow.
[Intelligence Bureau Security Assistant, 2019]

A. plan   **B.** planning   **C.** plans   **D.** think

Q.39 Direction: Identify the interjection in the following sentence.
Oops! The plate broke.
A. Oops   **B.** The   **C.** plate   **D.** broke

Q.40 Generally, gender is of___types.
A. 2   **B.** 3   **C.** 4   **D.** 5

Q.41 Out of the given words, one word is misspelt find the misspelt word.
A. Phlegm   **B.** Mnemonic
C. Apropos   **D.** Rendezvos

Q.42 Direction: Select the related word from the given alternatives.
Ignominy : Disloyalty :: Fame :
A. Heroism   **B.** Fool   **C.** Victory   **D.** Man

Q.43 Fill in the blank with the correct pronoun.
Please give _____ a pen.
A. I   **B.** you   **C.** me   **D.** they

Q.44 Direction: Select the word which means the same as the group of words given.
A person who loves everybody
A. Cosmopolitan   **B.** Fratricide
C. Altruistic   **D.** Aristocrat

Q.45 Which of these is used to separate short co-ordinate clauses of a compound sentence?
A. Semicolon   **B.** Comma
C. Full stop   **D.** Colon

Ques (46-47):Direction: Choose the most appropriate synonym of the given word.

Q.46 Defer
A. Indifferent   **B.** Defy
C. Differ   **D.** Postpone

Q.47 Alacrity
A. Briskness   **B.** Fear
C. Frankness   **D.** Alarm

Ques (48-49):Direction: Choose the most appropriate antonym of the given word.

Q.48 Prosperous
A. Adverse   **B.** Advanced
C. Retarded   **D.** Impecunious

Q.49 Superiority
A. Seniority   **B.** Juniority
C. Inferiority   **D.** Urbanity

Q.50 Choose the meaningful word from the given jumbled word:
SEPARATE
A. Seert   **B.** Tears   **C.** Rasep   **D.** Septar

General Studies

Q.51 The Nobel Memorial Prize in Economic Sciences 2022 was awarded to three scientists for their research in which field?
A. Behavioural Economics
B. Global Poverty
C. Banks and Financial Crises
D. Quantitative Methods

Q.52 NASSCOM appointed _____ as Chairperson for 2022-2023.
A. Indira Hinduja
B. Madhabi Puri Buch
C. Krishnan Ramanujam
D. Hemant Soren

Q.53 Which state launched the Mukhya Mantri Bagwani Bima scheme portal in 2022 To compensate for the damage caused to the crops due to adverse weather and natural calamities?
A. Uttar Pradesh **B.** Tamil Nadu
C. Gujarat **D.** Haryana

Q.54 Iconic French filmmaker ___________ passed away in 2022.
A. Humbert Balsan
B. Jax Bar
C. Christophe Barretier
D. Jean-Luc Godard

Q.55 Which state has won "Ranji Trophy 2022" Title ?
A. Bihar **B.** Madya Pradesh
C. Maharashtra **D.** Odisha

Q.56 In Uttar Pradesh, the cow slaughter prevention act was passed in which year?
A. 1954 **B.** 1956 **C.** 1958 **D.** 1955

Q.57 The Indian state of Uttar Pradesh is divided into how many divisions?
A. 18 **B.** 12 **C.** 75 **D.** 15

Q.58 The Hathnikund barrage irrigation project is located in which district of Uttar Pradesh?
A. Balia **B.** Firozpur
C. Mirzapur **D.** Saharanpur

Q.59 In which of the following areas of Uttar Pradesh is the main crop of soybean grown?
A. Vindhya Region
B. Bundelkhand Region
C. Baghelkhand Region
D. None of the above

Q.60 Uranium is found in which of the following district of Uttar Pradesh?
A. Lalitpur **B.** Prayagraj
C. Kanpur **D.** Sonbhadra

Q.61 Scissor term is associated with which of the following sport?
A. Hockey **B.** Kabaddi

C. Wrestling **D.** Polo

Q.62 The boundary between Germany and Poland is called the _______.
A. Oder–Neisse line **B.** Maginot Line
C. Durand Line **D.** 17th Parallel

Q.63 Branch of biology which deal with the study of heredity is called:
A. Cytology **B.** Evolution
C. Genetics **D.** Physiology

Q.64 World Braille Day is celebrated on ______.
A. 5th January **B.** 4th January
C. 6th January **D.** 8th January

Q.65 Hampi, the ancient capital of Vijayanagara is located in:
A. Tamil Nadu **B.** Kerala
C. Telengana **D.** Karnataka

Q.66 Which of the following vitamin deficiency causes Beriberi?
A. Vitamin A **B.** Vitamin B
C. Vitamin C **D.** Vitamin D

Q.67 Milk is a:
A. Emulsion **B.** Suspension
C. Foam **D.** Gel

Q.68 Nylon is made up of:
A. Polyamide **B.** Polyester
C. Polyethylene **D.** Polypropylene

Q.69 The Currency "Dong" belongs to which country?
A. Cambodia **B.** Laos
C. Myanmar **D.** Vietnam

Q.70 Which of the following is the capital of Japan?
A. Tokyo **B.** Luanda
C. Saint John's **D.** Buenos Aires

Q.71 Who had been appointed as Prime Minister Narendra Modi's advisor?
A. Atul Kumar Goel
B. Praveen Kumar
C. Soma Sankara Prasad
D. Tarun Kapoor

Q.72 The Chilika Lake is located in _________.
A. West Bengal **B.** Odisha
C. Kerala **D.** Tamil Nadu

Q.73 Teak, Sal, Sandalwood are important species of:
A. Tropical Thorn Forests
B. Montane forests
C. Tropical Evergreen forests
D. Tropical Deciduous Forests

Q.74 Which one among the following Union Territories of India is the smallest in geographical area?
[Indian Military Academy (IMA), 2020], [Officers Training Academy (OTA), 2020]

A. Chandigarh
B. Puducherry
C. Dadra and Nagar Haveli and Daman and Diu
D. Lakshadweep

Q.75 The Buddhist text Majjhima Nikaya is in:
[UPSC Central Armed Police Forces AC, 2018]

A. Sanskrit   B. Pali   C. Prakrit   D. Telugu

Mathematics

Ques (76-80):Direction: What value will come in place of the question mark (?) in the following question?

Q.76 $1888 \div 32 \div 8 =?$
A. 7.375   B. 9.485   C. 29.5   D. 472

Q.77 $4848 \times 222 =?$
A. 2,076,256   B. 1,076,256
C. 1,176,256   D. 1,076,25

Q.78 $8888 \div 22 =?$
A. 400   B. 402   C. 444   D. 404

Q.79 0.06 × ? × 0.216 = 1.944
A. 120   B. 110   C. 150   D. 130

Q.80 $788 \times 546 =?$
A. 430,240   B. 430,248   C. 431,248   D. 430,245

Q.81 Find the HCF of 18 and 36.
A. 4   B. 12   C. 18   D. 15

Q.82 If the circumference of a circle is equalto the perimeter of square, then whichone of the following is correct?
[HTET TGT Mathematics, 2018]

A. Area of circle $=$ Area of square
B. Area of circle $>$ Area of square
C. Area of circle $<$ Area of square
D. None of these

Q.83 The circumference of a circle, whose area is $24.64 \ m^2$, is :
A. 14.64 m   B. 16.36 m   C. 17.60 m   D. 18.40 m

Q.84 Find the simple interest on Rs. 900 for 3 years 4 months at 5% per annum.
A. Rs. 350   B. Rs. 150   C. Rs. 250   D. Rs. 155

Q.85 Solve for x:
3x + 4 (x+3) = 26
A. 3   B. 2   C. 4   D. 5

Q.86 Find the Square root of the following:
$\sqrt{441}$
A. 23   B. 20   C. 22   D. 21

Q.87 The roots of the equation $3x^2 - 2x + 4 = 0$ are:
A. Real and equal   B. Imaginary

C. Real and unequal   D. None of these

Q.88 Direction: What should come in place of the question mark '?' in the following number series?
22, 46, 94, 190, ?
A. 412   B. 370   C. 382   D. 394

Q.89 If $x\%$ of y is 100 and $y\%$ of z is 200, then find the relation between x and z.
[Sainik School Entrance Class VI, 2021]

A. $z = x$ B. $2z = x$ C. $z = 2x$ D. $z = 3x$

Q.90 A man buys a fan for Rs. 1000 and sells it at a loss of 15%. What is the selling price of the fan?
A. 725   B. 750   C. 850   D. 875

Q.91 The mean of 13 numbers is 24. If 3 is added to each number, then what will the new mean?
A. 24   B. 21   C. 27   D. 25

Q.92 A man completes $\frac{6}{11}$ of a 231 km journey by train, $\frac{3}{7}$ by bus and the rest on foot. What distance did the man walk?
A. 4 km   B. 5 km   C. 6 km   D. 10 km

Q.93 The first two common multiples of 6 and 5 are:
A. 30, 60   B. 80, 60   C. 40, 60   D. 30, 40

Q.94 Which of the following number we multiply by $\frac{5}{3}$ gives 145?
A. 97   B. 27   C. 67   D. 87

Q.95 Write decimal number for the following:
Five thousand five hundred ninety two point three five
A. 5592.35   B. 5092.35
C. 5592.035   D. 5592.0035

Q.96 Write down the place value of digit 9 in the following number.
8795
A. Hundred   B. Tens
C. Ones   D. Thousands

Q.97 Arrange the following in ascending order:
2032, 2006, 2036, 2045, 2039
A. 2032, 2006, 2036, 2039, 2045
B. 2006, 2032, 2036, 2039, 2045
C. 2006, 2032, 2039, 2036, 2045
D. 2006, 2032, 2036, 2045, 2039

Q.98 What are the two consecutive numbers after 4999?
A. 4998, 4997   B. 5000, 5001
C. 5001, 5002   D. 4998, 5001

Q.99 Convert the given number into Roman numeral:
35
A. XXXV   B. XXXVI   C. XXV   D. XV

Q.100 Five pens cost Rs. 115. How many pens can you buy in Rs. 207?

A. 9   **B.** 8   **C.** 10   **D.** 11

// Smart Answer Sheet //

Correct Indicates percentage of students who answered questions correctly.

Skipped Indicates percentage of students who skipped questions.

Q.	Ans.	Correct / Skipped	Q.	Ans.	Correct / Skipped	Q.	Ans.	Correct / Skipped	Q.	Ans.	Correct / Skipped	Q.	Ans.	Correct / Skipped
1	A	56.77 % / 1.39 %	17	A	48.69 % / 1.08 %	33	B	68.26 % / 1.4 %	49	C	53.38 % / 1.89 %	65	D	29.45 % / 3.84 %
2	C	68.13 % / 1.17 %	18	A	66.89 % / 1.81 %	34	B	53.75 % / 1.66 %	50	B	58.95 % / 1.75 %	66	B	84.16 % / 0.0 %
3	A	84.84 % / 0.0 %	19	C	88.72 % / 0.0 %	35	A	61.49 % / 1.99 %	51	C	22.04 % / 3.59 %	67	A	86.87 % / 0.0 %
4	A	83.86 % / 0.0 %	20	A	89.81 % / 0.0 %	36	A	29.04 % / 4.28 %	52	C	83.27 % / 0.0 %	68	A	78.77 % / 0.0 %
5	C	40.04 % / 1.56 %	21	B	64.92 % / 1.9 %	37	C	58.39 % / 1.21 %	53	D	55.41 % / 1.5 %	69	D	27.01 % / 3.26 %
6	C	60.91 % / 1.0 %	22	B	81.13 % / 0.0 %	38	B	12.05 % / 4.56 %	54	D	17.03 % / 4.3 %	70	A	14.45 % / 3.6 %
7	D	61.74 % / 1.54 %	23	B	87.15 % / 0.0 %	39	A	80.06 % / 0.0 %	55	B	53.88 % / 1.02 %	71	D	82.26 % / 0.0 %
8	D	48.1 % / 1.21 %	24	A	50.72 % / 1.53 %	40	C	78.05 % / 0.0 %	56	D	54.76 % / 1.9 %	72	B	42.76 % / 1.17 %
9	A	84.11 % / 0.0 %	25	A	82.61 % / 0.0 %	41	D	53.58 % / 1.82 %	57	A	66.91 % / 1.26 %	73	D	57.2 % / 1.25 %
10	A	58.55 % / 1.07 %	26	B	67.25 % / 1.13 %	42	A	12.78 % / 4.33 %	58	D	45.66 % / 1.68 %	74	D	54.17 % / 1.6 %
11	C	80.13 % / 0.0 %	27	B	54.97 % / 1.95 %	43	C	69.66 % / 1.43 %	59	B	57.97 % / 1.18 %	75	B	82.84 % / 0.0 %
12	C	63.75 % / 1.49 %	28	C	76.11 % / 0.0 %	44	C	32.88 % / 4.87 %	60	A	56.97 % / 1.2 %	76	A	32.99 % / 4.1 %
13	B	54.45 % / 1.61 %	29	C	47.63 % / 1.32 %	45	B	81.62 % / 0.0 %	61	C	89.3 % / 0.0 %	77	B	55.24 % / 1.21 %
14	A	46.22 % / 1.43 %	30	C	77.69 % / 0.0 %	46	D	54.51 % / 1.18 %	62	A	65.87 % / 1.73 %	78	D	63.3 % / 1.68 %
15	C	43.6 % / 1.21 %	31	C	66.32 % / 1.17 %	47	A	46.45 % / 1.96 %	63	C	76.83 % / 0.0 %	79	C	80.69 % / 0.0 %
16	D	64.86 % / 1.5 %	32	C	40.7 % / 1.37 %	48	D	69.43 % / 1.16 %	64	B	45.75 % / 1.64 %	80	A	77.07 % / 0.0 %

Q.	Ans.	Correct / Skipped
81	C	80.22 %
		0.0 %
82	B	11.98 %
		3.17 %
83	C	54.1 %
		1.23 %
84	B	68.67 %
		1.8 %

Q.	Ans.	Correct / Skipped
85	B	56.84 %
		1.81 %
86	D	60.36 %
		1.89 %
87	B	23.42 %
		3.35 %
88	C	52.65 %
		1.99 %

Q.	Ans.	Correct / Skipped
89	C	78.95 %
		0.0 %
90	C	46.28 %
		1.63 %
91	C	57.9 %
		1.09 %
92	C	58.72 %
		1.22 %

Q.	Ans.	Correct / Skipped
93	A	41.82 %
		1.9 %
94	D	67.24 %
		1.87 %
95	A	87.22 %
		0.0 %
96	B	79.98 %
		0.0 %

Q.	Ans.	Correct / Skipped
97	B	58.49 %
		1.65 %
98	B	87.72 %
		0.0 %
99	A	43.43 %
		1.96 %
100	A	43.88 %
		1.58 %

Performance Analysis

Avg. Score (%)	31.0%
Toppers Score (%)	63.0%
Your Score	

//Hints and Solutions//

1. 'कार्य करने वाला व्यक्ति' के लिए एक शब्द 'कार्यकर्ता' होगा। 'कार्यकर्ता' का विलोम 'आलसी' होता है।

एक शब्द	वाक्यांश
कल्पनातीत	जो कल्पना से परे हो
केन्द्राभिमुख	जो केन्द की ओर उन्मुख होता हो
खड्गहस्त	जो सदैव हाथ में खड्ग लिए रहता हो

अत: विकल्प (A) सही है।

2. 'जो स्त्री सूर्य भी न देख सकें' के लिए एक शब्द है - 'असूर्यपश्या'।

'असूर्यपश्या' शब्द में 'अ' उपसर्ग का योग है।

विदुषी - जो स्त्री विद्वान हो

अलक्ष्या - जो स्त्री अदृश्य/ अज्ञेय हो

शास्त्रज्ञा - जिस स्त्री को शास्त्रों का ज्ञान हो

अत: विकल्प (C) सही है।

3. दिए गए वाक्य "वह कानपुर जा रहा था।" में भूतकाल है।

वे शब्द जो केवल बीते समय का बोध कराते है, उसे भूतकाल कहते हैं। भूतकाल का मतलब कार्य की समाप्ति। भूतकाल के वाक्यों के अंत में सामान्यतः था, थे, थी, चुका, चुके, चुकी आते हैं।

जैसे : बस जा चुकी थी।

अत: विकल्प (A) सही है।

4. दो समान शब्दों के मध्य लगाया जाने वाला चिन्ह 'योजक चिह्न (-)' है। दो शब्दों को जोड़ने के लिए प्रयुक्त विराम चिह्न 'योजक चिह्न (-)' कहलाता है। व्याकरण में वह चिन्ह (-) जो शब्दों, पदों, उपवाक्यों आदि को जोड़ता है, योजक चिन्ह कहलाता है।

उदाहरण के लिए, लाभ-हानि, लेनी-देनी आदि।

अत: विकल्प (A) सही है।

5. जब किसी भाव या शब्द की व्याख्या करना चाहते हैं, किन्तु उस अंश को मूल वाक्य से अलग ही रखना चाहते हैं, तो कोष्ठक चिन्ह का प्रयोग किया जाता है।

नाटक या एकांकी में निर्देश के लिए कोष्ठक का प्रयोग होता है।

प्राय: बड़े [] और मझले {} कोष्ठकों का उपयोग गणित के कोष्ठक वाले सवालों को हल करने के लिए किया जाता है।

अत: विकल्प (C) सही है।

6. जो शब्द किसी व्यक्ति, वस्तु या स्थान की संपूर्ण जाति का बोध कराते हैं, उन शब्दों को जातिवाचक संज्ञा कहते हैं। यानी, जातिवाचक संज्ञा शब्दों से एक जाति के अंतर्गत आने वाले सभी व्यक्तियों, वस्तुओं व स्थानों का बोध होता है।

जैसे-

वस्तु – मोबाइल, टीवी, कम्प्यूटर, पुस्तक, कार, ट्रक आदि।

स्थान – गाँव, स्कूल, शहर, बगीचा, नदी आदि।

प्राणी – आदमी, जानवर, पशु पक्षी, गाय, लड़का आदि।

अत: विकल्प (C) सही है।

7. "घड़ो पानी पड़ना " से तात्पर्य किसी के द्वारा जाने अनजाने में किये गए उस कृत्य से जिसकी वजह से करने वाले को बहुत अधिक शर्मिंदगी उठानी पड़ती है।

वाक्य प्रयोग: चोरी करते रंगे हाथ पकड़े जाने पर मोहन पर घड़ों पानी पड़ गया।

अत: विकल्प (D) सही है।

8. "एक पन्थ दो काज" लोकोक्ति का अर्थ "एक काम से दूसरा काम हो जाना" है।

वाक्य प्रयोग: विद्यालय बंद होने से एक संग दो कार्य हुए जहां बच्चों को संक्रामक बीमारी से बचाया गया वहीं दूसरी ओर बिजली और पानी का अनावश्यक खर्च भी बचा।

अत: विकल्प (D) सही है।

9. दिए गए विकल्पों में 'से' 'करण कारक' का चिह्न है।

संज्ञा या सर्वनाम के जिस रूप की सहायता से क्रिया सम्पन्न होती हैं, उसे करण कारक कहते हैं। जैसे- रामा ने मोहन को डंडे से मारा।

अत: विकल्प (A) सही है।

10. 'संहार' का संधि विच्छेद 'सम् + हार' है, इसलिए संहार में 'सम्' उपसर्ग का प्रयोग हुआ है।

उपसर्ग ऐसे शब्दांश जो किसी शब्द के पूर्व जुड़ कर उसके अर्थ में परिवर्तन कर देते हैं या उसके अर्थ में विशेषता ला देते हैं।

उप (समीप) + सर्ग (सृष्टि करना) का अर्थ है - किसी शब्द के समीप आ कर नया शब्द बनाना।

उदाहरण:

प्र + हार = प्रहार

आ + हार = आहार

सम् + हार = संहार

अत: विकल्प (A) सही है।

11. 'सावधानी' में 'ई' प्रत्यय है।

'सावधान (मूल शब्द) + ई (प्रत्यय) = सावधानी'

'ई' प्रत्यय से बने अन्य शब्द 'हँसी, बोली, त्यागी, रेती, चालाकी' आदि हैं।

अत: विकल्प (C) सही है।

12. मेरे तो गिरधर गोपाल दूसरो न कोई। जाके सिर मोर मुकुट मेरो पति सोई ।।

दी गई पँक्तियों में श्रृंगार रस का प्रयोग किया गया है। इसका स्थायी भाव 'रति' है। इसका आलंबन 'नायक-नायिका' है। इसका उद्दीपन विभाव आलंबन का सौन्दर्य है।

अत: विकल्प (C) सही है।

13. 'उबटन' शब्द का तत्सम रूप 'उद्वर्तन' है। अन्य शब्द उबटन के तत्सम रूप नहीं है। उबटन शब्द उद्वर्तन का तद्भव रूप होता है।

अत: विकल्प (B) सही है।

14. दंश, डंक शब्द का तत्सम रूप है। युवान, जवान शब्द का तत्सम रूप है और यज्ञोपवीत, जनेऊ शब्द का तत्सम रूप है, जबकि झीना जीर्ण का तद्भव रूप है।

अत: विकल्प (A) सही है।

15. 'यशोदा' का सन्धि विच्छेद है - यश: + दा। 'यशोदा' में विसर्ग संधि है। विसर्ग के साथ स्वर अथवा व्यंजन के मिलने से जो विकार उत्पन्न होता है, उसे विसर्ग संधि कहते हैं।

जैसे- नम: + कार = नमस्कार आदि।

अतः विकल्प (C) सही है।

16. "ईश्वर तुम्हें सफलता दें।" इच्छावाचक वाक्य है। जिन वाक्यों से किसी इच्छा, आशा, आशीर्वाद या शुभकामना का बोध होता है, उन्हें इच्छावाचक वाक्य कहते हैं।

उदाहरण:

भगवान तुम्हें दीर्घायु करे।

नववर्ष मंगलमय हो।

ईश्वर करे, सब कुशल लौटें।

अत: विकल्प (D) सही है।

17. "उस मैदान में पाँच लड़के खेल रहे हैं।" वाक्य में प्रयुक्त संख्यावाचक विशेषण है। वह विशेषण, जो अपने विशेष्यों की निश्चित या अनिश्चित संख्याओं का बोध कराए, 'संख्यावाचक विशेषण' कहलाता है। दिए गए वाक्य में 'पाँच' लड़कों की निश्चित संख्या बतायी गयी है।

अत: विकल्प (A) सही है।

18. 'वह' निश्चयवाचक सर्वनाम है। जिन सर्वनाम शब्दों से किसी समीप वस्तु, व्यक्ति प्राणियों या स्थान, घटना-व्यापार की निश्चितता का बोध हो, उन शब्दों को निश्चयवाचक सर्वनाम कहा जाता है। जैसे- यह, ये, उस, इस, वे आदि।

वे शब्द जो संज्ञा के स्थान पर प्रयोग किये जाते हैं, सर्वनाम कहलाते हैं।

अत: विकल्प (A) सही है।

19. अनुरोध का अर्थ निवेदन, विनती, प्रार्थना होता है।

अनुग्रह का अर्थ कृपा, प्रसाद, ईश्वरीय कृपा होता है।

कामना का अर्थ हार्दिक इच्छा, मनोरथ होता है।

आरक्षण का अर्थ रिज़र्व करना होता है।

दिए गए वाक्य में विनती की जा रही है। इसीलिए उपरोक्त शब्दों के अर्थों के अनुसार दिए गए विकल्पों में से 'अनुरोध' उचित है।

वाक्य है,

आपसे सादर अनुरोध है कि आप हमारे समारोह में मुख्य अतिथि के रुप में पद पधारें।

अत: विकल्प (C) सही है।

20. वाक्य है,

उसे मेरी सफलता से ईर्ष्या है।

ईर्ष्या एक भावना है जो आमतौर पर विचारों व असुरक्षा की भावना को दर्शाता है।

अत: विकल्प (A) सही है।

21. मात्रा के आधार पर स्वर 3 प्रकार के होते हैं।

- हस्व स्वर: जिनके उच्चारण में कम समय लगता है। जैसे - 'अ', 'इ', 'उ', 'ऋ'।
- दीर्घ स्वर: जिनके उच्चारण में ज्यादा समय लगता है। जैसे - 'आ', 'ई', 'ऊ', 'ए', 'ऐ', 'ओ', 'औ'।
- प्लुत स्वर: जिस स्वर के उच्चारण में तीन गुना समय लगे, उसे 'प्लुत' कहते हैं। इसका चिह्न (S) है। जैसे- सुनोSS, राSSम, ओSSम्।

अत: विकल्प (B) सही है।

22. संज्ञा का एक से अधिक का बोध करानेवाला रूप, बहुवचन कहलाता है।

"आँख" का बहुवचन- "आँखें" होगा।

अत: विकल्प (B) सही है।

23. दिए गए विकल्पों में से शोकाकुल सही वर्तनी वाला शब्द है, इसका अर्थ 'शोक से व्याकुल' है। अन्य विकल्प असंगत है।

अत: विकल्प (B) सही है।

24. दिए गए शब्द 'अश्व' का पर्यायवाची शब्द 'घोड़ा' है।

दृग: आँख

अभिलाषा: इच्छा

मघवा: इंद्र

अत: विकल्प (A) सही है।

25. 'कृतघ्न' शब्द 'कृतज्ञ' का विलोम शब्द है।

शब्द: विलोम

ऋषि: संसारी

भय: निर्भय

ऋजु: वक्र

अत: विकल्प (A) सही है।

26. Given sentence 'The peon is ringing the bell.' is of Present continuous tense.

The present continuous verb tense indicates that an action or condition is happening now, frequently, and may continue into the future.

The Present Continuous Formula: Subject + helping verb [am, is, are] + verb+ing form + object

Example:

Mary is going to a new school.

The children are growing up quickly.

Hence, the correct option is (B).

27. Given sentence 'It rains all year round here.' is of Present indefinite tense.

Present indefinite tense can be defined as the action that is done in the present however there is no definite time limit given of it being accomplished. Present indefinite tense can also be used to express true events, near future, habit, nature, etc.

Example:

Shally loves chocolate cake.

Adam eats an apple every day.

Hence, the correct option is (B).

28. 'Dog' is not an adjective. Dog is a common noun.

Adjectives are words that describe the qualities or states of being of nouns: beautiful, enormous, doglike, silly, yellow, fun, fast.

Hence, the correct option is (C).

29. Correct sentence:

Ram as well as his brothers is coming today.

In a sentence, the verb is used according to person and number.

If the main subject is followed by the following words/phrases, the verb will conform to the 1st subject:

As well as, and not, in addition to, with/along with/together with, like/unlike, except, nothing but, etc. The verb 'were/are' seems correct due to the noun 'brothers' but the actual subject in the given sentence is 'Ram'.

Hence, the correct option is (C).

30. Of is a preposition that indicates relationships between other words, such as belonging, things made of other things, things that contain other things, or a point of reckoning.

The sentence is,

He picked up a piece of wood.

Hence, the correct option is (C).

31. The sentence is,

Is there a fitness centre near your house?

In the given sentence, 'fitness centre' is an indefinite singular countable noun. The indefinite article 'a' is grammatically and contextually correct. The indefinite article (a, an) is used before a noun that is general or when its identity is not known.

Hence, the correct option is (C).

32. The sentence is,

He has hardly read the book.

Article 'the' is a definite article used before a noun to indicate that the identity of the noun is known to the reader. In the given sentence "book" is a noun, therefore usage of 'the' is grammatically and contextually correct.

Hence, the correct option is (C).

33. "An" is used before words that begin with vowels.

Then the sentence is,

Give me an apple.

Hence, the correct option is (B).

34. There are a few adjectives that are accompanied by 'to', like, senior, junior, superior, inferior, preferable, prefer, elder.

The sentence is,

He is superior to me.

Hence, the correct option is (B).

35. 'From' is used to talk about origins, sources, and starting points and can be used to talk about distance. From is also used after specific adjectives and verbs.

The sentence is,

We were prevented from seeing the prisoner.

Hence, the correct option is (A).

36. The sentence is,

I have been to the doctor, whose name figured in the Times of India.

Article 'the' is a definite article used before a noun to indicate that the identity of the noun is known to the reader. In the given sentence "doctor" is a noun and when we use 'the', it means a "particular doctor" that we may be referring to.

Hence, the correct option is (A).

37. All the options, except option (C) has the pairs where persons do not denote masculine or feminine of same class or type.

Only option (C) has a pair where boy and girl belong to masculine and feminine genders respectively.

Hence, the correct option is (C).

38. Correct Sentence: We are planning to go out for a picnic tomorrow.

From the given sentence one thing is clear that an action is going to take place soon or in the near future. The "planning" is still in the process which means that it is a continuous process.

When we refer to an action which is in continuation, the tense will be present continuous (am/is/are + present participle). Thus the usage of "planning" is grammatically and contextually correct.

Hence, the correct option is (B).

39. 'Oops!' is an interjection used in the above statement which is used when a small mistake or slight accident has happened. They are usually followed by an exclamation mark (!)

Whereas other options are not the form of interjections.

Hence, the correct option is (A).

40. Generally, gender is of 4 types, the four genders of noun are masculine, feminine, common, and neuter.

Masculine- Father, Boy, Uncle, Husband etc. are example of masculine gender.

Feminine- Mother, Girl, Aunt, Wife etc. are example of feminine gender.

Common- Animal, Artist, Children, Servant, Enemy, Pupil, Neighbor, Minister, Doctor, Employee, Singer, Peon, Musician, Dancer etc. are example of commongender.

Neuter- Table, Hair, City etc. are example of neuter gender.

Hence, the correct option is (C).

41. Rendezvos is the misspelt word. Correct spelling is Rendezvous.

Rendezvous: an agreement to be present at a specified time and place

Hence, the correct option is (D).

42. The logic is:

Ignominy : Disloyalty → Ignominy is the result of disloyalty.

Similarly,

Fame : Heroism → Fame is the result of Heroism.

Just as a disloyal person gets ignominy or disgrace, a heroic person gets fame.

Hence, the correct option is (A).

43. The correct sentence is 'Please give me a pen.'

A pronoun is a word that is used instead of a noun or noun phrase. Pronouns refer to either a noun that has already been mentioned or to a noun that does not need to be named specifically.

Example: He, She, I, Me, They, You

Hence the correct option is (C).

44. One word substitute is Altruistic.

Altruistic: a person who loves everybody, showing a disinterested and selfless concern for the well-being of others, unselfish.

Cosmopolitan: including people from many different countries

Fratricide: the killing of one's brother or sister

Aristocrat: nobleman

Hence, the correct option is (C).

45. The comma is used to separate short co-ordinate clauses of a compound sentence.

For example: "She came, she stopped, she conquered."

Hence, the correct option is (B).

46. The most appropriate synonym of the given word 'Defer' is 'Postpone'.

Defer : Put off (an action or event) to a later time; postpone.

Postpone : Cause or arrange for (something) to take place at a time later than that first scheduled.

Indifferent : Having no particular interest or sympathy, unconcerned.

Defy : Openly resist or refuse to obey.

Differ : Be unlike or dissimilar.

Hence, the correct option is (D).

47. The most appropriate synonym of the given word 'Alacrity' is 'Briskness'.

Alacrity : Brisk and cheerful readiness.

Briskness : Active, fast, and energetic.

Fear : An unpleasant emotion caused by the belief that someone or something is dangerous, likely to cause pain, or a threat.

Frankness : Open, honest, and direct in speech or writing, especially when dealing with unpalatable matters.

Alarm : An anxious awareness of danger, warning, alert, caveat, caution, admonition.

Hence, the correct option is (A).

48. The most appropriate antonym of the given word 'Prosperous' is 'Impecunious'.

Prosperous : Successful in material terms, flourishing financially, wealthy.

Impecunious : Having little or no money.

Adverse : Preventing success or development, harmful, unfavorable.

Advanced : Far on or ahead in development or progress.

Retarded : Less advanced in mental, physical, or social development than is usual for one's age.

Hence, the correct option is (D).

49. The most appropriate antonym of the given word 'Superiority' is 'Inferiority'.

Superiority : Excellence, eminence, transcendence, mastery.

Inferiority : The condition of being lower in status or quality than another or others.

Seniority : The fact or state of being older or higher in rank or status than someone else.

Juniority : For or denoting young or younger people.

Urbanity : Urban life.

Hence, the correct option is (C).

50. The given set of letters: SEPARATE

The only meaningful word that can be made using the given letters is 'TEARS'.

So, Tears is the correct answer.

Hence, the correct option is (B).

51. The Nobel Memorial Prize in Economic Sciences was awarded to Ben S Bernanke, the former chair of the US Federal Reserve, Douglas W Diamond and Philip H Dybvig of USA for research into banks and financial crises.

As per the committee, 'the laureates have provided a foundation for our modern understanding of why banks are needed, why they're vulnerable, and what to do about it'.

Hence, the correct option is (C).

52. The National Association of Software and Services Companies (NASSCOM), has appointed Krishnan Ramanujam, President, Enterprise Growth Group at TCS, as its Chairperson for the period 2022-23. NASSCOM also announced the appointment of Anant Maheshwari, President of Microsoft India as its Vice-Chairperson for 2022-23.

Hence, the correct option is (C).

53. To compensate for the damage caused to the crops due to adverse weather and natural calamities, Haryana has launched the Mukhya Mantri Bagwani Bima scheme portal in 2022 with an initial corpus of Rs 10 crore for the scheme. The scheme compensates a sum of Rs 30,000 per acre for vegetables and Spices and Rs 40,000 per acre for fruits, which will be compensated to the farmers upon claim via four categories such as 25 per cent, 50 per cent, 75 per cent and 100 per cent based on the survey. The farmer's contribution will be only 5 per cent of the insured amount i.e., Rs 750 per acre for vegetables and Spices and Rs 1000 per acre for fruits.

Hence, the correct option is (D).

54. Iconic French filmmaker Jean-Luc Godard passed away at the age of 91 in Switzerland.

He revolutionized cinema with his debut film 'Breathless' in 1960 and remains one of the world's most celebrated and provocative directors.

He started his career as a film critic in the 1950s.

In December 2007, he was honored with the Lifetime Achievement Award by the European Film Academy.

Hence, the correct option is (D).

55. Madya Pradesh has won "Ranji Trophy 2022" Title by defeating Mumbai by six wickets in the final at the M. Chinnaswamy Stadium in Bengaluru. Mumbai and Uttar Pradesh played the second semi-final which was a draw and it led to the advancing of Mumbai in the final due to their first-innings lead.

Hence, the correct option is (B).

56. In Uttar Pradesh, the cow slaughter prevention act was passed in 1955.

- The objective of the act was to stop cow slaughtering in the state.
- In order to promote cattle rearing in the state, gauseva aayog was set up in the year 1999.
- Uttar Pradesh is an agricultural state.
- It has a vast resource of livestock and poultry.
- It plays a vital role in improving the socio-economic conditions of rural masses.
- Around 59% population of the state depends on agriculture and allied activities.
- These allies' activities consist of animal husbandries like poultry farming, dairy farming, and fisheries.

Hence, the correct option is (D).

57. There are 18 divisions in Uttar Pradesh.

- Uttar Pradesh was formed on 1 April 1937 as United province.
- It got its statehood on 26 January 1950 and renamed as Uttar Pradesh.
- Uttar Pradesh's capital is Lucknow.
- Smt. Anandiben Patel is the current Governor of Uttar Pradesh.
- Uttar Pradesh's Chief Minister is Yogi Adityanath.
- Uttar Pradesh's official language is Hindi.
- Uttar Pradesh's area stretches 2,40,928 Square km.
- Uttar Pradesh is the 4th largest in terms of area in India.

- Uttar Pradesh has 75 districts.

Hence, the correct option is (A).

58. The Hathnikund barrage irrigation project is located in the Saharanpur district of Uttar Pradesh.

- It is a joint project of 5 states namely Delhi, Uttar Pradesh, Himachal Pradesh, Haryana, and Rajasthan.
- This barrage has been constructed in 1872 in Saharanpur on the Yamuna River.
- Due to destruction by the heavy flood of 1978, the central government planned a pact among these 5 states on the demand of Yamuna River water on 12th May 199.
- Thus, the construction of the new barrage was started in 1994 and completed in 1999.

Hence, the correct option is (D).

59. The farming of Soybean is mainly in the Bundelkhand region in Uttar Pradesh.

- The other major crops grown in the Bundelkhand region are rice, jwar, maize, bajra, kodo, kutki, gram, tuar, mung, urad, alsi, til, mungfali, jute and vegetables.
- Rice is the principal crop of the Baghelkhand Region.
- The region grew wheat, corn (maize), and gram (chickpeas).
- Mandarin, Acidlime, Mosambi, Aonla, Pomegranate, Mango Ber, Chiku, Papaya, Turmeric, Chillies, Coriander, Ajwine are the crops mainly recommended to the Vindhya Region.

Hence, the correct option is (B).

60. Uranium is found in the Lalitpur district of Uttar Pradesh.

- This zone is 300 meters wide and contains 0.01 to 0.09% uranium.
- Bauxite is also found in Lalitpur.

Other Minerals in Uttar Pradesh:

Minerals	District
Dolomite	Bari (Sonbhadra), Banda
Andalusite	Sonbhadra, Mirzapur
Ocher	Banda
Calcite	Mirzapur
Pyrites	Sonbhadra

Hence, the correct option is (A).

61. The term scissors are related to the sport of wrestling. This is a wrestling hold in which you wrap your legs around the opponent's body or head and put your feet together and squeeze.

Hence, the correct option is (C).

62. The Germany–Poland border the state border between Poland and Germany, is currently the Oder–Neisse line. It has a total length of 467 km (290 mi) and has been in place since 1945.

Hence, the correct option is (A).

63. Genetics is the study of heredity and the variation of inherited characteristics.

Cytology is the branches of biology and medicine concerned with the structure and function of plant and animal cells.

In biology, evolution is the change in the characteristics of a species over several generations and relies on the process of natural selection.

Physiology is the branch of biology that deals with the normal functions of living organisms and their parts.

Hence, the correct option is (C).

64. World Braille Day is celebrated on 4th January. Louis Braille was born on this day. It was Louis Braille who gave birth to the Braille script. Blind, blind or partially blind people can read through this script. It was decided to celebrate the birthday of Louis Braille, the inventor of the Braille script, as World Braille Day in his honour.

Hence, the correct option is (B).

65. Hampi was the capital of the medieval Hindu kingdom of the Vijayanagara Empire. It is located on the banks of the Tungabhadra River in the present-day Karnataka state.

Hence, the correct option is (D).

66. Vitamin B deficiency causes Beriberi. Beriberi symptoms include:

- Shortness of breath during physical activity
- Waking up short of breath
- Rapid heart rate
- Swollen lower legs

Hence, the correct option is (B).

67. An emulsion is a mixture of two or more liquids that are normally immiscible (unblendable). The emulsion is used when both the dispersed and the continuous phase are liquid. Examples of emulsions include vinaigrettes, milk, and some cutting fluids for metalworking.
Hence, the correct option is (A).

68. Nylon is a generic designation for a family of synthetic polymers, more specifically aliphatic or semi-aromatic polyamides. They can be melt-processed into fibers, films, or shapes.
Hence, the correct option is (A).

69. Currency "Dong" belongs to Vietnam.

Country	Currency	Capital
Cambodia	Cambodian riel	Phnom Penh
Laos	Lao kip	Vientiane
Myanmar	Burmese kyat	Naypyitaw/Naypyidaw
Vietnam	**Dong**	**Hanoi**

Hence, the correct option is (D).

70. The capital of Japan is Tokyo.

Tokyo is a very famous city situated under Japan, which was made the capital of Japan under the year 1868. About 9.5 million people live under Tokyo, mainly people who follow the culture of Japan live here. Tokyo, the capital of Japan, has the world's largest fish market.

Hence, the correct option is (A).

71. Former petroleum secretary Tarun Kapoor had been appointed as an advisor to Prime Minister Narendra Modi, according to a government order issued. Kapoor, a 1987-batch IAS officer of the Himachal Pradesh cadre, superannuated as the secretary of the ministry of petroleum and natural gas.

Hence, the correct option is (D).

72. The Chilika Lake is located in Odisha. The Chilika Lake is a brackish water lake and a shallow lagoon with estuarine character spread across the districts of Puri, Khurda and Ganjam in the state of Odisha in eastern India. It is fed by several streams and flows east into the Bay of Bengal. Chilika Lake is 70 km long and 30 km wide.

Hence, the correct option is (B).

73. Teak, Sal, Sandalwood are important species of Tropical Deciduous Forests.

Tropical Deciduous Forests:

- These are the most widespread forests in India.
- They are also called the monsoon forests because the trees in these forests shed their leaves during the dry season and re-grow during the monsoon.
- They spread over regions that receive rainfall between 70-200 cm.
- The average temperature of Tropical Deciduous forests is 30°C.
- The humidity in these forests lies in the range of 80-90 percent.
- The prime feature of these forests as trees shed their leaves in the dry season and grow back leaf in rainy seasons.

Hence, the correct option is (D).

74. Lakshadweep is the Union Territories of India which is the smallest in the geographical area. Lakshadweep is India's smallest Union Territory. Our country, Indian consists of 28 states and 8 union territories.

- The Kavaratti is the capital of the Union Territory Lakshadweep in India.
- India's smallest Union Territory Lakshadweep is an archipelago consisting of 36 islands with an area of 36 sq km^2 only.
- The population on this island is approximately 65,000.

Hence, the correct option is (D).

75. The Buddhist text Majjhimnikaya is written in Pali language. Majjhimnikaya is a Buddhist scripture. It is the second of the five Buddhist bodies of the Suttapitaka. It was composed between the third century BC to the second century BC.

Hence, the correct option is (B).

76. Given:

$$1888 \div 32 \div 8 =?$$

$$? = \frac{1888}{32} \div 8$$

$$? = 59 \div 8$$

$$? = \frac{59}{8}$$

$$? = 7.375$$

Hence, the correct option is (A).

77. Given:

$$4848 \times 222 =?$$

? = 1,076,256

Hence, the correct option is (B).

78. Given:

$$8888 \div 22 =?$$

? = 404

Hence, the correct option is (D).

79. Follow the BODMAS rule:

0.06 × ? × 0.216 = 1.944

⇒ ? × 0.01296 = 1.944

$$\Rightarrow ? = \frac{1.944}{0.01296} = 150$$

∴ ? = 150

Hence, the correct option is (C).

80. Given:

$$788 \times 546 =?$$

? = 430,240

Hence, the correct option is (A).

81. Factors of 18 and 36:

$$18 = 2 \times 3 \times 3$$

$$36 = 2 \times 2 \times 3 \times 3$$

Common factor $= 2 \times 3 \times 3$

$$\therefore \text{HCF} = 18$$

So, the HCF of 18 and 36 is 18.

Hence, the correct option is (C).

82. As we know,

Area of circle $= \pi r^2$

Circumference of circle $= 2\pi r$

Perimeter of square $= 4a$

Area of square $= a^2$

Where,

$r =$ radius of circle and

$a =$ side of the square

Let the radius of the circle is r and the side of the square is a.

Then the area of a circle

$$A = \pi r^2 = 3.14 r^2 \text{ .... (1)}$$

According to the question,

Circumference of a circle $=$ perimeter of the square

$$\Rightarrow 2\pi r = 4a$$

$$\Rightarrow a = \frac{\pi r}{2}$$

So, the area of square

$$a^2 = \left(\frac{\pi r}{2}\right)^2$$

$$\Rightarrow a^2 = 2.46 r^2 \text{ ...(2)}$$

From the equation (1) and (2), we can say that, Area of circle $>$ Area of the square.

Hence, the correct option is (B).

83. Given,

Area of circle, $A = 24.64 \ m^2$

As we know,

Area of circle $A = \pi R^2$

$$R^2 = \left(\frac{24.64}{22} \times 7\right)$$

$$R^2 = 7.84$$

$$R = \sqrt{7.84}$$

$$R = 2.8 \ m$$

$$\therefore \text{Circumference} = \left(2 \times \frac{22}{7} \times 2.8\right)$$

$$= 17.60 \ \text{m}$$

Hence, the correct option is (C).

84. Given,

P = Rs. 900

R = 5% per annum

T = 3 years 4 months = $\frac{40}{12}$ years = $\frac{10}{3}$ years

S.I. = $\frac{PRT}{100}$

$$= \frac{(900 \times 5 \times 10)}{(100 \times 3)}$$

= Rs. 150

Hence, the correct option is (B).

85. Given,

3x + 4 (x+3) = 26

3x + 4x + 12 = 26

7x = 26 - 12

7x = 14

x = 2

Hence, the correct option is (B).

86. By using prime factorization method we are going to find square root of given number,

441 = 3 × 147

= 3 × 3 × 49

= 3 × 3 × 7 × 7

$= 3^2 \times 7^2$

$\sqrt{441} = \sqrt{3^2 \times 7^2}$

$\sqrt{441} = 3 \times 7$

$\therefore \sqrt{441} = 21$

Hence, the correct option is (D).

87. The given equation is,

$$3x^2 - 2x + 4 = 0$$

On comparing the above equation with $ax^2 + bx + c = 0,$

$$a = 3, b = -2, c = 4$$

Discriminant,

$$b^2 - 4ac = (-2)^2 - 4 \times 3 \times 4$$

$$= 4 - 48$$

$$= -44 \text{ (Negative)}$$

So, the roots are imaginary.
Hence, the correct option is (B).

88. The logic is as:

22 + 24 = 46

46 + 48 = 94

94 + 96 = 190

190 + 192 = 382

Thus, 382 is the next number in the series.

Hence, the correct option is (C).

89. Given:

$$x\% \text{ of } y = 100$$

$$\Rightarrow y \times \frac{x}{100} = 100 \quad \text{.....(i)}$$

$$\Rightarrow \frac{y}{100} = \frac{100}{x}$$

$$y\% \text{ of } z = 200$$

$$z \times \frac{y}{100} = 200 \quad \text{.....(ii)}$$

Put the value of $\left(\frac{y}{100}\right)$ in equation (ii) from the equation (i),

$$z \times \left(\frac{100}{x}\right) = 200$$

$$\Rightarrow \frac{z}{x} = 2$$

$$\Rightarrow z = 2x$$

Hence, the correct option is (C).

90. Given:

Cost Price of the fan is Rs.1000.

Loss percentage is 15%.

As we know,

$$\text{Loss percentage} = \frac{\text{Loss}}{\text{Cost Price}} \times 100$$

$$15 = \frac{\text{Loss}}{1000} \times 100$$

Therefore, Loss = Rs. 150

As we know,

Loss = Cost Price – Selling Price

So, Selling Price = Cost Price – Loss

= 1000 – 150

Selling Price = Rs. 850

Hence, the correct option is (C).

91. Given,

Mean of 13 numbers is 24.

Now 3 added to each number

$$\text{Mean} = \frac{\text{Total of observation}}{\text{Number of observation}}$$

$$\Rightarrow 24 = \frac{\text{total of observation}}{13}$$

⇒ Total of observation = 13 × 24

⇒ Total of observation = 312

Now 3 is added to all 13 numbers.

⇒ New total = 312 + 13(3)

$\Rightarrow$ New total = 312 + 39

$\Rightarrow$ New total = 351

New mean $= \dfrac{351}{13}$

$\Rightarrow$ New mean = 27

$\therefore$ The new mean will be 27.

Hence, the correct option is (C).

92. Given,

A man completes $\dfrac{6}{11}$ of a 231 km journey by train, $\dfrac{3}{7}$ by bus and the rest on foot.

Distance covered by train $= \left(\dfrac{6}{11}\right) \times 231$

= 126 km

Distance covered by bus $= \left(\dfrac{3}{7}\right) \times 231$

= 99 km

$\therefore$ Distance covered by walk = 231 −(126 + 99) = 6 km

Hence, the correct option is (C).

93. Given:

6 and 5

Multiples of 5 = 5, 10, 15, 20, 25, 30, 35, 40, 45, 50, 55, 60

Multiples of 6 = 6, 12, 18, 24, 30, 36, 48, 54, 60

So we can conclude that the common multiples of 6 and 5 are 30, 60.

Hence, the correct option is (A).

94. Let the number be x.

According to the question,

$\dfrac{5}{3} \times x = 145$

We multiply the above equation by $\dfrac{3}{5}$ on both side.

$\Rightarrow x = 145 \times \dfrac{3}{5}$

$\Rightarrow x = 29 \times 3$

$\Rightarrow x = 87$

$\therefore$ The number is 87.

Hence, the correct option is (D).

95. Given,

Five thousand five hundred ninety two point three five

In the decimal number,

5592.35

Hence, the correct option is (A).

96. Given,

8795

Ones digit = 5

Tens digit =9

Hundred digit =7

Thousands digit = 8

Hence, the correct option is (B).

97. Given,

2032, 2006, 2036, 2045, 2039

In ascending order,

2006, 2032, 2036, 2039, 2045

Hence, the correct option is (B).

98. Two consecutive numbers after 4999 are, (4999+1), (4999+2)

= 5000, 5001

Hence, the correct option is (B).

99. We can write,

30 = 10 + 10 + 10 + 5

Roman numeral of 10 = X

Roman numeral of 10 = V

So roman numeral of 35 = XXXV

Hence, the correct option is (A).

100. Given,

Rs. 115 is cost of 5 pens.

Rs. 1 is cost of $= \dfrac{5}{115}$ pens

$\therefore$ Rs. 207 is cost of $= \dfrac{207 \times 5}{115}$

$= \dfrac{207}{23} = 9$ pens

Hence, the correct option is (A).

Hindi

Ques (1-2):निर्देश: वाक्यांश के लिए एक शब्द का चयन कीजिये।

Q.1 आवश्यकता से अधिक वर्षा

A. अत्वृष्टि   B. अल्पवृष्टि   C. ओलावृष्टि   D. अतिवृष्टि

Q.2 आड़ या परदे के लिये रथ या पालकी को ढकनेवाला कपड़ा

A. अंडज   B. आगत   C. ओहार   D. औरस

Q.3 निम्नलिखित वाक्य में कौन सा वाक्य आसन्न भूत काल है?

A. महेश अभी -अभी गया है
B. आप लोगों ने खाना खा लिया
C. मैं आया हूँ
D. उस समय मैं सोया होऊँगा

Q.4 किसी के द्वारा कहे गए वचन को ज्यों का त्यों लिखने के लिए किस चिह्न का प्रयोग किया जाता है?

A. अवतरण चिह्न   B. उद्धरण चिह्न
C. कोष्ठक चिह्न   D. विवरण चिह्न

Q.5 मुंबई कौन सी संज्ञा है?

A. जातिवाचक   B. भाववाचक
C. व्यक्तिवाचक   D. एक देश

Q.6 "होनहार बिरवान के होत चीकने पात" कहावत का अर्थ है:

A. दूर से सब चीजें अच्छी लगना
B. बचपन में सुन्दर होना
C. बड़ा होशियार बच्चा
D. बचपन से ही बड़प्पन का संकेत

Q.7 निम्नलिखित चार मुहावरे में से तीन मुहावरे सही हैं शेष एक गलत मुहावरे का चयन कीजिए।

A. खरी मजूरी   B. खाक छानना
C. चिकना घड़ा रहना   D. घर फूंक तमाशा देखना।

Q.8 'को' और 'के लिए' कारक के चिह्न है:

A. संप्रदान कारक   B. अपादान कारक
C. कर्म कारक   D. करण कारक

Q.9 किस शब्द में 'इन' प्रत्यय का प्रयोग सही नहीं हुआ है?

[Haryana Primary Teacher (PRT), 2020]

A. कुँजड़िन   B. नागिन   C. नाईन   D. ईसाइन

Q.10 'आंजनेय' शब्द में प्रयुक्त प्रत्यय है:

[Haryana Primary Teacher (PRT), 2020]

A. एय   B. य   C. नेय   D. ऐय

Q.11 रस कितने प्रकार के होते हैं?

A. चार   B. छह   C. नौ   D. आठ

Q.12 'पसीना' शब्द का तत्सम क्या होता है?

A. पशीना   B. प्रस्विन्न   C. पश्मीना   D. पषीना

Q.13 कौन-सा तत्सम शब्द नहीं है?

A. अज्ञानी   B. एला   C. उष्ट्र   D. कपूर

Q.14 'व्यवहार' का सही संधि-विच्छेद है:

[UPSSSC Junior Assistant, 2020]

A. वि + अव + हार   B. व्यव + हार
C. व्य + वहार   D. व्य + व + हार

Q.15 "रात होते ही तारे निकल आये" कौन सा वाक्य है?

A. मिश्र वाक्य   B. सरल वाक्य
C. संयुक्त सूचक वाक्य   D. इच्छा सूचक वाक्य

Q.16 निर्देश: निम्नलिखित वाक्य में क्रियाविशेषण बताइये।
कछुआ (धीरे धीरे) चलता है।

A. परिमाण वाचक क्रिया विशेषण
B. रीतिवाचक क्रिया विशेषण
C. स्थानवाचक क्रियाविशेषण
D. काल वाचक क्रिया विशेषण

Q.17 "कोई" शब्द किस सर्वनाम का उदाहरण है?

A. निश्चय वाचक   B. अनिश्चय वाचक
C. निजवाचक   D. प्रश्न वाचक

Q.18 जो स्वर केवल मुख से उच्चारित होता है, उसे क्या कहते हैं?

A. अनुनासिक   B. निरनुनासिक
C. दीर्घ   D. हस्व

Q.19 निम्नलिखित में से कौन सा शब्द 'आँख' का बहुवचन होगा?

A. आँखों   B. आँखें   C. अँखियाँ   D. आँखी

Q.20 नीचे दिए गए विकल्पों में से शुद्ध वर्तनी का चयन कीजिए ।

A. प्रतियोगिता   B. प्रतियोगिता
C. प्रतियोगिता   D. प्रतीयोगिता

Q.21 'सन्धि' का विलोम शब्द है:

[UPPSC Staff Nurse, 2017]

A. उपसंधि   B. शत्रुता   C. विग्रह   D. वैमनस्य

Q.22 इनमें से 'मछली' किसका पर्यायवाची है?

A. कबूतर   B. शफरी   C. काला   D. आकाश

Ques (23-24):निर्देश: रिक्त स्थान को भरने के लिए उपयुक्त शब्द का चयन करें।

Q.23 बाहर के देशों में वस्तुओं को भेजने के लिए हिंदी में __________ कहते हैं।

A. पर्याप्त   B. साकार
C. निर्यात   D. इनमें से कोई नहीं

Q.24 आज हमारे देश में बनने वाली अधिकांश फिल्म बाजारू बन कर रह गई है। उनका उद्देश्य सस्ती लोकप्रियता प्राप्त करना तथा __________ कमाना मात्र रह गया है।

A. गर्व   B. पैसा   C. अधिकार   D. प्रचार

Q.25 'मुझे आज बाहर घूमने का मन हो रहा है।' यह वाक्य किस प्रकार का वाक्य है?

A. आज्ञा वाचक वाक्य   B. संकेत वाचक वाक्य

C. इच्छा वाचक वाक्य   **D.** विस्मयादिबोधक वाक्य

English

Ques (26-33):Direction: Select the most appropriate option to fill in the blank.

Q.26 The teacher, as well as the students, ________ responsible for the agitation in the school campus.
A. are   **B.** is   **C.** shall   **D.** were

Q.27 Nanny died last week. She ______ from cancer for some time.
A. suffering   **B.** is suffering
C. had been suffering   **D.** suffers

Q.28 Susan watched a movie at the theatre ________ a friend.
A. of   **B.** on   **C.** in   **D.** with

Q.29 She often goes for a walk ___ night.
A. on   **B.** in   **C.** for   **D.** at

Q.30 I ______ to take a vacation from the office, tomorrow.
A. will be plan   **B.** planned
C. am planning   **D.** will plan

Q.31 The author's wife was a good editor, ______ being a great writer herself.
A. besides   **B.** by   **C.** into   **D.** on

Q.32 If it ______, we will cancel the party.
A. were raining   **B.** rain
C. rains   **D.** rained

Q.33 Nobody but ________ is responsible for this fiasco.
A. I   **B.** me
C. mine   **D.** Both 'I' and 'me'

Q.34 Select the wrongly spelt word.
[SSC Sub Inspector (CPO), 2020]
A. Custody   **B.** Custom   **C.** Cursory   **D.** Curtesy

Q.35 Which is indefinite pronoun in sentence "I saw someone running in street."
A. I   **B.** in   **C.** someone   **D.** saw

Q.36 Direction: Select single word or phrase which means most nearly the same as the given phrase.
An accomplished musician
A. Virtuoso   **B.** Dilettante
C. Termagant   **D.** Agnostic

Q.37 Direction: Identify the tense used in the following sentence.
I will give him a gift.
A. Simple Present   **B.** Simple Past
C. Present Continuous   **D.** Simple Future

Q.38 Which of the following words is not an adjective?
A. Miserly   **B.** Historical
C. Momentary   **D.** None of these

Q.39 Direction: Choose the correct option to fill in the blank with the help of the hint in the brackets.
We ____ respect our elders. (duty/obligation)
A. should   **B.** could   **C.** will   **D.** would

Q.40 Choose the word which is the antonym of the FLEXIBLE.
A. Rigid   **B.** Flatter
C. Bending   **D.** Disregard

Q.41 Choose the synonym of the FOSTERING.
A. Safeguarding   **B.** Neglecting
C. Ignoring   **D.** Nurturing

Q.42 Direction: Select the most appropriate synonym of the given word.
Deepen
A. Soothe   **B.** Neutralize
C. Relieve   **D.** Intensify

Q.43 Choose the word opposite in meaning to the Height.
A. Length   **B.** Depth   **C.** Width   **D.** Breadth

Q.44 Direction: Identify the interjection in the sentence given below.
Hey! You left me behind.
A. Hey   **B.** You   **C.** left   **D.** behind

Q.45 Direction: Change the gender of the underlined noun and rewrite the sentence.
My father is sleeping.
A.   My sister is sleeping.
B.   My aunt is sleeping.
C.   My cousin is sleeping.
D.   My mother is sleeping.

Q.46 Direction: Choose the meaningful word from the given jumbled words.
YRTNUOC
A. Country   **B.** Conutry   **C.** Conutyr   **D.** Cotyrnu

Q.47 Select the grammatically correct sentence from among the given options.
A.   She replied, "Amazing!"
B.   She replied, "Amazing!
C.   She replied, Amazing!"
D.   She replied, "Amazing"

Q.48 Select the correctly punctuated sentence.
A.   "Get out, of the car. Ordered the policeman."
B.   "Get out of the car!" ordered the policeman.
C.   Get out of the car, Ordered the policeman.
D.   "Get out of the car?" ordered the policeman.

Q.49 Direction: Fill in the blanks with the most appropriate option.
I feel very ______ in some of our ________ meetings.
A. bored, bored   **B.** board, board
C. bored, board   **D.** board, bored

Q.50 Direction: In the following question, select the related word from the given alternatives.

Blissful : Sad:: Melancholy : ?

A. Thoughtfulness
B. Unrelenting
C. Ecstasy
D. Promising

General Studies

Q.51 Special ASEAN-India Foreign Ministers' Meeting (SAIFMM) will be held on the 16th and 17th June 2022 in ______________.

A. New Delhi, India
B. Islamabad, Pakistan
C. Dhaka, Bangladesh
D. Colombo, Sri Lanka

Q.52 Union Minister Sarbananda Sonowal on 28th Oct 2022 inaugurated the 'Ayush Utsav' in which of the following region?

A. Uttrakhand
B. Himachal Pradesh
C. Uttar Pradesh
D. Kashmir

Q.53 Which of the following districts belongs to the Bundelkhand region of Uttar Pradesh?

[UP Police Constable, 2018]

A. Fatehpur
B. Jaunpur
C. Mahoba
D. Shravasti

Q.54 The area of Uttar Pradesh is approximately ______ of the total area of the country.

[UP Police Constable, 2018]

A. 13.5%
B. 9.4%
C. 8.4%
D. 7.30%

Q.55 In which year was it made legally binding to use Hindi in all official works in Uttar Pradesh?

[UP Police Constable, 2018]

A. 1947
B. 1957
C. 1968
D. 1951

Q.56 Which is the main folk song of Uttar Pradesh?

A. Dhamar
B. Birha
C. Tappa
D. Qawwaali

Q.57 The ______ is a colourful and mesmeric fair which is held a few days after Holi, every year in Meerut in Uttar Pradesh.

[UP Police Constable, 2018]

A. Kumbh Mela
B. Nauchandi Mela
C. Ganga Mela
D. Sikri Mela

Q.58 Where is the Tulsi Manas temple located?

A. Ayodhya
B. Allahabad
C. Varanasi
D. Agra

Q.59 Which one of the following countries is called the 'country of winds'?

[UPSC NDA, 2020]

A. India
B. China
C. Denmark
D. Germany

Q.60 In which of the following insects, a pigment called luciferin is found?

A. Housefly
B. Firefly
C. Sandfly
D. Fruitfly

Q.61 Which of the following is an example of binary fertilizer?

A. MOP
B. Ammonia
C. Urea
D. DAP

Q.62 What is the capital of Moldova?

A. Chişinău
B. Bucharest
C. Minsk
D. Kyiv

Q.63 A deep valley characterized by a steep step-like slope is known as:

A. U-shaped valley
B. Blind valley
C. Gorge
D. Canyon

Q.64 India has decided to set up a Fast Track Mechanism to resolve issues faced by Indian businesses and investors in ______ in October 2022.

A. Australia
B. Japan
C. Canada
D. United Arab Emirates (UAE)

Q.65 In which Indian city is Panch Mahal Located?

[Allahabad High Court Review Officer (RO), 2019]

A. Lucknow
B. Golconda
C. Agra
D. Fatehpur Sikri

Q.66 India's first marine national park is located in:

A. Gulf of Kutch
B. Bay of Bengal
C. Arabian Sea
D. Gulf of Khambhat

Q.67 Which of the following systems in man is affected by the bite of the cobra?

A. Digestive system
B. Nervous system
C. Excretory system
D. Circulatory system

Q.68 The alluvial soil of India is generally rich in:

A. Lime
B. Nitrogen
C. Phosphorus
D. Humus

Q.69 The first Cricket player to be awarded Rajiv Gandhi Khel Ratna award is ______.

A. Sachin Tendulkar
B. Rahul Dravid
C. Mahendra Singh Dhoni
D. Kapil Dev

Q.70 Who defeated Humayun in the battle of Chausa in 1539?

[Territorial Army Officer, 2019]

A. Sher Shah
B. Bahadur Shah
C. Rana Sanga
D. None of these

Q.71 Rashid Khan born in Sahaswan, Uttar Pradesh, was awarded Padma Bhushan 2022 in which field?

A. Science
B. Literature
C. Art
D. Social Work

Q.72 Who launched India's first virtual school for students in August 2022?

A. Arvind Kejriwal
B. Shivraj Singh Chauhan

C. Amit Shah

D. Jitendra Singh

Q.73 Which of the following is the outermost range of the Himalayas?

A. Pir Panjal

B. Lesser Himalaya

C. Dhaula Dhar

D. Shivaliks

Q.74 In June 2022 who launched Single Nodal Agency (SNA) dashboard to provide a platform for ministries/departments to monitor the fund transfers?

A. Narendra Modi

B. Amit Shah

C. Anurag Thakur

D. Nirmala Sitharaman

Q.75 Who is considered the father of white revolution in India?

[RRB (NTPC), 2021]

A. Arun Krishnan

B. MS Swaminathan

C. Verghese Kurien

D. Indira Gandhi

Mathematics

Q.76 Simplify $\frac{6}{5} \times 4\frac{1}{2}$.

A. $\frac{27}{5}$

B. $\frac{6}{5}$

C. $\frac{11}{5}$

D. None of these

Q.77 Find the LCM of $30, 45$ and 60.

A. 180

B. 190

C. 18

D. 1800

Q.78 The ratio of diagonals of a rhombus is $5:6$ and its area is $375cm^2$. Find the length of larger diagonal.

A. $30cm$

B. $36cm$

C. $18cm$

D. $24cm$

Q.79 The total surface area of a circular cylinder which has a height of 14 metres and a base of radius 3 metres, is:

[HTET TGT Mathematics, 2020]

A. 302.75 sq. metre

B. 203.57 sq. metre

C. 320.57 sq. metre

D. 230.75 sq. metre

Q.80 A sum becomes five times of itself in 8 years at simple interest. What is the rate of interest per annum?

A. 37.5%

B. 25%

C. 62.5%

D. 50%

Q.81 The sum of the digits of a two digit number is 9. If the digits are reversed, the number is 63 more than the original. Find the number.

A. 19

B. 17

C. 16

D. 18

Q.82 Find out the square root of 3969.

A. 53

B. 63

C. 43

D. 83

Q.83 Direction: What should come in place of the question mark (?) in the following number series?

8, 13, 20, ?, 40, 53

A. 25

B. 27

C. 29

D. 31

Q.84 The rational number lying between $\sqrt{2}$ and $\sqrt{3}$ is:

[Territorial Army Officer, 2019]

A. $\frac{49}{28}$

B. $\frac{56}{35}$

C. $\frac{63}{45}$

D. $\frac{85}{66}$

Q.85 Number name for $83,07,80,120$ is:

A. Eighty three crore seven thousand eighty lakh one hundred twenty

B. Eighty three crore seven lakh eighty thousand one hundred twenty

C. Eighty three crore seventy thousand eighty lakh one twenty

D. None of these

Q.86 Successor of 100000000 is:

A. 99999999

B. 100000001

C. 10000002

D. None of these

Q.87 2 dozens of oranges cost Rs. 60. Find the cost of 120 similar oranges.

A. 300

B. 400

C. 500

D. 600

Q.88 $\frac{9}{4}$ of 36 equals:

A. 81

B. 79

C. 70

D. 80

Q.89 Evaluate $1\frac{2}{5} - \frac{3}{8} + \frac{1}{4}$.

A. $\frac{51}{40}$

B. $\frac{61}{40}$

C. $\frac{51}{50}$

D. $\frac{71}{40}$

Q.90 The difference between the smallest 6-digit number and the greatest 4-digit number is:

A. 1

B. 90000

C. 90001

D. 900001

Q.91 Sum of 10 and 40 in roman number is:

A. C

B. V

C. L

D. D

Q.92 Find H.C.F. of 805, 1127 and 1449.

A. 161

B. 165

C. 170

D. 175

Q.93 Find the value of $2\frac{3}{11} + 4\frac{1}{9} + \frac{1}{3}$.

A. $6\frac{71}{99}$

B. $6\frac{71}{9}$

C. $8\frac{71}{99}$

D. $6\frac{7}{99}$

Q.94 Calculate the average.

74, 56, 89, 92, 68 & 35

A. 89

B. 75

C. 69

D. 96

Q.95 Three numbers are in the ratio $4:5:6$ and their average is 30. The largest number is:

A. 28

B. 32

C. 36

D. 42

Q.96 If 20% of n is equal to 40, what is n?

A. 200

B. 2000

C. 800

D. 80

Q.97 Find the simple interest on Rs. 78000 at $15\left(\frac{2}{5}\right)\%$ per annum for 9 months.

A. Rs. 7804

B. Rs. 8979

C. Rs. 8046

D. Rs. 9009

Q.98 Sunandabai bought milk for Rs 475. She converted it into yoghurt and sold it for Rs 700. How much profit did she make?

A. Rs 225

B. Rs 245

C. Rs 235

D. Rs 325

Q.99 Simplify the $(4x + 1)(4x - 1)$.

A. $16x^2 + 8x + 2$

B. $16x^2 + 8x + 1$

C. $16x^2 - 1$

D. $16x^2 + 1$

Q.100 Find the factor of the following number:

13

A. 1

B. 13

C. 26

D. Both (A) and (B)

// Smart Answer Sheet //

Correct   Indicates percentage of students who answered questions correctly.

Skipped   Indicates percentage of students who skipped questions.

Q.	Ans.	Correct / Skipped	Q.	Ans.	Correct / Skipped	Q.	Ans.	Correct / Skipped	Q.	Ans.	Correct / Skipped	Q.	Ans.	Correct / Skipped
1	D	55.4 % / 1.12 %	17	B	86.99 % / 0.0 %	33	B	81.53 % / 0.0 %	49	C	85.73 % / 0.0 %	65	D	78.86 % / 0.0 %
2	C	42.8 % / 1.33 %	18	B	58.61 % / 1.01 %	34	D	82.08 % / 0.0 %	50	C	84.04 % / 0.0 %	66	A	59.43 % / 1.08 %
3	A	56.0 % / 1.98 %	19	B	61.88 % / 1.6 %	35	C	42.87 % / 1.13 %	51	A	78.41 % / 0.0 %	67	B	51.84 % / 1.7 %
4	B	46.57 % / 1.19 %	20	C	86.86 % / 0.0 %	36	A	63.04 % / 1.66 %	52	D	57.67 % / 1.3 %	68	A	85.65 % / 0.0 %
5	C	62.08 % / 1.13 %	21	C	84.7 % / 0.0 %	37	D	77.74 % / 0.0 %	53	C	41.89 % / 1.82 %	69	A	79.64 % / 0.0 %
6	D	53.3 % / 1.91 %	22	B	85.81 % / 0.0 %	38	D	89.92 % / 0.0 %	54	D	49.42 % / 1.49 %	70	A	49.86 % / 1.54 %
7	C	76.25 % / 0.0 %	23	C	55.93 % / 1.99 %	39	A	82.91 % / 0.0 %	55	D	66.27 % / 1.32 %	71	C	89.47 % / 0.0 %
8	A	42.13 % / 1.0 %	24	B	61.77 % / 1.37 %	40	A	84.01 % / 0.0 %	56	B	66.63 % / 1.46 %	72	A	63.47 % / 1.42 %
9	C	85.83 % / 0.0 %	25	C	88.52 % / 0.0 %	41	D	81.89 % / 0.0 %	57	B	67.52 % / 1.12 %	73	D	51.92 % / 1.91 %
10	A	87.28 % / 0.0 %	26	B	65.03 % / 1.95 %	42	D	82.33 % / 0.0 %	58	C	56.16 % / 1.71 %	74	D	60.97 % / 1.45 %
11	C	47.95 % / 1.68 %	27	C	42.75 % / 1.95 %	43	B	55.29 % / 1.09 %	59	C	82.73 % / 0.0 %	75	C	47.76 % / 1.94 %
12	B	83.81 % / 0.0 %	28	D	53.76 % / 1.77 %	44	A	88.0 % / 0.0 %	60	B	56.42 % / 1.23 %	76	A	57.43 % / 1.64 %
13	D	82.15 % / 0.0 %	29	D	48.8 % / 1.66 %	45	D	80.73 % / 0.0 %	61	D	28.46 % / 3.38 %	77	A	41.74 % / 1.82 %
14	A	66.69 % / 1.56 %	30	C	64.03 % / 1.99 %	46	A	88.16 % / 0.0 %	62	A	14.01 % / 4.94 %	78	A	48.66 % / 1.55 %
15	A	57.08 % / 1.59 %	31	A	51.36 % / 1.8 %	47	A	42.03 % / 1.26 %	63	D	80.08 % / 0.0 %	79	C	83.38 % / 0.0 %
16	B	49.78 % / 1.36 %	32	C	79.93 % / 0.0 %	48	B	40.57 % / 1.42 %	64	D	54.56 % / 2.0 %	80	D	50.23 % / 1.23 %

Q.	Ans.	Correct / Skipped	Q.	Ans.	Correct / Skipped	Q.	Ans.	Correct / Skipped	Q.	Ans.	Correct / Skipped	Q.	Ans.	Correct / Skipped
81	D	57.26 % 1.41 %	85	B	61.78 % 1.3 %	89	A	56.12 % 1.71 %	93	A	63.98 % 1.35 %	97	D	58.77 % 1.19 %
82	B	86.57 % 0.0 %	86	B	43.71 % 1.74 %	90	C	52.76 % 1.21 %	94	C	68.96 % 1.7 %	98	A	89.24 % 0.0 %
83	C	40.9 % 1.62 %	87	A	43.35 % 1.18 %	91	C	45.0 % 1.66 %	95	C	64.06 % 1.99 %	99	C	77.65 % 0.0 %
84	B	77.45 % 0.0 %	88	A	53.87 % 1.51 %	92	A	54.0 % 1.88 %	96	A	42.07 % 1.65 %	100	D	80.94 % 0.0 %

Performance Analysis

Avg. Score (%)	46.0%
Toppers Score (%)	67.0%
Your Score	

//Hints and Solutions//

1. 'आवश्यकता से अधिक वर्षा' के लिए एक शब्द 'अतिवृष्टि' होगा।

- 'अतिवृष्टि' का विलोम - अनावृष्टि
- अल्पवृष्टि- आवश्यकता से कम बरसात
- ओलावृष्टि- ओले की बरसात

अतः विकल्प (D) सही है।

2. आड़ या परदे के लिये रथ या पालकी को ढकनेवाला कपड़ा के लिए वाक्यांश के लिए एक शब्द ओहार है।

- अंडज: अंडे से उत्पन्न
- आगत: आया हुआ
- औरस: विवाहित स्त्री से उत्पन्न

अतः विकल्प (C) सही है।

3. दिए गए विकल्पों में आसन्न भूत काल का उदाहरण विकल्प "महेश अभी - अभी गया है"।

आसन्न भूतकाल: भूतकाल कि जिस क्रिया से यह पता चले कि यहाँ कार्य कुछ समय पहले ही समाप्त हुआ हो वहाँ आसन्न भूतकाल कहते है ।

अत: विकल्प (A) सही है।

4. किसी के द्वारा कहे गए वचन को ज्यों का त्यों लिखने के लिए उद्धरण चिह्न (" ") या (' ') का प्रयोग किया जाता है।

जैसे - हरिवंश राय बच्चन ने कहा है - "मन का हो तो अच्छा, मन का न हो तो भी अच्छा"

अतः विकल्प (B) सही है।

5. मुंबई व्यक्तिवाचक संज्ञा है।

किसी भी विशेष व्यक्ति, वस्तु या स्थान के नाम का बोध कराने वाली संज्ञा ही व्यक्तिवाचक संज्ञा कहलाती हैं। यानी, व्यक्तिवाचक संज्ञा सभी व्यक्ति, वस्तु या स्थान की संपूर्ण जाती में से ख़ास का नाम बताती हैं।

जैसे:

व्यक्ति- महात्मा गाँधी, भगत सिंह, रमेश, पवन, सीमा, विकास आदि।

वस्तु- कुरान, बाइबल, रामायण आदि।

स्थान- बैंगलोर, दिल्ली, मुंबई, लखनऊ आदि।

अत: विकल्प (C) सही है।

6. लोकोक्ति - होनहार बिरवान के होत चीकने पात

अर्थ - बचपन से ही बड़प्पन का संकेत अर्थात होनहार के लक्षण पहले से ही दिखायी पड़ने लगते है।

वाक्य - अब्दुल कलाम बचपन से ही मेधावी एवं मां बाप की आज्ञा का पालन करने वाले थे। सच ही कहा है– होनहार बिरवान के होत चीकने पात।

अतः विकल्प (D) सही है।

7. उपर्युक्त मुहावरों में से गलत मुहावरा है - 'चिकना घड़ा रहना।' यहाँ 'रहना' के स्थान पर 'होना' शब्द उपयुक्त है। शेष मुहावरे सही हैं।

मुहावरे	अर्थ	वाक्य प्रयोग
चिकना घड़ा होना	बेशर्म होना, बात का असर न पड़ना	राशिद को हर अध्यापक होमवर्क कर लाने को कहते हैं पर वह इतना चिकना घड़ा है कि वह कभी भी होमवर्क करके नहीं आया।

अतः विकल्प (C) सही है।

8. 'को' और 'के लिए' सम्प्रदान कारक के चिह्न है। अन्य विकल्प असंगत है।

सम्प्रदान कारक: जिसके लिए कोई क्रिया (काम)की जाती है, उसे सम्प्रदान कारक कहते है।

जैसे:

शिष्य ने अपने गुरु के लिए सब कुछ किया।

गरीब को धन दीजिए।

वह अरुण के लिए मिठाई लाया।

अत: विकल्प (A) सही है।

9. 'नाईन' में 'इन' प्रत्यय नही लगा हुआ है।

नाईन शब्द में ईन, प्रत्यय लगा हुआ है, 'इन' प्रत्यय नही।

- कुँजड़ + इन = कुँजड़िन
- नाग + इन = नागिन
- ईसा + इन = ईसाइन

अत: विकल्प (C) सही है।

10. 'आंजनेय' शब्द में प्रयुक्त प्रत्यय 'एय' है।

'एय' प्रत्यय से बने शब्द:- राधा - राधेय, कुंती - कौन्तेय

शब्द के उपरांत जिस शब्द का प्रयोग किया जाता है वह प्रत्यय है। जैसे - ता, औना, अन, अत

अत: विकल्प (A) सही है।

11. मुख्यतः रस 9 प्रकार के होते है। लेकिन कई विद्वानों ने अपने तर्क से रस को 11 प्रकार के बताये है।

1- श्रृंगार रस
2- हास्य रस
3- करुण रस
4- रौद्र रस
5- वीभत्स रस
6- भयानक रस
7- अद्भुत रस
8- वीर रस
9- शांत रस

अत: विकल्प (C) सही है।

12. पसीना शब्द का तत्सम 'प्रस्विन्न' होता है। ऐसे शब्द जिसे हम संस्कृत से बिना कोई बदलाव करे उपयोग में लाते है, तत्सम शब्द कहलाते हैं। पसीना शब्द प्रस्विन्न का तद्भव रूप होता है।

अत: विकल्प (B) सही है।

13. 'कपूर' तद्भव शब्द है, इसका तत्सम शब्द 'कर्पूर' होता है। शेष विकल्पों में तत्सम शब्द का प्रयोग किया गया है।

अत: विकल्प (D) सही है।

14. 'व्यवहार' का सही संधि-विच्छेद वि + अव + हार है, इसमें यण संधि है।

यण संधि: जब संधि करते समय इ, ई के साथ कोई अन्य स्वर हो तो ' य ' बन जाता है, जब उ, ऊ के साथ कोई अन्य स्वर हो तो ' व् ' बन जाता है, जब ऋ के साथ कोई अन्य स्वर हो तो ' र ' बन जाता है।

अत: विकल्प (A) सही है।

15. "रात होते ही तारे निकल आये" मिश्र वाक्य है।

"रात होते ही तारे निकल आये" वाक्य में दो वाक्य एक साथ मिश्रित किए गए है।

ऐसे वाक्य जिनमें सरल वाक्य के साथ-साथ कोई दूसरा उपवाक्य भी हो, वे वाक्य मिश्र वाक्य कहलाते हैं।

अतः विकल्प (A) सही है।

16. उपर्युक्त वाक्य में रीतिवाचक क्रिया विशेषण प्रयोग हुआ है।

ऐसे अविकारी शब्द जो हमें क्रिया के होने के तरीके या विधि के बारे में बताते हैं, वे शब्द रीतिवाचक क्रियाविशेषण कहलाते हैं। जैसे: खरगोश तेज़ दौड़ता है। इस वाक्य में दौड़ना क्रिया है एवं तेज़ शब्द से हमें दौड़ने कि रफ्तार अथवा विधि पता चल रही है। इसलिए, जो भी शब्द हमें किसी क्रिया के होने के तरीके का बोध कराते हैं वे शब्द रीतिवाचक क्रियाविशेषण कहलाते हैं।

अतः विकल्प (B) सही है।

17. कोई" शब्द अनिश्चय वाचक सर्वनाम का उदाहरण हैं।

जिन सर्वनामों से किसी निश्चित वस्तु का पता नहीं चलता है उसे अनिश्चय वाचक सर्वनाम कहते हैं। जैसे:- कोई, कुछ, आदि।

अतः विकल्प (B) सही है।

18. जो स्वर केवल मुख से उच्चारित होता है, उसे निरननासिक स्वर कहते है। जैसे – अ-सवार, आ-बाट, ऊ-पूछ, ओ-गोद इत्यादि। हवा के नाक व मुँह से निकलने के आधार पर स्वर दो प्रकार के होते हैं:

- निरननासिक स्वर
- अनुनासिक स्वर

अतः विकल्प (B) सही है।

19. 'आँख' का बहुवचन शब्द 'आँखें' होता है।

वचन	परिभाषा	उदाहरण
एकवचन	संज्ञा के जिस रूप से एक वस्तु, प्राणी या पदार्थ आदि का पता चलता है।	लड़का, गाय, बेटी आदि।
बहुवचन	संज्ञा के जिस रूप से एक से अधिक वस्तु, प्राणी या पदार्थ आदि का पता चलता है।	लड़के, गायें, बेटियाँ आदि।

अतः विकल्प (B) सही है।

20. प्रतियोगिता शब्द वर्तनीगत शुद्ध शब्द है।

प्रतियोगिता शब्द का अर्थ प्रतिद्वंदिता या होड़ होता है।

वर्तनी भाषा में शब्दों को वर्णों से अभिव्यक्त करने की क्रिया को कहते हैं। वर्तनी का सीधा सम्बन्ध भाषागत ध्वनियों के उच्चारण से है।

अतः विकल्प (C) सही है।

21. 'सन्धि' का विलोम शब्द विग्रह है।

- संधि का अर्थ : जोड़ना
- विग्रह का अर्थ : अलग होना, करना

अतः विकल्प (C) सही है।

22. 'मछली' का पर्यायिवाची शब्द शफरी है।

अन्य पर्यायिवाची - मतस्य, झख, झष, मच्छी, जलजीवन

अन्य विकल्प:

शब्द	पर्यायवाची
कबूतर	कपोत, रक्तलोचन, पारावत, कलरव, हारिल।
काला	श्याम, कृष्ण, कलूटा, साँवला, स्याह।
आकाश	पुष्कर, व्योम, विष्णुपद, फलक

अतः विकल्प (B) सही है।

23. बाहर के देशों में वस्तुओं को भेजने के लिए हिंदी में निर्यात कहते हैं।

अन्य विकल्प :

शब्द	अर्थ	शब्द का वाक्य मे प्रयोग
पर्याप्त	जितना चाहिए उतना	सौ लोगों के लिए पर्याप्त भोजन बनाइए।
साकार	जिसका कोई आकार हो	राम गोस्वामी तुलसीदास के साकार ईश्वर हैं।

अतः विकल्प (C) सही है।

24. आज हमारे देश में बनने वाली अधिकांश फिल्म बाजारू बन कर रह गई है। उनका उद्देश्य सस्ती लोकप्रियता प्राप्त करना तथा पैसा कमाना मात्र रह गया है।

अन्य विकल्प :

शब्द	अर्थ	शब्द का वाक्य मे प्रयोग
गर्व	घमंड	हमेशा गर्व से सीना तानकर चलने वाले साहूकार को आज सबके सामने लज्जित होना पड़ा।
अधिकार	हक	कुछ लोग अपने अधिकार का दुरुपयोग करते हैं।
प्रचार	जनता में किसी बात को प्रसिद्ध करना	कम्पनियाँ टीवी आदि के माध्यम से अपने उत्पादों का प्रचार करती हैं।

अतः विकल्प (B) सही है।

25. 'मुझे आज बाहर घूमने का मन हो रहा है।' यह इच्छा वाचक वाक्य है।

जिन वाक्यों से किसी इच्छा, आशा, आशीर्वाद या शुभकामना का बोध होता है, उन्हें इच्छावाचक वाक्य कहते हैं।

अतः विकल्प (C) सही है।

26. Correct Sentence: The teacher, as well as the students, is responsible for the agitation in the school campus.

Subject-verb agreement refers to the rules for using verbs according to the subject.

- Example: They play every day. (plural)
- He eats every day. (Singular)

According to the subject-verb agreement, when we use words like as well as, along with, the verb works according to the first subject.

Hence, the correct option is (B).

27. Correct sentence: Nanny died last week. She had been suffering from cancer for some time.

An activity that started in the past, continued and finished in the past comes under Past Perfect Continuous Tense.

The formula is as follows:

- Sub + had + been + V1 + ing + obj + for/since + time.

In the given sentence, the incident of the subject dying and suffering from cancer have occurred in the past.

Hence, the correct option is (C).

28. Correct sentence: Susan watched a movie at the theatre with a friend.

With is used to indicate in the company or in the presence of something or in the company of someone, using something or having something.

For example: She lives with her parents.

In the given sentence, Susan was accompanied to the theatre by a friend, so with will be used.

Hence, the correct option is (D).

29. Correct sentence: She often goes for a walk at night.

According to grammar, we can use "at" with the time of day. Also use "at" with noon, night, and midnight.'

Example: They go to bed at midnight.

Hence, the correct option is (D).

30. Complete Sentence: I am planning to take a vacation from the office, tomorrow.

The given sentence is talking about something that is unfinished or incomplete.

Therefore, the present continuous tense should be used in the blank.

The present continuous tense indicates that an action or condition is happening now, frequently, and may continue into the future.

This tense is formed by to be (am, is, are) + verb (the present participle).

Therefore, the most appropriate option to be filled in the blank is 'am planning'.

Hence, the correct option is (C).

31. Correct sentence: The author's wife was a good editor, besides being a great writer herself.

Besides: in addition to; apart from.

Ex: I have no other family besides my parents.

Hence, the correct option is (A).

32. Correct sentence: If it rains, we will cancel the party.

The sentence starts with 'if' which indicates that the first part is a condition and the second part is the result.

The given sentence is in an example of first conditional which is of the form (if + present simple, ... will + infinitive)

So, clearly we will use the present tense form of verb i.e. rains.

Hence, the correct option is (C).

33. Complete sentence: Nobody but me is responsible for this fiasco.

'But' means 'except' when it is used after words such as all, everything/nothing, everyone/no one, everybody/nobody.

In such cases we always use 'objective case of pronouns' after it.

- Ex: No one but him would get a job like that.
- Ex: Everybody but me has paid.

In the given sentence also, the similar condition is available. So, object pronoun 'me' is the correct choice to fill in the blank.

Hence, the correct option is (B).

34. The correct answer is 'curtesy'.

Courtesy: Polite and pleasant behaviour that shows respect for other people

Example: His abilities, his courtesy and his upright character made him a universal favourite.

Hence, the correct option is (D).

35. An indefinite pronoun does not refer to any specific person, thing or amount. It is vague and "not definite". Some typical indefinite pronouns are: all, another, any, anybody/anyone, anything, each, everybody/everyone, everything, few, many, nobody, none, one, several, some, somebody/someone.

In sentence "I saw someone running in street."

someone is An indefinite pronoun

Hence the correct option is (C).

36. 'Virtuoso' is 'a person highly skilled in music or another artistic pursuit'.

The other given options,

'Dilettante' is 'a person who cultivates an area of interest, such as the arts, without real commitment or knowledge.

'Termagant' is 'a harsh-tempered or overbearing woman'.

'Agnostic' is 'a person who believes that nothing is known or can be known of the existence or nature of God'.

Hence, the correct option is (A).

37. The sentence is in the simple future tense.

A simple way to identify this tense is that in the future tense the helping verbs 'will' or 'shall' is used with the base form of the verb, 'give' in this case.

Hence, the correct option is (D).

38. All the given words are adjective.

Although Miserly looks like an adverb, it is an adjective actually.

"In a miserly manner" is used as an adverb for adjective miserly.

Hence, the correct option is (D).

39. We **should** respect our elders.

Modal Verbs show us the attitude of the speaker to what is being said or done. The term "modal" means expressing mood and mood is a way to express the attitude of the speaker.

Option (A) expresses the mood of duty/ obligation according to the sentence. Whereas, option (B) expresses ability, option (C) expresses assurance to act in future, and option (D) expresses assurance and likely to act in the future.

Hence, the correct option is (A).

40. The meaning of the given words:

- Flexible means 'bending and not breaking'.

- Rigid meaning 'firm'.

- Flatter means 'lavish praise on someone with the idea of furthering one's interest.

- Bending means the same as flexible.

- Disregard means 'unmindful'.

From the meanings of the given words, we can conclude that Rigid is the most appropriate antonym of flexible.

Hence, the correct option is (A).

41. The meaning of the given words:

- Fostering: encourage the development of (something, especially something desirable).

- Nurturing: care for and protect (someone or something) while they are growing.

- Safeguarding: a measure taken to protect someone or something or to prevent something undesirable.

- Neglecting: fail to care for properly.

- Ignoring: refuse to take notice of or acknowledge; disregard intentionally.

From the meanings of the given words, we can conclude that Nurturing is the most appropriate synonym for fostering.

Hence, the correct option is (D).

42. Meaning of the given words:

- Deepen means to make deep or deeper and heighten something.

- Intensify - to make intense or increase the density.

- Soothe - to calm and pacify.

- Neutralize - to make something neutral or less severe.

- Relieve - to set free from an obligation.

From the meanings of the given words, we can conclude that intensify is the most appropriate synonym of deepen.

Hence, the correct option is (D).

43. The meaning of the given words:

- Height: measurement from base to top.

- Depth: distance from top to surface.

- Length: measurement from end to end.

- Width: measurement from side to side.

- Breadth: distance from side to side.

From the meanings of the given words, we can conclude that Depth is the most appropriate opposite of Height.

Hence, the correct option is (B).

44. 'Hey' is the interjection.

In the particular sentence, Hey, is the right one, as it expresses sudden burst of emotions and the function of an interjection is the same. It is helpful to note that interjection is a part of speech that is used in informal language than in formal writing.

Hence, the correct option is (A).

45. The feminine of a father is mother.

The word father describes a single man.

Hence, the correct option is (D).

46. The meaningful word from the words "YRTNUOC" is "country".

"country" means an area of land with its own people, government, etc.

Example: I prefer to live in a hot country

Hence, the correct option is (A).

47. Correct sentence: She replied, "Amazing!"

- The given sentence is in direct speech.

- Punctuation is used in direct speech to separate spoken words, or dialogue, from the rest of a story.

- The words spoken by a character sit inside speech marks.

- Here the spoken word is "Amazing," so it should be within inverted commas or quotation marks (" ").

- In the given sentence, "Amazing" is used as an exclamation and used for expression of extremely surprising.

- Therefore, we need to use an exclamatory mark (!) after this word. Example: This stain remover really works - it's amazing!

Hence, the correct option is (A).

48. Correct sentence - "Get out of the car!" ordered the policeman.

- From the given options, it is clear that we have to punctuate a direct speech.

- Punctuation is used in direct speech to separate spoken words, or dialogue, (reporting clause) from the rest of a sentence (reported clause).

- The reporting clause comes inside inverted commas (" ...").

- In direct speech, we usually put a comma between the reporting clause and the reported clause.

- If the direct speech is a question or exclamation, we use a question mark or exclamation mark, not a comma: - 'Is there a reason for this?' she asked.

- The reporting clause in the given sentence is 'Get out of the car'. This is a command and hence should end with an exclamation mark (!).

- The reported clause in the given sentence is 'ordered the policeman'.

- Based on the above-mentioned rules we get the following punctuated sentence: "Get out of the car!" ordered the policeman.

Hence, the correct option is (B).

49. Correct Sentence: I feel very bored in some of our board meetings.

The given words are examples of a homonym.

- Homophones are words that sound the same but are different in meaning or spelling. Example: "Mail" and "Male" are easy to confuse because they sound identical (i.e., they are perfect homonyms).

- In the given sentence the word 'bored' should be used in the first blank because it means 'feeling tired and perhaps slightly annoyed because something is not interesting or because you do not have anything to do'. Example: The children get bored on long journeys.

- And in the second filer 'board' should be used because it means 'a group of people who control an organization, company, etc. Example: The board of directors is/are meeting to discuss the firm's future.

Hence, the correct option is (C).

50. The pattern followed here is:

Sad is an antonym of Blissful.

Similarly, Ecstasy is an antonym of Melancholy.

Hence, the correct option is (C).

51. Special ASEAN-India Foreign Ministers' Meeting (SAIFMM) will be held on the 16th and 17th June 2022 in New Delhi, India to commemorate 30 years of ASEAN-India Dialogue Relations. In recognition of this milestone, the year 2022 is being celebrated as the ASEAN-India Friendship Year as announced by ASEAN and Indian leaders at the 18th ASEAN-India Summit in October 2021.

Hence, the correct option is (A).

52. Union Minister Sarbananda Sonowal on 28th Oct 2022 inaugurated the 'Ayush Utsav' in Ganderbal, Kashmir.

It was launched with the inauguration of a seminar titled 'Bridging the Gaps in Healthcare: Ayush, a Promising Recourse'. It has been launched to enable traditional medicinal practices to supplement modern patient care.

Hence, the correct option is (D).

53. Mahoba district belongs to the Bundelkhand region of Uttar Pradesh.

The Bundelkhand region has an area of around 70,000 sq km.

Bundelkhand comprises seven districts of southern Uttar Pradesh and six districts of northern Madhya Pradesh.

Hence, the correct option is (C).

54. The area of Uttar Pradesh is approximately 7.30% of the total area of the country.

Uttar Pradesh is the fourth largest state in the country while Rajasthan is the largest state in the country in terms of area.

Uttar Pradesh is the most populous state in the country.

Uttar Pradesh has 75 districts under 18 divisions.

The state of Uttar Pradesh has 80 Lok Sabha seats while it has 31 Rajya Sabha seats.

The Legislative Assembly of Uttar Pradesh has 404 members while its Legislative Council comprises of 100 members.

Hence, the correct option is (D).

55. In the year 1951, it was made legally binding to use Hindi in all official works in the Indian State of Uttar Pradesh.

Under the Official Language Act of 1951 Hindi became the language of state administration in Uttar Pradesh.

In 1989 an amendment to the act was done which added Urdu, as an additional language of the state.

The other languages majorly used in the state include Awadhi, Bhojpuri, Bundeli, Braj Bhasha, Kannauji and Hindustani.

The main script used to write the languages of Uttar Pradesh is Devanagari.

Hence, the correct option is (D).

56. Birha is the main folk song of Uttar Pradesh.

This genre is mood based and the basic theme revolves around the separation of lover and his beloved. Actually 'Birha' in Hindi means separation. The history of this genre is not very old and the earliest reference goes back to 17th century.

Hence, the correct option is (B).

57. The Nauchandi Mela is a colourful and mesmeric fair which is held a few days after Holi, every year in Meerut in Uttar Pradesh.

The Kumbh Mela is the largest fair of the world organized in Prayag, Allahabad.

It is organized for approximately 48 days to bathe at the holy confluence of Ganga, Yamuna, and the mysterious Saraswati.

Kumbh Mela, in Hinduism, is a religious pilgrimage that is celebrated four times over a course of 12 years.

Hence, the correct option is (B).

58. The Tulsi Manas temple is located at Varanasi district of Uttar Pradesh.

- It is believed that the epic Ramcharitmanas was composed at this place by Goswami Tulsidas in the 16th century.

- The walls of the temple are craved with Dohas, Chaupayees, Chhandas and paintings of the scenes from Ramcharitmanas.

- It was reconstructed in the year 1964 and was inaugurated by Dr Sarvapalli Radhakrishanan.

Hence, the correct option is (C).

59. Denmark is called the 'Country of Winds' as it has the highest proportion of wind power in the world.

- Wind dominated, with 47% of the green energy coming from wind turbines.

- Denmark fulfill 50% of its power requirements from renewable energy.

Hence, the correct option is (C).

60. A pigment called luciferin is found in firefly. Luciferin is a light-emitting compound which is found in organisms that generate bioluminescence. Luciferins typically undergo an enzyme-catalyzed reaction with molecular oxygen.

Hence, the correct option is (B).

61. DAP is an example of binary fertilizer.

- DAP i.e. Diammonium phosphate is a very famous fertilizer.

- Fertilizers are substances which when added to the soil, help in supplying nutrients that are essential for the growth of plants and also help in aeration and water retention of soil.

- They may be natural or synthetic.

- Natural fertilizers include manure, compost, etc.

- Synthetic or artificial fertilizers are the man-made ones that provide specific nutrients that the soil lacks.

- Nitrogen (N), Phosphorous (P), and Potassium(K) are the macronutrients essential for the growth of plants.

Hence, the correct option is (D).

62. The capital of Moldova is Chișinău.

Chișinău is the capital and largest city of the Republic of Moldova. The city is Moldova's main industrial and commercial center, and is located in the middle of the country, on the river Bâc, a tributary of the Dniester.

Hence, the correct option is (A).

63. A deep valley characterized by a steep step-like slope is known as Canyon.

- A U–shaped valley is formed by strong lateral erosion of glaciers at high altitudes.

- Blind valley is a narrow, deep, and flat-bottomed valley which has an abrupt ending.

- Gorge is a narrow valley between steep mountains or hills.

Hence, the correct option is (D).

64. India has decided to set up a Fast Track Mechanism to resolve issues faced by Indian businesses and investors in UAE. Union Minister Piyush Goyal announced this while Co-chairing the 10th Meeting of the India-UAE High-Level Joint Task Force on Investments in Mumbai on 11th Oct 2022. This Joint Task Force was established in 2013 to promote trade, investment and economic ties between UAE and India.

Hence, the correct option is (D).

65. Panch Mahal is Located in Fatehpur Sikri.

- Panch Mahal is a palace in Fatehpur Sikri, Uttar Pradesh, India.

- Akbar commissioned the Panch Mahal, which means 'Five Level Palace.'

- This edifice is located adjacent to the Zenana quarters (Harem), implying that it was utilized for entertainment and relaxation.

Hence, the correct option is (D).

66. India's first marine national park is located in Gulf of Kutch.

India's first Marine Wildlife Sanctuary and first Marine National Park were created in the Gulf of Kutch in 1980 and 1982, respectively. It is an archipelago of 42 tropical islands along the northern coast of Jamnagar district and the southern coast of Kutch.

Hence, the correct option is (A).

67. The venom of elapids, including sea snakes, kraits, cobras, king cobra, mambas, and many Australian species, contains toxins which attack the nervous system, causing neurotoxicity. The person may present with strange disturbances to their vision, including blurriness.

Hence, the correct option is (B).

68. The alluvial soil of India is generally rich in Lime.

- Alluvial soils are widespread in the northern plains and the river valleys. These soils cover almost 40% of the total area of the country.

- They are depositional soils, transported and deposited by rivers and streams.

- Zonal Soil- These types of soil have the same mineral properties that of the parent rock and are found in the same area where they are weathered.

- The alluvial soils vary in nature from sandy, loam to clay.

- Alluvial soils lack nitrogen, phosphorus and humus. However, they are generally rich in potash and lime.

Hence, the correct option is (A).

69. The first Cricket player to be awarded Rajiv Gandhi Khel Ratna award is Sachin Tendulkar.

The Rajiv Gandhi Khel Ratna Award is the highest sporting honour given in India in the field of sports and games.

Hence, the correct option is (A).

70. Sher Shah defeated Humayun in the battle of Chausa in 1539.

- The Battle of Chausa was a notable military engagement between the Mughal emperor, Humayun, and the Afghan, Sher Shah Suri.

- It was fought on 26 June 1539 at Chausa.

- Sher Shah was victorious and crowned himself Farid al-Din Sher Shah.

Hence, the correct option is (A).

71. Hindustani classical music exponent Rashid Khan was conferred with the Padma Bhushan on the eve of Republic Day.

- Rashid Khan belongs to the Rampur-Sahaswan Gharana and is an Indian classical musician.

- Pandit Bhimsen Joshi said that Rashid Khan was the assurance for the future of Indian vocal music.

- He was born in Sahaswan, Badayun, Uttar Pradesh.

- He has sung in many Bollywood movies.

- He was awarded the Padma Shri and Sangeet Natak Akademi Award in 2000.

Hence, the correct option is (C).

72. Delhi Chief Minister Arvind Kejriwal on 31 August 2022 launched country's first virtual school. Students from all across the country will be eligible for admission. The school is for classes 9-12 and the application process for the Delhi Model Virtual School (DMVS) began on the same day. The classes will be online and recorded lectures will also be uploaded online.

Hence, the correct option is (A).

73. Shivaliks is the outermost range of the Himalayas.

- The Himalayas consist of three parallel ranges, the Greater Himalayas known as the Himadri, the Lesser Himalayas called the Himachal, and the Shivalik hills, which comprise the foothills.

- Siwalik Range, also called Siwalik Hills or Outer Himalayas, Siwalik also spelled Shiwalik, is the sub-Himalayan range of the northern Indian subcontinent.

Hence, the correct option is (D).

74. In June 2022 Nirmala Sitharaman launched Single Nodal Agency (SNA) dashboard to provide a platform for ministries/departments to monitor the fund transfers.

Union Finance Minister Nirmala Sitharaman in June 2022 launched the Single Nodal Agency (SNA) Dashboard of Public Financial Management System (PFMS) in New Delhi as a part of the 'Azadi ka Amrit Mahotsav' (AKAM) celebrations by the Ministry of Finance. The SNA dashboard will provide a platform for ministries and departments to monitor the transfer of funds to states and their utilisation.

Hence, the correct option is (D).

75. Verghese Kurien is considered the father of the white revolution in India.

- The White Revolution, known as Operation Flood, was launched in 1970.

- It was an initiative by India's National Dairy Development Board (NDDB) and was the world's biggest dairy development programme.

- It transformed India from a milk deficient nation into the world's largest milk producer.

Hence, the correct option is (C).

76. Given,

$$\frac{6}{5} \times 4\frac{1}{2}$$

$$= \frac{6}{5} \times \frac{9}{2}$$

$$= \frac{54}{10}$$

$$= \frac{27}{5}$$

Hence, the correct option is (A).

77. $30 = 5 \times 3 \times 2$

$45 = 5 \times 3 \times 3 = 5 \times 3^2$

$60 = 5 \times 3 \times 2 \times 2 = 5 \times 3 \times 2^2$

$\therefore \text{LCM} = 5 \times 3^2 \times 2^2 = 180$

Hence, the correct option is (A).

78. Let the length of diagonals be $5a$ and $6a$.

Area of rhombus $= \frac{1}{2} \times d_1 \times d_2$

$\Rightarrow 375 = \frac{1}{2} \times 5a \times 6a$

$\Rightarrow 375 = 15a^2$

$\Rightarrow a = 5$

$6a = 6 \times 5 = 30cm$

Hence, the correct option is (A).

79. Given,

Height of cylinder $= 14$ metre

Radius of cylinder $= 3$ metre

As we know,

Total surface area of cylinder $= 2\pi r(r + h)$

Total surface area of cylinder $= 2 \times \frac{22}{7} \times 3(3 + 14)$

$\therefore$ Total surface area of cylinder $= 320.57$ sq. metre

Hence, the correct option is (C).

80. Given,

The sum becomes five times itself.

Time $= 8$ years

As we know,

Simple interest $= \frac{(P \times R \times T)}{100}$

$P = $ Principal

$R = $ Rate of interest

$T = $ Time

Let the sum of money be P.

After 8 years it becomes 5 times.

Simple interest $= 5P - P = 4P$

$$4P = \frac{(P \times R \times 8)}{100}$$

$$\Rightarrow R = \frac{400}{8}$$

$$\Rightarrow R = 50\%$$

$\therefore$ The Rate of interest per annum is 50%.

Hence, the correct option is (D).

81. Let the units digit be x.

Then the tens digit is $9 - x$.

Therefore the original number is $10(9 - x) + x = 90 - 10x + x = 90 - 9x$.

On reversing the order of the digits the number obtained is $10x + 9 - x = 9x + 9$

According to question,

$$9x + 9 = 63 + (90 - 9x)$$

$$(9x + 9) - (90 - 9x) = 63$$

$$9x + 9 - 90 + 9x = 63$$

$18x = 144$ (Transposing 9 and -90 to the R.H.S.)

$$x = 8$$

Therefore the original number is $90 - 9 \times 8 = 90 - 72 = 18$.

Hence, the correct option is (D).

82. Given number, 3969

The factors of 3969 $= 3 \times 3 \times 3 \times 3 \times 7 \times 7$

Therefore the square root of 3969,

$$\Rightarrow \sqrt{3969} = \sqrt{3 \times 3 \times 3 \times 3 \times 7 \times 7}$$

$$\Rightarrow \sqrt{3969} = 3 \times 3 \times 7$$

$$\Rightarrow \sqrt{3969} = 63$$

So, the square root of 3969 is 63.

Hence, the correct option is (B).

83. Given:

8, 13, 20, ?, 40, 53

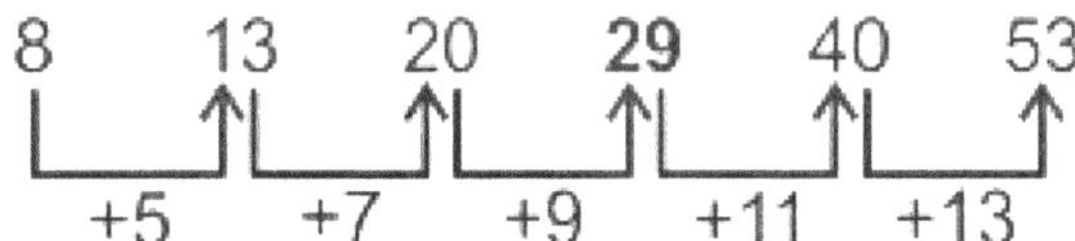

In the above series, there is a difference of odd consecutive numbers so the number missing after 20 is 29.

$\therefore$ The required number in the series is 29.

Hence, the correct option is (C).

84. Decimal values of the given numbers:

$$\sqrt{2} = 1.42 \quad \sqrt{3} = 1.73$$

So the number inserted must be between 1.42 and 1.73.

Now checking the options:

(A): $\dfrac{49}{28} = 1.75$

(B): $\dfrac{56}{35} = 1.6$

(C): $\dfrac{63}{45} = 1.4$

(D): $\dfrac{85}{66} = 1.28$

We can see that only $\dfrac{56}{35}$ can be put between $\sqrt{2}$ and $\sqrt{3}$.

Hence, the correct option is (B).

85. $83, 07, 80, 120 = 83 \times 1,00,00,000 + 07 \times 1,00,000 + 80 \times 1,000 + 100 + 20$

So this will equal to Eighty three crore seven lakh eighty thousand one hundred twenty.

Hence, the correct option is (B).

86. Successor is the number that occurs just after the given number.

So, Successor of $100000000 = 100000000 + 1 = 100000001$

Hence, the correct option is (B).

87. 2 dozens of oranges means $2 \times 12 = 24$ oranges cost Rs. 60.

Then cost of 1 orange $=$ Rs. $\dfrac{60}{24} = 2.5$

So, the cost of 120 similar oranges $=$ Rs. $2.5 \times 120 = 300$

Hence, the correct option is (A).

88. $\dfrac{9}{4}$ of $36 =?$

$$\dfrac{9}{4} \times 36 =?$$

$$9 \times 9 =?$$

$$= 81$$

$\dfrac{9}{4}$ of 36 equals 81.

Hence, the correct option is (A).

89. Given,

$$1\dfrac{2}{5} - \dfrac{3}{8} + \dfrac{1}{4}$$

$$= \frac{7}{5} - \frac{3}{8} + \frac{2}{8}$$

$$= \frac{7}{5} - \frac{1}{8}$$

$$= \frac{56-5}{40}$$

$$= \frac{51}{40}$$

Hence, the correct option is (A).

90. Smallest 6 -digit number $= 100000$

Greatest 4-digit number $= 9999$

Required Difference $= 100000 - 9999 = 90001$

Hence, the correct option is (C).

91. The sum of 10 and $40 = 10 + 40$

$= 50$

50 is written as the symbol L in Roman numerals.

So, $50 =$ L

Hence, the correct option is (C).

92. Factors of 805=1,5,7,23,35,115,161,805

Factors of 1127=1,7,23,49,161,1127

Factors of 1449=1,3,7,9,21,23,63,69,161,207,483,1449

Common factors =1,7,23,161

So, HCF =161

Hence, the correct option is (A).

93. Given,

$$2\frac{3}{11} + 4\frac{1}{9} + \frac{1}{3}$$

$$= \frac{25}{11} + \frac{37}{9} + \frac{1}{3}$$

$$= \frac{25}{11} + \frac{37}{9} + \frac{3}{9}$$

$$= \frac{25}{11} + \frac{40}{9}$$

$$= \frac{25 \times 9 + 40 \times 11}{11 \times 9}$$

$$= \frac{225 + 440}{99}$$

$$= \frac{665}{99}$$

$$= 6\frac{71}{99}$$

Hence, the correct option is (A).

94. Given:

74, 56, 89, 92, 68 & 35

Average = (Sum of Observations) ÷ (Total Numbers of Observations)

Sum of Observations = 74 + 56 + 89 + 92 + 68 + 35 = 414

Total Numbers of Observations = 6

Average $= \frac{414}{6}$

Average = 69

Hence, the correct option is (C).

95. Let the numbers be $4x, 5x$ and $6x$.

Therefore,

$$\Rightarrow \frac{(4x + 5x + 6x)}{3} = 30$$

$$\Rightarrow 15x = 90$$

$$\Rightarrow x = 6$$

Largest number $= 6x = 36$

Hence, the correct option is (C).

96. Given,

20% of $n = 40$

According to question,

$20\% \times n = 40$

$$\Rightarrow \left(\frac{20}{100}\right) \times n = 40$$

$$\Rightarrow \left(\frac{20n}{100}\right) = 40$$

$$\Rightarrow 20n = 40 \times 100$$

$$\Rightarrow 20n = 4000$$

$$\Rightarrow n = \frac{4000}{20}$$

$$\Rightarrow n = 200$$

Hence, the correct option is (A).

97. Given,

Principal $(P) =$ Rs. 78000 , Rate $(R) = \frac{77}{5}\%$ p.a and $T = \frac{9}{12}$ years $= \frac{3}{4}$ years

As we know,

Simple interest $= \frac{(P \times R \times T)}{100}$

$$= \frac{\left(78000 \times \frac{77}{5} \times \frac{3}{4}\right)}{1000}$$

$$= \frac{390 \times 77 \times 3}{100}$$

$$= \frac{90900}{100}$$

$= $ Rs. 9009

Hence, the correct option is (D).

98. Given,

Cost price = Rs 475

Selling price = Rs 700

Since selling price is more than cost price, so there is a profit.

Profit = Selling price − Cost price

=700−475

= Rs 225

∴ Sunandabai made a profit of Rs 225 in this transaction.

Hence, the correct option is (A).

99. Given,

$$(4x + 1) \times (4x - 1)$$
$$= 4x \times (4x - 1) + 1 \times (4x - 1)$$
$$= (4x \times 4x) - (4x \times 1) + (1 \times 4x) - (1 \times 1)$$
$$= 16x^2 - 4x + 4x - 1$$
$$= 16x^2 - 1$$

Hence, the correct option is (C).

100. Given number is 13.

13 is a prime number so there are only two factors of 13, which are 1 and 13.

∴ Factors of 13 are 1 and 13.

Hence, the correct option is (D).

Hindi

Q.1 एक ही वाक्य या वाक्यांश में एक ही तरह के पद, शब्द, पदबंध या वाक्यांश एक साथ आने पर कौन सा चिन्ह लगाया जाता है?

A. उद्धरण- चिह्न
B. प्रश्नवाचक-चिह्न
C. अर्द्धविराम
D. अल्पविराम

Q.2 रमेश कल दिल्ली जाएगा' इस वाक्य में रमेश क्या है?

A. संज्ञा
B. सर्वनाम
C. क्रिया
D. विशेषण

Q.3 निम्न में से कौन-सा 'रौद्र रस' का स्थायी भाव है?

A. क्रोध
B. उत्साह
C. जुगुप्सा
D. निर्वेद

Q.4 'अनाड़ी' का तत्सम रूप कौन-सा होगा?

[UP Police Sub Inspector, 2021]

A. अनार्य
B. अन्यत
C. अट्टालिका
D. अन्यत्र

Q.5 इनमें से तद्भव शब्द का चयन कीजिए।

[UP Police Sub Inspector, 2021]

A. आधा
B. कूप
C. व्योम
D. विद्या

Q.6 संयोजक शब्द से जुड़े हुए एक से अधिक साधारण वाक्यों से बनने वाला वाक्य क्या कहलाता है?

[Rajasthan Teachers Eligibility Test - Level 1 Primary Level (RTET), 2017]

A. मिश्र वाक्य
B. संयुक्त वाक्य
C. आश्रित उपवाक्य
D. प्रधान वाक्य

Q.7 निम्नलिखित प्रश्न में, चार विकल्पों में से, उस विकल्प का चयन करें जो दिए गए वाक्य में विशेषण शब्द की विशेषता प्रकट करता है।
सुनील बहुत अच्छा निशानेबाज है।

A. बहुत
B. अच्छा
C. निशानेबाज
D. बहुत अच्छा

Q.8 'स्वत:' में कौन-सा सर्वनाम है?

A. निजवाचक सर्वनाम
B. संबंधवाचक सर्वनाम
C. निश्चयवाचक सर्वनाम
D. पुरूषवाचक सर्वनाम

Ques (9-10):निर्देश: सही शब्द का चयन करते हुए रिक्त स्थान की पूर्ति कीजिए।

Q.9 व्याकरण के नियमों में बँधे, वाक्य में प्रयुक्त शब्द _____ कहलाते हैं।

A. व्याकरण
B. वाक्य
C. शब्द
D. पद

Q.10 भाषा के लिखने के ढंग को _____ कहते हैं।

A. वर्ण
B. शब्द
C. वाक्य
D. लिपि

Q.11 ओष्ठों की स्थिति के अनुसार स्वरों को कितने प्रकार में वर्गीकरण किया गया है?

A. 5
B. 4
C. 3
D. 2

Q.12 निम्नलिखित में से शुद्ध वर्तनी का चयन कीजिए:

A. औपचारीक
B. पारियाग
C. निषेध
D. शिल्पि

Q.13 'अनादर' का विलोम शब्द है:

A. मान
B. सम्मान
C. आदर
D. सत्कार

Q.14 'वाह ! कितना सुन्दर दृश्य है !' यह वाक्य अर्थ की दृष्टि से है:

A. संभावनार्थक
B. संकेतार्थक
C. विस्मयादिबोधक
D. प्रश्नवाचक

Q.15 'जो मापा न जा सके' वाक्यांश के लिए एक शब्द है:

A. परिमेय
B. परिमाप
C. आयतन
D. अपरिमेय

Q.16 'जिसको त्यागा न जा सके' वाक्यांश के लिए एक शब्द है:

A. त्यक्त
B. त्याग
C. अत्याज्य
D. त्याज्य

Q.17 निम्न में से कौन- सा वाक्य भविष्य काल का है?

A. मैं कहानी पढ़ती हूँ।
B. मैंने कहानी पढ़ी थी।
C. मैं कहानी पढ़ रही हूँ।
D. मैं शायद कहानी पढ़ूंगी।

Q.18 'घबरा जाना' के अर्थ के लिए सही मुहावरा क्या है?

A. चेहरे की हवाइयाँ उड़ना
B. चिकनी चुपड़ी बात करना
C. चुल्लू भर पानी में डूब मारना
D. चिकना घड़ा होना

Q.19 'मनमानी करना' के अर्थ के लिए उपयुक्त लोकोक्ति का चयन कीजिए।

A. थोथा चना बजे घना
B. सइयाँ भए कोतवाल अब डर काहे का
C. अंधे के हाथ बटेर लगना
D. साँप मरे पर लाठी न टूटे

Q.20 'राजा सेवक को कम्बल देता है', वाक्य में रेखांकित पद में कौन-सा कारक है?

A. सम्प्रदान कारक
B. कर्ता कारक
C. कर्म कारक
D. सम्बन्ध कारक

Q.21 विराम चिह्न की दृष्टि से शुद्ध वाक्य है:

A. चारों भाई सुंदर, सुशील, नम्र, दयालु और सबल थे।
B. चारों भाई सुंदर- सुशील, नम्र-दयालु और सबल थे।
C. चारों भाई, सुंदर, सुशील, नम्र, दयालु और सबल थे।
D. चारों भाई-- सुंदर, सुशील, नम्र, दयालु और सबल थे।

Q.22 'अहंकार' का संधि-विच्छेद कीजिए।

A. अहम् + कार
B. अहं + कार
C. अ + हंकार
D. अहङ + कार

Q.23 वृक्ष का पर्यायवाची नहीं है:

A. तरू
B. द्रुम
C. पेड़
D. कानन

Q.24 दिए गए शब्द का प्रत्यय ज्ञात कीजिए।
तैराक

A. राक
B. आक
C. अक
D. तै

Q.25 निम्नलिखित में से कौन सा शब्द बहुवचन है?

A. भीड़
B. मिठास
C. चाय
D. हस्ताक्षर

English

Q.26 Identify the tense used in the given sentence. "You are always working on your laptop."
A. Present indefinite tense
B. Present perfect tense
C. Present continuous tense
D. Present perfect continuous tense

Ques (27-33):Directions: Fill in the blanks in the following sentences with the help of options that follow.

Q.27 We _______ the City Palace in the afternoon as per the schedule.
A. are visiting
B. will visiting
C. will be visit
D. visiting

Q.28 When my father visits him, he ______ good.
A. felt
B. feel
C. feels
D. has felt

Q.29 My father was not hungry; ______, he ate a heavy lunch.
A. nevertheless
B. further
C. besides
D. instead

Q.30 There was a time when the national marriage rate was ________ too high.
A. fairly
B. fair
C. rather
D. None of these

Q.31 My husband _____ play the piano very well because he's a professional pianist.
A. might
B. can
C. shall
D. may

Q.32 Everyone _____ save the natural resources of the earth.
A. must
B. might
C. could
D. dare

Q.33 She is industrious _____ is not recognized in her field.
A. else
B. since
C. yet
D. and

Q.34 Direction: Fill in the blank with correct alternative.

Once upon a time, _____English ruled over the whole world.
A. an
B. a
C. the
D. None of these

Q.35 Direction: Fill in the blank with correct gender.
All monks and ______ of this church are invited to the program.
A. Monkes
B. Monkies
C. Monkixes
D. Nuns

Q.36 Choose the correctly spelled word:
A. Sattellite
B. Satelite
C. Sattelite
D. Satellite

Q.37 Direction: Fill in the blank with the appropriate pronoun.
He was so afraid that his knees knocked ______ other.
A. Every
B. One
C. Each
D. None

Q.38 Direction: Select the option that can be used as a one-word substitute for the given group of words.
A person who knows everything:
[SSC Constable (GD), 2021]

A. Naive
B. Omniscient
C. Intelligent
D. Omnipresent

Q.39 Choose the correctly punctuated sentence.
A. He said, I do not like video games.
B. He said, I do not like video games?
C. He said, I do not like video games!
D. He said, "I do not like video games."

Q.40 Direction: Select the most appropriate option to fill in the blank.
Simran is ______ officer, but her husband owns ______café.
A. an, a
B. the, a
C. a, a
D. an, the

Ques (41-42):Direction: Select the most appropriate synonym of the given word.

Q.41 ACTIVE
A. Lazy
B. Similar
C. Quiet
D. Busy

Q.42 ELEGANT
A. Rough
B. Common
C. Intelligent
D. Graceful

Ques (43-44):Direction: Select the most appropriate ANTONYM of the given word.

Q.43 PERMANENT
[SSC MTS, 2021]
A. Temporary
B. Stable
C. Lasting
D. Constant

Q.44 NEGLECT
A. Taste
B. Care
C. Wish
D. Mock

Q.45 Direction: Choose a meaningful word from the given jumbled words:
EVCOL
A. Clove
B. Colve
C. Ceovl
D. Clevo

Q.46 Direction: Identify the interjection in the following sentence:
Whoa, this city view is amazing!
A. Adverb
B. Interjection
C. Pronoun
D. Noun

Q.47 Direction: Choose the correct option which has the same relation as that given in the words.
Big : Enormous :: Small : _____
A. Tidy
B. Compact
C. Stubborn
D. Insufficient

Q.48 Direction: Fill in the blank with a suitable alternative.
He wanted ______ in the pool.
A. swim
B. to swim
C. to swims
D. to swimming

Q.49 Which of the words is an adjective?
A. Quickly
B. Adorable
C. Annually
D. Extremely

Q.50 Direction: Fill in the blank with the correct tense.
Julie _____ like to visit Kyoto when she is in Japan.
A. should
B. could
C. would
D. will

General Studies

Q.51 Which Indian company has entered the Fortune Global 500 list for the first time in August 2022?

[RBI Assistant, 2020]

A.   Reliance Industries
B.   Infosys
C.   Tata Motors
D.   Life Insurance Corporation

Q.52 What is name of the digital app which has been launched by the Parliament of India?
A.   Internet Sansad App
B.   Digital Sansad App
C.   Sansad Vichaar App
D.   Connect Your Sansad App

Q.53 What is the structure of local self-government in Uttar Pradesh?

A. Unilateral
B. Quadrilateral
C. Three-tier
D. Two-tier

Q.54 In which year United Provinces was renamed as Uttar Pradesh?
A. 1937
B. 1935
C. 1950
D. 1961

Q.55 Where is the famous Buland Darwaza located in Uttar Pradesh?
A. Fatehpur Sikri
B. Lucknow
C. Jaunpur
D. Agra

Q.56 Where is Chaukhandi Stupa located in Uttar Pradesh?
A. Allahabad
B. Gorakhpur
C. kaushambi
D. Sarnath

Q.57 Which city of Uttar Pradesh is famous for the lock industry?
A. Agra
B. Ghaziabad
C. Aligarh
D. Mirzapur

Q.58 Where is Keetham lake situated?

[SBI PO, 2021]

A. Agra
B. Jaipur
C. Kanpur
D. Bhopal

Q.59 The radioactive isotope of hydrogen is _______.
[Indian Military Academy (IMA), 2020], [Officers Training Academy (OTA), 2020]

A. Protium
B. Deuterium
C. Tritium
D. Hydronium

Q.60 Choose the correct pair of country and capital.
A. Latvia - Beirut
B. Lebanon - Maseru
C. Libya - Tripoli
D. Lesotho - Riga

Q.61 Coal, Petroleum and Natural Gas are examples of
A. Fossil Fuels
B. Cryogenic Fuels
C. Indigenous Fuels
D. Radioactive Fuels

Q.62 Which of the following planet is the fastest spinning planet of the solar system?

A. Mercury
B. Venus
C. Saturn
D. Jupiter

Q.63 Ibn Battuta, the Moroccan traveler, visited India during the reign of:
A.   Muhammad-bin-Tughlaq
B.   Babar
C.   Akbar
D.   Mahmood Ghazni

Q.64 Identify the leaf:

A. Banana leaf
B. Coconut leaf
C. Papaya leaf
D. None of the above

Q.65 What is the intermediate level in the Panchayati Raj Institutions called?
A. Zilla Panchayat
B. Kshettra Panchayat
C. Panchayat Samiti
D. Gram Panchayat

Q.66 The Gondwana rock system is famous for which mineral?
A. Coal
B. Limestone
C. Copper
D. Diamond

Q.67 Who was the first Ramon Magsaysay Award winner from India?
A.   C.D. Deshmukh
B.   Jayaprakash Narayan
C.   Dr. Verghese Kurien
D.   Acharya Vinoba Bhave

Q.68 Who is known as the 'Father of the Indian Nuclear Programme'?
A.   C.N.R. Rao
B.   M.S. Swaminathan
C.   Vikram Sarabhai
D.   Homi Jehangir Bhabha

Q.69 Lime reacts with baking soda to liberate which gas?
A. Carbon di oxide
B. Sodium
C. Sulphur di oxide
D. Oxygen

Q.70 In which city, PM Narendra Modi inaugurated 'Akhil Bhartiya Shiksha Samagam' on 7 July 2022?
A. Haridwar
B. Ayodhya
C. Ujjain
D. Varanasi

Q.71 Which country won the 2022 U19 Men's Cricket World Cup title?
A. India
B. England
C. West Indies
D. Sri Lanka

Q.72 Which missilie has been successfully test fired by India on 15 June 2022?

A. Agni IV   **B.** BrahMos
C. Agni II   **D.** Prithvi II

Q.73 Bonalu is the "state festival" of which state?

A. Andhra Pradesh   **B.** Karnataka
C. Kerala   **D.** Telangana

Q.74 Who wrote the play "Uttararamacharita"?

A. Harsha   **B.** Tulsidas
C. Bhavabhuti   **D.** Sudraka

Q.75 Which of the following do not produce flame on burning?

A. Flame
B. Only glow
C. Both flame and glow
D. None of these

Mathematics

Q.76 Evaluate: $\dfrac{-(4-6)^2-3(-2)+|-6|}{18-9\div3\times5}$

A. $\dfrac{3}{8}$ **B.** $\dfrac{4}{7}$ **C.** $\dfrac{8}{3}$ **D.** $\dfrac{7}{4}$

Q.77 Direction: What will come in place of question mark (?) in the following question?

$$18\dfrac{2}{3} + 7\dfrac{1}{2} = ?$$

A. $26\dfrac{1}{3}$ **B.** $19\dfrac{1}{2}$ **C.** $26\dfrac{1}{6}$ **D.** $25\dfrac{2}{3}$

Q.78 Direction: Find the value of '?' in the given equation:

$72 \times 25 + 45 \times 20 = 15^3 - ?$

A. 525   **B.** 675   **C.** 575   **D.** 625

Q.79 Direction: Find the value of ' ?' in the given equation.

$$\sqrt[3]{8000} - \sqrt[3]{4096} - \sqrt[3]{64} = ?$$

A. -8 **B.** -7 **C.** 0 **D.** 6

Q.80 Simplify:

$$9\dfrac{1}{7} + 9\dfrac{2}{7} + 9\dfrac{3}{7} + 9\dfrac{4}{7} + 9\dfrac{5}{7} + 9\dfrac{6}{7}$$

A. 57   **B.** 12   **C.** 17   **D.** 97

Q.81 Find the HCF of $1152, 1664$.

A. 128   **B.** 18   **C.** 182   **D.** 281

Q.82 If side of an equilateral triangle is ' a', then area of this triangle is equal to:

[HTET TGT Mathematics, 2018]

A. $\dfrac{3a^2}{2}$ **B.** $\dfrac{\sqrt{3}a^2}{2}$ **C.** $\dfrac{\sqrt{3}a^2}{4}$ **D.** $\sqrt{3}a^2$

Q.83 If the circumference of a circle is 18.6 cm more than its diameter, then what is the diameter of the circle?

[UPSSSC Rajasva Lekhpal, 2015]

A. 7.84 cm   **B.** 8.68 cm   **C.** 8.84 cm   **D.** 7.54 cm

Q.84 If sum of money becomes $\dfrac{7}{4}$ of itself in 3 years at certain rate of simple interest then find rate per annum:

A. 22% p.a   **B.** 25% p.a   **C.** 24% p.a   **D.** 20% p.a

Q.85 $3x - 5 = x + 5$ Find the value of x.

A. 5   **B.** 4   **C.** 3   **D.** 2

Q.86 Find the value of $\dfrac{x}{\sqrt{128}} = \dfrac{\sqrt{162}}{x}$.

A. 12   **B.** 14   **C.** 144   **D.** 196

Q.87 If the number when subtracted from 37.5% of itself gives the result as 35, find the original number.

A. 90   **B.** 49   **C.** 56   **D.** 72

Q.88 Find the median of the first nine prime numbers.

A. 5   **B.** 7   **C.** 11   **D.** 13

Q.89 Which number amongst $2^{40}, 3^{21}, 4^{18}$ and 8^{12} is the smallest?

[UPSC Prelims, 2022]

A. 2^{40} **B.** 3^{21} **C.** 4^{18} **D.** 8^{12}

Q.90 How many 3-digit natural numbers (without repetition of digits) are there such that each digit is odd and the number is divisible by 5?

[UPSC Prelims, 2022]

A. 8   **B.** 12   **C.** 16   **D.** 24

Q.91 What will come in place of question mark (?) in the following number series?

$$1, 1, 4, 8, 9, 27, ?, ?$$

A. 15,36   **B.** 16,25   **C.** 16,64   **D.** 25,49

Q.92 Which fraction is largest among $\dfrac{3}{13}, \dfrac{2}{15}, \dfrac{4}{17}$

A. $\dfrac{3}{13}$ **B.** $\dfrac{2}{15}$
C. $\dfrac{4}{17}$ **D.** All are equal

Q.93 The decimal expansion of $\dfrac{10}{3}$ will be:

A. Terminating
B. Non-terminating recurring (repeating)
C. Non-terminating non-recurring (repeating)
D. None of these

Q.94 Find the largest of the following fractions.

A. $\dfrac{9}{62}$ **B.** $\dfrac{6}{11}$ **C.** $\dfrac{10}{49}$ **D.** $\dfrac{31}{42}$

Q.95 If $x - 2y + 6y = 3x - 4x + 10$ and $x = 3$, then find the value of y.

A. 1   **B.** 2   **C.** 3   **D.** 4

Q.96 An umbrella is marked for Rs. 150 and sold for Rs. 138. The rate of discount is:

A. 10%   **B.** 5%   **C.** 8%   **D.** 6%

Q.97 Find the lowest common multiple of $24, 36$ and 42.

A. 520   **B.** 540   **C.** 504   **D.** 580

Q.98 What are the prime factors of 38760?

A. $2 \times 2 \times 2 \times 3 \times 3 \times 5 \times 17 \times 29$
B. $2 \times 2 \times 2 \times 3 \times 5 \times 7 \times 7 \times 29$
C. $2 \times 2 \times 2 \times 3 \times 5 \times 17 \times 19$
D. None of the above

Q.99 The sum of all prime numbers between 15 and 35 is:

A. 119   **B.** 121   **C.** 129   **D.** 131

Q.100 Find the remainder when 4^{13} divided by 3?

A. 1   **B.** 2   **C.** 0   **D.** 3

// Smart Answer Sheet //

Correct   Indicates percentage of students who answered questions correctly.

Skipped   Indicates percentage of students who skipped questions.

Q.	Ans.	Correct / Skipped	Q.	Ans.	Correct / Skipped	Q.	Ans.	Correct / Skipped	Q.	Ans.	Correct / Skipped	Q.	Ans.	Correct / Skipped
1	D	50.43 % / 1.53 %	17	D	46.5 % / 1.76 %	33	C	40.23 % / 1.31 %	49	B	40.07 % / 1.16 %	65	C	11.35 % / 3.48 %
2	A	82.9 % / 0.0 %	18	A	52.16 % / 1.28 %	34	C	88.38 % / 0.0 %	50	C	45.78 % / 1.07 %	66	A	46.93 % / 1.14 %
3	A	63.81 % / 1.87 %	19	B	65.49 % / 1.59 %	35	D	53.14 % / 1.97 %	51	D	61.06 % / 1.03 %	67	D	69.45 % / 1.48 %
4	A	42.52 % / 1.11 %	20	A	86.36 % / 0.0 %	36	D	59.65 % / 1.77 %	52	B	46.19 % / 1.79 %	68	D	69.71 % / 1.41 %
5	A	85.44 % / 0.0 %	21	A	53.4 % / 1.5 %	37	C	58.73 % / 1.8 %	53	C	79.82 % / 0.0 %	69	A	32.63 % / 4.55 %
6	B	47.83 % / 1.81 %	22	A	67.31 % / 1.62 %	38	B	64.05 % / 1.04 %	54	C	62.95 % / 1.19 %	70	D	58.53 % / 1.33 %
7	A	41.76 % / 1.08 %	23	D	84.4 % / 0.0 %	39	D	40.87 % / 1.56 %	55	A	80.12 % / 0.0 %	71	A	52.1 % / 1.36 %
8	A	59.58 % / 1.77 %	24	B	40.98 % / 1.62 %	40	A	51.91 % / 1.36 %	56	D	49.58 % / 1.98 %	72	D	41.08 % / 1.6 %
9	D	67.51 % / 1.32 %	25	D	54.66 % / 1.22 %	41	D	66.14 % / 1.33 %	57	C	81.93 % / 0.0 %	73	D	46.64 % / 1.83 %
10	D	31.96 % / 4.07 %	26	C	78.0 % / 0.0 %	42	D	57.15 % / 1.25 %	58	A	59.64 % / 1.79 %	74	C	47.5 % / 1.83 %
11	D	68.24 % / 1.67 %	27	A	60.5 % / 1.29 %	43	A	67.12 % / 1.25 %	59	C	62.61 % / 1.39 %	75	B	86.24 % / 0.0 %
12	C	42.81 % / 1.59 %	28	C	69.6 % / 1.1 %	44	B	79.78 % / 0.0 %	60	C	31.54 % / 4.29 %	76	C	26.66 % / 4.42 %
13	C	80.69 % / 0.0 %	29	A	46.61 % / 1.62 %	45	A	60.55 % / 1.22 %	61	A	62.93 % / 1.8 %	77	C	79.07 % / 0.0 %
14	C	68.83 % / 1.2 %	30	C	66.58 % / 1.91 %	46	B	41.98 % / 1.4 %	62	D	68.42 % / 1.23 %	78	B	76.77 % / 0.0 %
15	D	64.16 % / 1.91 %	31	B	68.57 % / 1.18 %	47	B	55.23 % / 1.94 %	63	A	52.95 % / 1.17 %	79	C	48.89 % / 1.47 %
16	C	84.39 % / 0.0 %	32	A	57.35 % / 1.99 %	48	B	61.66 % / 1.63 %	64	C	86.15 % / 0.0 %	80	A	49.48 % / 1.48 %

Q.	Ans.	Correct / Skipped
81	A	14.56 %
		4.31 %
82	C	86.18 %
		0.0 %
83	B	19.25 %
		3.62 %
84	B	59.83 %
		1.61 %

Q.	Ans.	Correct / Skipped
85	A	82.29 %
		0.0 %
86	A	81.81 %
		0.0 %
87	C	60.07 %
		1.75 %
88	C	87.9 %
		0.0 %

Q.	Ans.	Correct / Skipped
89	B	61.2 %
		1.05 %
90	B	69.56 %
		1.85 %
91	C	68.45 %
		1.3 %
92	C	69.84 %
		1.15 %

Q.	Ans.	Correct / Skipped
93	B	57.91 %
		1.8 %
94	D	50.5 %
		1.43 %
95	A	57.63 %
		1.78 %
96	C	32.45 %
		4.86 %

Q.	Ans.	Correct / Skipped
97	C	88.2 %
		0.0 %
98	C	62.11 %
		1.22 %
99	A	62.15 %
		1.4 %
100	A	53.65 %
		1.84 %

Performance Analysis

Avg. Score (%)	60.0%
Toppers Score (%)	74.0%
Your Score	

//Hints and Solutions//

1. जहाँ भावातिरेक के कारण शब्दों की पुनरावृत्ति होती है, वहाँ अल्प विराम का प्रयोग होता है।

- जहाँ एक तरह के कई शब्द, वाक्यांश या वाक्य एक साथ आते हैं. तो उनके बीच अल्प विराम का प्रयोग होता है।
- पर, परन्तु, इसलिए, अत:, क्योंकि, बल्कि, तथापि, जिससे आदि के पूर्व अल्प विराम का प्रयोग होता है।
- सम्बोधन के समय जिसे सम्बोधित किया जाता है, उसके बाद अल्प विराम का प्रयोग होता है।
- उद्धरण से पूर्व अल्प विराम का प्रयोग होता है।
- यह, वह, तब, तो, और, अब, आदि के लोप होने पर वाक्य में अल्प विराम का प्रयोग होता है।
- बस, वस्तुत:, अच्छा, वास्तव में आदि से आरम्भ होने वाले वाक्यों में इनके पश्चात् अल्प विराम का प्रयोग होता है।
- तारीख के साथ महीने का नाम लिखने के बाद तथा सन्, संवत् के पूर्व अल्प विराम का प्रयोग किया जाता है।
- अंकों को लिखते समय भी अल्प विराम का प्रयोग किया जाता है।

अत: विकल्प (D) सही है।

2. रमेश कल दिल्ली जाएगा' इस वाक्य में रमेश संज्ञा है।

किसी भी व्यक्ति, वस्तु, जाति, भाव या स्थान के नाम को ही संज्ञा कहते हैं। जैसे – मनुष्य (जाति), अमेरिका, भारत (स्थान), बचपन, मिठास(भाव), किताब, टेबल(वस्तु) आदि।

अत: विकल्प (A) सही है।

3. 'रौद्र रस' का स्थायी भाव क्रोध है।

"रौद्र रस" की विशेषताएँ निम्नलिखित है:

- "रौद्र रस" काव्य का एक रस है, जिसमें स्थायी भाव अथवा 'क्रोध' का भाव होता है।
- धार्मिक महत्व के आधार पर इसका वर्ण रक्त एवं देवता रुद्र है।

अत: विकल्प (A) सही है।

4. 'अनाड़ी' का तत्सम रूप 'अनार्य' होगा।

तत्सम का अर्थ होता है "उसके समान"। अर्थात, ऐसे शब्द जो संस्कृत के समान है, जो शब्द संस्कृत भाषा से हिंदी भाषा मे आये है और उन्हें ज्यों का त्यों प्रयुक्त कर रहे है, उन्हें तत्सम शब्द कहते है।

अत: विकल्प (A) सही है।

5. 'आधा' शब्द तद्भव शब्द है जिसका तत्सम 'अर्द्ध' होता है।

तद्भव का शाब्दिक अर्थ है – उससे बने (तत् + भव = उससे उत्पन्न), अर्थात जो उससे (संस्कृत से) उत्पन्न हुए हैं। यहाँ पर तत् शब्द भी संस्कृत भाषा की ओर इंगित करता है।

अत: विकल्प (A) सही है।

6. संयोजक शब्द से जुड़े हुए एक से अधिक साधारण वाक्यों से बनने वाला वाक्य 'संयुक्त वाक्य' कहलाता है। जैसे - राधा गयी और रीता आयी।

अत: विकल्प (B) सही है।

7. 'सुनील बहुत अच्छा निशानेबाज है।' इस वाक्य में 'अच्छा' विशेषण शब्द है और 'बहुत' शब्द 'अच्छा' की विशेषता बता रहा है जो प्रविशेषण है।

विशेषण की भी विशेषता बताने वाले शब्द प्रविशेषण कहलाते हैं।

जो शब्द संज्ञा या सर्वनाम की विशेषता बताते हैं, विशेषण कहलाते हैं।

अत: विकल्प (A) सही है।

8. निजवाचक सर्वनाम: जहाँ स्वयं के लिए 'आप, अपना, अपने आप' शब्दों का प्रयोग हो।

उदाहरण: आप, अपना, अपने आप, स्वत:

अत: विकल्प (A) सही है।

9. व्याकरण के नियमों में बँधे, वाक्य में प्रयुक्त शब्द पद कहलाते हैं।

- जब कोई शब्द वाक्य में प्रयोग किया जाता है तो पद कहलाता है।
- जैसे - 'परिश्रम' एक शब्द है, जब इस शब्द को वाक्य में प्रयोग कर दें जैसे 'परिश्रम का फल मीठा होता है, तो यह पद कहलाता है।

अन्य विकल्प असंगत है।

अत: विकल्प (D) सही है।

10. पूर्ण वाक्य है - भाषा के लिखने के ढंग को लिपि कहते हैं।

- भाषा- भाषा वह साधन है जिसके द्वारा हम अपने विचारों को व्यक्त कर सकते हैं और इसके लिये हम वाचिक ध्वनियों का प्रयोग करते हैं।

विकल्प:

- वर्ण – अक्षर
- शब्द – वर्णों का सार्थक समूह, ध्वनि
- वाक्य – सार्थक शब्द समूह
- लिपि - भाषा के लघुतम ध्वनि अक्षरों का समूह।

अत: विकल्प (D) सही है।

11. ओष्ठों की स्थिति के अनुसार स्वरों का 2 प्रकार से वर्गीकरण किया गया है, वे अवृत्तमुखी और वृत्तमुखी हैं।

- वृत्तमुखी स्वर: ओष्ठों को वृत्ताकार (गोल) करके जिन स्वरों का उच्चारण होता है, उन्हें वृत्तमुखी या वृत्ताकार स्वर कहते हैं। इनकी संख्या पाँच है – उ, ऊ, ओ, औ तथा गृहीत स्वर ऑ।
- अवृत्तमुखी स्वर: जिन स्वरों के उच्चारण में ओष्ठ गोल होने की बजाए फैल जाते हैं, उन्हें अवृत्तमुखी स्वर कहते हैं। इनकी संख्या छः है – आ, इ, ई, ऋ, ए तथा ऐ।

अत: विकल्प (D) सही है।

12. दिए गए विकल्पों में 'निषेध' शब्द वर्तनीगत शुद्ध शब्द है।

जिसका अर्थ मनाही, रोक या बाधा होता है।

'निषेध' का विलोम शब्द 'विधि' होगा।

वर्तनी: लिखने की रीति को वर्तनी कहते हैं। 'वर्तनी' शब्द का अर्थ उच्चारित होने वाले शब्द के लेखन में प्रयोग होने वाले लिपि चिह्नों के व्यवस्थित रूप को वर्तनी कहा जाता है।

अत: विकल्प (C) सही है।

13. 'अनादर' का विलोम 'आदर' है। शेष विकल्प असंगत हैं।

अन्य विकल्प:

- मान : अपमान
- सम्मान : असम्मान
- सत्कार : तिरस्कार

अत: विकल्प (C) सही है।

14. दिए गए विकल्पों में 'वाह ! कितना सुन्दर दृश्य है।' यह विस्मयादिबोधक वाक्य का उदाहरण है।

वह वाक्य जिससे किसी प्रकार की गहरी अनुभूति का प्रदर्शन किया जाता है, वह विस्मयादिबोधक या विस्मयादिवाचक वाक्य कहलाता हैं।

उपर्युक्त वाक्य में खुशी कि गहरी अनुभूति हो रही है। इसका चिह्न (!) है।

अत: विकल्प (C) सही है।

15. 'जो मापा न जा सके' वाक्यांश के लिए एक शब्द है - 'अपरिमेय'

जिसका परिमाण जाना जा सके - परिमेय

जिसे मापा या तौला जा सके - परिमाप

त्रि-विमीय स्थान की मात्रा की माप - आयतन

अत: विकल्प (D) सही है।

16. 'जिसको त्यागा न जा सके' के लिए एक शब्द 'अत्याज्य' होगा।

अन्य विकल्प:

- त्यक्त: जिसे त्यागा जा चुका हो
- त्याग: नाता तोड़ देने की क्रिया
- त्याज्य: त्याग करने योग्य

अत: विकल्प (C) सही है।

17. 'मैं शायद कहानी पढ़ूंगी' वाक्य सम्भाव्य भविष्य काल का है।

अन्य विकल्प :

- मैं कहानी पढ़ती हूँ - सामान्य वर्तमान
- मैंने कहानी पढ़ी थी - सामान्य भूत
- मैं कहानी पढ़ रही हूँ - तात्कालिक वर्तमान

अत: विकल्प (D) सही है।

18. 'घबरा जाना' अर्थ के लिए उचित मुहावरा 'चेहरे की हवाइयाँ उड़ना' है।

वाक्य-प्रयोग: जैसे ही श्रवण का नाम बुलाया गया उसके चेहरे की हवाइयाँ उड़ गई।

अत: विकल्प (A) सही है।

19. दिए गए विकल्पों में से 'सइयाँ भए कोतवाल अब डर काहे का' सही विकल्प है।

'मनमानी करना' के अर्थ के लिए उपयुक्त लोकोक्ति दिए गए विकल्पों में 'सइयाँ भए कोतवाल अब डर काहे का' ये है। अन्य असंगत हैं।

वाक्य- मीरा बिना हेलमेट के अपनी स्कूटी से निकली तो उसकी सहेली ने कहा कि हेलमेट तो लगा लो तो उसने बहुत घमंड से कहा 'सइयाँ भए कोतवाल अब डर काहे का'।

अत: विकल्प (B) सही है।

20. 'राजा <u>सेवक को</u> कम्बल देता है', वाक्य में रेखांकित पद में सम्प्रदान कारक है।

दिए गए वाक्य में किसी को कुछ देने का बोध हो रहा है। अत: यहाँ सम्प्रदान कारक है। जिस शब्द से किसी के लिए कुछ करने या देने का बोध हो, इसकी विभक्ति 'को' और 'के लिए' है।

अत: विकल्प (A) सही है।

21. विराम चिह्न की दृष्टि से शुद्ध वाक्य चारों भाई सुंदर, सुशील, नम्र, दयालु और सबल थे।

'चारों भाई सुंदर, सुशील, नम्र, दयालु और सबल थे।' प्रस्तुत वाक्य में उचित स्थानों पर अल्पविराम और पूर्ण विराम का प्रयोग किया गया है।

जब हम एक से अधिक वस्तुओं की बात करते हैं कुछ अंतराल देने के लिए अल्पविराम का प्रयोग करते हैं। जैसा कि सुंदर, सुशील, नम्र, दयालु के बीच में किया गया है।

अत: विकल्प (A) सही है।

22. अहंकार का संधि-विच्छेद - 'अहम् + कार'।

अहंकार शब्द में व्यंजन संधि है।

अहंकार में संधि का नियम - म् + क = ङ्क।

अत: विकल्प (A) सही है।

23. वृक्ष का पर्यायवाची 'कानन' नहीं है।

वृक्ष का पर्यायवाची : तरू, अगम, पेड़, पादप, विटप, गाछ, दरख्त, शाखी, विटप, द्रुम।

कानन का पर्यायवाची : जंगल, अरण्य, वन, अटवी, कान्तार, विपिन।

अत: विकल्प (D) सही है।

24. तैराक शब्द में तैर मूल शब्द है और 'आक' प्रत्यय है।

तैराक - जो खूब अच्छी तरह तैरना जानता हो।

'अक' प्रत्यय से बने शब्द - लेखक, पाठक, कारक, गायक।

अत: विकल्प (B) सही है।

25. उपरोक्त विकल्पों में 'हस्ताक्षर' शब्द बहुवचन है।

अन्य विकल्प:

शब्द	वचन
भीड़	एकवचन
मिठास	एकवचन
चाय	एकवचन

शब्द के जिस रुप से एक अथवा अनेक होने का बोध हो उसे 'वचन' कहते हैं।

अत: विकल्प (D) सही है।

26. The present continuous tense is formed with the subject plus the present particle form (-ing) of the main verb and the present continuous tense of the verb to be: am, is, are. One simple example of this tense is: He is swimming.

Then, the given sentence is of present continuous tense.

Hence, the correct option is (C).

27. The structure is given below:

Subject + is/am/are + V1 + ing + Object

For events that will take place in the near future, Present Continuous Tense is used.

Complete sentence: We are visiting the City Palace in the afternoon as per the schedule.

Hence, the correct option is (A).

28. Correct sentence: When my father visits him, he feels good.

- The given sentence is the type Zero conditional.

- The zero conditional is used for when the time being referred to is now or always and the situation is real and possible.

- The zero conditional is often used to refer to general truths.

- The tense in both parts of the sentence is the simple present.

- In zero conditional sentences, the word "if" can usually be replaced by the word "when" without changing the meaning.

Hence, the correct option is (C).

29. Complete Sentence: My father was not hungry; nevertheless, he ate a heavy lunch.

The given sentence is talking about a father who ate a heavy lunch even though he was not hungry.

Let us explore the given options:

- The adverb 'nevertheless' means in spite of that.

- The adverb 'further' means more; to a greater degree.

- The adverb 'besides' means in addition; as well.

- The adverb 'instead' means as an alternative or substitute.

Conclusion: In spite of the fact that his/her father was not hungry, he ate a heavy lunch.

Hence, the correct option is (A).

30. Correct sentence: There was a time when the national marriage rate was rather too high.

- 'Fairly' is used to a positive degree and it is not followed by 'too'.

- 'Fair' is an adjective.

- 'Rather' is used to a positive and comparative degree and it is followed by 'too'.

- So, the word 'rather' should be used to make the sentence grammatically correct.

- So, the correct answer is 'rather'.

Hence, the correct option is (C).

31. Correct Sentence: My husband can play the piano very well because he's a professional pianist.

Let us explore the options:

- 'Might' is a modal verb most commonly used to express possibility. It is also often used in conditional sentences. 'Might' is also used to make suggestions or requests.

- 'Can' is a modal verb most commonly used to express; ability, opportunity, a request, to grant permission, to show possibility or impossibility.

- 'Shall' is a modal verb used to indicate future action and is often found in suggestions. It is frequently used in promises or voluntary actions.

- 'May' is a modal verb most commonly used to express possibility. It can also be used to give or request permission.

In the given sentence, the ability to play the piano is shown.

Hence, the correct option is (B).

32. Complete Sentence: Everyone must save the natural resources of the earth.

The given sentence is talking about saving the natural resources of the earth.

Let us explore the given options:

- 'Must' means be obliged to; should (expressing necessity).

- 'Might' is used for expressing a possibility based on an unfulfilled condition.

- 'Could' is used to indicate possibility.

- 'Dare' means have the courage to do something.

Hence, the correct option is (A).

33. The complete sentence will be: She is industrious yet is not recognized in her field.

- In order to fill in the blank, we need to select the appropriate conjunction.

- Conjunctions are words or groups of words used to connect two or more than two words, phrases, or clauses.

- For eg.- and, but, yet, where, etc.

- Conjunctions such as but, yet, still, only, however, etc are known as adversative conjunctions, used to join such nouns, pronouns, sentences, etc, that denote the result is opposite.

- For example- I am going to the market however I will not buy you ice cream.

- In the given sentence, we can see that the woman is industrious but still the results are opposite.

- She is not appreciated.

- We will therefore use the conjunction 'yet' to fill in the blank.

Hence, the correct option is (C).

34. Once upon a time, **the** English ruled over the whole world.

- Articles are words that define a noun as specific or unspecific.

- The definite article 'the' is used with the name of things that are unique or already mentioned before.

- 'The' isn't used with the name of a language though it can be used before 'nationality'.

- As per the context of the given sentence, peoples/rulers from England are being talked about.

- So, the article 'the' will be appropriate here.

Hence, the correct option is (C).

35. All monks and nuns of this church are invited to the program. The feminine gender of monk is nun. So using nun is suitable here in this context.

Feminine nouns refer to female figures or female members of a species (i.e. woman, girl, actress, mare, etc.)

Hence, the correct option is (D).

36. The correctly spelled word is Satellite.

A satellite is a moon, planet, or machine that orbits a planet or star. Usually, the word "satellite" refers to a machine that is launched into space and moves around Earth or another body in space.

Hence, the correct option is (D).

37. From the given options, the correct choice to fill in the blank is 'each.'

We know that each other is used to denote the mutual relationship between two person or things.

Example: The sibling loves each other.

From the above mentions information, it is clear that 'each' is the correct answer.

Correct sentence: He was so afraid that his knees knocked each other.

Hence, the correct option is (C).

38. A person who knows everything: Omniscient

Omniscient means someone having complete or unlimited knowledge.

Example: They give the impression that the book is omniscient.

Hence, the correct option is (B).

39. The correct punctuated sentence is: He said, "I do not like video games."

The given sentence is a direct speech, so 'quotation marks' should be used here.

The question mark is used after asking a question.
Example: What is her name?

The exclamation mark is used to express wonder, surprise or to emphasize. Example: I have found the lost photo album!

Hence, the correct option is (D).

40. Simran is an officer, but her husband owns a café.

If any word starts with these vowels or has any vowel sound then the article 'an' is used before them. In the given sentence 'honest' starts with a 'vowel sound'.

Some words start with 'vowel sound' but start with 'consonant letter'. We use 'an' article before these kinds of words.

Hence, the correct option is (A).

41. "Busy" is the synonym of "Active".

Active: Engaging or ready to engage in physically energetic pursuits.

Busy: (of a time or place) full of activity.

Hence, the correct option is (D).

42. The most appropriate synonym of the given word 'Elegant' is 'Graceful'.

Elegant: having a good or attractive style

Graceful: having a smooth, attractive movement or form

Hence, the correct option is (D).

43. 'Temporary' is the correct antonym of 'Permanent'.

Permanent - lasting for long time or forever.

Temporary - lasting for very short time.

Hence, the correct option is (A).

44. The most appropriate antonym of the given word 'Neglect' is 'Care'.

Neglect: to give too little or no attention or care to somebody/something.

Care: looking after somebody/something so that he/she/it has what he/she/it needs for his/her/its health and protection.

Hence, the correct option is (B).

45. The meaningful word from the words "EVCOL" is "Clove".

Clove is a tree native to Indonesia. Its dried flower buds are a popular spice and are also used in Chinese and Ayurvedic medicine.

Hence, the correct option is (A).

46. The part of speech of the word 'why' is an interjection.

- Interjections are words used to express strong feelings or sudden emotions.
- They are included in a sentence (usually at the start) to express a sentiment such as surprise, disgust, joy, excitement, or enthusiasm.
- Example: Wow, that's so beautiful!
- In the given sentence, the word 'whoa' is showing emotion.

Hence, the correct option is (B).

47. Big and enormous are both synonyms.

Now we need to find a word which is the synonym of 'small'.

Compact means having all the necessary components or features neatly fitted into a small space.

Clearly, 'compact' is the correct word.

Hence, the correct option is (B).

48. He wanted to swim in the pool.

- An infinitive verb is essentially the base form of a verb with the word "to" in front of it.
- When we use an infinitive verb, the "to" is a part of the verb. It is not acting as a preposition in this case.

- The infinitive is the base form of a verb.

- Structure: To + Base form of the verb.

- Example: I decided not to go to London.

- Infinitives are never conjugated with -ed or -ing at the end because they are not used as verbs in a sentence.

- When want, learn and offer are followed by another verb, it must be in the to + infinitive form.

- For Example - I want to speak to the manager.

- Here, "to swim" is an infinitive verb.

Hence, the correct option is (B).

49. Adorable is an adjective.

Adorable means inspiring great affection or delight. An adjective is a word that describes the traits, qualities, or the number of a noun.

Hence, the correct option is (B).

50. Julie would like to visit Kyoto when she is in Japan.

The sentence talks about the imaginary situation.

Would: We use "would" as the past of "will" and it is used to make hypotheses. In this condition, we imagine a situation.

- Example: I would give you a lift, but my wife has the car today.

Hence, the correct option is (C).

51. LIC entered the Fortune Global 500 list for the first time in August 2022.

- Meanwhile, Reliance Industries which is the largest company in terms of market capitalization in India, jumped 51 places.

- However, LIC was at the top of the list from India.

- A total of nine Indian companies have entered the list, out of which, five of them were state-owned and four were private sector firms.

Hence, the correct option is (D).

52. The Parliament has launched a new app, Digital Sansad, that will make it easier for people to follow proceedings in Parliament, and also their own lawmakers. In addition, it will also help members of parliament access services such as checking personal updates. In the future, the MPs can log in for attendance, give questions for the Question Hour, or submit notices for debates.

Hence, the correct option is (B).

53. There is a 3 tier structure of local self-government in Uttar Pradesh:

1. Zila Panchayat at District Level
2. Kshetra Panchayat at Intermediary (Block) level
3. Gram Panchayat at the Village level

Hence, the correct option is (C).

54. With the adoption of a new Indian constitution in 1950, the United Provinces were renamed Uttar Pradesh and became a constituent state of the Republic of India.

Hence, the correct option is (C).

55. The famous Buland Darwaza located in Fatehpur Sikri in Uttar Pradesh.

Buland Darwaza, or the "Door of victory", was built in 1575 A.D. by Mughal emperor Akbar to commemorate his victory over Gujarat.Hence, the correct option is (A).

56. Chaukhandi Stupa is a Buddhist stupa in Sarnath, located 8 kilometers from Cantt Railway Station Varanasi, Uttar Pradesh, India. Stupas have evolved from burial mounds and serve as a shrine for a relic of the Buddha.
Hence, the correct option is (D).

57. Aligarh is an important business center of Uttar Pradesh and it is well known as the city of locks in India. Due to the easy of availability of the raw materials and power supply, Aligarh has emerged as good business centre. Aligarh locks are exported across the world.
Hence, the correct option is (C).

58. Keetham lake, also known as Sur Sarovar, in Agra of Uttar Pradesh has been added to the list of Ramsar sites.

- More than 106 species of migratory birds rest in Sur Sarovar lake.

- The water of the lake is obtained from Agra Canal.

- The canal originates from Okhla barrage on River Yamuna in Delhi.

Hence, the correct option is (A).

59. The radioactive isotope of hydrogen is tritium.

The most stable radioactive isotope is tritium, with a half-life of 12.32 years. Hydrogen is the first element in the periodic table and has the atomic number one. Those elements which have the same atomic number but a different mass number are called isotopes. The isotopes are different because of the different numbers of neutrons present in them.

Hence, the correct option is (C).

60. The correct pair of country and capital are Libya - Tripoli.

Libya officially the State of Libya is a country in the Maghreb region in North Africa. It is bordered by the Mediterranean Sea to the north, Egypt to the east, Sudan to the southeast, Chad to the south, Niger to the southwest, Algeria to the west, and Tunisia to the northwest. Libya is made of three historical regions: Tripolitania, Fezzan, and Cyrenaica.

Tripoli is the capital and largest city of Libya, with a population of about 1.1 million people in 2019. It is located in the northwest of Libya on the edge of the desert, on a point of rocky land projecting into the Mediterranean Sea and forming a bay.

Hence, the correct option is (C).

61. Fossil fuel is formed by natural processes.

Fossil fuels range from volatile materials with low carbon-to-hydrogen ratios (like methane) to liquids (like petroleum), to nonvolatile materials composed of almost pure carbon, like Anthracite coal.

It is formed such as the anaerobic decomposition of buried dead organisms. These types of organisms and their resulting fossil fuels typically have an age of millions of years, and sometimes more than 650 million years. These types of fuels (Fossil fuels) contain high percentages of carbon and include coal, natural gas, and petroleum. Commonly used derivatives of fossil fuels include propane and kerosene. Till 2018, the world's main primary energy sources which amount to 85% share for fossil fuels in primary energy consumption in the world consists of

- Coal (27%)
- Petroleum (34%), and
- Natural gas (24%)

Hence, the correct option is (A).

62. Ganymede, a satellite of Jupiter is the largest satellite in the Solar system.

Jupiter has the shortest days of all the planets in the solar system.

Planet	No. of Satellites	Important Points
Mercury	None	• It is the closest planet to the Sun. • A year in mercury is just 88 days long. • It is the smallest planet in the solar system.
Venus	None	• It is also known as 'morning star' and 'evening star'. • It is an earth-like planet in size and mass therefore it is also called 'Earth's twin'. • It is the hottest planet of the solar system.
Saturn	82	• It is the second-largest planet of the solar system. • Titan is the largest satellite of Saturn.

Hence, the correct option is (D).

63. Ibn Battuta was a Moorish traveler who visited India during the reign of Muhammad-bin-Tughlaq. His book Rehal (The travelogue) throws a lot of light on the reign of Muhammad-bin-Tughlaq and the geographical, economic, and social conditions in India. He was appointed as the chief Qazi of Delhi.

Hence, the correct option is (A).

64. It is a papaya leaf.

Papaya leaf is often consumed as an extract, tea, or juice and has been found to treat symptoms related to dengue fever. Other common uses include reducing inflammation, improving blood sugar control, supporting skin and hair health, and preventing cancer.

Hence, the correct option is (C).

65. The intermediate level in the Panchayati Raj Institutions called Panchayat Samiti.

The Panchayat Samiti is the intermediate level in the Panchayati Raj Institutions. It is the tehsil or taluka or block level of the rural local-self government system in India. Panchayat Samiti at the block level is an Administrative Authority that is responsible for enforcing the law and carrying it into effect. They form the middle level of the Panchayati Raj Institutions in India.

Hence, the correct option is (C).

66. The Gondwana rock system is famous for coal.

Gondwana rocks contain nearly 98% of India's coal reserves. The carbon content is very low. The Gondwana rock system is also called the Carboniferous rock system. They are deposits ordered down in synclinal troughs on ancient tableland surfaces.

Hence, the correct option is (A).

67. Acharya Vinoba Bhave was the first Indian who won the Ramon Magsaysay award. Human rights activist Vinoba Bhave was among the first five individuals to receive the Ramon Magsaysay Award in its year of inception in 1958.

Hence, the correct option is (D).

68. Homi Jehangir Bhabha is known as the 'Father of the Indian Nuclear Programme'.

Homi Jehangir Bhabha was an Indian nuclear physicist, founding director, and professor of physics at the Tata Institute of Fundamental Research. In 1954, Bhabha founded a nuclear research centre at Trombay which was later renamed the Bhabha Atomic Research Centre (BARC).

Hence, the correct option is (D).

69. Lime reacts with baking soda to liberate carbon di oxide gas.

Baking soda is sodium bicarbonate. Lime contains citric acid which is an organic acid of formula $C_6H_8O_7$.

Acids when reacted with sodium bicarbonate liberates carbon dioxide gas. Citric Acid on reaction with baking soda produces carbonic acid. Carbonic acid then decomposes further to give water and carbon dioxide CO_2.

Hence, the correct option is (A).

70. PM Narendra Modi on 7 July 2022 inaugurated 'Akhil Bhartiya Shiksha Samagam' on implementation of the National Education Policy (NEP) in Varanasi.

The Ministry of Education is organising Shiksha Samagam from 7th to 9th July '22. It will provide a platform for academicians & policymakers to deliberate, share their experiences & discuss the roadmap for effective implementation of the NEP 2020.

Hence, the correct option is (D).

71. India win the 2022 U19 World Cup title, by beating England by 4 wickets

Shaik Rasheed and Nishant Sindhu cracked the 50s in chase of 190 as India clinched record-extending fifth U19 World Cup title in Antigua. Raj Bawa claimed a fifer while Ravi Kumar bagged 4 wickets to fold England for 189.

Hence, the correct option is (A).

72. Prithvi II has been successfully test fired by India on 15 June 2022.

Prithvi-II is capable of carrying 500-1,000 kilogram of warheads and is powered by liquid propulsion twin engines. It is a surface-to-surface short-range ballistic missile developed by Defence Research and Development Organisation (DRDO).

Hence, the correct option is (D).

73. Bonalu is the "state festival" of Telangana state.

Bonalu is a Hindu festival in which Goddess Mahakali is worshipped. Bonalu, the annual festival of Telangana which is celebrated in Hyderabad, Secunderabad and Telangana apart from many other parts of India. It is celebrated in the month of Ashadha i.e. in July/August. Special pujas are performed for Yellamma on the first and last day of the festival. This festival is celebrated to thank the Goddess for fulfillment of vows.

Hence, the correct option is (D).

74. Bhavabhuti wrote the play "Uttararamacharita".

Bhavabhuti, Indian dramatist and poet, whose dramas, written in Sanskrit and noted for their suspense and vivid characterization, rival the outstanding plays of the better-known playwright Kalidasa.

Hence, the correct option is (C).

75. Only glow do not produce flame on burning.

Coal burns directly without getting vaporised. So it does not produce the flame. It burns with a glow.

Hence, the correct option is (B).

76. Given:

$$\frac{-(4-6)^2 - 3(-2) + |-6|}{18 - 9 \div 3 \times 5}$$

$$= \frac{-(-2)^2 - (-6) + 6}{18 - 3 \times 5}$$

$$= \frac{-4 + 6 + 6}{18 - 15}$$

$$= \frac{8}{3}$$

Hence, the correct option is (C).

77. Given:

$$= 18\frac{2}{3} + 7\frac{1}{2}$$

$$= \frac{56}{3} + \frac{15}{2}$$

$$= \frac{112 + 45}{6}$$

$$= \frac{157}{6}$$

$$= 26\frac{1}{6}$$

Hence, the correct option is (C).

78. The given equation is:

$$\Rightarrow 72 \times 25 + 45 \times 20 = 15^3 - ?$$

By simplifying the above equation, we get:

$$\Rightarrow 1800 + 900 = 3375 - ?$$

$$\Rightarrow ? = 3375 - 2700 = 675$$

Hence, the correct option is (B).

79. The given equation is:

$$= \sqrt[3]{8000} - \sqrt[3]{4096} - \sqrt[3]{64}$$

$$= 20 - 16 - 4$$

$$= 0$$

Hence, the correct option is (C).

80. Separating the whole part and the fraction part of the expression, we get

$$9 + 9 + 9 + 9 + 9 + 9 + \frac{1}{7} + \frac{2}{7} + \frac{3}{7} + \frac{4}{7} + \frac{5}{7} + \frac{6}{7}$$

$$= 54 + \frac{21}{7}$$

$$= 54 + 3$$

$$= 57$$

Hence, the correct option is (A).

81. Factor of $1152 = 2 \times 2 \times 2 \times 2 \times 2 \times 2 \times 2 \times 3 \times 3$

Factor of $1664 = 2 \times 2 \times 2 \times 2 \times 2 \times 2 \times 2 \times 13$

So, HCF $= 128$

Hence, the correct option is (A).

82. Given:

Side of an equilateral triangle is a

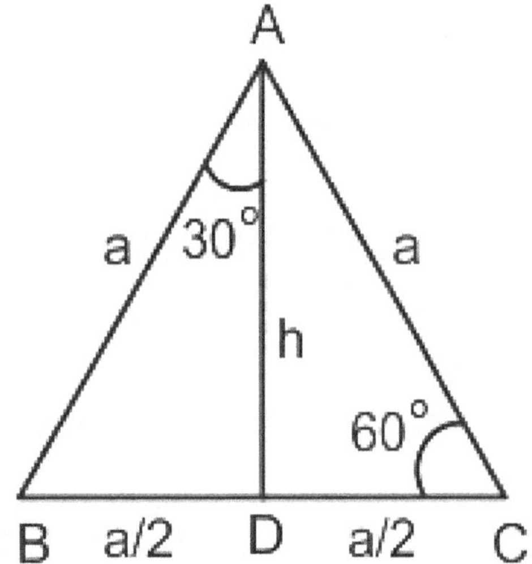

As we know,

$$A = \frac{1}{2}(b \times h)$$

We know that perpendicular AD bisects the side BC

$$\Rightarrow BD = DC = \frac{a}{2}$$

In a triangle, ABD, using Pythagoras theorem,

$$AB^2 = AD^2 + BD^2$$

$$\Rightarrow a^2 = \left(\frac{a}{2}\right)^2 + h^2$$

$$\Rightarrow h = \sqrt{3}\frac{a}{2}$$

So, the area of triangle ABD

$$A' = \frac{1}{2}\left(\frac{a}{2} \times \frac{a\sqrt{3}}{2}\right) = \frac{\sqrt{3}}{4}a^2$$

Since,

Area of triangle $ABC = 2 \times$ area of a triangle ABC

$$A = \frac{\sqrt{3}}{4}a^2$$

Hence, the correct option is (C).

83. Given:

The circumference of a circle is 18.6 cm.

We know that,

Diameter of circle $= d$,

Circumference of circle $= \pi d$

According to the question:

$$\pi d - d = 18.6$$

$$\Rightarrow d(\pi - 1) = 18.6$$

$$\Rightarrow d\left(\frac{22}{7} - 1\right) = 18.6$$

$$\Rightarrow d\left(\frac{22-7}{7}\right) = 18.6$$

$$\Rightarrow d \times \frac{15}{7} = 18.6$$

$$\Rightarrow d = 18.6 \times \frac{7}{15} = 8.68 \text{ cm}$$

So, the diameter of the circle is 8.68 cm.

Hence, the correct option is (B).

84. Given,

Time $= 3$ years

Amount : Principal $= 7:4 = \frac{7}{4}$

As we know,

Interest $=$ Amount $-$ Principal

$$\text{SI} = \frac{P \times R \times T}{100}$$

Where $P =$ principal, $R =$ rate and $T =$ time

Let principal be $4x$ and amount be $7x$.

Interest $=$ Amount $-$ Principal

$$= 7x - 4x$$

$$= 3x$$

$$\text{SI} = \frac{P \times R \times T}{100}$$

$$\Rightarrow 3x = \frac{4x \times R \times 3}{100}$$

$$\Rightarrow 3x \times 100 = 4x \times R \times 3$$

$$\Rightarrow 300x = 4x \times R \times 3$$

$$\Rightarrow \frac{300x}{4x \times 3} = R$$

$$\Rightarrow R = 25\% \text{ p.a.}$$

$\therefore$ The rate of interest is 25% p.a.

Hence, the correct option is (B).

85. Given: $3x - 5 = x + 5$

$$3x - x = 5 + 5$$

$$2x = 10$$

$$x = 5$$

Hence, the correct option is (A).

86. Given,

$$\frac{x}{\sqrt{128}} = \frac{\sqrt{162}}{x}$$

Then,

$$x^2 = \sqrt{128 \times 162}$$

$$\Rightarrow x^2 = \sqrt{64 \times 2 \times 18 \times 9}$$

$$\Rightarrow x^2 = \sqrt{8^2 \times 6^2 \times 3^2}$$

$$\Rightarrow x^2 = 8 \times 6 \times 3$$

$$\Rightarrow x^2 = 144$$

$$\Rightarrow x = \sqrt{144}$$

$$\therefore x = 12$$

Hence, the correct option is (A).

87. Given:

Let the original number be 100x.

The number when subtracted from 37.5%

So, New number $= 100x \times \left(\frac{100-37.5}{100}\right) = 62.5x$

Resulting number = 35 = 62.5x

$\Rightarrow$ x = 0.56

$\Rightarrow$ 100x = 0.56 × 100 = 56

$\therefore$ Original value of number is 56.

Hence, the correct option is (C).

88. As we know,

Prime numbers are those numbers that have only 2 factors i.e.,1 and themselves.

The first nine prime numbers are $2,3,5,7,11,13,17,19$ and 23.

Total numbers, $n = 9$ (odd number)

Median $= \left[\frac{(n+1)}{2}\right]^{\text{th}} = \left[\frac{(9+1)}{2}\right] = 5^{\text{th}}$

Here, 5th term is 11.

So, the median of the first nine prime numbers is 11.

Hence, the correct option is (C).

89. Given,

Numbers are: $2^{40}, 3^{21}, 4^{18},$ and 8^{12}.

We can also write them as: $2^{40}, 3^{21}, 2^{36},$ and 2^{36}. (as $4 = 2^2$, and $8 = 2^3$)

So, we basically need to find the smallest one from among 2^{36}, and 3^{21}. As we cannot have two correct answers, it must be 3^{21}.

We can rewrite $2^{36} = 2^{3^{12}}$ and $3^{21} = 3^{3^7}$

$$4096 > 2187$$

So, 3^{21} is the smallest number.

Hence, the correct option is (B).

90. Given,

Number of $3 -$ digit numbers without repetition of digits in which each digit is odd and the number is divisible by 5.

We have odd numbers as $1,3,5,7,9$

In $3 -$ digit numbers we have three positions of digits i.e. units, tens and hundreds in which units digit will always be 5 because number is divisible by 5.

For remaining two positions we have 4 numbers i.e., $1,3,7,9$.

So, for arranging these numbers we use permutation as:

$${}^4P_2 = \frac{4!}{(4-2)!}$$

$$= \frac{4 \times 3 \times 2 \times 1}{2 \times 1}$$

$$= 12$$

Hence, the correct option is (B).

91. Given:

$$1,1,4,8,9,27,?,?$$

There are two series in the given number series.

The first series is of the square of the numbers,

$$\Rightarrow 1,4,9,\underline{16}$$

The second series is of the cube of the numbers,

$$\Rightarrow 1,8,27,\underline{64}$$

$\therefore 16,64$ will come in the place of $?$.

Hence, the correct option is (C).

92. Given:

$$\frac{3}{13}, \frac{2}{15}, \frac{4}{17}$$

To know the largest fraction we need to compare the three fractions.

Comparing two fractions $\frac{3}{13}$ and $\frac{2}{15}$,

$$\Rightarrow 3 \times 15 = 45$$

$$\Rightarrow 13 \times 2 = 26$$

So, $\frac{3}{13}$ is larger.

Comparing $\frac{3}{13}$ and $\frac{4}{17}$,

$\Rightarrow 3 \times 17 = 51$

$\Rightarrow 13 \times 4 = 52$

$\frac{4}{17}$ is larger.

Comparing $\frac{4}{17}$ and $\frac{2}{15}$,

$\Rightarrow 4 \times 15 = 60$

$\Rightarrow 17 \times 2 = 34$

Comparing all three we get $\frac{4}{17}$ is the largest among all.

Hence, the correct option is (C).

93. Given:

Decimal expansion $= \frac{10}{3}$

$\Rightarrow \frac{10}{3} = 3.333$

$\therefore$ Decimal expansion is non-terminating recurring.

Hence, the correct option is (B).

94. Given:

$\frac{9}{62}, \frac{6}{11}, \frac{10}{49}, \frac{31}{42}$

According to the question,

$\Rightarrow \frac{9}{62} = 0.1451$

$\Rightarrow \frac{6}{11} = 0.5454$

$\Rightarrow \frac{10}{49} = 0.2040$

$\Rightarrow \frac{31}{42} = 0.7380$

$\therefore$ The largest fraction is $\frac{31}{42}$.

Hence, the correct option is (D).

95. Given:

$x - 2y + 6y = 3x - 4x + 10$

$x = 3$

Now,

$3 - 2y + 6y = 3(3) - 4(3) + 10$

$\Rightarrow 3 + 4y = 9 - 12 + 10$

$\Rightarrow 3 + 4y = -3 + 10$

$\Rightarrow 3 + 4y = 7$

$\Rightarrow 4y = 7 - 3$

$\Rightarrow 4y = 4$

$\Rightarrow y = 1$

Hence, the correct option is (A).

96. Given:

Marked price of umbrella $=$ Rs. 150

Selling price of umbrella $=$ Rs. 138

We know that,

$D\% = \frac{(MP - SP)}{MP} \times 100$

$= \frac{(150 - 138)}{150} \times 100$

$= \frac{12}{150} \times 100$

$= 8\%$

Hence, the correct option is (C).

97. The lowest common multiple of $24, 36$ and 42 is the smallest number which is divisible by $24, 36$ and 42.

Now, $24 = 2 \times 2 \times 2 \times 3$

$36 = 2 \times 3 \times 2 \times 3$

$42 = 3 \times 2 \times 7$

So, the lowest common multiple of $24, 36$ and 42 is:
$2 \times 3 \times 2 \times 2 \times 3 \times 7 = 504$

Hence, the correct option is (C).

98. To find the factors,

2	38760
2	19380
2	9690
3	4845
5	1615
17	323
19	19
	1

$\therefore 38760 = 2 \times 2 \times 2 \times 3 \times 5 \times 17 \times 19$

Hence, the correct option is (C).

99. Prime numbers between 15 and 35 are $17, 19, 23, 29$ and 31.

Now, $17 + 19 + 23 + 29 + 31 = 119$

$\therefore$ Sum of all prime numbers between 15 and 35 is 119.

Hence, the correct option is (A).

100. As per the given data,

Let us consider $4^1 = 4$, when divided by 3 gives the remainder 1.

Four power odd number when divided by 3 gives the remainder 1.

Similarly, $4^3 = 64$, when divided by 3 gives the remainder 1.

$\therefore 4^{13}$ divided by 3 also gives the remainder 1.

Hence, the correct option is (A).

Hindi

Q.1 वाक्यांश के लिए एक शब्द का चयन कीजिये:
आदि से अंत तक
A. अनादि
B. आद्योपान्त
C. समकालीन
D. समीचीन

Q.2 संरचना के आधार पर किए गए वाक्य के वर्गीकरण में इनमें से कौन सा प्रकार नहीं है?
[Rajasthan Teachers Eligibility Test - Level 1 Primary Level (RTET), 2015]
A. सरल वाक्य
B. मिश्र वाक्य
C. आज्ञार्थक वाक्य
D. संयुक्त वाक्य

Q.3 निम्नलिखित प्रश्न में, चार विकल्पों में से, उस सही विकल्प का चयन करें, जो वाक्य के काल के भेद का सही विकल्प हो:
मैंने खाना बनाया है।
A. सामान्य वर्तमान काल
B. आसन्न भूतकाल
C. अपूर्ण वर्तमान काल
D. संभाव्य वर्तमान काल

Q.4 हिन्दी में पूर्ण विराम चिह्न को छोड़कर शेष चिह्न किस भाषा के है?
A. संस्कृत
B. अंग्रेजी
C. फारसी
D. चीनी

Q.5 प्रश्नवाचक चिह्न का प्रयोग किस वाक्य में होगा?
A. राम की आय सुरेश से अधिक है
B. सीता जानना चाहती है
C. मोहन बाजार गया था
D. मोहन को बाजार क्यों जाना था

Q.6 जिन शब्दों से किसी व्यक्ति, वस्तु, स्थान के गुण, दोष, दशा आदि का ज्ञान हो, उसे क्या कहते हैं?
A. व्यक्तिवाचक संज्ञा
B. भाववाचक संज्ञा
C. जातिवाचक संज्ञा
D. समुदायवाचक संज्ञा

Q.7 'बहुत ही कठिन कार्य करना' के लिए किस वाक्य में सही मुहावरा प्रयोग में लाया गया है?
A. संस्कृत पढ़ना लोहे के चने चबाना है, कोई आसान काम नहीं।
B. प्रताप ने ज्योंही लगाम लगाई, चेतक हवा से बातें करने लगा।
C. वह तो मेरी मुट्ठी में है, उससे तो जो चाहो काम करवा दूँ।
D. भारतीय जवानों से लोहा लेना सरल काम नहीं है।

Q.8 'कहाँ राजा भोज और कहाँ गंगू तेली' लोकोक्ति का अर्थ है:
A. बहुत बड़ा होना
B. बहुत अंतर होना
C. बहुत चतुर होना
D. बहुत छोटा होना

Q.9 'कानों सुनी बात सच्ची नहीं है।' - वाक्य के रेखांकित पद में कारक है:
A. कर्ता
B. अधिकरण
C. कर्म
D. करण

Q.10 'प्रत्येक' शब्द में कौन सा उपसर्ग है?
A. प्र
B. प्रति
C. एक
D. इक

Q.11 निम्नलिखित शब्द में प्रयुक्त उपसर्ग के सही विकल्प का चयन कीजिए:
निश्चल
[Sainik School Entrance Class VI, 2021]
A. निश्
B. निर
C. निः
D. निश

Q.12 "मन रे तन कागद का पुतला। लागै बूँद बिनसि जाय छिन में, गरब करे क्या इतना।।"
इन पंक्तियों में कौन-सा रस है?
A. भक्ति रस
B. श्रृंगार रस
C. करुण रस
D. शांत रस

Q.13 'अखरोट' शब्द का तत्सम शब्द क्या होता है?
A. अक्षोट
B. अख्रोट
C. आखरोट
D. अकरोट

Q.14 निम्न में से 'नकुल' का तद्भव शब्द है:
A. नेउता
B. नेवला
C. नींबू
D. नीम

Q.15 'छात्रावास' में कौन सी सन्धि है?
A. दीर्घ
B. गुण
C. वृद्धि
D. अयादि

Q.16 जिस वाक्य में किसी काम या बात का होना पाया जाता है, वह है:
[Rajasthan Teachers Eligibility Test - Level 1 Primary Level (RTET), 2021]
A. आज्ञावाचक वाक्य
B. विधानवाचक वाक्य
C. इच्छावाचक वाक्य
D. संकेतार्थक वाक्य

Q.17 'पानी निरंतर बह रहा है।' वाक्य किस क्रिया विशेषण का है?
A. कालवाचक क्रिया-विशेषण
B. स्थानवाचक क्रिया-विशेषण
C. परिमाणवाचक क्रिया-विशेषण
D. रीतिवाचक क्रिया-विशेषण

Q.18 'किसी को बुलाओ' वाक्य में 'किसी' इनमें से क्या है?
[UP Police Sub Inspector, 2021]
A. यौगिक सार्वनामिक विशेषण
B. सार्वनामिक विशेषण
C. संयुक्त सर्वनाम
D. अनिश्चयवाचक सर्वनाम

Q.19 प्रस्तुत पंक्ति को पूर्ण करने के लिए दिए गए विकल्पों में से सही का चयन कर रिक्त स्थान भरें।
'एक _____ मोतियों से _____'
[UP Police Sub Inspector, 2017]
A. बूँद, जड़ा
B. थाल, भरा
C. जाल, जड़ा
D. घड़ा, खड़ा

Q.20 दिए गए विकल्पों में से सही का चयन कर रिक्त स्थान भरें:
इस ग्रंथ को इतिहास की _____ से भी एक महत्त्वपूर्ण रचना माना गया है।
[UP Police Sub Inspector, 2017]
A. दृष्टि
B. तुलना
C. पन्ने
D. ओर

Q.21 निम्नलिखित में से कौन सा स्वर कंठतालव्य है?
A. ई
B. आ
C. औ
D. ए

Q.22 'बाल' का उचित वचन है:
A. एकवचन
B. बहुवचन
C. दोनों
D. इनमें से कोई नहीं

Q.23 दिए गए शब्दों की सही वर्तनी के साथ विकल्प को चिन्हित करें:
A. अतीथी
B. अतिथि
C. आतिथी
D. अथिति

Q.24 दिए गए विकल्पों में से 'सुषुप्ति' शब्द का विलोम क्या होगा?

A. सुप्त   **B.** अचेतन   **C.** स्तुति   **D.** जागरण

Q.25 'तलवार' का पर्यायवाची है:

[UPPSC Staff Nurse, 2022]

A. तूणीर   **B.** तीर   **C.** चंद्रहास   **D.** वाण

English

Q.26 Which tense is formed by using "was/were + verb (ing)"?

A. Past Indefinite   **B.** Past Continuous

C. Past Perfect   **D.** Present Perfect

Q.27 'Regret' may be expressed by the following interjection:

A. Alas!   **B.** Hush!   **C.** Bravo!   **D.** Hurrah!

Q.28 Direction: Fill in the blank with an appropriate adjective.

His attitude was the _______ offensive among all the guys.

A. fewest   **B.** least   **C.** fewer   **D.** less

Q.29 Direction: Choose the correct verb in the given sentence.

I persuaded the boys ____ the room before the teacher entered.

A. leave   **B.** to leave   **C.** left   **D.** leaving

Ques (30-31):Direction: Fill in the blank with correct alternative.

Q.30 Have they ______ the broken window?

A. fix   **B.** fixed   **C.** fixing   **D.** fixes

Q.31 All ______ glitters is not gold.

A. that   **B.** who   **C.** which   **D.** whom

Ques (32-37):Direction: From the given option choose the correct word to fill in the blank space.

Q.32 It is necessary to be very careful in irrigating during _______ weather.

A. hot   **B.** sultry   **C.** torrid   **D.** frosty

Q.33 They had to travel everywhere by ______. (bus)

A. busis   **B.** buses   **C.** busses   **D.** busess

Q.34 In the test, we will______ your work and then give you detailed feedback.

A. assess   **B.** check   **C.** measure   **D.** judge

Q.35 She got into a car accident while driving through a _______ intersection.

A. harmless   **B.** safe

C. dangerous   **D.** positive

Q.36 I have nobody _____ I can confide in.

A. which   **B.** whose   **C.** whoever   **D.** whom

Q.37 The idea was both __________ and painfully disappointing.

A. sad   **B.** boring

C. exciting   **D.** moderate

Q.38 Choose the option that best punctuates the given sentence:

I'm not sure yet but I think I'll become a teacher.

A. I'm not sure yet, but I think I'll become a teacher.

B. I'm not sure yet, but I think I'll become a teacher.

C. I'm not sure yet, but I think I'll Become a teacher.

D. I'm not sure yet but I think I'll become a teacher.

Q.39 Direction: Choose the correct option.

My father was angry ________ me. My mother was angry _______ my talking to Riya.

A. at, at   **B.** at, with

C. with, at   **D.** with, with

Ques (40-41):Direction: Select the most appropriate synonym of the given word.

Q.40 VERSATILE

A. Multi-purpose

B. Greedy

C. Having no specific interest

D. Ambitious

Q.41 CRUX

A. Core   **B.** Part   **C.** Idea   **D.** Tip

Q.42 Direction: Choose the masculine gender of the given term.

Nun

A. Maid   **B.** Monk

C. Steward   **D.** Man-servant

Q.43 Select the combination of numbers so that the letters arranged accordingly will form a meaningful word:

I L B O E M

1 2 3 4 5 6

A. 6, 4, 3, 2, 5, 1   **B.** 3, 4, 5, 6, 2, 1

C. 6, 4, 3, 1, 2, 5   **D.** 3, 4, 6, 2, 1, 5

Q.44 Direction: Select the most appropriate antonym of the given word.

Discourage

A. Crushed   **B.** Demoralize

C. Dishearten   **D.** Encourage

Q.45 Select the correctly spelt word.

[SSC Sub Inspector (CPO), 2020]

A. Recommend   **B.** Recomend

C. Reccommend   **D.** Recommened

Q.46 Direction: In the following question find out the alternative which will replace the question mark.

Dexterity : Ability :: Timid : ?

A. Bold   **B.** Energetic

C. Afraid   **D.** Agility

Q.47 Which is the subjective pronoun in sentence, "We should be honest in every aspects of life."?

A. we   **B.** be   **C.** every   **D.** of

Q.48 Direction: Select the option that can be used as a one-word substitute for the given group of words.

The sound of owls

[SSC Constable (GD), 2021]

A. Hoot   **B.** Caw   **C.** Cluck   **D.** Moo

Q.49 Which of these is not a punctuation mark?

A. Full stop   **B.** Comma   **C.** Colon   **D.** Hashtag

Q.50 Direction: Select the most appropriate antonym of the given word.
SUBMISSIVE

A. Miserly   **B.** Dutiful   **C.** Obedient   **D.** Stubborn

General Studies

Q.51 Defence Research and Development Organisation (DRDO) launched the Hull Module of the Submersible Platform for Acoustic Characterization & Evaluation (SPACE) facility at Kochi in November 2022. Who is the current chairman of DRDO?

A. Dr. Samir V Kamat   **B.** G. Satheesh Reddy
C. S. Somnath   **D.** Dr. K. Sivan

Q.52 Bharat Kala Bhawan Museum is situated in
________________.

A. Agra   **B.** Lucknow
C. Allahabad   **D.** Varanasi

Q.53 In which of the following districts of the state, 'Mango' is not cultivated?

A. Varanasi   **B.** Lucknow
C. Mirzapur   **D.** Agra

Q.54 Anpara Thermal Power Station is located in which of the following state?

A. Lucknow   **B.** Sonbhadra
C. Jhansi   **D.** Hamirpur

Q.55 Which is the capital of Australia?

A. Sydney   **B.** Canberra
C. Queensland   **D.** None of the above

Q.56 Which one of the following is the first State in India to have 100 percent households with tap water connection?
[Indian Military Academy (IMA), 2022]

A. Gujarat   **B.** Goa
C. Delhi   **D.** Andhra Pradesh

Q.57 The oldest High Court in India is the ________.
A. Calcutta High Court
B. Bombay High Court
C. Allahabad High Court
D. Madras High Court

Q.58 Who is known as the Iron Man of India?
A. Sardar Vallabhbhai Patel
B. Morarji Desai
C. PV Narsimha Rao
D. Atal Bihari Vajpayee

Q.59 Thalassemia is a hereditary disease which affects:
[Uttarakhand Public Service Commission (UKPSC), 2016]

A. Blood   **B.** Lungs   **C.** Heart   **D.** Kidney

Q.60 In which city Yamuna river meets Ganga river?
A. Varanasi   **B.** Prayagraj
C. Agra   **D.** Unnao

Q.61 In which one of the following soils, the salt content is so high that common salt is obtained by evaporating the saline water in some areas?
A. Peaty soil   **B.** Alluvial soil
C. Laterite soil   **D.** Arid soil

Q.62 Recently, coastal clean up day campaign launched in India, which institute lead this day?
A. Indian Coast Guard   **B.** NCC
C. Indian Navy   **D.** NSS

Q.63 Which Indian city was the host of 'Global Fintech Conference' in 2022?
A. Mumbai   **B.** New Delhi
C. Ahmedabad   **D.** Bengaluru

Q.64 The New Naval Ensign features the national emblem inside which shape?
A. Green Hexagon   **B.** Blue Octagon
C. Orange Hexagon   **D.** White Octagon

Q.65 Which is the first e-commerce company to set up solar farms in India?
A. Walmart   **B.** Amazon   **C.** Flipkart   **D.** ebay

Q.66 Which country has won gold medal in men's table tennis event at the 2022 Commonwealth Games in Birmingham on 2 August 2022?
A. Malaysia   **B.** Canada
C. India   **D.** South Africa

Q.67 Amarkantak Temple is located in which of the following states?
A. Uttar Pradesh   **B.** Jharkhand
C. Madhya Pradesh   **D.** Bihar

Q.68 Central Institute for research on buffaloes is situated in ________.

A. Hisar   **B.** Gurgaon   **C.** Jhajjar   **D.** Panipat

Q.69 In which one of the following States has the President's Rule been imposed most number of times?
[Indian Military Academy (IMA), 2022]

A. Bihar   **B.** Karnataka
C. Manipur   **D.** Punjab

Q.70 Mohiniattam is the dance form of which Indian state?
A. Kerala   **B.** Andhra Pradesh
C. Karnataka   **D.** Tamil Nadu

Q.71 The product of mass and velocity is called:
[RRB/RRC Group D, 2018]

A. Potential energy   **B.** Momentum
C. Force   **D.** Kinetic energy

Q.72 What is the value of pH of a neutral solution?

A. 7.0 **B.** 6.5 **C.** 7.5 **D.** 6.0

Q.73 Black soil is helpful for which type of following crop?
A. Wheat **B.** Rice **C.** Cotton **D.** Pulses

Q.74 Which of the following is one of the sacred books of Buddhism?
A. Torah **B.** The Avesta
C. Kalpa Sutra **D.** Tripitaka

Q.75 During the swadeshi movement, a National College was started in calcutta under the principalship of:

[UPSC NDA, 2019]

A. Rabindranath Tagore
B. Aurobindo Ghosh
C. Rajani Kant Sen
D. Syed Abu Mohammad

Mathematics

Q.76 The area of a rhombus with side 13 cm and one diagonal 10 cm will be:

[HTET TGT Mathematics, 2020]

A. 100 cm ^{2} **B.** 105 cm ^{2} **C.** 110 cm ^{2} **D.** 120 cm ^{2}

Q.77 At what rate the simple interest will be $\frac{2}{5}$ times to the original sum in 10 years?

[Rajasthan Teachers Eligibility Test - Level 1 Primary Level (RTET), 2015]

A. 4% **B.** $5\frac{2}{3}\%$ **C.** 6% **D.** $6\frac{2}{3}\%$

Q.78 Find the value of x:

$$9x - 3 = 7x + 3$$

A. 8 **B.** 4 **C.** 5 **D.** 3

Q.79 Find the next number in the series:

$$12, 17, 24, 33, 44, ?$$

[UP Police Sub Inspector, 2021]

A. 52 **B.** 51 **C.** 57 **D.** 48

Q.80 The median of the following data is:

$$31, 37, 43, 42, 25, 46, 45, 39, 32$$

[UPSESSB TGT Mathematics, 2013]

A. 25 **B.** 42 **C.** 46 **D.** 39

Q.81 The sum of the digits of a number is subtracted from the number. The resulting number is always divisible by:

[Jawahar Navodaya Entrance Class VI, 2022], [Jawahar Navodaya Entrance Class VI, 2018]

A. 2 **B.** 5 **C.** 8 **D.** 9

Q.82 Find the number of factor of 54:
A. 2 **B.** 4 **C.** 6 **D.** 8

Q.83 Which is correct option for $6\sqrt{2} - \sqrt{32}$?
A. Difference $2\sqrt{2}$ is an irrational number
B. Difference $2\sqrt{2}$ is a rational number
C. Difference 2 is an irrational number
D. Difference $\sqrt{2}$ is a rational number

Q.84 If Ankit purchased 10 more apples, his carton will weigh 25 kilograms. If the weight of one apple is 500 grams. How many apples did he initially had in his carton?
A. 48 **B.** 40 **C.** 46 **D.** 44

Q.85 Write the given number in Roman numerals:
98
A. XCI **B.** XLVI **C.** XCVIII **D.** XXXIV

Q.86 Every rational number is:
A. Whole number **B.** Natural number
C. Integer **D.** Real number

Q.87 Find which of the following are twin Primes:
A. (37, 41) **B.** (3, 7) **C.** (43, 47) **D.** (71, 73)

Q.88 Direction: Arrange the following integers in descending order.
-101, -88, -125, 45, 98, 88
A. 90 > 88 > 45 > -88 > -101 > -125
B. 90 > 88 > 45 > -101> -88> -125
C. 101> 88 > 45 > -88 > -90> -125
D. 88> 90> 45 > -88 > -101 > -125

Q.89 If $15 - 15 \div 15 \times 6 = x$, then x is:

[Jawahar Navodaya Entrance Class VI, 2020]

A. 6 **B.** 0 **C.** 9 **D.** 84

Q.90 140.75×0.01 is:

[Jawahar Navodaya Entrance Class VI, 2020]

A. 140.75 **B.** 14000.75
C. 1.4075 **D.** 0.14075

Q.91 Select the correct answer of:
4 + 4.44 + 4.04 + 44.4 + 444 = ?
A. 472.88 **B.** 495.22
C. 577.2 **D.** None of these

Q.92 Simplify $16 - 2 \div 14 + 6 \times 2$:
A. $27\frac{12}{14}$ **B.** $29\frac{5}{7}$ **C.** $26\frac{5}{7}$ **D.** $27\frac{5}{8}$

Q.93 LCM of $\frac{2}{5}, \frac{3}{10}$ and $\frac{4}{15}$ is:
A. $\frac{2}{5}$ **B.** $\frac{1}{15}$ **C.** $\frac{9}{5}$ **D.** $\frac{12}{5}$

Q.94 The product of two numbers is 4107. If the HCF of those two numbers is 37, find the ratio of HCF and LCM:
A. $1:3$ **B.** $3:1$ **C.** $1:5$ **D.** $2:3$

Q.95 If the height of the triangle is 24 cm, and the area of the triangle is 168 sq. cm. The perimeter of the rectangle is 84 cm. If it were given that the base of a triangle is equal to the breadth of a rectangle. Find length of rectangle:
A. 30 cm **B.** 32 cm **C.** 28 cm **D.** 40 cm

Q.96 The area of a trapezium is 480 cm^2, the distance between two parallel sides is 15 cm and one of the parallel side is 20 cm. The other parallel side is:

A. 20 cm   **B.** 34 cm   **C.** 44 cm   **D.** 50 cm

Q.97 What is the square root of 8281?

A. 81   **B.** 91   **C.** 89   **D.** 99

Q.98 If $(a - b) = 3$ and $ab = 70$, then find the value of $(a^3 - b^3)$:

A. 657   **B.** 783   **C.** 840   **D.** 580

Q.99 800 is first increased by 10% and then it is again increased by 20%. What is the final value?

A. 1034   **B.** 1140   **C.** 1056   **D.** 1086

Q.100 A shopkeeper sold an article for Rs. 2500. If the cost price of the article is 2000, find the profit percent:

A. 23%   **B.** 25%   **C.** 27%   **D.** 29%

// Smart Answer Sheet //

Correct — Indicates percentage of students who answered questions correctly.

Skipped — Indicates percentage of students who skipped questions.

Q.	Ans.	Correct / Skipped	Q.	Ans.	Correct / Skipped	Q.	Ans.	Correct / Skipped	Q.	Ans.	Correct / Skipped	Q.	Ans.	Correct / Skipped
1	B	51.05 % / 1.63 %	17	A	16.32 % / 4.45 %	33	B	87.23 % / 0.0 %	49	D	79.95 % / 0.0 %	65	B	87.47 % / 0.0 %
2	C	51.31 % / 1.28 %	18	D	85.26 % / 0.0 %	34	A	48.42 % / 1.49 %	50	D	12.34 % / 4.14 %	66	C	64.39 % / 1.9 %
3	B	48.88 % / 1.85 %	19	B	68.58 % / 1.93 %	35	C	54.14 % / 1.32 %	51	A	32.06 % / 3.86 %	67	C	78.02 % / 0.0 %
4	C	17.56 % / 3.34 %	20	A	43.36 % / 1.14 %	36	D	59.78 % / 1.91 %	52	D	78.58 % / 0.0 %	68	A	53.01 % / 1.71 %
5	D	63.88 % / 1.97 %	21	D	84.3 % / 0.0 %	37	C	40.81 % / 1.42 %	53	D	48.07 % / 1.03 %	69	C	82.37 % / 0.0 %
6	B	10.1 % / 3.38 %	22	B	46.47 % / 1.89 %	38	B	64.86 % / 1.61 %	54	B	78.71 % / 0.0 %	70	A	58.61 % / 1.85 %
7	A	42.58 % / 1.38 %	23	B	87.47 % / 0.0 %	39	C	84.54 % / 0.0 %	55	B	19.43 % / 3.56 %	71	B	89.24 % / 0.0 %
8	B	50.92 % / 1.05 %	24	D	55.11 % / 1.79 %	40	A	55.39 % / 1.97 %	56	B	64.49 % / 1.23 %	72	A	50.69 % / 1.09 %
9	D	53.32 % / 1.27 %	25	C	87.69 % / 0.0 %	41	A	48.59 % / 1.48 %	57	A	85.44 % / 0.0 %	73	C	61.7 % / 1.99 %
10	B	77.86 % / 0.0 %	26	B	49.3 % / 1.94 %	42	B	87.04 % / 0.0 %	58	A	62.74 % / 1.95 %	74	D	48.27 % / 1.65 %
11	C	79.68 % / 0.0 %	27	A	47.85 % / 1.3 %	43	C	22.76 % / 4.12 %	59	A	32.52 % / 4.23 %	75	B	41.58 % / 1.85 %
12	D	43.39 % / 1.16 %	28	B	45.24 % / 1.44 %	44	D	52.46 % / 1.03 %	60	B	81.79 % / 0.0 %	76	D	63.51 % / 1.42 %
13	A	56.5 % / 1.49 %	29	B	56.0 % / 1.12 %	45	A	80.57 % / 0.0 %	61	D	69.08 % / 1.47 %	77	A	41.48 % / 1.03 %
14	B	67.72 % / 1.93 %	30	B	54.23 % / 1.53 %	46	C	27.36 % / 3.21 %	62	A	49.9 % / 1.23 %	78	D	52.53 % / 1.28 %
15	A	44.27 % / 1.72 %	31	A	76.58 % / 0.0 %	47	A	76.78 % / 0.0 %	63	A	65.84 % / 1.46 %	79	C	43.54 % / 1.91 %
16	B	53.68 % / 1.27 %	32	D	44.65 % / 1.02 %	48	A	49.68 % / 1.13 %	64	B	47.71 % / 1.79 %	80	D	87.49 % / 0.0 %

Q.	Ans.	Correct	Skipped
81	D	69.31 %	1.24 %
82	D	68.32 %	1.97 %
83	A	11.89 %	4.88 %
84	B	66.13 %	1.72 %

Q.	Ans.	Correct	Skipped
85	C	69.23 %	1.13 %
86	D	85.53 %	0.0 %
87	D	61.28 %	1.63 %
88	A	26.42 %	4.64 %

Q.	Ans.	Correct	Skipped
89	C	55.39 %	1.3 %
90	C	87.19 %	0.0 %
91	D	55.63 %	1.37 %
92	A	28.72 %	3.03 %

Q.	Ans.	Correct	Skipped
93	D	48.15 %	1.03 %
94	A	47.14 %	1.4 %
95	C	68.62 %	1.81 %
96	C	47.59 %	1.06 %

Q.	Ans.	Correct	Skipped
97	B	66.73 %	1.76 %
98	A	45.97 %	1.82 %
99	C	62.64 %	1.56 %
100	B	13.96 %	4.47 %

Performance Analysis

Avg. Score (%)	71.0%
Toppers Score (%)	74.0%
Your Score	

//Hints and Solutions//

1. वाक्यांश 'आदि से अंत तक' के लिए एक शब्द आद्योपान्त है, जबकि जिसका प्रारम्भ न हो - अनादि, उसी समय होने वाला - समकालीन अथवा समयोचित तथा तर्क-पूर्ण के लिए, एक शब्द समीचीन होगा।

अतः विकल्प (B) सही है।

2. संरचना के आधार पर किए गए वाक्य के वर्गीकरण में 'आज्ञार्थक' वाक्य का प्रकार नहीं है। संरचना के आधार पर वाक्य तीन प्रकार के होते हैं - सरल वाक्य, मिश्र वाक्य और संयुक्त वाक्य। इस प्रकार सही विकल्प 'आज्ञार्थक वाक्य' है।

विशेष:

आज्ञार्थक या अज्ञावाचक वाक्य अर्थात ऐसे वाक्य जिनमें आदेश, आज्ञा या अनुमति का पता चले या बोध हो। जैसे - सभी अपना-अपना काम करो, यह पाठ तुम्हें पढ़ना होगा आदि।

अतः विकल्प (C) सही है।

3. 'मैंने खाना बनाया है।' इस वाक्य में क्रिया कुछ ही समय पहले पूर्ण हुई है। अतः यह आसन्न भूतकाल का वाक्य है।

आसन्न भूतकाल- क्रिया के जिस रूप से यह पता चले कि क्रिया अभी कुछ समय पहले ही पूर्ण हुई है या खत्म हुई है उस क्रिया को आसन्न भूतकाल कहते हैं।

अतः विकल्प (B) सही है।

4. हिन्दी में पूर्ण विराम चिन्ह को छोड़कर शेष चिन्ह 'फारसी भाषा' के है।

अंग्रेजी, फारसी, चीनी विदेशी भाषा है, इनके शब्द ज्यों के त्यों हिन्दी भाषा में लिए गये है।

संस्कृत भारत तथा विश्व की प्राचीनतम भाषा मानी जाती है।

अतः विकल्प (C) सही है।

5. 'मोहन को बाजार क्यों जाना था' वाक्य में प्रश्नवाचक चिह्न का प्रयोग होगा।

प्रश्नवाचक चिह्न एक विरामचिह्न है जिसका प्रयोग प्रश्नवाची वाक्यों के अन्त में किया जाता है।

इसका उपयोग अधिकांश भाषाओं में लिखी हुई सामग्री में प्रश्नवाची वाक्यों के अन्त में किया जाता है।

अतः विकल्प (D) सही है।

6. जो शब्द किसी चीज़ या पदार्थ की अवस्था, दशा या भाव का बोध कराते हैं, उन शब्दों को भाववाचक संज्ञा कहते हैं।

जैसे- बचपन, बुढ़ापा, मोटापा, मिठास, उमंग, थकावट, मानवता, चतुराई, जवानी, लम्बाई, मित्रता, मुस्कुराहट, अपनापन, परायापन, भूख, प्यास, चोरी, क्रोध, सुन्दरता आदि।

अतः विकल्प (B) सही है।

7. 'लोहे के चने चबाना' मुहावरे का अर्थ कठिन परिश्रम करना है।

वाक्य प्रयोग: संस्कृत पढ़ना लोहे के चने चबाना है, कोई आसान काम नहीं।

अन्य मुहावरे:

मुहावरा	अर्थ	वाक्य
हवा से बातें करना	बहुत तेज़ दौड़ना	प्रताप ने ज्योंही लगाम लगाई, चेतक हवा से बातें करने लगा।
मुट्ठी में करना	वश में करना	वह तो मेरी मुट्ठी में है, उससे तो जो चाहो काम करवा दूँ।
लोहा लेना	साहसपूर्वक	भारतीय जवानों से लोहा लेना सरल
मुकाबला करना		काम नहीं है।

अतः विकल्प (A) सही है।

8. 'कहाँ राजा भोज और कहाँ गंगू तेली' लोकोक्ति का अर्थ 'बहुत अंतर होना' होता है। शेष सभी अर्थ सही नहीं हैं।

वाक्य प्रयोग: कंपनी के बॉस आजकल विदेश क्या गये हैं, कंपनी के मैनेजर साहब खुद को ही मालिक समझने लगे हैं, कहाँ राजा भोज कहाँ गंगू तेली।

अतः विकल्प (B) सही है।

9. 'करण' का अर्थ साधन है। संज्ञा का वह रूप जिससे किसी क्रिया के साधन का बोध हो, उसे करण कारक कहते हैं।

दिए गये 'कानों सुनी बात सच्ची नहीं है।' वाक्य में '' कान करण कारक है। यहाँ 'से' के प्रयोग से 'द्वारा', का भाव बोध हो रहा है।

करण कारक के चिन्ह के चिन्ह – 'से', 'के द्वारा', 'के कारण', 'के साथ', 'के बिना' आदि हैं।

अतः विकल्प (D) सही है।

10. प्रत्येक में उपसर्ग है – 'प्रति', [प्रति + एक = प्रयेक]

प्रत्येक में उपसर्ग 'प्रति' का अर्थ है: प्रतिदिन, **प्रत्येक**, प्रतिकूल, प्रतिहिंसा, प्रतिरूप, प्रतिध्वनि

अतः विकल्प (B) सही है।

11. निश्चल में 'निः' उपसर्ग है।

निश्चल :जो अपने स्थान से ज़रा भी इधर-उधर चलता या हिलता-डोलता न हो,

जैसे: अचल, स्थिर, अटल

अतः विकल्प (C) सही है।

12. "मन रे तन कागद का पुतला। लागै बूँद बिनसि जाय छिन में, गरब करे क्या इतना।।" इन पंक्तियों में शांत रस है।

शांत रस की विशेषताएँ निम्नलिखित है:

- शांत रस का स्थायी भाव निर्वेद होता है।
- शांत रस में तत्व ज्ञान कि प्राप्ति या संसार से वैराग्य मिलने पर, परमात्मा के वास्तविक रूप का ज्ञान प्राप्त होने पर मन को जो शांति मिलती है, वहाँ पर शांत रस की उत्पत्ति होती है।
- जहाँ पर न दुःख होता है, न ही द्वेष होता है, मनुष्य का मन सांसारिक कार्यों से मुक्त हो जाता है और मनुष्य वैराग्य प्राप्त कर लेता है, शांत रस कहा जाता है।

अतः विकल्प (D) सही है।

13. 'अखरोट' शब्द का तत्सम शब्द 'अक्षोट' होता है। ऐसे शब्द जिसे हम संस्कृत से बिना कोई बदलाव करे उपयोग में लाते है, तत्सम शब्द कहलाते हैं। 'अखरोट' शब्द, 'अक्षोट' का तद्भव रूप होता है।

अतः विकल्प (A) सही है।

14. दिए गए विकल्पों में सही उत्तर विकल्प (B) 'नेवला' होगा। अन्य विकल्प इसके अनुचित उत्तर हैं।

'दिए गए शब्दों में 'नकुल' शब्द तत्सम है जिसका तद्भव रूप 'नेवला' होगा।

अतः विकल्प (B) सही है।

15. दीर्घ सन्धि: हस्व या दीर्घ अ, इ, उ के बाद यदि हस्व या दीर्घ अ, इ, उ आ जाएँ तो दोनों मिलकर दीर्घ आ, ई और ऊ हो जाते हैं।

जैसे: आ + आ = आ (विद्या + आलय = विद्यालय)

छात्रावास = छात्र + आवास

अतः विकल्प (A) सही है।

16. जिस वाक्य में किसी काम या बात का होना पाया जाता है, वह विधानवाचक वाक्य है। विधानवाचक वाक्यों को विधिवाचक वाक्य भी कहा जाता है। जैसे:

1. ममता ने खाना खा लिया।
2. सूर्य गर्मी देता है।
3. भारत हमारा देश है।

अत: विकल्प (B) सही है।

17. 'पानी निरंतर बह रहा है।' वाक्य 'कालवाचक क्रिया-विशेषण' का है।

इस क्रिया विशेषण में अभी, फिर कभी और निरन्तर शब्दों के द्वारा काल का पता लगाया जाता है। यदा, कदा, जब, तब, हमेशा, तभी, तत्काल, निरन्तर, आदि शब्द कालवाचक क्रिया विशेषण के अंतर्गत आते हैं।

अतः विकल्प (A) सही है।

18. 'किसी को बुलाओ' वाक्य में 'किसी' 'अनिश्चयवाचक सर्वनाम' है।

जिस सर्वनाम से किसी व्यक्ति या पदार्थ का निश्चित बोध न हो, उसे अनिश्चयवाचक सर्वनाम कहते हैं।

जैसे: दुकान पर कोई आया था।

अतः विकल्प (D) सही है।

19. 'एक थाल मोतियों से भरा' यह निम्न पहेली की एक पंक्ति है:

एक थाल मोतियों से भरा, सबके सिर पर औंधा धरा। चारों ओर वह थाल फिरे, मोती उससे एक ना गिरे।

अतः विकल्प (B) सही है।

20. दृष्टि का अर्थ नजर होता है, जो इस वाक्य को सही अर्थ प्रदान करता है।

इसलिए, वाक्य होगा:

इस ग्रंथ को इतिहास की दृष्टि से भी एक महत्वपूर्ण रचना माना गया है।

अन्य विकल्प दिए गए वाक्य को पूर्ण अर्थ प्रदान नहीं करते।

अतः विकल्प (A) सही है।

21. कंठतालव्य स्वर जिन स्वर के उच्चारण में कंठ और तालु दोनों का प्रयोग होता है, उन्हें कंठतालव्य स्वर कहते हैं। ए, ऐ, कंठ और तालु के स्पर्श से उच्चारित होते हैं, इसलिए ये कंठतालव्य वर्ण कहलाते हैं।

अतः विकल्प (D) सही है।

22. दिए गए विकल्पों में से सही विकल्प 'बहुवचन' है।

कुछ पुल्लिंग शब्द ऐसे भी हैं, जिनका सदैव ही बहुवचन में प्रयोग होता है।

बाल शब्द भी सदा बहुवचन में प्रयुक्त होता है।

यदि उसका प्रयोग एक वचन में करना होता है तो उसके आगे एक लिखेंगे।

जैसे - मेरा एक बाल सफ़ेद हो गया |

अतः विकल्प (B) सही है।

23. सही वर्तनी वाला शब्द अतिथि है। अन्य विकल्प असंगत है।

भाषा के शब्दों के शुद्ध लेखन को वर्तनी कहते हैं।

अतः विकल्प (B) सही है।

24. दिए गए विकल्पों में से 'सुषुप्ति' शब्द का विलोम जागरण है।

सुषुप्ति का अर्थ - निद्रावस्था

जागरण का अर्थ- जागना

अत: विकल्प (D) सही है।

25. चंद्रहास शब्द तलवार का पर्यायवाची है।

तलवार के अन्य पर्यायवाची- असि, करवाल, कृपाण, खडग, शम्शीर, शायक, खंज है।

अत: विकल्प (C) सही है।

26. The tense formed by using "was/were + verb (ing)" is past continuous tense. Past continuous tense is a tense which is used to indicate a continuing action or event that was happening at some point in time in the past. It uses the auxiliary verb i.e. was or were present participle. The past continuous tense, also known as the past progressive tense.

Hence, the correct option is (B).

27. As we know that, the given options are:

Option (A): Alas!

Alas! is used to express regret, grief, pity or concern.

Option (B): Hush!

Hush! is used for making someone be quiet or stop talking.

Option (C): Bravo!

Bravo! is used to express approval when a performer or other person has done something well.

Option (D): Hurrah!

Hurrah! is used to express joy or approval.

So, we can conclude that, the 'Regret' is expressed by an interjection Alas!

Hence, the correct option is (A).

28. As we know that, a superlative adjective is an adjective used in comparisons to describe something as being of the highest degree or extreme. We use superlative adjectives when making comparisons of three or more people or things. The words biggest, smallest and fastest are examples of superlative adjectives.

Thus, the most appropriate adjective of all the options is least. The meaning of least is the smallest form.

So, the correct sentence is, "His attitude was the least offensive among all the guys".

Hence, the correct option is (B).

29. Correct sentence: I persuaded the boys to leave the room before the teacher entered.

There are some verbs like 'advise', 'allow', 'ask', 'beg', 'persuade', etc which are succeeded by infinitive after them.

Example:

- I beg to differ.
- My parents didn't allow me to go to the concert.
- He advise me not to take this job.

- They persuaded him to tell the truth.

Thus, 'to leave' will be used in the blank.

Hence, the correct option is (B).

30. As we know that,

The structure of the Present Perfect Tense for the interrogative sentence is: Question word + have/has + Sub + V3 + obj +?

- For example: Have you read this poem before?

From the above information, we can say that the most appropriate answer is 'fixed'.

Thus the correct sentence is, "Have they fixed the broken window?"

Hence, the correct option is (B).

31. All **that** glitters is not gold.

- From the given options, the correct choice to fill in the blank is 'that.'
- We know that, if all denotes non-living things, 'that' is used and not 'who' or 'whom.' Example: All the money that I gave her has been spent.

Hence, the correct option is (A).

32. As we know that, the given options are having meaning such as:

Option (D): Frosty means (of the weather) very cold, with frost forming on surfaces.

Option (A): Hot means having a high degree of heat or a high temperature.

Option (B): Sultry means (of the air or weather) hot and humid.

Option (C): Torrid means very hot and dry.

The correct word suitable for fill in the blank space is frosty.
So, the sentence is, "It is necessary to be very careful in irrigating during frosty weather".

Hence, the correct option is (D).

33. The correct word suitable for the blank is buses. The plural of "bus" is "buses." "Busses" is an archaic plural now considered a spelling mistake.

The correct sentence is, "They had to travel everywhere by buses".

Hence, the correct option is (B).

34. The correct word for the blank is assess.

Assess: To judge or form an opinion about something.

Check: To examine or test something in order to make sure that it is safe or correct, in good condition, etc.

Measure: To find the size, weight, quantity, etc. of somebody/something in standard units by using an instrument.

Judge: A person in a court of law whose job is to decide how criminals should be punished and to make legal decisions.

The correct sentence is, "In the test, we will assess your work and then give you detailed feedback".

Hence, the correct option is (A).

35. The correct word for the blank is dangerous.

Dangerous means able or likely to cause harm or injury.

Harmless means not able or likely to cause harm.

Safe means protected from or not exposed to danger or risk; not likely to be harmed or lost.

Positive means consisting of or characterized by the presence rather than the absence of distinguishing features.

The correct sentence is, "She got into a car accident while driving through a dangerous intersection".

Hence, the correct option is (C).

36. The correct word suitable for the blank is whom. 'Whom' is used instead of 'who' as the object of a verb or preposition. 'Which' is used to add extra information to a previous clause, in writing usually after a comma. 'Whose' is used especially in questions when asking about which person owns or is responsible for something. 'Whoever' is used where any person who; used in questions as a way of expressing surprise.

The correct sentence is, "I have nobody whom I can confide in".

Hence, the correct option is (D).

37. The correct word suitable for the blank is exciting.

Exciting means causing great enthusiasm and eagerness.

Sad means feeling or showing sorrow, unhappy.

Boring means not interesting, tedious.

Moderate means average in amount, intensity, quality or degree.

The sentence is, "The idea was both exciting and painfully disappointing".

Hence, the correct option is (C).

38. The comma (,) represents the shortest pause. We use commas (,) to separate independent clauses when they are joined by any of these seven coordinating conjunctions: and, but, for, or, nor, so, yet. So, we need to insert a comma (,) after the two independent clauses "I'm not sure yet" and "but I think I'll become a teacher".

The full stop (.) represents the greatest pause and separation and it is used to mark the end of a declarative or an Imperative sentence. So, we need to use a full stop (.) at the end of the sentence.

Also, the verb "become" must be in the lower case as it is used in the middle of the sentence.

Thus, the correct sentence is, "I'm not sure yet, but I think I'll become a teacher".

Hence, the correct option is (B).

39. As we know that,

Angry (adjective): Having a strong feeling against someone who has behaved badly, making you want to shout at them or hurt them.

When 'anger' is directed towards a person or living things, we should use 'angry with'. Example: I got really angry with her.

When 'anger' is directed towards a non-living thing, we should use 'angry at'. Example: She was so angry at her car's weird features.

In the first blank, 'anger' is directed towards a living thing, therefore, 'with' should be used.

In the second blank, 'anger' is directed towards the action of speaker's talking to Riya. So, 'at' should be used.

The complete sentences will be, "My father was angry with me. My mother was angry at my talking to Riya."

Hence, the correct option is (C).

40. The correct synonym of versatile is multi-purpose.

Versatile: Able to adapt or be adapted to many different functions or activities.

Example: A leather jacket is a timeless and versatile garment that can be worn in all seasons.

Hence, the correct option is (A).

41. The correct answer is core.

Crux: The decisive or most important point at issue.

Core: The central or most important part of something.

So, the meaning of the other given options are:

- **Part:** An element or constituent that belongs to something and is essential to its nature.
- **Idea:** A thought or suggestion as to a possible course of action.
- **Tip:** The pointed or rounded end or extremity of something slender or tapering.

Thus, from the given meanings, we find that crux and core are synonyms.

Hence, the correct option is (A).

42. As we know that, the meaning of the given term in the question i.e. 'Nun' is a woman belonging to a religious order. Now, the meaning of the given options are:

Option (A): Maid

An unmarried girl or woman especially when young.

Option (B): Monk

A man who is a member of a religious order and lives in a monastery.

Option (C): Steward

An employee on a ship, airplane, bus, or train who manages the provisioning of food and attends passengers.

Option (D): Man-servant

A male servant.

Thus, we can conclude that, the masculine gender of the given term is Monk.

Hence, the correct option is (B).

43. As we know that,

Option (A):

6, 4, 3, 2, 5, 1 → MOBLEI → Not a meaningful word.

Option (B):

3, 4, 5, 6, 2, 1 → BOEMLI → Not a meaningful word.

Option (C):

6, 4, 3, 1, 2, 5 → MOBILE → Meaningful word.

MOBILE meaning able to move or be moved easily.

Option (D):

3, 4, 6, 2, 1, 5 → BOMLIE → Not a meaningful word.

Thus, the combination of numbers so that the letters arranged accordingly will form a meaningful word is 6, 4, 3, 1, 2, 5.

Hence, the correct option is (C).

44. 'Discourage' means cause (someone) to lose confidence or enthusiasm. The antonym of that would be 'Encourage'.

'Crushed' means feeling overwhelmingly disappointed or embarrassed.

'Demoralize' means cause (someone) to lose confidence or hope.

'Dishearten' means cause (someone) to lose determination or confidence.

'Encourage' means give support, confidence, or hope to (someone).

Hence, the correct option is (D).

45. Recommend is the correctly spelt word. Recommend means put forward (someone or something) with approval as being suitable for a particular purpose or role.

While the other options which are given are not giving the meaning sense of the word itself.

Hence, the correct option is (A).

46. According to the question,

Dexterity : Ability :: Timid : ?

Given pair of words,

Dexterity: Ability

They are synonyms of each other. Thus, we need a synonym of Timid. The meaning of Timid is showing a lack of courage or confidence or easily frightened. The meanings of the options given are:

Bold: Showing a willingness to take risks; confident and courageous.

Energetic: Showing or involving great activity or vitality.

Afraid: Feeling fear or anxiety; frightened.

Agility: Ability to move quickly and easily.

Thus, the correct pair of words are:

Dexterity : Ability :: Timid : Afraid

Hence, the correct option is (C).

47. A subjective pronoun acts as the subject of a sentence that means it performs the action of the verb. The subjective pronouns are he, I, it, she, they, we, and you.

In sentence, "We should be honest in every aspects of life."

"We" is a subjective pronoun.

Hence the correct option is (A).

48. As we know that, the meaning of the given words are:

Hoot: A low, wavering musical sound that is the typical call of many kinds of owls.

Caw: The harsh cry of a rook, crow, or similar bird.

Cluck means (of a hen) make a short, low sound.

Moo: Make the characteristic deep resonant vocal sound of cattle.

As per the meaning of the given words, "hoot" is the one-word substitute for the given group of words.

Hence, the correct option is (A).

49. The main punctuation marks are full stop, comma, colon, semicolon, question mark, exclamation mark, hyphen, dash, brackets, apostrophe. Hashtag isn't a punctuation mark. It is a symbol used in social networks, and it has no relevance in English Grammar.

Hence, the correct option is (D).

50. As we know that,

The meanings of all the words are defined so that we can find the antonym of 'Submissive'.

Submissive means ready to conform to the authority or will of others; meekly obedient or passive.

Example: After months of training, our aggressive dog finally became submissive.

- Miserly means being unwilling or showing unwillingness to share with others, stingy.
- Dutiful means obediently fulfilling one's duty.
- Obedient means complying or willing to comply with an order or request.
- Stubborn means difficult to move, remove or cure.

Example: My toddler is very stubborn when it comes to following directions.

Out of the given words, we can see that the word Stubborn is opposite in meaning to the word Submissive.

Miserly, Dutiful, and Obedient are in fact, near-synonyms of the word Submissive.

Hence, the correct option is (D).

51. Dr. Samir V Kamat is the current chairman of DRDO.

DRDO launched the Hull Module of the Submersible Platform for Acoustic Characterization & Evaluation (SPACE) facility at Kochi, in November 2022. It is a state of the art testing and evaluation facility for sonar systems developed for use by the Indian navy onboard various platforms. It has a specially designed submersible platform, which can be lowered up to depths of 100 meters.

Hence, the correct option is (A).

52. Bharat Kala Bhavan is a university museum located in Banaras Hindu University, Varanasi, India. It has been instrumental in the dissemination of knowledge on Indian art and culture. It is one of the important touristic attractions in the Banaras Hindu University and in the city of Varanasi.

Bharat Kala Bhavan has a collection of artefacts, Buddhist and Hindu sculptures, pictures, manuscripts, Mughal miniatures, paintings, brocade textiles, contemporary art form and bronze statues from 1st to 15th century.

Hence, the correct option is (D).

53. In Agra, 'Mango' is not cultivated.

In Uttar Pradesh, mango is produced in an area of 2.5 lakh hectares. Lucknow, Pratapgarh, Allahabad, Bulandshahar, Saharanpur, Faizabad, Varanasi, Moradabad, Barabanki, Meerut, Unnao, Sitapur, Hardoi, Gorakhpur, Basti, JP Nagar, Mirzapur, and Mathura are the major mango producing belts in the state.

Hence, the correct option is (D).

54. Anpara Thermal Power Station is located at Anpara in Sonbhadra district of Uttar Pradesh state, India. It is located on the Varanasi-Shaktinagar road at a distance of about 200 km from Varanasi. All the units of Anpara Thermal Power Station are coal-fired thermal power plants with a total generating capacity of 2630 MW.

Hence, the correct option is (B).

55. Canberra is the federal capital of Australia. It occupies part of the Australian Capital Territory in southeastern Australia and is about 150 miles (240 km) southwest of Sydney. It lies astride the Molonglo River.

It is Australia's largest inland city and the eighth-largest city overall. The city is conceived as an ideal city, a National Capital worthy of the aspirations, passions, values, and patriotism of the Federation movement for the fledgling Australian nation.

Hence, the correct option is (B).

56. Goa has become the first state in India to provide 100 percent tap water connections in the rural areas covering 2.30 lakh households. Goa to strengthen the water testing facilities is also in the process of getting 14 water quality testing laboratories that are accredited by the National Accreditation Board for Testing and Calibration Laboratories (NABL). Goa became the first 'Har

Ghar Jal State' in India with 100 percent tap water connections in October 2020.

Hence, the correct option is (B).

57. The Calcutta High Court is the oldest in India. It has jurisdiction over the state of West Bengal and the Union Territory of the Andaman and Nicobar Islands. The High Court building's design is based on the Cloth Hall, Ypres, in Belgium. The court has a sanctioned judge strength of 72.

Hence, the correct option is (A).

58. Sardar Vallabhbhai Patel popularly known as Sardar Patel was an Indian statesman. He served as the First Deputy Prime Minister of India. He was an Indian barrister and a senior leader of the Indian National Congress who played a leading role in the country's struggle for independence and guided its integration into a united, independent nation.

His commitment to national integration in the newly independent country was total and uncompromising, earning him the sobriquet "Iron Man of India".

Hence, the correct option is (A).

59. Thalassemia is the genetic disease of blood.

Thalassemia is an inherited (i.e., passed from parents to children through genes) blood disorder caused when the body doesn't make enough of a protein called hemoglobin, an important part of red blood cells.

Hence, the correct option is (A).

60. Prayagraj is one of the ancient pilgrimage centers of India, and it represents the confluence of the rivers Yamuna and Ganga, near the city of Allahabad in Uttar Pradesh. The Ganges and Yamuna have joined in the river Trivedi Sangam is at the confluence of the Ganges, Yamuna, and Sarasvati (a mythical river that should have dried up thousands of years ago), which is a very important spiritual place in India. In India, these three major rivers are considered holy, but it is clear that their meeting point is one of the energies of piety.

Hence, the correct option is (B).

61. In arid soil the salt content is so high that common salt is obtained by evaporating the saline water in some areas. The loose material or the upper layer of the mantle rock consisting mainly of very small particles and humus which can support the growth of plants is known as "soil".

Soil is formed under specific natural conditions and each of the elements of the natural environment contributes to this complex process of soil formation known as "pedogenesis".

Hence, the correct option is (D).

62. The International Coastal Clean-up Day (ICC) is observed worldwide on the third Saturday of September.

The Indian Coast Guard (ICG) has led this campaign in India since 2006. In 2022, the Coast Guard leaned beaches at 75 locations across the country as part of the International Coastal Clean-up Day and 'Swachh Sagar Abhiyan'. ICG's efforts align with the

programme of the Ministry of Earth Sciences, 'Swachh Sagar-Surakshit Sagar'.

Hence, the correct option is (A).

63. In 2022, the Indian city of Mumbai was the host of the 'Global Fintech Conference'.

Global Fintech Fest was organized by the National Payments Corporation of India (NPCI), the Payments Council of India (PCI) and the Fintech Convergence Council (FCC).

It was attended by Union Finance Minister Nirmala Sitharaman and RBI Governor Shaktikanta Das. The Finance Minister called upon fintech industry to take advantage of opportunities in green finance for building a sustainable financial environment.

Hence, the correct option is (A).

64. Prime Minister Narendra Modi unveiled the new Naval Ensign (Flag) at Cochin Shipyard Limited in Kochi on September 2, 2022, signifying tenacity. The Indian flag is placed on the top left of the flag, while a blue octagonal shape that encompasses the national emblem sits atop an anchor on the right, which depicts steadfastness. The octagonal shape has been designed to represent eight directions, depicting the multi-directional reach and of the Indian Navy. The twin golden borders surrounding it are inspired from Chhatrapati Shivaji.

Hence, the correct option is (B).

65. Amazon announced its first solar project in India with three new solar farms in Rajasthan, with a combined energy capacity of 420 megawatts.

Amazon aims to use 100% renewable energy across its business by 2025. The Indian project includes a 210-MW project to be developed by ReNew Power, a 100-MW project to be developed by Amp Energy India, and a 110-MW project to be developed by Brookfield Renewable Partners.

Hence, the correct option is (B).

66. The Indian men's table tennis team clinched the gold medal at the 2022 Commonwealth Games in Birmingham on 2 August 2022.

- India defeated Singapore by 3-1 in the final.
- This is India's third gold medal at the CWG in the men's team event having earlier won in 2010 and 2018.
- On 2 August 2022 , the Indian women's lawn bowls team also won its first-ever gold at the Commonwealth Games.

Hence, the correct option is (C).

67. Amarkantak is located in the Anuppur district of Madhya Pradesh, at an elevation of 1065 metres, near the confluence of the Vindhya and Satpura mountain ranges, in a sylvan setting. It is 1048 metres above sea level on average. It was constructed during 1042-1122 AD by the monarch Karan Chendi.

Hence, the correct option is (C).

68. The central institute for research on buffaloes is a public-funded institute situated in Hisar for buffalo research.

- It operates nationwide and has 10 research centers and over 20 laboratories working on breed improvement and buffalo research respectively.
- It is the world's largest institute for buffalo research and has the widest range of breeds under study. It was established on 1 February 1985.

Hence, the correct option is (A).

69. The state of Manipur has undergone the maximum number of President rule from 1951 to 2019. The number of times the President's rule is imposed here is 10.

Article 356 empowers the President to issue a proclamation if he is satisfied that a situation has arisen in which the government of a state cannot be carried out on in accordance with the provisions of the Constitution.

Hence, the correct option is (C).

70. Mohiniyattam literally interpreted as the dance of "Mohini", the celestial enchantress of the Hindu mythology, is the classical solo dance form of Kerala. Mohiniyattam dance gets its name from the word Mohini – a historical enchantress avatar of the Hindu god Vishnu, who helps the good prevail over evil by developing her feminine powers.

Hence, the correct option is (A).

71. The product of the mass and velocity of a body is called momentum.

Momentum: It is defined as the quantity of motion of the body. Momentum depends on both speed and direction. Momentum is a vector quantity; i.e., it has both magnitude and direction. Isaac Newton's second law of motion states that the time rate of change of momentum is equal to the force acting on the particle.

Hence, the correct option is (B).

72. The pH scale stands for potential of hydrogen and it ranges from 0-14 with 7 being at the center it is for a completely neutral solution.

7 is the value of the pH of a neutral solution. A pH value less than 7 is acidic. A pH value greater than 7 is basic.

Hence, the correct option is (A).

73. Black soil is helpful for cotton crop. Black soil is appropriate for the growth of cotton because it has a high clay content and a good capacity to retain water. Cotton cultivation requires high moisture retention. Black soils are very fine grained and dark, contain a high proportion of calcium and magnesium carbonates and highly argillaceous.

Hence, the correct option is (C).

74. Tripiṭaka is the traditional term for the Buddhist scriptures.

Tripitaka are of three types:

- Vinay Pitaka rules of monastic discipline for monks.
- Sutta Pitaka is a collection of Buddha's Sermon.
- Abhidhamma Pitaka is the philosophies of Buddha's teachings.

Hence, the correct option is (D).

75. Bengal National College was set up on August 14th, 1906 as a part of the swadeshi movement. It was started with Sri Aurobindo Ghosh as the first principal of the College. It was included as part of the four-fold Programme of the new Nationalist Party of the Extremists.

The boycott of Foreign Schools, colleges, and goods as a result of the Swadeshi Movement was a result of the Partition of Bengal announced by Lord Curzon.

Hence, the correct option is (B).

76. Given,

Side of the rhombus $= 13$ cm

Length of one diagonal $= 10$ cm

As we know,

Area of a rhombus $(A) = \dfrac{\text{Product of the diagonals}}{2}$

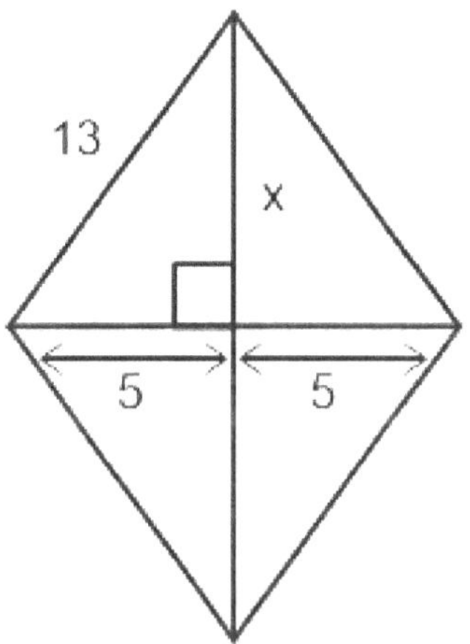

From Pythagoras theorom,

$$13^2 = 5^2 + x^2$$

$$\Rightarrow x = 12 \text{ cm}$$

Length of the other diagonal $= 2x$

$$= 2 \times 12$$

$$= 24 \text{ cm}$$

$$A = \dfrac{(24 \times 10)}{2}$$

$$= 120$$

$\therefore$ Area of the rhombus $= 120$ cm^2

Hence, the correct option is (D).

77. Given,

$T = 10$ years

$R = ?$

Now, let the original sum be Rs. 100.

$\therefore SI$ will be $\frac{2}{5}$ of $100 = 40$ Rs.

As we know that,

$$SI = \frac{P \times R \times T}{100}$$

$$R = SI \times \frac{100}{P \times T}$$

$$= 40 \times \frac{100}{100 \times 10}$$

$$= 4\%$$

Thus, at the rate of 4% the simple interest will be $\frac{2}{5}$ times to the original sum in 10 years.

Hence, the correct option is (A).

78. $9x - 3 = 7x + 3$

$2x = 6$

$x = 3$

The value of x is 3.

Hence, the correct option is (D).

79. The sequence of the given series is as follows:

$$a_n = (n + 1)^2 + 8$$

Now,

$$a_1 = (1 + 1)^2 + 8 = 2^2 + 8 = 4 + 8 = 12$$

$$a_2 = (2 + 1)^2 + 8 = 3^2 + 8 = 9 + 8 = 17$$

$$a_3 = (3 + 1)^2 + 8 = 4^2 + 8 = 16 + 8 = 24$$

$$a_4 = (4 + 1)^2 + 8 = 5^2 + 8 = 25 + 8 = 33$$

$$a_5 = (5 + 1)^2 + 8 = 6^2 + 8 = 36 + 8 = 44$$

$$a_6 = (6 + 1)^2 + 8 = 7^2 + 8 = 49 + 8 = 57$$

So, the next number in the series 57.

Hence, the correct option is (C).

80. The median is the middle number in a data set when the numbers are listed in either ascending or descending order.

If total number of observation (n) is odd then, Median $= \frac{(n+1)^{th}}{2}$ observation

Given data is:

$31, 37, 43, 42, 25, 46, 45, 39, 32$

Now, the given data is in ascending order:
$25, 31, 32, 37, 39, 42, 43, 45, 46$

The median of this data is the middlemost number of this data (as the total number of data is odd).

$$= [\tfrac{9+1}{2}]^{\text{th}} = [\tfrac{10}{2}]^{\text{th}} = 5^{\text{th}} \text{ number}$$

So, the required median is 39.

Hence, the correct option is (D).

81. Let the number be $10x + y$.

Sum of digits $= x + y$

According to the question,

Number $-$ Sum of digits $= (10x + y) - (x + y)$

$= 10x + y - x - y$

$= 10x - x + y - y$

$= 9x$

So, $9x$ has factors 9 and x.

Therefore, the resulting number is always divisible by 9.

Hence, the correct option is (D).

82. The factors of 54 are 1, 2, 3, 6, 9, 18, 27 and 54.

We add all the factors,

1+2+3+6+9+18+27+54 = 120

So, there are total 8 factors.

Hence, the correct option is (D).

83. Given,

$$6\sqrt{2} - \sqrt{32}$$

As we know that,

Rational numbers: A rational number is a number that can be express as the ratio of two integers.

Irrational numbers: An irrational number is a number that cannot be expressed as a fraction for any integers and. Irrational numbers have decimal expansions that neither terminate nor become periodic.

Now,

$$\sqrt{32} = \sqrt{2 \times 2 \times 2 \times 2 \times 2}$$

$$= 4\sqrt{2}$$

$$\therefore 6\sqrt{2} - \sqrt{32}$$

$$= 6\sqrt{2} - 4\sqrt{2}$$

$$= \sqrt{2}\,(6 - 4)$$

$$= 2\sqrt{2}$$

Thus, $2\sqrt{2}$ is an irrational number.

Hence, the correct option is (A).

84. Weight of 1 apple $= 500$ kg

Weight of 10 apples $= 500 \times 10$ kg

$= 5$ kg

Initial weight $= 25 - 5 = 20$ kg

A number of apples in his carton initially,

$= 20000 \div 500$

$= 40$ apples

Hence, the correct option is (B).

85. Given,

98

= 90 + 8

= XC + VIII

= XCVIII

Thus, the correct roman numeral of a given number that is 98 is XCVIII.

Hence, the correct option is (C).

86. Real number consist of all the rational and irrational numbers. A rational number is a number that is represented in the form of P/Q, where Q is not equal to zero and both P and Q are integers. For example, $\dfrac{1}{2}$ is a rational number, but not a whole number, not a natural number or not an integer.

Hence, the correct option is (D).

87. We know that,

A twin prime is a prime number that is either 2 less or 2 more than another prime number.

The difference between the twin prime number is always two.

In twin prime number, both the number should be the prime number.

Now,

Twin primes are pairs of successive primes that differ by two.

The primes from 1 to 100 are 2, 3, 5, 7, 11, 13, 17, 19, 23, 29, 31, 37, 41, 43, 47, 53, 59, 61, 67, 71, 73, 79, 83, 89, 97.

(71, 73) - Difference between them is 2.

Here, in the given option (71 and 73) are prime numbers and their difference is '2'.

Hence, the correct option is (D).

88. Given,

-101, -88, -125, 45, 98, 88

As we know that, the highest number with a negative sign is considered to be the smallest number.

So, the descending order of -101, -88, -125, 45, 98, 88 is:

Descending order = 90, 88, 45, -88, -101, -125

Symbolically, it is represented by 90 > 88 > 45 > -88 > -101 > -125.

Hence, the correct option is (A).

89. Given,

$$15 - 15 \div 15 \times 6 = x$$

$$x = 15 - 15 \times \dfrac{1}{15} \times 6$$

$$x = 15 - 15 \times \dfrac{1}{15} \times 6$$

$$x = 15 - 6$$

$$x = 9$$

Hence, the correct option is (C).

90. Given,

Any number when multiplied with 1, gives the same number as the result.

Here, 0.01 is actually $\dfrac{1}{100}$ so we first multiply the given number by 1.

$$140.75 \times 1 = 140.75$$

Now, since the result is to be divided by 100, we shift the decimal two places to the left.

$$140.75 \times 0.01 = 1.4075$$

Hence, the correct option is (C).

91. Given,

4 + 4.44 + 4.04 + 44.4 + 444 = ?

Adding decimals first:

0.44 + 0.04 + 0.4 = 0.88

Now, adding 4 + 4 + 4 + 44 + 444 = 500

$\Rightarrow$ 500 + 0.88

= 500.88

Hence, the correct option is (D).

92. Given,

$$16 - 2 \div 14 + 6 \times 2$$

$$= 16 - \dfrac{2}{14} + 12$$

$$= 28 - \dfrac{2}{14}$$

$$= \dfrac{28 \times 14 - 2}{14}$$

$$= \dfrac{392 - 2}{14}$$

$= \dfrac{390}{14}$

$= 27\dfrac{12}{14}$

Hence, the correct option is (A).

93. Given,

LCM of $\dfrac{2}{5}, \dfrac{3}{10}$ and $\dfrac{4}{15}$

Now,

LCM of $\dfrac{2}{5}, \dfrac{3}{10}$ and $\dfrac{4}{15}$

$\Rightarrow \dfrac{LCM(2,3,4)}{HCF(5,10,15)}$

$\Rightarrow LCM$ of $(2,3,4) = 12$

$\Rightarrow HCF(5,10,15) = 5$

$\therefore LCM$ of $\dfrac{2}{5}, \dfrac{3}{10}$ and $\dfrac{4}{15}$

$= \dfrac{12}{5}$

Hence, the correct option is (D).

94. Given,

The product of two numbers is 4107.

$HCF = 37$

According to the formula,

$HCF \times LCM = $ Product of two numbers

$\Rightarrow 37 \times LCM = 4107$

$\Rightarrow LCM = \dfrac{4107}{37}$

$\Rightarrow LCM = 111$

Ratio of HCF and LCM $= 37:111$

$= 1:3$

Hence, the correct option is (A).

95. If the height of the right angle triangle is 24 cm, and the area of the triangle is 168 sq.cm.

Area of right angle triangle,

$\Rightarrow \dfrac{1}{2} \times b \times h = 168$

$\Rightarrow \dfrac{1}{2} \times b \times 24 = 168$

$\Rightarrow b = \dfrac{168 \times 2}{12}$

$b = 14$ cm

The perimeter of the rectangle is 84 cm.

The base of a triangle is equal to the breadth of a rectangle.

So, $2(L + b) = 84$

$\Rightarrow 2L + 2 \times 14 = 84$

$\Rightarrow L = \left(\dfrac{56}{2}\right)$

$= 28$ cm

Hence, the correct option is (C).

96. As we know that,

Area of trapezium $= \dfrac{1}{2}h(a + b)$

Given,

$a = 20$ cm

$h = 15$ cm

Area $= 480$ sq.cm

Now,

$\Rightarrow 480 = \dfrac{1}{2} \times (15) \times (20 + b)$

$\Rightarrow 20 + b = \dfrac{(480 \times 2)}{15}$

$\Rightarrow 20 + b = 64$

$b = 44$ cm

Thus, the other parallel side of a trapezium is 44 cm.

Hence, the correct option is (C).

97. Given,

8281

As we know,

Prime factorisation of a number,

Prime factorisation of:

$8281 = 7 \times 7 \times 13 \times 13$

So, $\sqrt{8281} = 7 \times 13$

$= 91$

$\therefore$ Square root of 8281 is 91.

Hence, the correct option is (B).

98. Given,

$(a - b) = 3$ and $ab = 70$

Formula:

$a^3 - b^3 = (a - b)^3 + 3ab(a - b)$

$\Rightarrow a^3 - b^3 = 3^3 + 3 \times 70 \times 3$

$$\Rightarrow a^3 - b^3 = 27 + 630$$

$$\therefore a^3 - b^3 = 657$$

Hence, the correct option is (A).

99. When 800 is first increased by 10%,

$$\Rightarrow 800 + 800 \times \frac{10}{100}$$

$$= 880$$

It is again increased by 20%,

$$\Rightarrow 880 + 880 \times \frac{20}{100}$$

$$= 1056$$

Hence, the correct option is (C).

100. Given,

C.P. $=$ Rs. 2000

S.P. $=$ Rs. 2500

As we know that,

Profit or Gain = S.P. $-$ C.P.

$$= 2500 - 2000$$

$$= 500$$

$\therefore$ Profit $\% =$ Profit $\times 100$

$$= \frac{500}{2000} \times 100$$

$$= 25\%$$

Hence, the correct option is (B).

Q.1 निर्देश: दिए गए शब्दों का एक शब्द बताइए।
"जो इंद्रियों द्वारा न जाना जा सके"
A. अगोचर 　　　　　B. अतिशयोक्ति
C. अग्रणी 　　　　　D. अज्ञात

Q.2 निर्देश: दिए गए शब्दों का एक शब्द बताइए।
'जिसके पेट मे माँ ने रस्सी (दाम) बाँध दी हो'
A. अनिर्वचनीय 　　　　　B. अछूत
C. अटल 　　　　　D. दामोदर

Q.3 'किसान' का तत्सम रूप है:
A. कृषक 　　B. कषक 　　C. कृष 　　D. कृषकृ

Q.4 निम्नलिखित में 'अग्नि' का तद्भव रूप कौन सा है?
A. अटारी 　　B. दबाना 　　C. आग 　　D. दूब

Q.5 दिए गए वाक्य का सही काल निर्धारण कीजिए।
'राम घर जाता है।'
A. वर्तमान काल 　　　　　B. भूतकाल
C. भविष्य काल 　　　　　D. सामान्य भविष्य

Q.6 'किसी वाक्य में जब अर्थ की स्पष्टता हेतु थोड़ा रुकना पड़े' वहाँ किस विराम की आवश्यकता होती है?
A. अर्द्ध विराम 　　　　　B. पूर्ण विराम
C. अल्पविराम 　　　　　D. उपविराम

Q.7 जहाँ वाक्य की गति अंतिम रूप से ले, विचार के तार टूट जाएँ, वहाँ किस चिह्न का प्रयोग किया जाता है?
A. योजक 　　　　　B. अल्पविराम
C. उद्धरण चिह्न 　　　　　D. पूर्ण विराम

Q.8 "अधजल गगरी छलकत जाए" लोकोक्ति का अर्थ बताइये।
A. जिनमे ज्ञान की कमी होती है वह ज्ञान का दिखावा अधिक करते हैं।
B. मूर्ख व्यक्तियों की भीड़ में कम ज्ञानी व्यक्ति भी स्वयं को बुद्धिमान समझता है।
C. किसी का नाम उसके गुड़ो के बिल्कुल विपरीत होना।
D. किसी का अंतिम और एकमात्र सहारा।

Q.9 "खटाई में पड़ना" मुहावरे का आशय है:
A. बहुत कष्ट होना 　　　　　B. नुकसान होना
C. पछतावा होना 　　　　　D. निर्णय न होना

Q.10 'ओखली में सिर देना' लोकोक्ति का अर्थ है -
A. जान-बुझकर अपने को जोखिम में डालना।
B. सिर में दर्द होना।
C. अधिक जानने वाले को उपदेश देने वाला।
D. डर या दुःख से घबरा जाना।

Q.11 'रेखा खाना खा रही है।' इसमें कौन सा कारक हैं?
A. कर्ता कारक 　　　　　B. कर्म कारक
C. करण कारक 　　　　　D. संप्रदान कारक

Q.12 'विद्यार्थी' में संधि है:
A. वृद्धि संधि 　　B. दीर्घ संधि 　　C. यण संधि 　　D. गुण संधि

Q.13 'नौसिखिया' शब्द में कौन-सा उपसर्ग का प्रयोग हुआ है?
A. नौ 　　B. उत् 　　C. अप 　　D. अन

Q.14 'धावक' शब्द में कौन-सा प्रत्यय है?
A. क 　　B. अक 　　C. धाव 　　D. वक

Q.15 दिए गए विकल्पों में से निम्नलिखित वाक्य का भेद बताइए।
"उसने कहा कि मैं घर जाऊँगा।"
A. सरल वाक्य 　　　　　B. संयुक्त वाक्य
C. मिश्र वाक्य 　　　　　D. प्रश्नवाचक वाक्य

Q.16 'यह गाय अधिक दूध देती है' इस वाक्य में विशेषण है:
A. अधिक 　　B. गाय 　　C. दूध 　　D. यह

Q.17 'मैं अपने आप यह काम सीख लूँगा।' इस वाक्य में निजवाचक सर्वनाम है:
A. आप 　　B. सीख 　　C. यह 　　D. काम

Q.18 दिए गए विकल्पों में से रिक्त स्थान की पूर्ति कीजिए।
यह ________ सदियों से चली आ रही है।
A. समाटी 　　B. परिपाटी 　　C. उपपाटी 　　D. धरपाटी

Q.19 निम्नलिखित में से उक्षिप्त व्यंजन ________ हैं।
A. ट, ठ 　　B. ज, फ 　　C. ड़, ढ़ 　　D. ढ, ण

Q.20 "लड़के फुटबॉल खेल रहे हैं" इसमें लड़के में कौन वचन हैं?
A. एकवचन 　　　　　B. बहुवचन
C. द्विवचन 　　　　　D. इनमे से कोई नहीं

Q.21 निम्नलिखित में से शुद्ध वर्तनी का चयन कीजिए:
A. सूचिपत्र 　　B. त्रृकोण 　　C. एकान्त 　　D. भानू

Q.22 निम्नलिखित में से कौन-सा शब्द 'अपकार' का विलोम शब्द है?
A. उपकार 　　B. ऐच्छिक 　　C. ऐक्य 　　D. कीर्ति

Q.23 दिए गए शब्द का पर्यायवाची शब्द बताइए।
'अभिलाषा'
A. द्रग 　　B. इच्छा 　　C. नवीन 　　D. भय

Q.24 'ब्रज के बिरही लोग दुखारे' में कौन-सा रस है?
A. वीर रस 　　B. शांत रस 　　C. भक्ति रस 　　D. श्रृंगार रस

Q.25 संज्ञा का मुख्य भेद नहीं है?
A. व्यक्तिवाचक 　　　　　B. जातिवाचक
C. निजवाचक 　　　　　D. भाववाचक

// स्मार्ट उत्तर पुस्तिका //

सही उत्तर — उन छात्रों के प्रतिशत को इंगित करता है जिन्होंने प्रश्नों का सही उत्तर दिया था।

छोड़ दिया — उन छात्रों के प्रतिशत को इंगित करता है जिन्होंने प्रश्नों को छोड़ दिया था।

प्रश्न संख्या	उत्तर	सही उत्तर / छोड़ दिया	प्रश्न संख्या	उत्तर	सही उत्तर / छोड़ दिया	प्रश्न संख्या	उत्तर	सही उत्तर / छोड़ दिया	प्रश्न संख्या	उत्तर	सही उत्तर / छोड़ दिया	प्रश्न संख्या	उत्तर	सही उत्तर / छोड़ दिया
1	A	42.43 % / 1.97 %	6	C	64.92 % / 1.21 %	11	A	63.7 % / 1.17 %	16	A	89.62 % / 0.0 %	21	C	19.8 % / 3.53 %
2	D	47.46 % / 1.17 %	7	D	68.81 % / 1.21 %	12	B	79.56 % / 0.0 %	17	A	64.97 % / 1.6 %	22	A	58.98 % / 1.89 %
3	A	89.8 % / 0.0 %	8	A	77.8 % / 0.0 %	13	A	51.73 % / 1.77 %	18	B	28.88 % / 3.5 %	23	B	44.2 % / 1.5 %
4	C	85.76 % / 0.0 %	9	D	83.2 % / 0.0 %	14	B	50.8 % / 1.65 %	19	C	80.58 % / 0.0 %	24	D	56.66 % / 1.01 %
5	A	53.96 % / 1.72 %	10	A	89.75 % / 0.0 %	15	C	83.42 % / 0.0 %	20	B	50.6 % / 1.03 %	25	C	44.51 % / 1.21 %

कार्य विश्लेषण	
औसत अंक (%)	52.0%
टॉपर्स स्कोर (%)	60.0%
आपका स्कोर	

//Hints and Solutions//

1. जो इंद्रियों द्वारा न जाना जा सके - अगोचर

अत्यधिक बढ़ा–चढ़ा कर कही गई बात - अतिशयोक्ति

सबसे आगे रहने वाला - अग्रणी

जिसका पता न हो - अज्ञात

अतः विकल्प (A) सही है।

2. जिसके पेट मे माँ ने रस्सी (दाम) बाँध दी हो - दामोदर

जिसका भाषा द्वारा वर्णन असंभव हो - अनिर्वचनीय

जो अपनी बात से टले नहीं - अटल

जो छूने योग्य न हो - अछूत

अतः विकल्प (D) सही है।

3. 'किसान' का तत्सम रूप 'कृषक' है।

संस्कृत भाषा के वे शब्द जो हिंदी भाषा में ज्यों के त्यों ले लिए गए है, तत्सम शब्द कहलाते है। जैसे – अग्नि, अमूल्य, अज्ञान, कर्पूर

अतः विकल्प (A) सही है।

4. 'अग्नि' का तद्भव रूप 'आग' है। अन्य विकल्प इसके अनुचित उत्तर हैं।

आग - अग्नि

अटारी - अट्टालिका

दबाना - दमन

दूब - दूर्वा

अतः विकल्प (C) सही है।

5. दिए गए वाक्य 'राम घर जाता है।' में वर्तमान काल है।

क्रिया के जिस रूप से कार्य का वर्तमान समय में होना पाया जाता है, उसे वर्तमान काल कहते है।

जैसे: अंकित पुस्तक पढ़ता है।

अत: विकल्प (A) सही है।

6. अल्प विराम (,)- वाक्य को कहते या लिखते समय जब उसके अर्थ की स्पष्टता हेतु थोड़ी देर का विराम या ठहरना पड़े तो वहाँ पर अल्प विराम का उपयोग किया जाता है। इनका प्रयोग एक से अधिक वस्तुओं, व्यक्तियों या अन्य को अलग-अलग दर्शाने के लिए भी किया जाता है।

अल्पविराम को हम वाक्य में अर्थ को अधिक स्पष्ट करने के लिए उपयोग करते हैं।

जैसे-

वाक्य के अर्थ को अधिक स्पष्ट करने के लिए अल्प विराम का प्रयोग-

- कभी भी जरूरत पड़े, आ जाना।
- नहीं, मैं नहीं जाऊंगा।

एक से अधिक व्यक्तियों, वस्तुओं या अन्य को अलग-अलग दर्शाने हेतु अल्प विराम का प्रयोग-

- जयंत के साथ फ़ौजान, दीपक, रमेश और फ़ाहिम भी थे।
- लड्डू, मिठाई, बूंदी और समोसा लगभग सभी लोग पसंद करते हैं।

अतः विकल्प (C) सही है।

7. जहाँ वाक्य की गति अंतिम रूप से ले, विचार के तार टूट जाएँ, वहाँ पूर्ण विराम (।) चिह्न का प्रयोग किया जाता है।

पूर्ण विराम चिन्ह का प्रयोग किसी वाक्य की समाप्ति, किसी एक विचार या बात की समाप्ति या किसी वाक्यांश के अन्त में किया जाता है। पूर्ण विराम चिन्ह लगाने का अर्थ यह होता है की वाक्य समाप्त हो चुका है।

अतः विकल्प (D) सही है।

8. "अधजल गगरी छलकत जाए" लोकोक्ति का अर्थ "जिनमे ज्ञान की कमी होती है वह ज्ञान का दिखावा अधिक करते हैं।" है।

अंधों में काना राजा : मूर्ख व्यक्तियों की भीड़ में कम ज्ञानी व्यक्ति भी स्वयं को बुद्धिमान समझता है।

आंख का अंधा नाम नयन सुख : मूर्ख व्यक्तियों की भीड़ में कम ज्ञानी व्यक्ति भी स्वयं को बुद्धिमान समझता है।

अंधे की लकड़ी : किसी का अंतिम और एकमात्र सहारा।

अतः विकल्प (A) सही है।

9. निर्णय न होना, यहाँ सही विकल्प है। अन्य विकल्प असंगत है।

खटाई में पड़ना एक प्रचलित हिंदी मुहवरा है जिसका अर्थ किसी काम का अनिश्चित होने से है।

जैसे- इस बार की परीक्षा का परिणाम खटाई में पड़ गया है।

अतः विकल्प (D) सही है।

10. 'ओखली में सिर देना' एक प्रचलित लोकोक्ति है। इस लोकोक्ति का उपयुक्त अर्थ- 'जान-बुझकर अपने को जोखिम में डालना।

वाक्य प्रयोग – कल हथियारबंद बदमाशों से उलझकर केशव ने ओखली में सिर दे दिया।

अतः विकल्प (A) सही है।

11. 'रेखा खाना खा रही है।' इसमें कर्ता कारक हैं।

कोई भी वाक्य जिसमें कार्य करने वाले का पता लगता है, उन्हें कर्ता कारक कहा जाता है।

अतः विकल्प (A) सही है।

12. 'विद्यार्थी' में 'दीर्घ संधि' है।

'विद्यार्थी' का संधि-विच्छेद है - विद्या + अर्थी।

जब दो शब्दों की संधि करते समय (अ, आ) के साथ (अ, आ) हो तो 'आ' बनता है, जब (इ, ई) के साथ (इ, ई) हो तो 'ई' बनता है, जब (उ, ऊ) के साथ (उ, ऊ) हो तो 'ऊ' बनता है। उसे दीर्घ संधि कहते है।

जैसे- विद्या + अभ्यास = विद्याभ्यास (आ + अ = आ) आदि।

अतः विकल्प (B) सही है।

13. 'नौसिखिया' शब्द में 'नौ ' उपसर्ग का प्रयोग हुआ है।जिसमे मूल शब्द 'सिखिया' एवं उपसर्ग 'नौ' है। इसलिए सही विकल्प 'नौ' है।

अतः विकल्प (A) सही है।

14. 'धावक' शब्द में 'अक ' प्रत्यय है।

धावक शब्द का अर्थ 'दौड़नेवाला' है।

'अक' प्रत्यय से बने अन्य शब्द पाठक, गायक, लेखक, नायक आदि हैं।

अतः विकल्प (B) सही है।

15. "उसने कहा कि मैं घर जाऊँगा।" में वाक्य का भेद मिश्र वाक्य है। जिस वाक्य में एक प्रधान उपवाक्य तथा एक या एक से अधिक आश्रित उपवाक्य हों उसे मिश्र वाक्य कहते हैं।

उदाहरण:

जब भी मैं विकास के घर गया, मेरा आदर सत्कार हुआ।

अतः विकल्प (C) सही है।

16. 'यह गाय अधिक दूध देती है' इस वाक्य में विशेषण 'अधिक' है।

विशेषण संज्ञा या सर्वनाम के रूप गुण, संख्या, मात्रा, परिमाण, आदि के विशेषता बताते हैं।

अतः विकल्प (A) सही है।

17. वह सार्वनामिक शब्द जो स्वयं के लिए प्रयोग करते हैं जैसे – आप , अपना आदि जिससे स्वयं का बोध हो वह निजवाचक कहलाते हैं। जो सर्वनाम तीनों पुरुषों (उत्तम, मध्यम और अन्य) में निजत्व का बोध कराता है, उसे निजवाचक सर्वनाम कहते हैं। जैसे- मैं खुद लिख लूँगा। तुम अपने आप चले जाना।

उपरोक्त वाक्य में 'आप' निजवाचक सर्वनाम है।

अतः विकल्प (A) सही है।

18. वाक्य है,

यह परिपाटी सदियों से चली आ रही है।

परिपाटी का अर्थ क्रम, श्रेणी, सिलसिला होता है।

अतः विकल्प (B) सही है।

19. जिन व्यंजनों के उच्चारण में जीभ का अगला भाग थोड़ा ऊपर उठाकर झटके से नीचे गिरता है, उसे उक्षिप्त व्यंजन कहते हैं। ये संख्या में दो ही हैं। उक्षिप्त व्यंजन ड़, ढ़ हैं। इन्हें द्विगुण व्यंजन भी कहा जाता है।

अतः विकल्प (C) सही है।

20. "लड़के फुटबॉल खेल रहे हैं" इसमें लड़के में बहुवचन हैं।

संज्ञा के जिस रुप से किसी व्यक्ति, वस्तु प्राणी, पदार्थ आदि के एक से अधिक होने का बोध होता है या पता चलता है उसे बहुवचन कहते हैं। जैसे-लड़के, बच्चे कपड़े पुस्तकें स्त्रियां टोपिया, गाड़ियां, ठेले, नदियां आदि।

अतः विकल्प (B) सही है।

21. दिए गए विकल्पों में एकान्त शब्द की वर्तनी शुद्ध है।

'एकान्त' का अर्थ 'शांत या शोरगुल रहित ऐसा स्थान जहाँ कोई न हो' है।

अन्य विकल्प –

अशुद्ध वर्तनी	शुद्ध वर्तनी
सूचिपत्र	सूचीपत्र
तृकोण	त्रिकोण
भानू	भानु

अतः विकल्प (C) सही है।

22. 'अपकार' का विलोम शब्द 'उपकार' है।

अनैच्छिक : ऐच्छिक

अनैक्य : ऐक्य

अपकीर्ति : कीर्ति

अतः विकल्प (A) सही है।

23. दिए गए शब्द 'अभिलाषा' का पर्यायवाची शब्द 'इच्छा' है।

दृग: आँख

नवीन: नया

भय: डर

अतः विकल्प (B) सही है।

24. 'ब्रज के बिरही लोग दुखारे' में श्रृंगार रस है।

नायक और नायिका के मन में संस्कार रूप में स्थित रति या प्रेम जब रस की अवस्था को पहुँचकर आस्वादन के योग्य हो जाता है तो वह 'श्रृंगार रस' कहलाता है। श्रृंगार रस का स्थायी भाव 'रति' होता है।

अतः विकल्प (D) सही है।

25. मूलतः संज्ञा के तीन भेद (प्रकार) होते हैं- जातिवाचक संज्ञा, भाववाचक संज्ञा और व्यक्तिवाचक संज्ञा।

परन्तु निजवाचक संज्ञा का भेद नहीं सर्वनाम का भेद होता है। जिस सर्वनाम का प्रयोग कर्ता कारक स्वयं के लिए करता है, वह निजवाचक सर्वनाम होता है।

अतः विकल्प (C) सही है।

Ques (1-2):निर्देश: दिए गए शब्दों का एक शब्द बताइए।

Q.1 "सबसे आगे रहने वाला"

A. अग्रणी   **B.** अतिशयोक्ति

C. अज्ञात   **D.** अगोचर

Q.2 "जो सर्वत्र उपस्थित हो"

A. अनिर्वचनीय   **B.** अटल

C. अछूत   **D.** सर्वव्यापी

Q.3 नीचे दिए गये विकल्पों में से तत्सम - तद्भव शब्दों का कौन सा युग्म सही सुमेलित नहीं है?

A. धृष्ट - ढीठ   **B.** धूम्र - धुआँ

C. प्रहेलिका - फूल   **D.** प्रतिवेश्मिक - पड़ोसी

Q.4 "श्रृंग" का उचित तद्भव शब्द होगाः

A. श्रृग   **B.** सीख   **C.** सींग   **D.** साँकल

Q.5 'पिता जी समाचार सुनते है' इसमें कौन सा काल हैं ?

A. भूतकाल   **B.** वर्तमान काल

C. भविष्य काल   **D.** इसमें से कोई नहीं

Q.6 विराम चिह्न का क्या अर्थ है?

A. चलना   **B.** ठहराव या रुकना

C. वाक्यों का दोहराव   **D.** इनमें से कोई नहीं

Q.7 जहाँ वाक्य बीच में हल्का सा विराम लेना हो पर वाक्य को खत्म न किया जाये, वहाँ किस चिह्न का प्रयोग किया जाता है?

A. अर्द्ध विराम   **B.** योजक

C. उद्धरण चिह्न   **D.** पूर्ण विराम

Q.8 "आगे कुआं पीछे खाई" लोकोक्ति का अर्थ बताइये।

A. दोनों तरफ से मुसीबत आना अर्थात बचने का कोई रास्ता ना होना।

B. किसी के भरोसे पर ना रहकर अपना कार्य स्वंय करना।

C. किसी का नाम उसके गुणों के बिल्कुल विपरीत होना।

D. किसी का अंतिम और एकमात्र सहारा।

Q.9 "गूलर का फूल होना" मुहावरे का अर्थ बताईये।

A. लापता होना   **B.** क्रोध दबाना

C. डींग हाँकना   **D.** खूब याद रखना

Q.10 "गर्दन फँस गई" मुहावरे का अर्थ बताईये।

A. मूर्ख बनाना

B. झंझट या परेशानी में फँसना

C. किसी को ठगना

D. किसी को जिम्मेदार ठहराना

Q.11 'वेदांत सो रहा है।' इसमें कौन सा कारक हैं ?

A. कर्ता कारक   **B.** कर्म कारक

C. करण कारक   **D.** संप्रदान कारक

Q.12 'मतैक्य' शब्द का संधि विच्छेद क्या होगा?

A. मत + एक   **B.** मत + एक्य

C. मत + ऐक्य   **D.** म + तैक्य

Q.13 निम्नलिखित शब्दों में से किसमें 'अन' प्रत्यय का प्रयोग हुआ है?

A. चढ़ान   **B.** मोहन   **C.** वेदना   **D.** झाड़न

Q.14 'अतिपावन' शब्द में कौन-सा उपसर्ग का प्रयोग हुआ है?

A. पावन   **B.** अ   **C.** न   **D.** अति

Q.15 "संतोष से बढ़कर सुख नहीं।" किस प्रकार का वाक्य है?

A. मिश्र वाक्य   **B.** सरल वाक्य

C. संयुक्त वाक्य   **D.** इनमें से कोई नहीं

Q.16 निम्न में से विशेषण का उदाहरण नहीं है:

A. हरी   **B.** सुन्दर   **C.** कड़वाहट   **D.** दोहरा

Q.17 निश्चयवाचक सर्वनाम कौन सा है?

A. क्या   **B.** कुछ   **C.** कौन   **D.** यह

Q.18 रिक्त स्थान की पूर्ति उचित विकल्प से कीजिए। अनेक भाषाएँ बोलने वाले को _____ कहते हैं।

A. वक्ता   **B.** बहुभाषी   **C.** शाकाहारी   **D.** कटुभाषी

Q.19 निम्नलिखित में से पश्च स्वर कौन सा है?

A. इ   **B.** ए   **C.** क   **D.** आ

Q.20 'खूँटी' शब्द का बहुवचन बताइए:

A. खूँटियाँ   **B.** खूँटियों   **C.** खूँटिया   **D.** खूँटियौं

Q.21 निम्न में शुद्ध शब्द है:

A. केकेयी   **B.** केकैयी   **C.** कैकेयी   **D.** केकई

Q.22 'योम' का पर्यायवाची शब्द नहीं है:

A. सूर्यकाल   **B.** दिवस   **C.** अह   **D.** काल

Q.23 निम्नलिखित में से कौन-सा शब्द 'अनैच्छिक' का विलोम शब्द है?

A. ऐच्छिक   **B.** उपकार   **C.** ऐक्य   **D.** कीर्ति

Q.24 'झाँसी वाली रानी थी बुन्देलों हरबोलो के मुह हमने सुनी कहानी थी।' में कौन-सा रस है?

A. वीर रस   **B.** श्रृंगार रस   **C.** करूण रस   **D.** हास्य रस

Q.25 निम्न में से कौन सा शब्द व्यक्तिवाचक संज्ञा है?

A. गाय   **B.** पहाड़   **C.** यमुना   **D.** आम

// स्मार्ट उत्तर पुस्तिका //

सही उत्तर — उन छात्रों के प्रतिशत को इंगित करता है जिन्होंने प्रश्नों का सही उत्तर दिया था।

छोड़ दिया — उन छात्रों के प्रतिशत को इंगित करता है जिन्होंने प्रश्नों को छोड़ दिया था।

प्रश्न संख्या	उत्तर	सही उत्तर / छोड़ दिया
1	A	40.96 % / 1.65 %
2	D	68.67 % / 1.11 %
3	C	17.65 % / 4.24 %
4	C	89.67 % / 0.0 %
5	B	57.26 % / 1.21 %

प्रश्न संख्या	उत्तर	सही उत्तर / छोड़ दिया
6	B	45.93 % / 1.19 %
7	A	43.05 % / 1.48 %
8	A	49.58 % / 1.64 %
9	A	52.98 % / 1.6 %
10	B	59.81 % / 1.32 %

प्रश्न संख्या	उत्तर	सही उत्तर / छोड़ दिया
11	A	82.83 % / 0.0 %
12	C	17.97 % / 3.26 %
13	B	62.81 % / 1.38 %
14	D	50.1 % / 1.28 %
15	B	64.49 % / 1.64 %

प्रश्न संख्या	उत्तर	सही उत्तर / छोड़ दिया
16	C	51.26 % / 1.92 %
17	D	63.55 % / 1.93 %
18	B	11.91 % / 4.56 %
19	D	57.69 % / 1.51 %
20	A	77.13 % / 0.0 %

प्रश्न संख्या	उत्तर	सही उत्तर / छोड़ दिया
21	C	59.86 % / 1.35 %
22	D	46.27 % / 1.28 %
23	A	18.09 % / 3.82 %
24	A	42.23 % / 1.13 %
25	C	40.91 % / 1.24 %

कार्य विश्लेषण	
औसत अंक (%)	32.0%
टॉपर्स स्कोर (%)	52.0%
आपका स्कोर	

//Hints and Solutions//

1. सबसे आगे रहने वाला - अग्रणी

अत्यधिक बढ़ा–चढ़ा कर कही गई बात - अतिशयोक्ति

जिसका पता न हो - अज्ञात

जो इंद्रियों द्वारा न जाना जा सके - अगोचर

अतः विकल्प (A) सही है।

2. जो सर्वत्र उपस्थित हो - सर्वव्यापी

जिसका भाषा द्वारा वर्णन असंभव हो - अनिर्वचनीय

जो अपनी बात से टले नहीँ - अटल

जो छूने योग्य न हो - अछूत

अतः विकल्प (D) सही है।

3. दिए गए विकल्पो में "प्रहेलिका - फूल" युग्म सही सुमेलित नहीं है।

"प्रहेलिका" का सही तदभव "पहेली" होगा तथा "फूल" "पुष्प" का तदभव है।
अतः विकल्प (C) सही है।

4. "श्रृंग" का उचित तदभव शब्द "सींग" होगा।

"श्रृंग" का शाब्दिक अर्थ शिखर या चोटी होता है।
अतः विकल्प (C) सही है।

5. 'पिता जी समाचार सुनते है' इसमें वर्तमान काल हैं। क्रिया के जिस रूप से वर्तमान समय में मौजूद कोई स्थिति या किसी घटना के होने का संकेत मिलता है उसे 'वर्तमान काल' कहते हैं।

जैसे-

राम घर जाता है।

अत: विकल्प (B) सही है।

6. विराम चिन्ह का अर्थ ठहराव या रुकना है। अर्थात वाक्य लिखते समय विराम को प्रकट करने के लिए लगाये जाने वाले चिन्ह को ही विराम चिन्ह कहते हैं।

अतः विकल्प (B) सही है।

7. जहाँ वाक्य बीच में हल्का सा विराम लेना हो पर वाक्य को खत्म न किया जाये, वहाँ पर अर्द्ध विराम (;) चिन्ह का प्रयोग किया जाता है। जहाँ पूर्ण विराम की अपेक्षा कम विराम लेना हो और अल्प विराम (,) की अपेक्षा ज्यादा विराम (रुकना) हो वहां अर्द्ध विराम (;) का प्रयोग करते हैं।

अतः विकल्प (A) सही है।

8. "आगे कुआं पीछे खाई" लोकोक्ति का अर्थ "दोनों तरफ से मुसीबत आना अर्थित बचने का कोई रास्ता ना होना।" है।

अपना हाथ जगन्नाथ : किसी के भरोसे पर ना रहकर अपना कार्य स्वंय करना।

आंख का अंधा नाम नयन सुख : किसी का नाम उसके गुणों के बिल्कुल विपरीत होना।

अंधे की लकड़ी : किसी का अंतिम और एकमात्र सहारा।

अतः विकल्प (A) सही है।

9. मुहावरा – गूलर का फूल होना

अर्थ – लापता होना

वाक्य प्रयोग – वह तो ऐसा गूलर का फूल हो गया है कि उसके बारे में कुछ कहना मुश्किल है।

अतः विकल्प (A) सही है।

10. मुहावरा - गर्दन फँसना

अर्थ - झंझट या परेशानी में फँसना

वाक्य प्रयोग - उसे रुपया उधार देकर मेरी तो गर्दन फँस गई है।

अतः विकल्प (B) सही है।

11. 'वेदांत सो रहा है।' इसमें कर्ता कारक हैं।

कोई भी वाक्य जिसमें कार्य करने वाले का पता लगता है, उन्हें कर्ता कारक कहा जाता है।

अतः विकल्प (A) सही है।

12. 'मतैक्य' शब्द का संधि विच्छेद 'मत + ऐक्य' है।

'मतैक्य' शब्द में वृद्धि संधि है।

जब संधि करते समय जब अ, आ के साथ ए, ऐ हो तो 'ऐ' बनता है और जब अ, आ के साथ ओ, औ हो तो 'औ' बनता है। उसे वृद्धि संधि कहते हैं।

अत: विकल्प (C) सही है।

13. दिए गए विकल्पों में 'मोहन' शब्द में 'अन' प्रत्यय का प्रयोग हुआ है जिसका विच्छेद 'मोह + अन - मोहन' है।

प्रत्यय – ऐसे शब्दांश जो किसी शब्द के अंत में लगकर उसके अर्थ में परिवर्तन ला देता हैं, उन्हें प्रत्यय कहा जाता हैं।

जैसे – त्व, आ, इया, वाला, ना, नी, ता आदि।

अतः विकल्प (B) सही है।

14. 'अतिपावन' शब्द में 'अति' उपसर्ग का प्रयोग हुआ है। जिसमें मूल शब्द 'पावन' एवं उपसर्ग 'अति' है।

'अति' उपसर्ग से बने अन्य शब्द अत्यधिक, अतिरिक्त, अतिक्रमण, अत्याचार आदि हैं।

अत: विकल्प (D) सही है।

15. "संतोष से बढ़कर सुख नहीं।" एक सरल वाक्य है। ऐसा वाक्य जिसमे एक ही क्रिया एवं एक ही कर्ता होता है या जिस वाक्य में एक ही उद्देश्य एवं एक ही विधेय होता है, वे वाक्य सरल वाक्य कहलाते हैं।

अतः विकल्प (B) सही है।

16. निम्न में से विशेषण का उदाहरण कड़वाहट नहीं है।

यहाँ पर मूल शब्द 'कड़वा' एक संज्ञा-विशेषण है जिसमें तद्धित प्रत्यय (भाववाचक तद्धित प्रत्यय) 'आहट' जुड़ने से बना शब्द 'कड़वाहट' भाववाचक संज्ञा शब्द कहा जाएगा।

संज्ञा या सर्वनाम की विशेषता बताने वाले शब्द को विशेषण कहते हैं।

जैसे- अच्छा लड़का, तीन पुस्तकें, नई कलम इत्यादि।

अतः विकल्प (C) सही है।

17. जिन सर्वनाम शब्दों से किसी वस्तु, व्यक्ति या स्थान की निश्चितता का बोध हो वे शब्द निश्चयवाचक सर्वनाम कहलाते हैं।

जैसे- यह, वह, ये, वे आदे।

अतः विकल्प (D) सही है।

18. पूर्ण वाक्य है - अनेक भाषाएँ बोलने वाले को बहुभाषी कहते हैं।

- दिए गए विकल्पों में से रिक्त स्थान के लिए उचित शब्द 'बहुभाषी' होगा।

- अनेक भाषाएँ बोलने वाला यह एक वाक्यांश है जिसके लिए एक शब्द 'बहुभाषी' होता है।

अन्य विकल्प:

- वक्ता - भाषण आदि देने वाला।
- शाकाहारी - जो मांस न खाता हो।
- कटुभाषी - कटु (कड़वा) बोलने वाला।

अतः विकल्प (B) सही है।

19. जिन स्वरों के उच्चारण में जिह्वा का पिछला भाग सक्रिय रहता है, उन्हें 'पश्च स्वर' कहते हैं। हिंदी वर्णमाला के कुल 11 स्वरों में 5 पश्च स्वर होते हैं. जो निम्नलिखित हैं – आ, ऊ, उ, ओ ,औ। दिए गए विकल्पों में से 'आ' पश्च स्वर है।

मुखाकृति के आधार पर स्वरों का वर्गीकरण निम्न प्रकार से किया गया है:

- अग्र स्वर
- पश्च स्वर
- संवृत्त स्वर
- अर्द्धसंवृत्त स्वर
- विवृत्त स्वर
- अर्द्धविवृत स्वर

अतः विकल्प (D) सही है।

20. 'खूँटी' शब्द का बहुवचन खूँटियाँ होगा।

इकारान्त या ईकारान्त स्त्रीलिंग संज्ञाओं में अन्त्य 'ई' को ह्रस्व कर अन्तिम वर्ण के बाद 'याँ' जोड़ने से वहुवचन बनता है।

जैसे - तिथि-तिथियाँ, नारी-नारियाँ, नीति-नीतियाँ, रीति-रीतियाँ इत्यादि।

अतः विकल्प (A) सही है।

21. 'कैकेयी' शुद्ध शब्द है। अन्य विकल्प असंगत है।

कैकेयी शब्द का अर्थ : 'केकय देश की राजकुमारी' या कैकेयी रामायण की प्रमुख पात्र हैं।

अतः विकल्प (C) सही है।

22. दिए गए विकल्पों में काल 'योम' शब्द का पर्यायवाची शब्द नहीं है।

योम के अन्य पर्यायवाची शब्द हैं - दिनमान, दिन, दिवस, अह, सूर्यकाल।

अतः विकल्प (D) सही है।

23. 'अनैच्छिक' का विलोम शब्द 'ऐच्छिक' है।

अपकार : उपकार

अनैक्य : ऐक्य

अपकीर्ति : कीर्ति

अतः विकल्प (A) सही है।

24. 'झाँसी वाली रानी थी बुन्देलों हरबोलो के मुह हमने सुनी कहानी थी।' में वीर रस है।

जब कोई कार्य करने अथवा किसी रचना आदि के पढ़ने पर मन में जो उत्साह का भाव उत्पन्न होता है, उसे वीर रस कहते हैं। वीर रस का स्थाई भाव उत्साह होता है।

अतः विकल्प (A) सही है।

25. 'यमुना' शब्द व्यक्तिवाचक संज्ञा है। जिन शब्दों से किसी विशेष व्यक्ति, स्थान अथवा वस्तु के नाम का बोध हो, उसे व्यक्तिवाचक संज्ञा कहते हैं।

जैसे- जयपुर, दिल्ली, भारत, रामायण, अमेरिका, राम इत्यादि।

अतः विकल्प (C) सही है।

Q.1 Direction: Identify the interjection in the sentence given below.

Ugh! I don't like this vegetable.

A. I **B.** don't **C.** Ugh! **D.** Like

Q.2 Choose the correct spelt word out of the given alternatives.

A. Forcaust **B.** Forcast
C. Forecaste **D.** Forecast

Q.3 Select the correctly punctuated sentence.

A. Fortunately nobody was seriously injured in the accident?
B. Fortunately nobody was seriously injured in the accident.
C. Fortunately, nobody was seriously injured in the accident.
D. Fortunately nobody was seriously injured, in the accident!

Q.4 Select the correctly punctuated sentence.

A. Have you seen Smriti's new dress that she wore on Saturday.
B. Have you seen Smritis' new dress that she wore on Saturday?
C. Have you seen Smriti's new dress that she wore on Saturday?
D. Have you seen Smritis new dress that she wore on saturday!

Q.5 Which is interrogative pronoun in sentence "Why did you act like this? This matter has been perplexing me."

A. You **B.** This **C.** Why **D.** Me

Q.6 Direction: Choose the correct verb to fill in the blanks.

It _________ since early morning.

A. has been raining **B.** have been raining
C. had rained **D.** is been raining

Q.7 Direction: Choose the correct tense in the given sentence.

"The man is searching for his pet dog."

A. Simple present tense
B. Present continuous tense
C. Present perfect tense
D. Present perfect continuous tense

Q.8 Direction: Select the word which means the same as the group of words given.

One who plans the steps and moves in a dance

A. Composer **B.** Choreographer
C. Producer **D.** Director

Q.9 Direction: Choose the meaningful word from the given jumbled words.

EATRH

A. Hart **B.** Heart **C.** Harte **D.** Heatr

Q.10 Direction: Change the gender of the underlined noun and rewrite the sentence.

"My <u>sister</u> is sleeping"

A. My <u>brother</u> is sleeping
B. My <u>father</u> is sleeping
C. My <u>nephew</u> is sleeping
D. My <u>mother</u> is sleeping

Q.11 Which of the following is not an adjective?

A. Humble **B.** Humane **C.** Humid **D.** Humor

Q.12 Direction: Select the related word from the given alternatives.

Delicacy : Pride :: Decent : ?

A. Gentle **B.** Soft **C.** Noble **D.** Savage

Ques (13-20):Direction: Fill in the blanks with an appropriate word.

Q.13 He is not eligible ______ this post.

A. of **B.** for **C.** with **D.** to

Q.14 Don't _________ me you've lost your keys again.

A. say **B.** tell **C.** speak **D.** inform

Q.15 Would you like ___ apple?

A. a **B.** an
C. the **D.** no article

Q.16 Rohan ______ his leg when he played football last month.

A. broken **B.** breaks
C. broke **D.** was breaking

Q.17 After ______ (assess) the opposition, Abe suggested a strategy.

A. sizing up **B.** bringing up
C. breaking up **D.** showing up

Q.18 He was so afraid that his knees knocked ______ other.

A. Every **B.** One **C.** Each **D.** None

Q.19 "We walked ______ the beach, collecting small crabs in a bucket."

A. along **B.** below **C.** under **D.** over

Q.20 First language _________ the learning of second language.

A. hinders
B. works as an obstacle in
C. doesn't influence
D. supports

Ques (21-22):Direction: Choose the word which best expresses the opposite meaning of the word.

Q.21 BENEVOLENT

A. Generous **B.** Friendly
C. Stingy **D.** Liberal

Q.22 TACIT

[Territorial Army Officer, 2017]

A. Order **B.** Written
C. Oral **D.** Understanding

Ques (23-24):Direction: Select the most appropriate synonym of the given word.

Q.23 TIMID
A. Willful **B.** Shy **C.** Kind **D.** Strong

Q.24 Bitterness
A. Sourness **B.** Hoarseness
C. Acrimony **D.** Aspersion

Q.25 Direction: Fill in the blanks with the most appropriate option.
There are _____ takers for animal fur today, while ____ of the yesteryear stars were proud owners of mink coats.
A. few, quite a few **B.** quite a few, a few
C. few, a few **D.** a few, few

// Smart Answer Sheet //

Correct Indicates percentage of students who answered questions correctly.

Skipped Indicates percentage of students who skipped questions.

Q.	Ans.	Correct / Skipped
1	C	67.85 % / 1.89 %
2	D	46.19 % / 1.62 %
3	C	58.78 % / 1.8 %
4	C	49.63 % / 1.18 %
5	C	40.57 % / 1.19 %

Q.	Ans.	Correct / Skipped
6	A	50.29 % / 1.93 %
7	B	77.77 % / 0.0 %
8	B	54.66 % / 1.03 %
9	B	56.48 % / 1.72 %
10	A	83.66 % / 0.0 %

Q.	Ans.	Correct / Skipped
11	D	85.59 % / 0.0 %
12	D	84.88 % / 0.0 %
13	A	40.94 % / 1.91 %
14	B	63.4 % / 1.06 %
15	B	64.29 % / 1.42 %

Q.	Ans.	Correct / Skipped
16	C	49.71 % / 1.2 %
17	A	67.86 % / 1.03 %
18	C	52.28 % / 1.14 %
19	A	63.88 % / 1.01 %
20	D	57.9 % / 1.19 %

Q.	Ans.	Correct / Skipped
21	C	53.35 % / 1.96 %
22	C	64.53 % / 1.96 %
23	B	48.61 % / 1.79 %
24	C	56.15 % / 1.66 %
25	A	40.83 % / 1.13 %

Performance Analysis	
Avg. Score (%)	40.0%
Toppers Score (%)	56.0%
Your Score	

//Hints and Solutions//

1. Ugh! is interjection.

An interjection is a word or phrase that is grammatically independent of the words around it, and mainly expresses feeling rather than meaning.

Example : Oh! what a beautiful house

Hence, the correct option is (C).

2. The correctly spelt word is **forecast.**

Forecast means to say (with the help of information) what will probably happen in the future.

Example: Meanwhile, a tropical wave off the west coast of Africa is **forecast** to emerge offshore Sunday.

Hence, the correct option is (D).

3. The given sentence is a declarative sentence: a statement of fact.

There must be a comma (,) after "Fortunately" as it separates the imperative clause from the object clause, and makes it an easier sentence to read.

A period (.) marks the end of a declarative sentence.

Correct sentence: Fortunately, nobody was seriously injured in the accident.

Hence, the correct option is (C).

4. The given sentence is an interrogative sentence.

Interrogative sentences feature a word order with the predicate and primary verb before the subject.

"Have you seen Smriti's new dress that she wore on Saturday" is an Interrogative sentence, it must end with the question mark (?).

Structure: auxiliary verb + subject + verb...

Example: Have they lived together for over thirty years?

When a singular noun has possession over another noun (such as Mom's hat or the boy's dog), add an apostrophe (') + "S" to the end of the noun, so Smriti's is the correct format.

Example: The cat's kittens all began meowing at once.

Correct sentence: Have you seen Smriti's new dress that she wore on Saturday?

Hence, the correct option is (C).

5. An interrogative pronoun, like the name suggests, is used to ask questions. It refers to something or someone. What, which, who, whom and whose are the five interrogative pronouns in the English language.

In sentence **"Why did you act like this? This matter has been perplexing me."**

Why is interrogative pronoun.

Hence the correct option is (C).

6. The given sentence is in Present Perfect Continuous tense.

The present perfect continuous tense (also known as the present perfect progressive tense) shows that something started in the past and is continuing at the present time.

Structure: Subject + has\have + ing form of the verb + Object

Example : I have been reading War and Peace for a month now.

'Have' is used with the pronouns I, you, we, and they. 'Has' is used with he, she, and it.

In the given sentence, it is evident that the present perfect continuous tense is used to show that raining has started in the past and is continuing at the present time.

Thus, 'has been raining' is the correct option to fill in the blank.

Hence, the correct option is (A).

7. Present continuous tense is the correct tense in the given sentence.

Present continuous verb tense indicates that an action or condition is happening now, frequently, and may continue into the future.

Present Continuous Formula: to be [am, is, are] + verb [present participle] Aunt Christine is warming up the car while Scott looks for his new leather coat.

- Example: Children are going to school.

Hence, the correct option is (B).

8. Choreographer - one who plans the steps and moves in a dance. For Example: Lea Anderson is a choreographer who believes in making dance accessible.

Let's look at the meaning of the other options:

Composer: a person who writes music, especially as a professional occupation. For Example: The composer expresses his sorrow in his music.

Producer: a person, company, or country that makes, grows, or supplies goods or commodities for sale. For Example: a film producer.

Director: a person who is in charge of an activity, department, or organization. For Example: The director resigned in protest at the decision.

Hence, the correct option is (B).

9. The meaningful word from the words "JEUKAMTRXH" is "Heart".

"Heart" means the organ inside your chest that sends blood round your body.

Example: I could feel my heart pounding.

Hence, the correct option is (B).

10. The masculine of a **sister** is a **brother**.

The word **sister** describes a woman.

Hence, the correct option is (A).

11. Humor is not an adjective.

Humor is used as a noun. An adjective is a part of speech that can be used to describe or provide more information about a noun or pronoun that acts as the subject in a sentence. Adjectives are found after the verb or before the noun it modifies.

Hence, the correct option is (D).

12. Delicacy is the antonym of Pride.

Similarly;

Decent is the antonym of Savage.

Gentle is the antonym of Brutal.

Soft is the antonym of Hard.

Noble is the antonym of ignoble.

Hence, the correct option is (D).

13. Eligible always takes the fixed preposition 'for'.

It means to be suitable for something.

Eg: You may also not be eligible for the lowest interest rate, if you have poor credit.

Thus, the most correct option for the blank is - for.

Hence, the correct option is (A).

14. Correct sentence: Don't tell me you've lost your keys again.

Don't tell me you've lost your keys again.

- The verb 'tell' means to communicate information to someone in spoken or written words.
- The verb 'say' means to utter words so as to convey information, an opinion, a feeling or intention, or an instruction.
- The verb 'speak' means to say something in order to convey information or to express a feeling.
- The verb 'inform' means to give (someone) facts or information.

Hence, the correct option is (B).

15. Indefinite articles are used before unspecific, singular nouns. We use 'a' before nouns that begin with a consonant sound and 'an' before nouns that begin with a vowel sound.

Since 'apple' here refers to an unspecific one and begins with a vowel sound, we need to use the indefinite article 'an'.

Complete sentence: Would you like an apple?

Hence, the correct option is (B).

16. Complete sentence- Rohan broke his leg when he played football last month.

The past tense is used to express an action that has completed at some time in the past.

In the above sentence, the subject has done the action in the past.

The structure is- Subject + verb of the past form(V_2) + object.

Hence, the correct option is (C).

17. Correct sentence is "After sizing up (assess) the opposition, Abe suggested a strategy."

Meanings of the given options:

Size up = to examine something in order to make a judgment or form an opinion.

Break up = to make something separate into smaller pieces; to divide something into smaller parts.

Bring up = to mention a subject or start to talk about it.

Show up = to arrive where you have arranged to meet somebody or do something.

Hence, the correct option is (A).

18. He was so afraid that his knees knocked **each** other.

- From the given options, the correct choice to fill in the blank is 'each.'
- We know that each other is used to denote the mutual relationship between two people or things. Example: The sibling loves each other.
- From the above mentions information, it is clear that 'each' is the correct answer.

Hence, the correct option is (C).

19. Correct sentence: "We walked along the beach, collecting small crabs in a bucket."

A preposition is a word or group of words used before a noun, pronoun, or noun phrase to show direction, time, place, location, spatial relationships, or to introduce an object. Some examples of prepositions are words like "in," "at," "on," "of," and "to."

The preposition "along" means from one part of a road, river, etc., to another.

Hence, the correct option is (A).

20. First language supports the learning of second language.

First language: A native language or mother tongue that a child acquires since birth.

- use their previous knowledge when languages share identical rules.
- get motivated and gain a better understanding of how language works.
- feel secure and confident while building knowledge on prior experience.

Thus, it could be concluded that the first language supports the learning of the second language.

Hence, the correct option is (D).

21. The meaning of the given word:

- Benevolent- serving a charitable rather than a profit-making purpose.
- Stingy- unwilling to give or spend.
- Other words:

- Generous- showing kindness toward others.
- Friendly- kind and pleasant.
- Liberal- willing to respect or accept behavior or opinions different from one's own.

So from the given meanings, we find that Stingy is the antonym of benevolent.

Hence, the correct option is (C).

22. The meaning of the given words:

Tacit: The word 'Tacit' means understood or implied without being stated.

Oral: the word 'Oral' means relating to the transmission of information or literature by word of mouth.

So, from the given meanings, we find that tacit is the antonym for understanding.

Hence, the correct option is (C).

23. Let's look at the meanings of the given words:

- Timid- showing a lack of courage or confidence; easily frightened
- Shy- being reserved or having or showing nervousness or timidity in the company of other people
- Willful- (of an immoral or illegal act or omission) intentional; deliberate
- Kind- a group of people or things having similar characteristics
- Strong- having the power to move heavy weights or perform other physically demanding tasks

So from the given meanings, we find that Timid and Shy are synonyms.

Hence, the correct option is (B).

24. Bitterness: Sharpness of taste, lack of sweetness

Acrimony: Bitterness or ill-feeling

Sourness: Having an acid taste like lemon or vinegar

Hoarseness: Sounding rough and harsh, typically as the result of a sore throat or of shouting

Aspersion: An attack on the reputation or integrity of someone or something

Synonym of Bitterness is Acrimony.

Hence, the correct option is (C).

25. There are **few** takers for animal fur today, while **quite a few** of the yesteryear stars were proud owners of mink coats.

- Few: a small number of.
- Quite a few: being of a large but indefinite number.

It is appropriate to use 'few' and 'quite a few' respectively in the blanks of the sentence.

Hence, the correct option is (A).

Q.1 Direction: Choose the correct form of Adjective for the given word.

Danger

A. Dang　　　　　　　**B.** Dangerous

C. Dangerously　　　**D.** Dangers

Ques (2-9):Direction: Fill in the blank with the most appropriate alternative.

Q.2 I am having a dinner party for ___ close friends of mine at my residence.

A. Some　　　　　　**B.** A few

C. Many　　　　　　**D.** None of these

Q.3 May I ask you ___ questions?

A. A few　　　　　　**B.** Little

C. A little　　　　　**D.** None of these

Q.4 My servant ____ with all my money.

A. Have escaped　　**B.** Was run away

C. Has run off　　　**D.** Running away

Q.5 Hannah ___ her work till now.

A. Does not do　　　**B.** Did not do

C. Has not done　　 **D.** Will not do

Q.6 She ____ television when the accident occurred.

A. Watched　　　　　**B.** Was watching

C. Has been watching　**D.** Is watching

Q.7 He _______ in India.

A. live　　　　　　　**B.** lives

C. is living　　　　　**D.** are living

Q.8 After __________ smoking, they let the cigarette fall on the wood floor.

A. finished　　　　　**B.** finishing

C. had finished　　　**D.** finishes

Q.9 My brother is devoted ________ religion.

A. with　　　**B.** to　　　**C.** at　　　**D.** in

Q.10 Direction: Select the most similar meaning of the given word:

Enrage

A. Anger　　**B.** Crowd　　**C.** Answer　　**D.** Anxiety

Q.11 Choose the correct spelt word out of the given alternatives.

A. Itinaray　　**B.** Itinarery　　**C.** Itinerary　　**D.** Itinerary

Q.12 Choose the correctly punctuated sentence.

A. Bravo! You have recited the poem very well.

B. Bravo, You have recited the poem very well.

C. Bravo. You have recited the poem very well.

D. "Bravo" You have recited the poem very well.

Q.13 Choose the correctly punctuated sentence.

A. Do you know where the mall is!

B. Do you know where the mall is.

C. Do you know where the mall is?

D. Do you know where the mall is,

Q.14 Which is interrogative pronoun in sentence "To whom she was talking about?

A. was　　**B.** she　　**C.** to　　**D.** whom

Q.15 Direction: Fill in blank with the correct option:

Please don't _____ (medal /meddle) in my business, I will ask for your _____ (advice/advise).

A. medal, advice　　　**B.** meddle, advise

C. meddle, advice　　 **D.** medal, advise

Q.16 Direction: Select the most appropriate word to fill in the blank.

I _____ something burning now.

A. smell　　　　　　**B.** have smelt

C. smelt　　　　　　**D.** have been smelling

Q.17 Identify the interjection from the following sentence:

Why, is it really Sujata on the phone?

A. Why　　　　　　　**B.** On

C. The　　　　　　　**D.** None of these

Q.18 Direction: Choose the word which is most OPPOSITE of the given word.

Static

A. Steadfast　　**B.** Rooted　　**C.** Mobile　　**D.** Still

Q.19 Direction: Select the most similar meaning of the given word:

Wander

A. Think　　**B.** Run　　**C.** Roam　　**D.** Sing

Q.20 Direction: Name the form of tense for the bold word.

I was going to play badminton but decided to stay indoors.

A. Simple Present　　**B.** Present Perfect

C. Simple Past　　　　**D.** Past Continuous

Q.21 Direction: Select the most appropriate one-word substitution for the given words.

A very large impressive residence

[SSC CGL, 2020]

A. Cottage　　**B.** Cabin　　**C.** Igloo　　**D.** Mansion

Q.22 Direction: Change the gender of the underlined noun and rewrite the sentence:

When her <u>aunt</u> died, Katie moved in with Carmen.

A. When her brother died, Katie moved in with Carmen.

B. When her father died, Katie moved in with Carmen.

C. When her uncle died, Katie moved in with Carmen.

D. When her mother died, Katie moved in with Carmen.

Q.23 Direction: In each of the following questions find out the alternative which will replace the question mark.

Ornithologist : Bird :: Archaeologist : ?

A. Islands

B. Mediators

C. Archaeology

D. Aquatic

Q.24 Direction: Rearrange the letters to form meaningful words.

LUFTETR

A. Fluttre   **B.** Flutter   **C.** Fluettr   **D.** Flutetr

Q.25 Direction: Choose the word which best expresses the opposite meaning of the word.

SAPIENT

A. Wise   **B.** Foolish   **C.** Wasteful   **D.** Culvert

// Smart Answer Sheet //

Correct Indicates percentage of students who answered questions correctly.

Skipped Indicates percentage of students who skipped questions.

Q.	Ans.	Correct / Skipped
1	C	46.08 % / 1.75 %
2	B	49.35 % / 1.68 %
3	A	65.87 % / 1.6 %
4	C	61.24 % / 1.62 %
5	C	45.41 % / 1.09 %

Q.	Ans.	Correct / Skipped
6	B	68.02 % / 1.21 %
7	B	45.03 % / 1.67 %
8	B	45.5 % / 1.08 %
9	B	80.55 % / 0.0 %
10	A	40.09 % / 1.08 %

Q.	Ans.	Correct / Skipped
11	D	65.8 % / 1.04 %
12	A	17.44 % / 3.58 %
13	C	86.86 % / 0.0 %
14	D	46.9 % / 1.16 %
15	C	52.48 % / 1.72 %

Q.	Ans.	Correct / Skipped
16	A	52.38 % / 1.47 %
17	A	42.27 % / 1.07 %
18	C	55.05 % / 1.96 %
19	C	56.09 % / 1.05 %
20	D	65.39 % / 1.57 %

Q.	Ans.	Correct / Skipped
21	D	68.23 % / 1.97 %
22	C	54.14 % / 1.31 %
23	C	61.23 % / 1.5 %
24	B	61.57 % / 1.58 %
25	B	65.97 % / 1.99 %

Performance Analysis	
Avg. Score (%)	32.0%
Toppers Score (%)	60.0%
Your Score	

//Hints and Solutions//

1. The correct adjective form of the given Noun 'Danger' is **Dangerous**.

Danger (noun) means the possibility of harm or death to someone.

For example - He drove so fast that I really felt my life was in **danger**.

Dangerous (adjective) - A dangerous person, animal, thing, or activity could harm you.

For example - The men are armed and **dangerous**.

Hence, the correct option is (C).

2. A few means a small number of something.

Some means an unspecified number of something.

Many means a large number, amount of something.

A few fits appropriately in this context.

I am having a dinner party for **a few** close friends of mine at my residence.

Hence, the correct option is (B).

3. A few means a small number of something.

Little means small in size, amount, or degree.

A little also means small in size, amount, or degree but it refers to amount less than that of little.

A few fits appropriately in this context.

May I ask you **a few** questions?

Hence, the correct option is (A).

4. Has run off means a person who has run away already.

Have escaped means more than a person who have already escaped.

Was run away does not make sense as it is grammatically incorrect.

Running away means a present action in which someone is running.

Has run off fits appropriately in this context.

My servant **has run off** with all my money.

Hence, the correct option is (C).

5. Has not done means a task which was given earlier but it is not complete yet.

Does not do means a present action in which an action or a task is not done.

Did not do means to not have done something.

Will not do is a future action that tells that something will not be done.

Has not done fits appropriately in this context.

Hannah **has not done** her work till now.

Hence, the correct option is (C).

6. Was watching means a past action of seeing something.

Watched means that something has already been seen by someone.

Has been watching means that something is being still seen which was started earlier.

Is watching means to watch in the present moment.

Was watching fits appropriately in this context.

She **was watching** television when the accident occurred.

Hence, the correct option is (B).

7. Lives is a word in present tense and it means to stay somewhere. It is mostly used for a single being.

Lives fits appropriately in this context.

He **lives** in India.

Hence, the correct option is (B).

8. Finishing is a word in present continuous form which means to finish something in the present moment.

Finishing fits appropriately in this context.

After **finishing** smoking, they let the cigarette fall on the wood floor.

Hence, the correct option is (B).

9. The word **to** fits appropriately in this context. The other words with, at and in do not fit appropriately in this context.

My brother is devoted **to** religion.

Hence, the correct option is (B).

10. Let us see the meaning of Enrage:

Enrage: make (someone) very angry

Let us see the meanings of the words given in option:

Anger	fill (someone) with anger; provoke anger in
Crowd	(of a number of people) fill (space) almost completely, leaving little or no room for movement
Answer	say or write something as a reaction to someone or something
Anxiety	a feeling of worry, nervousness, or unease about something with an uncertain outcome

From the meaning of the given words, we can say that the word 'Anger' is the synonym of the word 'Enrage'.

Hence, the correct option is (A).

11. The correctly spelt word is **itinerary.**

Itinerary means a plan of a journey, including the route and the places that you will visit.

Example: On the Sea Paradise **itinerary** are several exciting dives each week, including a thrilling, must-do dive with manta rays

Hence, the correct option is (D).

12. The correct punctuated sentence is Bravo! You have recited the poem very well.

- Option (A) is the correctly punctuated sentence.
- Option (B) is incorrect. A comma is used when someone is directly addressed OR to separate two clauses/to separate ideas, objects, names in a sentence. Example: I will go to Goa, Mumbai and Pune.
- Option (C) is incorrect. The full stop is used at the end of a sentence. Example: She is my sister.
- Option (D) is incorrect. A quotation mark is used to introduce a direct speech. Example: She said, "I love cats."

Hence, the correct option is (A).

13. The correct punctuated sentence is Do you know where the mall is?

- Option (A) is incorrect. The exclamation mark is used to express strong feelings like sorrow, wonder, surprise or to emphasize. Example: I have found the lost photo album!
- Option (B) is incorrect. The full stop is used at the end of a sentence. Example: She is my sister.
- Option (D) is incorrect. The comma is used when someone is directly addressed OR to separate two clauses/to separate ideas, objects, names in a sentence.

Hence, the correct option is (C).

14. An interrogative pronoun, like the name suggests, is used to ask questions. It refers to something or someone. What, which, who, whom and whose are the five interrogative pronouns in the English language.

In sentence "**To whom she was talking about**?

whom is interrogative pronoun.

Hence the correct option is (D)

15. Let us see the meanings of the words in the brackets:

- Medal(noun): a metal disc typically of the size of a large coin and bearing an inscription or design, made to commemorate an event or awarded as a distinction to someone such as a soldier or athlete.
- Meddle (verb): interfere in something that is not one's concern.
- Advice (noun): guidance or recommendations offered with regard to prudent future action.
- Advise (verb): offer suggestions about the best course of action to someone.

Correct sentence: Please don't meddle in my business, I will ask for your advice.

Hence, the correct option is (C).

16. The given sentence is in the simple present tense, therefore the present simple tense form of the verb should be used.

Let us explore the given options:

- 'Smell' is the simple present form of the verb.
- 'Have smelt' is the past perfect form of the verb.
- 'Smelt' is the simple past form of the verb.
- 'Have been smelling' is the present perfect continuous form of the verb.

Complete Sentence: I **smell** something burning now.

Hence, the correct option is (A).

17. "Why" is used as an interjection.

As per the general rule, an interjection is a word or phrase that expresses something in a sudden or exclamatory way, especially an emotion.

Example:

- Congrats, You finally got your master's degree.
- Oh dear, I don't know what to do about this mess.

Here, in the given above examples, 'Congrats and Oh dear' can be used as an interjection.

Hence, the correct option is (A).

18. Static means 'staying in one place without moving, or not changing for a long time.

- Example: Oil prices have remained static for the past few months.

Marked option 'Mobile' means 'able to move or be moved freely or easily.

- Example: Hitesh remained fairly mobile despite his disabilities.

It is clear that Static and Mobile are opposite in meaning.

Hence, the correct option is (C).

19. Wander means 'to walk around slowly in a relaxed way or without any clear purpose or direction'

- Ex: We spent the morning wandering around the old part of the city.

Marked option 'Roam' means 'to move about or travel, especially without a clear idea of what you are going to do'

- Ex: After the bars close, gangs of youths roam the city streets.

It's clear that 'Wander' and 'Roam' are similar in meaning.

Hence, the correct option is (C).

20. Sentence in past continuous form is written as "Subject + was/were + ing + object".

Here, was going represents past continuous form.

Hence, the correct option is (D).

21. A very large impressive residence- Mansion

Cottage: a small and usually old house, especially in the country.

Cabin: a small room in a ship or boat, where a passenger sleeps.

Igloo: a small house that is built from blocks of hard snow.

Hence, the correct option is (D).

22. An opposite word can be defined as a word that expresses a meaning as opposed to the meaning of a particular word.

- In this case, the two words are called antonyms of each other.
- Let us explore the antonyms of the given options:
    - Brother: Sister
    - Father: Mother
    - Uncle: Aunt
    - Mother: Father
- Therefore, the gender of the underlined noun is "uncle."

Correct sentence: When her **uncle** died, Katie moved in with Carmen.

Hence, the correct option is (C).

23. As Ornithologist is a specialist of Birds similarly Archaeologist is a specialist of Archaeology.

Hence, the correct option is (C).

24. After rearranging 'LUFTETR' only meaningful word can be form - Flutter

Flutter : fly unsteadily or hover by flapping the wings quickly and lightly.

Hence, the correct option is (B).

25. Let's look at the meanings of the given word and marked option:

- Sapient- having or showing deep understanding and intelligent application of knowledge
- Foolish- showing or marked by a lack of good sense or judgment

Let's look at the meanings of the other given options:

- Wise- having or showing deep understanding and intelligent application of knowledge
- Wasteful- given to spending money freely or foolishly
- Culvert- a transverse drain

So, from the given meanings, we find that foolish and Sapient are antonyms.

Hence, the correct option is (B).

Ques (1-5):Direction: Simplify the given expression.

Q.1 $853 + ? \div 17 = 1000$

A. 2482   **B.** 2499   **C.** 2516   **D.** 16147

Q.2 $(? - 968) \div 79 \times 4 = 512$

A. 10185   **B.** 10190   **C.** 11075   **D.** 11080

Q.3 1-[5-{2+(-5+6-2) 2}]

A. -4   **B.** 2   **C.** 0   **D.** 2

Q.4 $1888 \div 4 \div 8 = ?$

A. 73   **B.** 94   **C.** 59   **D.** 47

Q.5 549 ÷ 3 × 54 - 25 × 321 + 31 = ?

A. 1888   **B.** 1887   **C.** 1886   **D.** 1898

Q.6 Find the HCF of $36, 54$, and 72.

A. 18   **B.** 3   **C.** 6   **D.** 12

Q.7 If (the place value of 6 in 16470) $-$ (the place value of 6 in 7605) $= 6 \times$ ____, then the number which comes in blank space is:

[CTET Paper - I, 2016]

A. 800   **B.** 900   **C.** 600   **D.** 700

Q.8 Arrange the following numbers in ascending order: 65, 98, 58, 49, 36, 62.

A. 36,49,58,62,65,98   **B.** 36,49,58,98,65,62
C. 49,36,58,62,65,98   **D.** 36,49,62,58,65,98

Q.9 In 42,365, identify the place value of 4:

A. four hundred
B. four million
C. four hundred thousand
D. four ten thousand

Q.10 The number of positive prime integer < 50 is:

[UPTET Paper - I, 2022]

A. 14   **B.** 25   **C.** 16   **D.** 15

Q.11 Which shows five hundred six million, seventy-three thousand, and eight in standard form?

A. 516,073,008   **B.** 506,073,008
C. 506,111,0008   **D.** 506,068,908

Q.12 What is $\frac{1}{8}$ as a decimal?

A. 0.5   **B.** 0.125   **C.** 0.73   **D.** 0.42

Q.13 Digit of unit place in the product of $(378 \times 236 \times 459 \times 312)$ is:

[UPTET Paper - I, 2022]

A. 6   **B.** 4   **C.** 2   **D.** 8

Q.14 If the difference and the product of two numbers are 5 and 36 respectively, then their reciprocals differ by:

[UPTET Paper - I, 2022], [UPTET Paper - I, 2019]

A. $\frac{5}{36}$ **B.** $\frac{9}{5}$ **C.** $\frac{5}{9}$ **D.** $\frac{31}{36}$

Q.15 A page is 25 cm long and 20 cm wide. Find the perimeter of this page:

A. 90 cm   **B.** 45 cm   **C.** 500 cm   **D.** 5 cm

Q.16 The perimeter of a square is 8 m. Find the length of the side.

A. 1 m   **B.** 2 m   **C.** 4 m   **D.** 8 m

Q.17 Find the area of the rectangle whose length is 15 cm and width is 4 cm.

A. 60 cm²   **B.** 50 cm²   **C.** 40 cm²   **D.** 30 cm²

Q.18 Find the Time when:

Principal $=$ Rs. 500, Rate $= 7.5\%$ p.a. and $S.I. =$ Rs. 150

A. 20 years   **B.** 15 years   **C.** 10 years   **D.** 4 years

Q.19 The solution of 2x-3=7 is:

A. 5   **B.** 7   **C.** 12   **D.** 11

Q.20 What is the square root of 1764?

A. 47   **B.** 46   **C.** 48   **D.** 42

Q.21 Write the expression for the statement: the sum of three times x and 11:

A. x + 3 + 11   **B.** 3x + 11
C. 3 + 11x   **D.** 3x – 11

Q.22 Look at this series: 7, 10, 8, 11, 9, 12, ... What number should come next?

[CLAT UG, 2018]

A. 7   **B.** 10   **C.** 12   **D.** 13

Q.23 What percent of 80 is 36?

A. 45%   **B.** 25%   **C.** 30%   **D.** 50%

Q.24 A man purchased a bike for his house for Rs. 45,000 and spent 10000 on its repairs. He had to sell it for Rs. 66,000. Find his profit:

A. Rs. 10,000   **B.** Rs. 11,000
C. Rs. 12,000   **D.** Rs. 13,000

Q.25 If the mean and median of a statistical data be 5 and 6 respectively, then the value of mode is:

A. 11   **B.** 9
C. 8   **D.** None of the above

// Smart Answer Sheet //

Correct   Indicates percentage of students who answered questions correctly.

Skipped   Indicates percentage of students who skipped questions.

Q.	Ans.	Correct / Skipped	Q.	Ans.	Correct / Skipped	Q.	Ans.	Correct / Skipped	Q.	Ans.	Correct / Skipped	Q.	Ans.	Correct / Skipped
1	B	42.09 % / 1.79 %	6	A	88.5 % / 0.0 %	11	B	84.07 % / 0.0 %	16	B	79.3 % / 0.0 %	21	B	22.54 % / 3.71 %
2	D	43.69 % / 1.45 %	7	B	85.16 % / 0.0 %	12	B	55.4 % / 1.21 %	17	A	59.89 % / 1.47 %	22	B	62.04 % / 1.08 %
3	A	56.04 % / 1.34 %	8	A	51.05 % / 1.37 %	13	B	61.02 % / 1.31 %	18	D	51.62 % / 1.69 %	23	A	69.26 % / 1.0 %
4	C	53.01 % / 1.55 %	9	D	87.08 % / 0.0 %	14	A	82.83 % / 0.0 %	19	A	44.15 % / 1.81 %	24	B	50.85 % / 1.16 %
5	A	89.0 % / 0.0 %	10	D	85.01 % / 0.0 %	15	A	47.42 % / 1.23 %	20	D	85.45 % / 0.0 %	25	C	89.36 % / 0.0 %

Performance Analysis	
Avg. Score (%)	48.0%
Toppers Score (%)	64.0%
Your Score	

//Hints and Solutions//

1. Let,

$$853 + x \div 17 = 1000$$

Then,

$$853 + \frac{x}{17} = 1000$$

$$\Rightarrow \frac{x}{17} = 1000 - 853 = 147$$

$$\Rightarrow x = 147 \times 17 = 2499$$

Hence, the correct option is (B).

2. Let,

$$(x - 968) \div 79 \times 4 = 512$$

Then,

$$\frac{x - 968}{79} \times 4 = 512$$

$$\Rightarrow x - 968 = \frac{512 \times 79}{4}$$

$$\Rightarrow x - 968 = 10112$$

$$\Rightarrow x = 10112 + 968$$

$$= 11080$$

Hence, the correct option is (D).

3. 1 - [5 - {2 + (- 5 + 6 - 2) 2}]

= 1 - [5 - {2 + (- 1) 2}]

= 1 - [5 - {2 - 2}]

= 1 - [5 - 0]

= 1 - 5

= -4

Hence, the correct option is (A).

4. $1888 \div 4 \div 8$

$$= \frac{1888}{4} \div 8$$

$$= 472 \div 8$$

$$= \frac{472}{8}$$

$$= 59$$

Hence, the correct option is (C)

5. Given:

$549 \div 3 \times 54 - 25 \times 321 + 31 = ?$

$183 \times 54 - 25 \times 321 + 31 = ?$

$9882 - 8025 + 31 = ?$

$9913 - 8025 = ?$

$? = 1888$

$\therefore$ The required answer is 1888.

Hence, the correct option is (A).

6. Given:

The numbers are $36, 54,$ and $72.$

Concept used:

HCF (highest common factor): this is the largest positive integer that divides each integer. This is sometimes called the greatest common divisor (G.C.D).

Factor of $36 = 1 \times 2 \times 2 \times 3 \times 3$

Factor of $54 = 1 \times 2 \times 3 \times 3 \times 3$

Factor of $72 = 1 \times 2 \times 2 \times 2 \times 3 \times 3$

So from the above, we can say that the highest common integer $= 3 \times 3 \times 2 = 18$

$\therefore$ The HCF of $36, 54,$ and 72 is $18.$

Hence, the correct option is (A).

7. Let the number which comes in blank space be ' a '.

The place value of 6 in $16470 = 6000$

The place value of 6 in $7605 = 600$

As given, $6000 - 600 = 6 \times a$

$$\Rightarrow 5400 = 6 \times a$$

$$\Rightarrow a = \frac{5400}{6}$$

$$\therefore a = 900$$

Hence, the correct option is (B).

8. Ascending order is a method of arranging numbers from smallest value to largest value.

Here smallest value is 36 and the largest value is 98 so ascending order of the given number is: 36,49,58,62,65,98

Hence, the correct option is (A).

9. The 4 is in the ten thousand place. It tells you there are 4 sets of ten thousand in the ten thousand place.

10,000+10,000+10,000+10,000 = 40,000

Hence, the correct option is (D).

10. As we know,

Prime number: The number which is divisible by only one and itself.

Ex:- $2,3,5,7$ etc

2 is the only even prime number.

1 is neither prime nor composite.

3 is the smallest odd prime number.

7 is the largest one-digit prime number.

Prime number less than $50 =$
$2,3,5,7,11,13,17,19,23,29,31,37,41,43,47$

∴ The total prime number less than 50 is 15.

Hence, the correct option is (D).

11. The standard form for five hundred six million, seventy-three thousand, eight is 506,073,008.

Hence, the correct option is (B).

12. Writing $\dfrac{1}{8}$ as a decimal using the division method.

To convert any fraction to decimal form, we just need to divide its numerator by the denominator.

Here, the fraction is $\dfrac{1}{8}$ which means we need to perform $1 \div 8$.

This gives the answer as 0.125.

So, $\dfrac{1}{8}$ as a decimal is 0.125.

Hence, the correct option is (B).

13. We can find the digit of unit place in $(378 \times 236 \times 459 \times 312)$ by multiplying the unit digit of $378, 236, 459,$ and 312.

Unit Digit of 378 is 8.

Unit Digit of 236 is 6.

Unit Digit of 459 is 9.

Unit Digit of 312 is 2.

$(8 \times 6 \times 9 \times 2) = 864$

Digit of unit place in $(378 \times 236 \times 459 \times 312)$ is 4.

Hence, the correct option is (B).

14. Given,

Difference $= 5$

Product $= 36$

As we know,

The reciprocal of a number is 1 divided by the number.

The reciprocal of $n = \dfrac{1}{n}$

Let the two numbers be a and b.

Reciprocal of a and b is $\dfrac{1}{a}$ and $\dfrac{1}{b}$ respectively.

$a - b = 5$

$ab = 36$

Difference of their reciprocals is $\left\{ \left(\dfrac{1}{b}\right) - \left(\dfrac{1}{a}\right) \right\}$

$= \dfrac{(a-b)}{ab}$

$= \dfrac{5}{36}$

Hence, the correct option is (A).

15. Given,

Length = 25 cm

Breadth = 20 cm

Perimeter of rectangle = 2(Length + Breadth)

= 2(25+20)

= 2 × 45

= 90 cm

Hence, the correct option is (A).

16. Given:

Perimeter of square = 8 m

Perimeter of = 4 × Length of side

Length of side $\dfrac{=}{\text{Perimeter of square}} 4$

$= \dfrac{8}{4}$

= 2 m

Hence, the correct option is (B).

17. Given,

Length = 15 cm

Width = 4 cm

Area of a rectangle = Length × Width

15 × 4 = 60

So the area of the rectangle = 60 cm²

Hence, the correct option is (A).

18. Given:

Principal $=$ Rs. 500

Rate $= 7.5\%$ p.a.

$S.I. =$ Rs. 150

As we know,

$S.I. = \dfrac{P \times R \times T}{100}$

Where, P = principal, R = rate and T = time

$$\therefore T = \frac{S.I. \times 100}{P \times R}$$

$$\therefore T = \frac{150 \times 100}{500 \times 7.5}$$

$$\Rightarrow T = \frac{150}{5 \times 7.5}$$

$$\Rightarrow T = \frac{150}{37.5}$$

$$\therefore T = 4 \text{ years}$$

Hence, the correct option is (D).

19. Given:

2x - 3 = 7

2x = 7 + 3 = 10

$x = \dfrac{10}{2} = 5$

Hence, the correct option is (A).

20. $\sqrt{1764} = \sqrt{42 \times 42}$

Here 42 × 42 makes a pair so they make a perfect square root for 1764.

Hence, the correct option is (D).

21. Three time x = 3x

Sum of three times x and 11 = 3x + 11

Hence, the correct option is (B).

22. In the given series 10 will come next.

This is a simple alternating addition and subtraction series. In the first pattern, 3 is added; in the second, 2 is subtracted.

Hence, the correct option is (B).

23. The two numbers are: 80 and 36

Therefore,

$= \dfrac{36}{80} \times 100\%$

$= \dfrac{9}{20} \times 100\%$

= 9 × 5%

= 45%

Therefore, 45 percent of 80 is 36.

Hence, the correct option is (A).

24. ⇒ CP of bike = Rs. 45000, he spent on bike's repair = Rs. 10000

⇒ Actual CP of bike = Rs. (45000 + 10000) = Rs. 55000

⇒ SP of bike = Rs. 66000

⇒ Now profit = Rs. (66000 - 55000) = Rs. 11000

Hence, the correct option is (B).

25. The mean (average) of a data set is found by adding all numbers in the data set and then dividing by the number of values in the set.

The median is the middle value when a data set is ordered from least to greatest.

The mode is the number that occurs most often in a data set.

Given

Mean = 5

Median = 6

Mode = 3(Median) − 2(Mean)

Mode = 3(6) - 2(5)

⇒ 18 - 10 = 8

Hence, the correct option is (C).

Q.1 What is the Least Common Multiple of 72, 84 and 108?
[Delhi Forest Guard, 2021]

A. 1632 **B.** 1234 **C.** 1512 **D.** 1108

Q.2 25450 expressed in standard form is:
[Jawahar Navodaya Entrance Class IX, 2021]

A. 2.545×10^{-4} **B.** 2545×10^{1}
C. 25.45×10^{2} **D.** 2.545×10^{4}

Q.3 The sum of four consecutive multiples of 7 is 322. Find the smallest multiple involved.
[Jawahar Navodaya Entrance Class IX, 2021]

A. 91 **B.** 84 **C.** 63 **D.** 70

Q.4 Out of the following rational numbers, which is the smallest?
[Jawahar Navodaya Entrance Class IX, 2021]

A. $\frac{2}{7}$ **B.** $\frac{-5}{7}$ **C.** $\frac{4}{-7}$ **D.** $\frac{3}{7}$

Q.5 What must be added to 269 to make the result a perfect square?
[Jawahar Navodaya Entrance Class IX, 2021]

A. 13 **B.** 20 **C.** 55 **D.** 44

Q.6 Direction: What will come in place of question mark (?) in the following number series?

$0.003 \times 0.0004 = ?$

A. 0.0012 **B.** 0.00012
C. 0.000012 **D.** 0.0000012

Q.7 If Rs. 1 produces Rs. 10.2 in 60 years at simple interest, find the interest rate.

A. 17% **B.** 14% **C.** 15% **D.** $12\frac{1}{2}\%$

Q.8 Complete the following series

19, 24, 30, 37, 45,__?

A. 57 **B.** 64 **C.** 49 **D.** 54

Q.9 Mohan sells fruits at their cost price but uses a weight of $850\,gm$ in place of $1\,kg$. What is his profit percentage?

A. $17\frac{11}{17}\%$ **B.** $15\frac{11}{17}\%$ **C.** $17\frac{11}{15}\%$ **D.** $19\frac{11}{17}\%$

Q.10 Direction: Simplify the following.

$\frac{8080}{16} + 16 = ?$

A. 552.5 **B.** 71 **C.** 568.5 **D.** 521

Q.11 If $0.13 \times p^{2} = 13$, then p is equal to:

A. 10 **B.** 0.01 **C.** 0.1 **D.** 100

Q.12 What is the LCM of 25, 30 and 45?

A. 25 **B.** 225 **C.** 450 **D.** 900

Q.13 Which of the following is the largest:
0.9999, 0.0001, 0.0025 and 1

A. 0.9999 **B.** 0.0001 **C.** 1 **D.** 0.0025

Q.14 Find the sum of the factors of 3240

A. 10890 **B.** 11000 **C.** 10800 **D.** 10190

Q.15 Find the number of factors of 40.

A. 2 **B.** 6 **C.** 8 **D.** 12

Q.16 Convert $0.\overline{1}$ into rational fraction.

A. $\frac{10}{11}$ **B.** $\frac{1}{9}$ **C.** $\frac{1}{10}$ **D.** $\frac{9}{10}$

Q.17 If perpendicular of a right angled triangle is $8\,cm$ and its area is $20\,cm^{2}$, the length of base is?

A. $20\,cm$ **B.** $05\,cm$ **C.** $40\,cm$ **D.** $08\,cm$

Q.18 45% of $? = 72.25$

A. 170 **B.** 165 **C.** 175 **D.** 160

Q.19 The mode of the data $3,5,4,5,4,3$ is:

A. 3 **B.** 5
C. 4 **D.** No mode

Q.20 If ABC is a triangle where AB = 3cm, BC = 5cm and AC = 4cm, then find its perimeter.

A. 12 cm **B.** 15 cm **C.** 18 cm **D.** 21 cm

Q.21 Direction: What should come in place of question mark (?) in the following questions?

1.5 × 78 ÷ 0.5 = ?

A. 243 **B.** 234 **C.** 238 **D.** 216

Q.22 Direction: Simplify the following.

$238 \div 238 = ?$

A. 0 **B.** 238 **C.** 28 **D.** 1

Q.23 The perimeter of a square whose side is 4 m is __________ m.

A. 8 **B.** 16 **C.** 12 **D.** 10

Q.24 The equation -7x + 1 = 5 - 3x will be satisfied for x = ?

A. 2 **B.** 1
C. -1 **D.** None of these

Q.25 Direction: Simplify the following.

102×103

A. 10506 **B.** 10505 **C.** 1050 **D.** 10504

// Smart Answer Sheet //

Correct Indicates percentage of students who answered questions correctly.

Skipped Indicates percentage of students who skipped questions.

Q.	Ans.	Correct / Skipped	Q.	Ans.	Correct / Skipped	Q.	Ans.	Correct / Skipped	Q.	Ans.	Correct / Skipped	Q.	Ans.	Correct / Skipped
1	C	56.34 % / 1.64 %	6	D	48.3 % / 1.85 %	11	A	55.43 % / 1.57 %	16	B	51.45 % / 1.63 %	21	B	65.88 % / 1.29 %
2	D	49.27 % / 1.04 %	7	A	66.26 % / 1.02 %	12	C	51.18 % / 1.23 %	17	B	57.64 % / 1.51 %	22	D	65.67 % / 1.54 %
3	D	49.95 % / 1.43 %	8	D	55.5 % / 1.13 %	13	C	65.07 % / 1.03 %	18	D	69.54 % / 1.91 %	23	B	66.84 % / 1.34 %
4	B	86.65 % / 0.0 %	9	A	45.76 % / 1.44 %	14	A	64.07 % / 1.72 %	19	D	55.81 % / 1.13 %	24	C	67.34 % / 1.35 %
5	B	77.99 % / 0.0 %	10	D	57.22 % / 1.86 %	15	C	63.22 % / 1.33 %	20	A	57.03 % / 1.45 %	25	A	52.24 % / 1.94 %

Performance Analysis	
Avg. Score (%)	56.0%
Toppers Score (%)	68.0%
Your Score	

//Hints and Solutions//

1. Prime factorisation:

72 = 2 × 2 × 2 × 3 × 3

84 = 2 × 2 × 3 × 7

108 = 2 × 2 × 3 × 3 × 3

LCM of (72, 84 and 108) = 2 × 2 × 2 × 3 × 3 × 3 × 7 = 1512

∴ The LCM of 72, 84, and 108 is 1512.

Hence, the correct option is (C).

2. Given:

The number 25450

For any given number Standard form is a way to express the number.

It is generally used to express a large or a small number

The standard form of any given number is:

$$= m \times 10^n$$

Where, m is a number such that $1 \leq m < 10$ and n is the exponent of 10

we can follow as:

Step 1: Write down the given number

Here, the given number is 25450

Step 2 : Express in standard form:

25450

$= 2.5450 \times 10000$

$= 2.5450 \times 10^4$

$= 2.545 \times 10^4$

Hence, the correct option is (D).

3. Given:

Four consecutive multiples of 7

$7k, 7(k + 1), 7(k + 2), 7(k + 3)$

Sum $= 322$

$7k + 7(k + 1) + 7(k + 2) + 7(k + 3) = 322$

$\Rightarrow 7(k + k + 1 + k + 2 + k + 3) = 322$

$\Rightarrow 7(4k + 6) = 322$

$\Rightarrow 4k + 6 = 46$

$\Rightarrow 4k = 40$

$\Rightarrow k = 10$

By putting the value of multiples of 7, we get $70, 77, 84, 91,$

Smallest multiple $= 70$

Hence, the correct option is (D).

4. Given:

$$\frac{2}{7}, \frac{-5}{7}, \frac{-4}{7}, \frac{3}{7}$$

On dividing the denominator by the numerator, we get

$$0.2, -0.71, -0.57, 0.42$$

The correct sequence on division: $-0.71 < -0.57 < 0.2 < 0.42$

So, the smallest number is $\dfrac{-5}{7}$.

Hence, the correct option is (B).

5. The nearest perfect square of 269 is 289 , i.e., the square of 17

$$\Rightarrow 289 - 269 = 20$$

So, the least number to be added to make 269 a perfect square is 20.

Hence, the correct option is (B).

6. Here,

$$\Rightarrow 0.003 \times 0.0004$$

$$\Rightarrow \frac{3}{1000} \times \frac{4}{10000}$$

$$\Rightarrow \frac{12}{10000000}$$

$$\Rightarrow 0.0000012$$

Hence, the correct option is (D).

7. Formula used:

$$I = \frac{(P \times t \times r)}{100}$$

$I =$ interest $= 1$

$P =$ principal $= 10.2$

$t =$ time $= 60$

$r =$ rate of interest

According to the given condition,

$$\Rightarrow 10.2 = \frac{(1 \times 60 \times r)}{100}$$

$$\therefore r = 17$$

∴ The rate is 17% p.a.

Hence, the correct option is (A).

8. Given:

19, 24, 30, 37, 45,__?

$\Rightarrow$ 19 + 5 = 24

$\Rightarrow$ 24 + 6 = 30

$\Rightarrow$ 30 + 7 = 37

$\Rightarrow$ 37 + 8 = 45

$\Rightarrow$ 45 + 9 = 54

$\therefore$ The complete series is 19, 24, 30, 37, 45, 54.

Hence, the correct option is (D).

9. Given:

Mohan sells fruits at their cost price but uses a weight of $850\ gm$ in place of $1\ kg$

Formula Used:

$$\text{Percentage} = \frac{\text{error}}{\text{true value}} \times 100$$

$\Rightarrow$ Error $= 1\ kg - 850gm = 1000 - 850 = 150gm$

According to the question,

$\Rightarrow$ Profit percentage $= \dfrac{\text{error}}{\text{true value}} \times 100 = \dfrac{150}{850} \times 100 = 17\dfrac{11}{17}$

So, The profit percentage is $17\dfrac{11}{17}\%$.

Hence, the correct option is (A).

10. Given:

$\Rightarrow \dfrac{8080}{16} = 505$

$\Rightarrow 505 + 16 = 521$

$\therefore$ The correct answer is 521.

Hence, the correct option is (D).

11. Given,

$$0.13 \times p^2 = 13$$

$\Rightarrow p^2 = \dfrac{13}{0.13}$

$\Rightarrow p^2 = \dfrac{13}{13} \times 100$

$\Rightarrow p^2 = 100$

$\Rightarrow p = 10$

Hence, the correct option is (A).

12. Given:

L.C.M of 25, 30, 45

Factors of 25 = 5 × 5 × 1

Factors of 30 = 2 × 3 × 5 × 1

Factors of 45 = 3 × 3 × 5 ×1

Now, the lowest common factor of the above numbers = 2 × 3 × 3 × 5 × 5 × 1 = 450

Hence, the correct option is (C).

13. Given,

0.9999 < 1

0.0001 < 1

0.0025 < 1

$\because$ All the values is less than 1.

Hence, the correct option is (C).

14. Given:

3240

Concept:

If $k = a^x \times b^y$, then

a, and b must be prime number

Sum of all factors = $(a^0 + a^1 + a^2 + ... + a^x)(b^0 + b^1 + b^2 + ... + b^y)$

$3240 = 2^3 \times 3^4 \times 5^1$

Sum of factors = $(2^0 + 2^1 + 2^2 + 2^3)(3^0 + 3^1 + 3^2 + 3^3 + 3^4)(5^0 + 5^1)$

$\Rightarrow$ (1 + 2 + 4 + 8) (1 + 3 + 9 + 27 + 81) (1 + 5)

$\Rightarrow$ 15 × 121 × 6

$\Rightarrow$ 10890

$\therefore$ Required sum is 10890.

Hence, the correct option is (A).

15. Concept used:

For finding number of factors of any number we do prime factorisation of that number.

If $X = p_1{}^a \times p_2{}^b$, then

Number of factors of X = (a + 1) × (b + 1)

Where, p_1, p_2 → Prime factors of X

Now, $40 = 2^3 \times 5^1$

$\Rightarrow$ Number of factors of 40 = (3 + 1) × (1 + 1) = 4 × 2 = 8

$\therefore$ The number of factors of 40 is 8.

Hence, the correct option is (C).

16. Given:

The number 0.1111

Let the number $0.1111 \ldots$ be x.

$\Rightarrow x = 0.111 \ .... \ \text{(i)}$

$\Rightarrow 10x = 1.1111 \ .... \ \text{(ii)}$

Subtracting (i) from (ii),

$\Rightarrow 10x - x = (1.11 \ ... \ ) - (0.111 \ ... \ )$

$\Rightarrow 9x = 1$

$\Rightarrow x = \dfrac{1}{9}$

Hence, the correct option is (B).

17. Given:

Perpendicular of right angled triangle $= 8 \ cm$

Area $= 20 \ cm^2$

Formula used:

Area of right angled triangle $= \left(\dfrac{1}{2}\right) \times$ perpendicular $\times$ base

$\Rightarrow 20 \ cm^2 = \left(\dfrac{1}{2}\right) \times 8 \times$ base

$\Rightarrow$ base $= \dfrac{20}{4}$

$\Rightarrow 5 \ cm$

$\therefore$ The length of base is $5 \ cm$.

Hence, the correct option is (B).

18. Formula used:

$X\% = \dfrac{X}{100}$

Using the above formula:

$\Rightarrow \dfrac{45}{100} \times ? = 72.25$

$\Rightarrow ? = \dfrac{72.25 \times 100}{45} = 160.55 \approx 160$

$\therefore$ The correct answer is 160.

Hence, the correct option is (D).

19. Concept:

Mode $=$ Maximum frequency

Analysis:

Arranging the data in increasing order, we get the distribution as:

$3,3,4,4,5,5$

The maximum occurring terms are $3,4,5$.

$\therefore$ Then there is no mode.

Hence, the correct option is (D).

20. Given,

ABC is a triangle.

AB = 3cm

BC = 5cm

AC = 4cm

As we know by the formula,

Perimeter = Sum of all three sides

P = AB + BC + AC

P = 3 + 5 + 4

P = 12 cm

Hence, the correct option is (A).

21. Given:

1.5 × 78 ÷ 0.5 = ?

$\Rightarrow$ 1.5 × 78 ÷ 0.5

$\Rightarrow$ 1.5 × 156 = 234

$\therefore$ The value of ? is 234.

Hence, the correct option is (B).

22. The number divided by itself and we get 1 as quotient except 0.

This is not valid for 0.

Now as per the question

The number 238 is divided by itself.

$238 \div 238 = \dfrac{238}{238} = 1$

Hence, the correct option is (D).

23. Given,

Side of square is 4 m.

Perimeter of a square is = 4 × side

So, Perimeter of square = 4 × 4 = 16 m

Hence, the correct option is (B).

24. Given:

$\Rightarrow$ -7x + 1 = 5 - 3x

$\Rightarrow$ -7x + 3x = 5 - 1

$\Rightarrow$ -4x = 4

$\Rightarrow$ x = -1

So, for the value of x = -1 , the equation will be satisfied.

Hence, the correct option is (C).

25. Given:

102 into 103

$(100 + 2) \times (100 + 3)$

[Using $(x + a)(x + b) = x^2 + (a + b)x + ab$]

$= (100)^2 + (2 + 3) \times 100 + 2 \times 3$

$= 10000 + 5 \times 100 + 6 = 10000 + 500 + 6 = 10506$

Hence, the correct option is (A).

Q.1 Phrygian cap has been unveiled as the mascot for the 2024 Olympics and Paralympics. The 2024 Olympics and Paralympics will be held in __________.

A. Paris　　　　　　　　**B.** San Fransico
C. New York　　　　　　**D.** Munich

Q.2 With __________ country India has signed an export order for missiles, rockets, and ammunition in October 2022.

A. Azerbaijan　　　　　　**B.** Iran
C. Mongolia　　　　　　 **D.** Armenia

Q.3 NSDC International (NSDCI) and Perdaman have partnered to create an interface between Indian skilled youth and market opportunities in __________ country.

A. Australia　　　　　　 **B.** Japan
C. South Korea　　　　　**D.** New Zealand

Q.4 In which city, the Election Commission of India (ECI) is hosting an international conference on the theme 'Role, Framework and Capacity of Election Management Bodies' from 31st October to 1st November?

A. New Delhi　　　　　　**B.** Lucknow
C. Bhopal　　　　　　　 **D.** Mumbai

Q.5 Union Minister and National Chairman of the Indian Institute of Public Administration (IIPA) Jitendra Singh on 12th Oct 2022 approved 111 new members of IIPA. Who is the President of IIPA?

A. Jagdeep Dhankhar　　　**B.** Amit Shah
C. Narendra Modi　　　　 **D.** Rajnath Singh

Q.6 Which one is the state flower of Uttar Pradesh?

A. Orchids　　　　　　　**B.** Palash
C. Lotus　　　　　　　　**D.** Siroi Lily

Q.7 Which one of the following minerals are not found in Uttar Pradesh?

A. Limestone　　　　　　**B.** Asbestos
C. Bauxite　　　　　　　**D.** Gypsum

Q.8 Which of the following is the drinking water project of Uttar Pradesh?

A. Sharda tributary canal project
B. Gyanpur Pump Canal Project
C. Gokul Barrage Project
D. Pathrai Dam

Q.9 Who was the first Governor of Uttar Pradesh after independence?

A. Sucheta Kriplani
B. Sarojini Naidu
C. Hormasji Peroshaw Mody
D. Biswanath Das

Q.10 Where is the headquarters of the Uttar Pradesh Police Department located?

A. Lucknow　　　　　　　**B.** Gonda
C. Barabanki　　　　　　 **D.** Kanpur

Q.11 The chairmanship/presidency of the UN Security Council rotates among the Council Members:

A. Every 6 months　　　　**B.** Every 3 months
C. Every year　　　　　　**D.** Every month

Q.12 Aam Admi Bima Yojana was launched on:

A. November 14, 2011　　 **B.** March 5, 2009
C. March 10, 2008　　　　**D.** October 2, 2007

Q.13 Which of the following river is originated from Aravalli Mountain?

A. Sabarmati　　　　　　 **B.** Ken
C. Chambal　　　　　　　**D.** Betwa

Q.14 Which of the following countries has Black Sea on one side and Mediterranean Sea on other side?

A. Turkey　　　　　　　　**B.** Azerbaijan
C. Syria　　　　　　　　　**D.** Bulgaria

Q.15 When is National Science Day celebrated in India?

A. 25 February　　　　　　**B.** 28 February
C. 27 February　　　　　　**D.** 24 February

Q.16 Which among the following is the most common method of pollination in flowers without petals?

A. Wind　　　　　　　　　**B.** Water
C. Insects　　　　　　　　**D.** All of the above

Q.17 Which of the following helps in blood clotting?

A. Vitamin A　　　　　　　**B.** Vitamin D
C. Vitamin K　　　　　　　**D.** Vitamin C

Q.18 Newton's second law of motion introduces the concept of ________.

A. force　　　　　　　　　**B.** angular momentum
C. velocity　　　　　　　　**D.** acceleration

Q.19 Apart from India, Pakistan, and Sri Lanka, which asian country has Rupee as its currency?

[Soldier GD, 2021]

A. Bhutan　　　　　　　　**B.** Myanmar
C. Indonesia　　　　　　　**D.** Nepal

Q.20 Which of the following is the capital of Egypt?

A. Cairo　　**B.** Rome　　**C.** Sydney　　**D.** Paris

Q.21 __________ famous personality founded the Marathi newspaper 'Kesari'.

A. Lokmanya Tilak　　　　 **B.** Vallabhbhai Patel
C. Lala Lajpat Rai　　　　　**D.** Mahatma Gandhi

Q.22 Most part of India receives rainfall from ______.

A. March to June
B. June to September
C. August to November
D. November to February

Q.23 Cycle of the seasons is caused due to:

A. Rotation
B. Revolution
C. Gravitation
D. None of these

Q.24 Which is the hottest planet in our solar system?

A. Venus
B. Venus
C. Mars
D. Mercury

Q.25 Which Indian mass movement began with the famous 'Dandi March' of Mahatma Gandhi?

A. Khilafat movement
B. Non-Co-operation movement
C. Civil Disobedience movement
D. Quit India movement

// Smart Answer Sheet //

Correct Indicates percentage of students who answered questions correctly.

Skipped Indicates percentage of students who skipped questions.

Q.	Ans.	Correct / Skipped
1	A	44.99 % / 1.04 %
2	D	44.01 % / 1.89 %
3	A	59.79 % / 1.82 %
4	A	56.04 % / 1.81 %
5	A	21.28 % / 3.13 %

Q.	Ans.	Correct / Skipped
6	B	59.1 % / 1.92 %
7	B	67.98 % / 1.94 %
8	C	57.77 % / 1.96 %
9	B	89.75 % / 0.0 %
10	A	77.09 % / 0.0 %

Q.	Ans.	Correct / Skipped
11	D	83.43 % / 0.0 %
12	D	42.57 % / 1.71 %
13	A	48.28 % / 1.46 %
14	A	64.67 % / 1.52 %
15	B	40.11 % / 1.66 %

Q.	Ans.	Correct / Skipped
16	A	49.28 % / 1.61 %
17	C	65.44 % / 1.72 %
18	A	84.5 % / 0.0 %
19	D	29.21 % / 4.22 %
20	A	59.71 % / 1.39 %

Q.	Ans.	Correct / Skipped
21	A	79.4 % / 0.0 %
22	B	54.04 % / 1.47 %
23	B	64.36 % / 1.54 %
24	A	44.38 % / 1.65 %
25	C	57.53 % / 1.92 %

Performance Analysis	
Avg. Score (%)	56.0%
Toppers Score (%)	60.0%
Your Score	

//Hints and Solutions//

1. Phrygian cap has been unveiled as the mascot for the 2024 Olympics and Paralympics. The 2024 Olympics and Paralympics will be held in Paris.

These red caps date back to ancient times & were a symbol of the pursuit of liberty in the French Revolution. The Paralympic version of the mascot features a prosthetic leg. Paris Olympics will take place from 26 July to 11 Aug 2024. The Games will feature the debut of breakdancing as an Olympic event.

Hence, the correct option is (A).

2. In a significant move to boost defence export, India has signed an export order for missiles, rockets, and ammunition to Armenia. Under this deal, military equipment worth over Rs. 2,000 crores will be exported by India to Armenia. It also includes six additional first-ever export of the indigenous Pinaka rocket launchers.

Hence, the correct option is (D).

3. NSDC International (NSDCI) and Perdaman have partnered to create an interface between Indian skilled youth and market opportunities in Australia. NSDCI plays role in steering national and international partnerships for overseas employment. Perdaman is a multinational group based in Western Australia with a long-standing track record in involvement within a diverse range of markets.

Hence, the correct option is (A).

4. The Election Commission of India (ECI) will host international conference on the theme 'Role, Framework and Capacity of Election Management Bodies' from 31st Oct to 1st Nov in New Delhi. ECI, as the lead for the Cohort on 'Election Integrity', has invited Greece, Mauritius and IFES to be co-leads for the cohort. The conference will be inaugurated by Chief Election Commissioner Rajiv Kumar.

Hence, the correct option is (A).

5. President of IIPA is Jagdeep Dhankhar (Vice President of India). Union Minister and National Chairman of the Indian Institute of Public Administration (IIPA) Jitendra Singh on 12th Oct 2022 approved 111 new members of IIPA. It includes 9 newly recruited IAS officers serving as Assistant Secretaries at the centre. The IIPA membership was earlier reserved for only retired officers.

Hence, the correct option is (A).

6. Palash is the state flower of Uttar Pradesh.

The Provincial flower of Uttar Pradesh is Palash or Tesu. Scientific name - Butea Monosperma. You can see it in summer with all the red flowers on tree and very less leave.

Hence, the correct option is (B).

7. Asbestos is a versatile mineral found in igneous and metamorphic rocks as blocks. It can be cut into very thin layers. It is colorless

or light yellow, green, or black. Asbestos is not found in Uttar Pradesh.

Hence, the correct option is (B).

8. Gokul Barrage project is a drinking water project of Uttar Pradesh. This project envisages ensuring water to Agra and Mathura. This project is being completed through the construction of a barrage on the Yamuna river near Gokul.

Hence, the correct option is (C).

9. Sarojini Naidu was the first Governor of Uttar Pradesh after independence.

Indian freedom fighter Sarojini Naidu became the first female Governor of a state in independent India when she was appointed as Governor of the United Provinces, now Uttar Pradesh, in 1947.

Hence, the correct option is (B).

10. The headquarters of the Uttar Pradesh Police Department is located in Lucknow.

The Uttar Pradesh Police is headquartered at Signature Building, Gomti Nagar Extension in Lucknow. Established in 1863 as the Office of the Inspector General of Police, United Provinces under the Police Act, of 1861. It is headed by the Director General of Police (DGP).

Hence, the correct option is (A).

11. The presidency of the United Nations Security Council rotates on a monthly basis alphabetically among all of the members based on their English name.

At its first meeting on 17 January 1946, the UNSC adopted provisional rule 18 and established the following method of selecting the president: the presidency rotates monthly among the fifteen members of the Security Council. The rotation takes place in alphabetical order of the member states' official names in English. As such, Australia was the first nation to hold the presidency. Such rotation makes the presidency unique among all United Nations organs. Terms began and ended on the 17 of every month until a suggestion by Australia in December 1946 to change led to the term being extended so the presidency would rotate on the first of every month. The president is the only non-elected head of a United Nations organization.

Hence, the correct option is (D).

12. The Aam Admi Bima Yojana was launched on 2nd October 2007. It is a social security scheme that is targeted toward the low-income families of India.

Hence, the correct option is (D).

13. Sabarmati river is originated from Aravalli Mountain.

- The Sabarmati basin extends over the states of Rajasthan and Gujarat having an area of 21,674 Sq.km with a maximum length and width of 300 km and 150 km.

- It lies between 70°58′ to 73°51′ east longitudes and 22°15′ to 24°47′ north latitudes.

- Sabarmati river originates from the Aravalli hills in Kotdi tehsil of Udaipur district of Rajasthan.
- The basin is bounded by Aravalli hills on the north and north-east, by Rann of Kutch on the west, and by the Gulf of Khambhat on the south.
- The basin is roughly triangular in shape with the Sabarmati River as the base and the source of the Vatrak River as the apex point.
- Sabarmati originates from Aravalli hills at an elevation of 762 m near village Tepur, in the Udaipur district of Rajasthan.
- Right Bank Tributaries are Sei, Siri and Dhamni.
- Left Bank Tributaries are Wakal, Harnav, Hathmati, Khari, Watrak.

Hence, the correct option is (A).

14. Turkey is located in the Middle East, with territory in both Europe and Asia. The country shares borders with Bulgaria, Greece, Iraq, Syria, Armenia, Azerbaijan, Iran, and Georgia. It also has coastal borders on the Black Sea, the Mediterranean Sea, and the Aegean Sea. With a total area of about 780,580 square kilometers (301,382 square miles), the country is slightly larger than the state of Texas. Turkey is administratively divided into eighty provinces.

Hence, the correct option is (A).

15. 28th February is celebrated as National Science Day (NSD) in India. NSD is celebrated to commemorate the discovery of the 'Raman Effect', which led to Sir Chandrasekhar Venkata Raman winning the Noble Prize.

Students from across the country present science-related projects and innovations at the state and national levels. The day is celebrated to encourage youth to understand the aspects of science and develop an interest in it.

Hence, the correct option is (B).

16. The wind is the most common media of pollination in flowers without petals. Pollination refers to the transfer of pollen from a male part of a plant to a female part of a plant which enables fertilisation and the production of seeds, most often by an animal or by the wind.

Hence, the correct option is (A).

17. Vitamin K helps in blood clotting.

Vitamin K helps to make four of the 13 proteins needed for blood clotting, which stops wounds from continuously bleeding so they can heal. People who are prescribed anticoagulants (also called blood thinners) to prevent blood clots from forming in the heart, lungs, or legs are often informed about vitamin K.

Hence, the correct option is (C).

18. Newton's second law of motion introduces the concept of force. It says that when a constant force acts on a massive body, it causes it to accelerate, i.e., to change its velocity, at a constant rate. In the simplest case, a force applied to an object at rest causes it to accelerate in the direction of the force.

Hence, the correct option is (A).

19. Apart from India, Pakistan, and Sri Lanka, Nepal country has Rupee as its currency.

Rupee is the common name for the currencies of India, Indonesia, the Maldives, Mauritius, Nepal, Pakistan, Seychelles, and Sri Lanka, and of former currencies of Afghanistan, Bahrain, Kuwait, Oman, the UAE (as the Gulf rupee), British East Africa, Burma, German East Africa (as Rupie/Rupien), and Tibet. In Indonesia and the Maldives the unit of currency is known as rupiah and rufiyaa respectively.

Hence, the correct option is (D).

20. Cairo is the capital of Egypt and the largest urban agglomeration in Africa, the Arab world, and the Middle East. The Greater Cairo metropolitan area, with a population of 21.9 million, is the 12th-largest in the world by population.

Hence, the correct option is (A).

21. Lokmanya Tilak founded the Marathi newspaper 'Kesari'. The Kesari newspaper is a Marathi-language Indian newspaper.

- The newspaper was initially founded in 1881 by a prominent personality of the Indian Independence Movement, Lokmanya Bal Gangadhar Tilak.
- The Kesari newspaper was originally started as a co-operative effort by Agarkar (the paper's first editor), Chiplunkar, and Tilak, and was published along with Tilak's English newspaper, the Mahratta, to encourage people to rise against the oppressive regime of the time, instead of being submissive.
- the Kesari is still published from the original offices in Pune. Reporting local, national, and international news, the paper today is still one of the leading dailies of Maharashtra.

Hence, the correct option is (A).

22. Most part of India receives rainfall from June to September.

India receives most of its rainfall from the southwest monsoon winds. Southwest Monsoon period is referred to as the period between June to September. South West monsoons are the rain-bearing seasonal winds that flow from the Arabian Sea towards India's mainland in the South-West direction.

Hence, the correct option is (B).

23. The cycle of the seasons is caused due to revolution.

The planet rotates around an (invisible) axis. At different times during the year, the northern or southern axis is closer to the sun, when it is closer and away from the Sun during the revolution we have different seasons.

Hence, the correct option is (B).

24. Venus is the hottest planet in our solar system.

Venus is the second planet from the Sun and our closest planetary neighbour. Its thick atmosphere traps heat in a runaway greenhouse effect, making it the hottest planet in our solar system with surface temperatures hot enough to melt lead.

Hence, the correct option is (A).

25. The Civil disobedience movement began with the famous 'Dandi March' of Mahatma Gandhi.

Civil disobedience was initiated under the stewardship of Mahatma Gandhi. It was launched after the observance of Independence Day in 1930. The civil disobedience movement commenced with the famous Dandi march when Gandhi left the Sabarmati Ashram at Ahmedabad on foot with 78 other members of the Ashram for Dandi on 12 March 1930.

Hence, the correct option is (C).

Q.1 Who won 'Outstanding Performance by a Female Actor in a Leading Role' award at the Screen Actor Guild Awards, held in California?

A. Jessica Chastain

B. Bryce Dallas Howard

C. Diane Kruger

D. Mackenzie Foy

Q.2 India won how many medals at the Singapore Weightlifting International?

A. 4   **B.** 6   **C.** 8   **D.** 10

Q.3 The government in November 2022 extended the term of Dr. VG Somani, the Drug Controller General of India (DCGI) by __________.

A. one year   **B.** 3 months

C. 6 months   **D.** two years

Q.4 Who was the Chief Minister of Uttar Pradesh for the shortest time?

A. Hemvati Nandan Bahuguna

B. Govind Ballabh Pant

C. Tribhuvan Narayan Singh

D. None of these

Q.5 Which one is the largest district in Uttar Pradesh by areawise?

A. Lakhimpur Kheri   **B.** Sonbhadra

C. Allahabad   **D.** Shahjahanpur

Q.6 Uttar Pradesh's first transgender toilet has been built in the Kamachha area of which city under the smart city project?

A. Agra   **B.** Kanpur

C. Varanasi   **D.** Lucknow

Q.7 The Banaras Hindu University was founded by:

A. Bal Gangadhar Tilak

B. Jawaharlal Nehru

C. Sir Syed Mohammad

D. Pandit Madan Mohan Malaviya

Q.8 Who invented the vaccination for smallpox?

A. Sir Fredrick Grant Banting

B. Sir Alexander Fleming

C. Louis Pasteur

D. Edward Jenner

Q.9 With the support of which country is the Rawatbhata nuclear power plant set up in Rajasthan?

A. U.S.A   **B.** France   **C.** Russia   **D.** Canada

Q.10 The headquarter of UNESCO is located at _____.

A. London   **B.** Paris   **C.** Moscow   **D.** Vienna

Q.11 Periyar Wildlife Sanctuary is located in _________ state.

A. Uttar Pradesh   **B.** Kerala

C. Madhya Pradesh   **D.** Maharashtra

Q.12 What is the chemical name of Vitamin K?

A. Phylloquinone   **B.** Ascorbic acid

C. Cholecalciferol   **D.** Tocopherols

Q.13 Red litmus paper is changed into blue in solution of __________.

A. Base   **B.** Acid   **C.** Salt   **D.** None

Q.14 Which of these has the highest frequency?

A. Gamma Rays   **B.** Radio Waves

C. Ultraviolet Light   **D.** Infrared Rays

Q.15 What is the capital of Bulgaria?

A. Beirut   **B.** Bucharest

C. Sofia   **D.** Tashkent

Q.16 Who among the following became the first transgender election Ambassador of India?

A. Gauri Sawant

B. Satyashree Sharmila

C. Joyita Mandal

D. Prithika Yashini

Q.17 The book 'India Wins Freedom' was written by?

A. Jawaharlal Nehru   **B.** Mahatma Gandhi

C. Vallabhbhai Patel   **D.** Abul Kalam Azad

Q.18 The Great Indian Desert is located along the:

A. Indo-Pak boundary

B. Indo-China boundary

C. Indo-Afgan boundary

D. None of the above

Q.19 Where is the origin of the river Tangri?

A. Gangotri

B. Yamunotri

C. Mewat Hills

D. Morni Hills of the Siwalik Hills

Q.20 In which of the following Himalayan ranges is the Banihal Pass situated?

A. Great Himalayas   **B.** Pir Panjal

C. Ladakh   **D.** Zaskar

Q.21 Which mobility firm has acquired Avail Finance?

A. Uber   **B.** Cabify

C. Yandex Taxi   **D.** Ola

Q.22 Reserve Bank of India (RBI) has inaugurated Reserve Bank Innovation Hub in which city?

A. New Delhi   **B.** Mumbai

C. Bengaluru   **D.** Kolkata

Q.23 Coringa Wildlife Sanctuary is situated in which among the following states in India?

A. Telangana

B. Andhra Pradesh

C. Karnataka

D. Kerala

Q.24 Who was the Prime Minister of India during Indo-Pak war in 1965?

A. Jawaharlal Nehru

B. Indira Gandhi

C. Lal Bahadur Shastri

D. Rajiv Gandhi

Q.25 Who was the Congress President when India became free?

A. Mahatma Gandhi

B. Jawaharlal Nehru

C. J.B. Kripalani

D. Sardar Patel

// Smart Answer Sheet //

Correct Indicates percentage of students who answered questions correctly.

Skipped Indicates percentage of students who skipped questions.

Q.	Ans.	Correct / Skipped
1	A	66.87 % / 1.09 %
2	C	85.44 % / 0.0 %
3	B	61.48 % / 1.85 %
4	C	65.88 % / 1.11 %
5	A	49.43 % / 1.0 %

Q.	Ans.	Correct / Skipped
6	C	56.65 % / 1.82 %
7	D	58.64 % / 1.63 %
8	D	50.7 % / 1.58 %
9	D	11.09 % / 3.76 %
10	B	42.18 % / 1.29 %

Q.	Ans.	Correct / Skipped
11	B	76.29 % / 0.0 %
12	A	67.31 % / 1.9 %
13	A	69.47 % / 1.9 %
14	A	69.22 % / 1.95 %
15	C	24.59 % / 4.01 %

Q.	Ans.	Correct / Skipped
16	A	47.89 % / 1.62 %
17	D	61.01 % / 1.46 %
18	A	52.47 % / 1.46 %
19	D	65.2 % / 1.62 %
20	B	57.43 % / 1.23 %

Q.	Ans.	Correct / Skipped
21	D	64.82 % / 1.47 %
22	C	57.49 % / 1.99 %
23	B	46.71 % / 1.49 %
24	C	52.97 % / 1.44 %
25	C	57.79 % / 1.42 %

Performance Analysis	
Avg. Score (%)	28.0%
Toppers Score (%)	56.0%
Your Score	

//Hints and Solutions//

1. Jessica Chastain won 'Outstanding Performance by a Female Actor in a Leading Role' award at the Screen Actor Guild Awards, held in California.

Screen Actor Guild Awards were held in California. Outstanding Performance by a Female Actor in a Leading Role was won by Jessica Chastain (The Eyes of Tammy Faye). Outstanding Performance by a Male Actor in a Leading Role Will Smith (King Richard). Outstanding Performance by a Cast in a Motion Picture was won by CODA, which included Eugenio Derbez, Daniel Durant, Emilia Jones, and more.

Hence, the correct option is (A).

2. India won 8 medals at the Singapore Weightlifting International.

Indian weightlifters Vikas Thakur and Venkat Rahul Ragala qualified for the Commonwealth Games by winning gold and bronze medals respectively at the Singapore Weightlifting International on 27 February 2022. India thus ended its campaign in the competition with 8 medals, including 6 gold, 1 silver, and 1 bronze.

Hence, the correct option is (C).

3. The government in November 2022 extended the term of Dr. VG Somani, the Drug Controller General of India (DCGI) by 3 months.

He was earlier given an extension in Aug 2022. Dr Somani was appointed as the DCGI for a term of three years on August 14, 2019. The DCGI heads the Central Drugs Standard Control Organisation (CDSCO), which is responsible for ensuring quality drugs supply across the country.

Hence, the correct option is (B).

4. Tribhuvan Narayan Singh (8 August 1904 – 3 August 1982) was an Indian politician and Chief Minister of Uttar Pradesh. He was the Chief Minister from 8 October 1970 to 4 April 1971. He later served as the Governor of West Bengal from 1970 to 1982.

Hence, the correct option is (C).

5. Lakhimpur Kheri is the largest district in Uttar Pradesh by areawise.

Lakhimpur Kheri is the largest district in Uttar Pradesh, India, on the border with Nepal. Its administrative capital is the city of Lakhimpur. Lakhimpur Kheri district is a part of Lucknow division, with a total area of 7,680 square kilometres (2,970 square mile).

Hence, the correct option is (A).

6. Uttar Pradesh's first transgender toilet has been built in the Kamachha area of Varanasi under the smart city project.

- This will ensure the participation of the community in the cleanliness of the city.
- It was inaugurated by Mrudula Jaiswal, Mayor of the city, on 18 February 2021.
- The government is also planning to open four more transgender toilets in different locations of the city.

Hence, the correct option is (C).

7. Banaras Hindu University was established in 1916 by Pandit Madan Mohan Malaviya.

- Pandit Madan Mohan Malaviya was an Indian reformer and he was the founder of Akhil Bharatiya Hindu Mahasabha.
- Bal Gangadhar Tilak was an Indian nationalist and leader of the Independence Movement.
- Jawaharlal Nehru was the first prime minister of India and the longest-serving prime minister.

Hence, the correct option is (D).

8. Edward Jenner invented the vaccination for smallpox in the year 1796.

Smallpox is caused by the Varicella virus. The symptoms include light fever, the eruption of bile on the body.

Inventor	Invented	Nationality
Sir Fredrick Grant Banting	Co-inventor of insulin	Canadian
Sir Alexander Fleming	Penicillin	Scottish
Louis Pasteur	Pasteurization	French
Edward Jenner	Smallpox vaccine	English

Hence, the correct option is (D).

9. Rawatbhata Nuclear Power Station located in Rajasthan was established in 1975.

- It was established in collaboration with the Government of Canada.
- It is the second nuclear power plant in India.
- India's first major nuclear power plant is at Tarapur Maharashtra (established 1969).
- Rawatbhata nuclear power plant is a 1240 MW capacity nuclear plant.
- Tarapur nuclear plant was established with the help of the USA.

Hence, the correct option is (D).

10. The headquarters of UNESCO is located in Paris.

UNESCO stands for United Nations Educational, Scientific and Cultural Organization. It was formed on 16 November 1945. Its headquarter is in Paris, France.

Hence, the correct option is (B).

11. Periyar Wildlife Sanctuary is located in Kerala state.

Some other famous National Parks and Sanctuaries in Kerala are:-

- Idukki Wildlife Sanctuary, Parambikulam Wildlife Sanctuary, Chinnar Wildlife Sanctuary, Thattekad Bird Sanctuary, Wayanad Wildlife Sanctuary, Muthanga Wildlife Sanctuary, Aralam Wildlife Sanctuary, Eravikulam National Park, and Silent Valley National Park.

Hence, the correct option is (B).

12. Phylloquinone is the chemical name of Vitamin K and its chemical formula is $C_{31}H_{46}O_2$. Vitamin K is an essential fat-soluble vitamin that is important in maintaining normal coagulation, serving as a cofactor in the activation of several clotting factors and anticoagulant proteins. Phylloquinone is a member of the class of phylloquinone that consists of 1,4-naphthoquinone having methyl and phytyl groups at positions 2 and 3 respectively.

Hence, the correct option is (A).

13. Red litmus paper is changed into blue in the solution of the base. Red litmus restrains a weak diprotic acid. A weak acid used in acid-base indicator usually has a different colour between the acid form and the conjugate base ion form. This is the reason when adding a water-soluble base into it, it turns blue, and allows the colour of the conjugate base ion.

Hence, the correct option is (A).

14. Gamma Rays have the highest frequency out of the above options. The frequency of a wave is the number of waves that pass through a single point in one second Frequency is measured in unit of Hertz (Hz), 1 Hertz is equal to one wave passing a point per second Gamma Rays have frequencies in order of greater than 10^{19} Hz. The energy of a wave is directly related to its frequency which makes gamma rays the most high energy form of electromagnetic radiation

Hence, the correct option is (A).

15. Sofia is the capital of Bulgaria and it is the 15th largest city in the European Union with a population of around 13 million people. It has been ranked by the Globalization and World Cities Research Network as a Beta city. Many of the major universities, cultural institutions, and commercial companies of Bulgaria are concentrated in Sofia.

Hence, the correct option is (C).

16. Gauri Sawant is a transgender activist from Mumbai, India.

- She is the director of Sakhi Char Chowghi which helps transgender people and people with HIV/AIDS.
- She was made the goodwill ambassador of the Election Commission in Maharashtra.
- Sawant was born in Ganesh and raised in Pune.

Hence, the correct option is (A).

17. The book 'India Wins Freedom' was written by Abul Kalam Azad. The book gives a first-hand account of the Indian freedom struggle. So, statement 4 is correct.

Abul Kalam Azad: He was one of the leaders of the Indian independence movement against British rule in the first half of the 20th century. He was born in Mecca, Saudi Arabia. Azad became active in journalism when he was in his late teens, and in 1912 he began publishing a weekly Urdu-language newspaper in Calcutta, Al-Hilal ("The Crescent").

Hence, the correct option is (D).

18. The Great Indian Desert is located along the Indo-Pak boundary.

The Great Indian Desert is called the Thar Desert. It is one of the hot deserts of the world. Many National Parks and Wildlife Sanctuaries are located in this area. It is the world's 17th largest desert and the world's 9th largest subtropical desert.

Hence, the correct option is (A).

19. The Tangri river originates from the Morni Hills of the Siwalik Hills of south-eastern Himachal Pradesh in India. It is a tributary of the Ghaggar River in the Indian state of Haryana.

Hence, the correct option is (D).

20. The Banihal Pass is situated in Pir Panjal Himalayan Range.

The Pir Panjal Range is a range of Inner Himalayan mountains stretching from east-southeast (ESE) to west-northwest (WNW) through Himachal Pradesh, the Indian state, and Jammu and Kashmir, Indian Union Territory. Pir Panjal is the greatest range of the Lesser Himalayas. The Pir Panjal Railway Tunnel, a rail tunnel of 11,215 meters passes through Jammu and Kashmir's Pir Panjal Range.

Hence, the correct option is (B).

21. Mobility firm Ola has signed an agreement to acquire neo bank Avail Finance. This acquisition provides financial services to working class. The acquisition will strengthen the Ola in the fintech space.

Hence, the correct option is (D).

22. RBI governor Shaktikanta Das inaugurated the Reserve Bank Innovation Hub (RBIH) in Bengaluru. The RBI has set up the RBIH as a Section 8 under Companies Act, 2013. RBIH is a wholly-owned subsidiary of RBI with an initial capital contribution of Rs 100 crore.

Hence, the correct option is (C).

23. Coringa Wildlife Sanctuary is situated in the southern state of Andhra Pradesh. It is the second largest mangrove stretch of the country with around 24 kinds of mangroves, 120 kinds of birds and animals etc. It is home to the critically endangered white-backed vulture and the long-billed vulture.

Hence, the correct option is (B).

24. Lal Bahadur Shastri was the second Prime Minister of India. He served as the Prime Minister of India from 1964 to 1965.

He was the Prime Minister of India during the Indo-Pak war in 1965. He signed the Tashkent Declaration on 10 January 1966 with Muhammad Ayub Khan, the then President of Pakistan. He is the first Prime Minister to die abroad. He was awarded the Bharat Ratna in 1966. He was the first person to receive the Bharat Ratna posthumously.

Hence, the correct option is (C).

25. When India became independent in 1947, JB Kriplani was the President of the Congress.

JB Kriplani was an Indian politician, Gandhian socialist, mystic and independence activist. Sucheta Kriplani, wife of JB Kripalani, was the first woman Chief Minister of India, she served as the Chief Minister of Uttar Pradesh from 1963 to 1967.

Hence, the correct option is (C).

// Notes //

// Notes //